RESEARCH ON MEN AND MASCULINITIES SERIES

Series Editor:
MICHAEL S. KIMMEL, SUNY Stony Brook

Contemporary research on men and masculinity, informed by recent feminist thought and intellectual breakthroughs of women's studies and the women's movement, treats masculinity not as a normative referent but as a problematic gender construct. This series of interdisciplinary, edited volumes attempts to understand men and masculinity through this lens, providing a comprehensive understanding of gender and gender relationships in the contemporary world. Published in cooperation with the Men's Studies Association, a Task Group of the National Organization for Men Against Sexism.

EDITORIAL ADVISORY BOARD

Volumes in this Series

Men's Health and Illness

Gender, Power, and the Body

EDITED BY

DONALD SABO & DAVID FREDERICK GORDON

RESEARCH ON MEN AND MASCULINITIES

Published in cooperation with the Men's Studies Association,
A Task Group of the National Organization for Men Against Sexism

SAGE Publications
International Educational and Professional Publisher
Thousand Oaks   London   New Delhi

For information address:

SAGE Publications, Inc.
2455 Teller Road
Thousand Oaks, California 91320
E-mail: order@sagepub.com

SAGE Publications Ltd.
6 Bonhill Street
London EC2A 4PU
United Kingdom

SAGE Publications India Pvt. Ltd.
M-32 Market
Greater Kailash I
New Delhi 110 048 India

Printed in the United States of America

Library of Congress Cataloging-in-Publication Data

Men's health and illness: Gender, power, and the body / edited by
   Donald Sabo and David Frederick Gordon.
      p. cm. —(Research on men and masculinities series; 8)
   Includes bibliographical references and index.
      ISBN 0-8039-4814-X (cloth: alk. paper). — ISBN 0-8039-5275-9
   (pbk.: alk. paper)
         1. Men—Health and hygiene—Social aspects. 2. Men—Health and
hygiene—Psychological aspects. I. Sabo, Donald F. II. Gordon,
David (David Frederick). III. Men's Studies Association (U.S.)
IV. Series
RA567.83.M46 1995
613'.04234—dc20   95-17398

This book is printed on acid-free paper.

95 96 97 98 99 10 9 8 7 6 5 4 3 2 1

Sage Production Editor: Gillian Dickens

Contents

Series Editor's Introduction

The data are as startling as they are familiar: Men are nearly six times more likely to die of lung cancer than women, five times as likely to die of other bronchopulmonic diseases, three times as likely to die in motor vehicle accidents, nearly three times as likely to commit suicide, and two times as likely to die of cirrhosis of the liver and heart disease. AIDS, now the leading cause of death for all Americans ages 25 to 44, is perhaps the most highly gendered disease in our history, affecting men at a rate of about nine to one.

Some have used these data to complain that feminist initiatives to improve women's health are misguided in that women already "have it made." But such complaints only hint at the larger point: Most of the leading causes of death among men are the result of men's behaviors—gendered behaviors that leave men more vulnerable to certain illnesses and not others. Masculinity is among the more significant risk factors associated with men's illness.

As with women, men are also fragile and vulnerable creatures, susceptible to a wide variety of health-related problems. Feminist women, it seems to me, have been able to theorize vulnerability and susceptibility to disease into a social movement to promote women's health. But masculinity is not only a risk factor in disease etiology but it is also among the most significant barriers to men developing a consciousness about health and illness. "Real men" don't get sick, and when they do, as we all do, real men don't complain about it, and they don't seek help until the entire system begins to shut down.

Pointing out simple sex differences in rates of various diseases only scratches the surface of the issue. We must look inside these health issues, inside the mechanics and symbolic structures of specific diseases to understand better men's experiences of health and illness. This volume begins that process.

This volume is the eighth in the **Sage Series on Research on Men and Masculinities.** The purpose of the series is to gather together the finest empirical research in the social sciences that focuses on the experiences of men in contemporary society.

Following the pioneering research of feminist scholars over the past two decades, social scientists have come to recognize gender as one of the primary axes around which social life is organized. Gender is now seen as equally central as class and race, both at the macrostructural level of the allocation and distribution of rewards in a hierarchical society, and at the micropsychological level of individual identity formation and interpersonal interaction.

Social scientists distinguish gender from sex. *Sex* refers to biology, the biological dimorphic division of male and female; *gender* refers to the cultural meanings that are attributed to those biological differences. Although biological sex varies little, the cultural meanings of gender vary enormously. Thus, we speak of gender as socially constructed; the definitions of masculinity and femininity as the products of the interplay among a variety of social forces. In particular, we understand gender to vary spatially (from one culture to another), temporally (within any one culture over historical time), and longitudinally (through any individual's life course). Finally, we understand that different groups within any culture may define masculinity and femininity differently, according to subcultural definitions; race, ethnicity, age, class, sexuality, and region of the country all affect our different gender definitions. Thus, it is more accurate to speak of "masculinities" and "femininities" than positing a monolithic gender construct.

It is the goal of this series to explore the varieties of men's experiences, remaining mindful of specific differences among men, and also be aware of the mechanisms of power that inform both men's relations with women and men's relations with other men. This volume helps us understand those dynamics as men relate to the inner workings of their bodies.

MICHAEL S. KIMMEL
Series Editor

Acknowledgments

We gratefully acknowledge the support and vision of Michael Kimmel, who nudged and inspired us at critical junctures. We thank Jim Doyle for his generous support and Judith Lorber for her feedback of our earlier ideas. This book was spun on the webwork of supportive colleagues, friends, and loved ones, including Sheila Dunn, Debbie Gordon, Sally Harrington, Dave Kelly, Michael Messner, Charlie Sabatino, Linda Sabo, Leon Shkolnik, Pat Stacey, and Jim Watson. We much appreciate the expertise of Gillian Dickens, Gavin Lockwood, and other stalwarts of Sage Publications. Finally, we thank our contributors for their insights, labor, and sticktuitiveness.

Don dedicates this book to his father, Donald F. Sabo, Sr., with great love and admiration. Dave dedicates this book to his parents, Fred and Viola, with thanks for their love, guidance, and encouragement.

1

Rethinking Men's Health and Illness

The Relevance of Gender Studies

DONALD SABO
DAVID FREDERICK GORDON

Someone once said that "the fish are the last ones to discover the ocean." So it is with men and patriarchy. Feminist scholars long have emphasized the analysis of patriarchy—that is, social hierarchies that are male domi-nated. Gerda Lerner (1986), for example, defines patriarchy as,

> the manifestation and institutionalization of male domination over women and children in the family and the extension of male dominance over women in society in general. It implies that men hold power in all the important institutions of society and that women are deprived of access to such power. It does not imply that women are either totally powerless or totally deprived of rights, influence, and resources. (p. 239)

Heidi Hartmann (1981) defines patriarchy as,

> a set of social relations between men, which have a material base, and which, though hierarchical, establish or create interdependence and solidarity among men that enable them to dominate women. Though patriarchy is hierarchical and men of different classes, races, or ethnic groups have different places in the patriarchy, they also are united in their shared relationship of dominance over their women. . . . In the hierarchy of patriarchy, all men, whatever their

1

rank in the patriarchy, are bought off by being able to control at least some women. (pp. 14-15)

Although feminist scholars differ in the ways they define patriarchy, none fail to recognize its historical longevity and societal pervasiveness. Unlike most feminist scholars, who have been *women,* men inside academia and the health professions have generally failed to reckon with the fundamental realities of sexism, male dominance, and social grouping by sex. Centuries of efforts of feminist scholars and women's rights activists to get men's attention were often met with derision, puzzlement, and resistance. Yet as Kimmel and Mosmiller (1992) have documented, there have always been pro-feminist men, such as Thomas Paine, Matthew Vassar, Robert Owen, Horace Greeley, Ralph Waldo Emerson, Frederick Douglass, Charles Beard, Lester Ward, Thorstein Veblen, Herbert Marcuse, Isaac Asimov, and Kalamu ya Salaam, who sided with women's bid for equal rights and reformist visions. Most recently, men have begun to attune to feminist writings and analyses under the bannerhead of "men's studies." Men's studies practitioners are attempting to re-vision men and masculinity in the context of historical and modern permutations of patriarchy and in light of feminist theory and practice.

The authors in this book attempt to see the patriarchal "ocean" for what it is and to forge new understandings of men's health and illness from these intellectual, empirical, and theoretical trends. One does not have to be a card-carrying feminist to realize that patriarchy and contemporary patterns of gender relations profoundly influence our customs, religious beliefs, political institutions, family relations, sexuality, medicine, and, in the context of this book, our understandings of men's health and illness. The contributors to this book contend that gender influences the patterning of men's health risks, the ways men perceive and use their bodies, and men's psychosocial adjustments to illness itself.

Gender and Men's Health and Illness

Beginning in the 1960s, initial thinking about gender and health issues was grounded in the "sociocultural model" that challenged the prevailing biological determinism and reductionism of the traditional "biomedical model." Critics of the biomedical model cited its mechanistic approach, the overemphasis on biochemical processes, and overly simplistic explanations that attribute disease to one or two specific etiological factors (Cockerham, 1986; Dubos, 1959; Wolinsky, 1980). Within the socio-cultural model, in contrast, health and illness are understood primarily in light of cultural values and practices, social conditions, and human emotion and perception.

The development of the sociocultural model during the 1960s fostered a reconceptualization of health and illness in light of gender. At first, researchers followed a basic "add and stir" approach, which treated gender as just another demographic variable for identifying health patterns and risk factors. The additive approach proved useful in epidemiological research that uncovered differential rates of illness between males and females or across male populations subgrouped by domain sociological variables such as race or ethnicity, socioeconomic status, or residential area. For example, descriptive research findings revealed that (a) men experience more life-threatening diseases and die younger than women, (b) women experience more non-life-threatening illnesses and live longer than men, and (c) women see doctors more frequently than men. By the late 1970s, gender had become accepted as a standard demographic variable to be included in epidemiological research. A growing body of research findings made it evident that variations in women's and men's health could not be adequately accounted for by biomedical explanations alone. It was also increasingly evident that sociocultural explanations of health and illness were not complete unless gender was taken into account.

During the 1970s and 1980s, researchers developed more comprehensive theoretical approaches to understanding linkages between gender and health issues. Most of the advances in theory and research on gender and health were fostered by the women's health movement[1] and the growth of feminist scholarship. Researchers studied the ways that differential gender socialization influenced perceptions of illness and adjustments to death. Sex discrimination in the health care delivery system and sex stratification in the health professions were documented (Muff, 1982). Feminist historians documented the oppression of women healers by the male-dominated clergy and physicians during the Middle Ages (Ehrenreich & English, 1973, 1974), whereas feminist philosophers of science argued that medical "science" was tainted by patriarchal and androcentric biases (Daly, 1978). Sexism and structured sex inequality were believed to lead to the misdiagnosis and maltreatment of women (Coopersmith, 1978; Corea, 1977; Scully & Bart, 1973). By the mid-1980s, the growing salience of gender in understanding patterns of health and illness were an undeniable presence in epidemiology, medical sociology, and interdisciplinary studies of psychosocial aspects of illness (Stillion, 1985).

One limitation of most of this pioneering scholarly work was that until recently researchers tended to equate the study of *gender and health* to studies of *women's* health and illness. While women were in the gender-analytical spotlight, men resided backstage. Even men who were affiliated with the American "men's movement," which budded in the early 1970s, were slow to cultivate awareness around men's physical health issues.[2] Some early work on men and masculinity by Marc Feigen-Fasteau (1974) and Warren Farrell (1975) did make connections between conformity to traditional masculinity and men's emotional and physical health. In 1979, physician Sam Julty published *Men's Bodies, Men's Selves,* which integrated a biomedical tour of male physiology and medical hygienic concerns with rudimentary commentary on masculine psychology. Others focused on men's sexual and emotional health. For example, Michael Castleman (1980) couched his therapeutic suggestions for men to transform their sexual conduct and experiences within a critique of traditional masculinity. In the 1980s, scrutiny of men's health issues got a boost from scholarly dialogue under areas variously dubbed the "study of men and masculinity," "men's critique of gender," or the "new men's studies."[3]

Professional scholars and researchers have been slow to study connections between gender and *men's* health and illness. This collection of readings helps to correct this lack of knowledge. We owe our intellectual origins to the sociocultural model in mainline social science, feminist theory and research, and the incipient efforts of feminist-identified men to rethink men's health issues.

Theorizing Men's Health and Illness

Efforts to explore how gender influences men's health derive from the sociocultural model that underpins interdisciplinary studies of health and illness as well as research and theory generated by feminist scholars and researchers. In addition, the writings in this book represent a variety of approaches that when taken collectively point toward the development of an "inclusive feminism" that facilitates systematic study of men and masculinity (Brod, 1987; Kimmel & Messner, 1993). Men's health and illness can be explained as a gendered phenomenon in several frameworks.

Gender, Nature, and Nurture

The nature-nurture debate has infused much thinking about differences in gender identity and behavior. Biologistic thinkers have argued that gender differences are natural in origin, deriving from instinctual, hormonal, morphological, neurological, or phylogenetic endowments. Proponents of the nurture thesis, in contrast, contend that gender differences are learned via socialization, social conditioning, or cultural adaptation.

Ingrid Waldron (1983) has pioneered research that explores the border crossings between biogenetic and sociocultural explanations for variations in men's and women's health (see also Verbrugge, 1985). In Chapter 2 she examines recent historical trends in mortality among women and men. She finds that some changes in behavioral patterns between the sexes, such as increased smoking among women, have narrowed the gap between men's formerly higher mortality rates from lung cancer, chronic obstructive pulmonary disease, and ischemic heart disease. In contrast, the trend toward decreased alcohol consumption during the 1980s was more marked among females than males and, in part, was responsible for increases in men's mortality from chronic liver disease and cirrhosis. In Chapter 3, Judith Stillion presents an analysis of premature death among men that depicts a "hierarchy of risks" that men incur as a result of both their biogenetic makeup and lifestyle and psychology. Waldron and Stillion discuss gender differences in health and illness that provide theoretical frameworks that take into account the complex interplay between biogenetic and sociocultural processes. Indeed, each chapter in this volume represents an application of the sociocultural model to understanding men's health and illness.

Masculine Identity
and Sex Role Theory

Sex role theorists called attention to the lethal aspects of the male role (Fasteau, 1974; Filene, 1974; Sabo & Runfola, 1980). In the words of Harrison, Chin, and Ficarrotto (1992),

> It is time that men especially begin to comprehend that the price paid for belief in the male role is shorter life expectancy. The male sex-role will become less hazardous to our health only insofar as it ceases to be defined as opposite to the female role, and comes to be defined as one genuinely human way to live. (p. 282)

Just how does masculinity or men's roles put men at risk for illness and early death? Researchers have varied in the ways they have conceptualized and measured *masculinity, masculine identity,* or *men's sex role identity.* As Vicki Helgeson details in Chapter 4, psychologists in the 1970s initially saw masculinity as a conglomeration of traits that in turn could be identified and measured (Bem, 1974; Spence, Helmreich, & Stapp, 1974). Consonant with the tenets of sex role theory, researchers recognized that masculinity as an inner, psychic process was intricately tied to an outer web of sex roles and gender expectations. Robert Brannon (1976), for example, identified the following four major components of the male role:

1. No Sissy Stuff: the need to be different from women
2. The Big Wheel: the need to be superior to others
3. The Sturdy Oak: the need to be independent and self-reliant
4. Give 'Em Hell: the need to be more powerful than others, through violence if necessary

Gender socialization influences the extent to which boys adopt masculine behaviors, which, in turn, can impact on their susceptibility to illness or accidental deaths. A give 'em hell approach to life can lead to hard drinking and fast driving, which account for about half of male adolescent deaths. As Helgeson suggests in Chapter 4, the need to be a sturdy oak and to avoid the semblances of feminine dependency may account for the tendency men have to deny symptoms of coronary heart disease.

In Chapter 5, Alan Klein analyzes why bodybuilders put their health at risk by using steroids, overtraining, and engaging in extreme dietary practices. He reports on years of ethnographic research in the muscled world of the bodybuilding subculture, where masculinity is equated to maximum muscularity and men's normative strivings for bigness and physical strength hide a psychic substratum of insecurity and low self-esteem. The links between masculinity and muscle have been embodied in cult heroes such as Joe Weider, Charles Atlas, Arnold Schwartzenegger, and Sylvester Stallone, who have served as male role models for generations of American boys and men. Klein's analysis lays bare a tragic irony in American culture; that the powerful male athlete, a symbol of strength and health, has often sacrificed his health in pursuit of ideal masculinity (Glassner, 1989; Messner & Sabo, 1995). Klein also emphasizes the theoretical necessity of linking sex role theory's focus on gender identity and socialization to a critical analysis of the political, economic, and cultural contexts of gender relations.

Social Inequality and
Critical Feminist Perspectives

Social scientists have long observed that social inequality influences the types and patterns of health and illness (Conrad & Kern, 1994). Freund (1982) contended that power is the central feature of social organization that is related to differences in health. Health is thus conceptualized as an important and complex component of social inequality. The quality of health is viewed as an inherently valuable resource that is differentially distributed to positions in various social hierarchies; for example, economic, political, racial, age, and gender hierarchies.

Health can also be understood as an important social resource for attaining and maintaining status within social hierarchies (Frank, 1991). Those at the bottom of the American class hierarchy, for example, have the highest rates of disease and disability, which in turn erodes their capacity to compete within the larger economy (Dutton, 1989). Powerful groups can attribute inferior health to less powerful groups as a justification for their oppression: for example, the diagnosis of upper-class women as hysterics by the male-dominated medical profession during the 19th century enhanced men's patriarchal status and authority in the family and society (Ehrenreich & English, 1973); the labeling of prostitutes as criminals and carriers of sexually transmitted disease heightens their political and economic marginalization in relation to middle-class women or men (Walkowitz, 1980).

Critical feminist analyses build on the premise that social inequality and power struggles profoundly inform gender relations and health outcomes. In addition to sex role theory's focus on gender identity, socialization, and conformity to role expectations, critical feminist thinkers emphasize the power differences that suffuse relational processes between men and women, women and women, and men and men. Critical feminists also contend that gender identity and behavior are not simply imposed on individuals through structured forms of socialization, but that individuals actively participate in the construction of their gender identity and behavior (West & Zimmerman, 1987). Gender identity is actively worked out, revamped, and maintained by individuals who are immersed in socially and historically constructed webs of power relations.

Elements of social constructionist and critical feminist approaches congeal in the theory of "hegemonic masculinity" developed by Robert Connell (1987). Connell's perspective integrated and synthesized Gayle Rubin's (1975) feminist analysis of the sex, or gender, system with a

Gramscian (1971) approach to theorizing hegemony. Connell used the term *gender order* to refer to a "historically constructed pattern of power relations between men and women and definitions of femininity and masculinity" (1987, pp. 98-99) that emerge and are transformed within varying institutional contexts. The prevailing cultural definitions of masculinity or hegemonic masculinity are essentially ideological constructions that serve the material interests of dominant male groups.[4] Hegemonic masculinity reflects, supports, and actively cultivates sex inequality (i.e., men's domination of women), but it also allows elite males to extend their influence and control over lesser-status males in various intermale dominance hierarchies (Sabo & London, 1992).

Pleck and Sonenstein's (1991) research on problem behaviors and masculine ideology in adolescent males provides an application of critical feminist approaches to understanding men's health. A national sample of adolescent, never-married males aged 15 to 19 were interviewed in 1980 and 1988. Hypothesis tests revolved around links between *masculine ideology* (which measured the presence of traditional male role attitudes) and *problem behaviors* (which, directly or indirectly, put boys at risk). Multiple regression analyses showed that traditional male role attitudes showed a significant, independent association with 7 of 10 problem behaviors. Specifically, traditional attitudes were associated with ever being suspended from school, drinking and use of street drugs, frequency of being picked up by the police, being sexually active, number of heterosexual partners in the last year, and tricking or forcing someone to have sex.

As Ingrid Waldron, Judith Stillion, and Robert Staples show in this book, these kinds of behaviors, which are in part expressions of the pursuit of hegemonic masculinity, elevate boys' risk for sexually transmitted diseases, HIV transmission, and early death by accident or homicide. Reciprocally, conformity to such hegemonic masculine values and behaviors also victimizes women through sexual assault, men's violence, and sexually transmitted disease. The importance of this research in the present context is that Pleck and Sonenstein's interpretation of this survey data combined elements of sex role theory and social constructionist theory within a larger critical framework that recognized structured sex inequality and the oppression of women by men.

A wedding of sex role theory and critical feminist perspectives helps explain the complexities surrounding men's reactions to breast cancer in a spouse. Initial studies of men's reactions and adjustments to a wife's mastectomy revealed that traditional conjugal role expectations influenced men's approach to caregiving (Sabo, 1984; Sabo, Brown, & Smith, 1986). During the early stages of caregiving, men took on more expressive functions that are traditionally associated with femininity and the home-maker-mother role. In later stages of recovery, however, men denied their fears about their spouse's mortality, anxieties about their own health, and perceived strains in the marital relationship by enacting a traditionally masculine protector-provider role. The enactment of traditional conjugal roles helped wife and husband get through the difficult period of diagno-sis, hospitalization, and short-range treatment. In the long run, however, men's denial (cloaked in well-intended bravery and paternal caring) tended to inhibit communications between spouses and, ultimately, steered the marital relationship in the direction of husbands' psychosocial interests and not wives. In short, denial reflected a power struggle between husband and wife to define the postmastectomy conjugal relationship (Sabo, 1990). Although sex role theory helps highlight changing role relations in cou-ples faced with breast cancer, critical feminist theory shows that power struggles are also operative.

Critical feminists point out that socialization theory underemphasizes the extent that patterns of gender socialization express and reproduce struc-tured sex inequality and men's institutional domination of women. This means that within male-dominated institutions and cultures, men learn to function psychologically in ways that maintain their authority and psy-chosocial priorities rather than women's. When Chodorow (1978) com-pares female and male psychology, for example, she holds that women's social orientation is personal and men's is positional. Girls learn to attune to and accept the needs of others, whereas boys, in contrast, become much more individuated and status conscious. There is much truth in her scheme. However, critical feminists would ground these psychological distinc-tions in social structure and patriarchal ideology; that is, one reason why boys learn to separate themselves from others and evaluate themselves and others according to status is that they are striving to fit into male-dominated, hierarchically organized institutions such as marriage, sports, government, and business. Hence, male psychology or gender identity derives from and revolves around status and power differences between the sexes and among men.

Critical feminists recognize that gender identity "develops and persists as a social, economic, and political category" (Anderson, 1988, p. 320). Many of the role expectations and psychological traits attached to mascu-linity in the current gender order, such as aggressiveness, ambition, success-striving, virility, asceticism, and competitiveness are intricately tied to men's preoccupation with power over others and attempts to impose their definitions of reality on others.

Masculinities and Men's Health

There is no such thing as masculinity; there are only masculinities. A limitation of early feminist theory was its "categoricalism"; that is, its treatment of all men as monolithic oppressors of women (Connell, 1987). The fact is, however, that all men are not alike; nor do all male groups share the same stakes in the gender order. At any given historical moment, there are competing masculinities—some hegemonic, some marginalized, and some stigmatized—each with their respective structural, psychosocial, and cultural moorings.

The gender order possesses two main structural aspects. First, it is a hierarchical system in which men dominate women in crude and debased, slick and subtle ways. Feminist scholars have made great progress exposing and analyzing this dimension of the edifice of sexism. Second, there also exists a system of intermale dominance in which a minority of men dominates the masses of men. These two hierarchical systems (male domination of women and the intermale dominance hierarchies) are economically, politically, and culturally synergistic. They reflect and feed one another. For example, male violence in one sector (e.g., training for aggression in the homosocial worlds of football, the military, or street gangs) can amplify or fuel violence in the other sector (e.g., bar fighting or assaults by men on women in the form of date rape or wife beating).

Although the comparative health status and life chances of some male groups in the gender order are minimized, other subgroups are systematically advantaged. Indeed, within the intermale dominance hierarchies that constitute the gender order, the comparative health of male elites is in part established through the exploitation of lesser-status male subgroups. Part of the mission for researchers of men's health and illness, therefore, is to describe and document substantial differences between the health options of homeless men, professional athletes, working-class men, underclass men, gay men, men with AIDS, prison inmates, men of color, and their comparatively advantaged middle- and upper-class, white, male counterparts.

The research reported in Part II of this book shows how men's health and illness vary tremendously in relation to socioeconomic status, race, and ethnicity, to the extent of physical disability, and to status in the criminal justice system. In Chapter 6, Robert Staples details a long list of health indicators that document the abysmally poor health status of African American males. That inner-city black men in the United States have a lower life expectancy than men in some Third World countries or that young black men have about a 1 in 20 chance of becoming a homicide victim, have led scholars such as Staples and Jewelle Taylor Gibbs to describe young black men in America as an "endangered species" (Gibbs, 1988). Staples contends that the health plight of African American men derives from an interrelated pattern of institutionalized racism, gender politics, and systematic political and economic marginalization that leaves them alienated and powerless.

It is difficult to find a population of men in North American society who are more politically and economically disenfranchised than prison inmates. They are housed in institutions that are geared more to the infliction of punishment than to rehabilitative practices. They are feared and regarded as pariahs by the public. Many come from lower socioeconomic backgrounds and are members of racial and ethnic minority groups. In Chapter 7, Carol Polych and Don Sabo document the greater risk for transmission of HIV among prisoners. The etiological processes surrounding HIV transmission in prison, they argue, extend far beyond the prison walls into the larger gender order. They present a theoretical framework that examines how men's pursuit of masculinity unfolds within multiple systems of domination (i.e., class, race, and gender) that converge upon the life chances of inmates. Polych and Sabo challenge feminist theorists to deal with the profound contradiction that many male prisoners are at once victims of a patriarchal politics of neglect yet perpetrators of crimes against women and society.

Chapter 8 presents a critical feminist analysis of sports injury. Athletes are held up as symbols of health and vitality in athletic and fitness subcultures. The healthy athlete is also a staple image in corporate advertising. Although it is true that many forms of athletic and fitness activities enhance physical and emotional health of tens of thousands of individuals, it is also true that in some of the more hypercompetitive and exploitative hierarchies that exist in the institution of sport, athletes incur greater risk for severe injury and long-term chronic illnesses. Phil White, Kevin Young, and William McTeer report on interview data that explores how some male athletes are enjoined by gender ideologies to deny pain, sacrifice health, and accept heightened risk for injury. Their description of male athletes' experiences shows how the pursuit of greater athletic achievement entails developing disregard for the body. Paradoxically, as the body is built up to move up the competitive hierarchies of modern athletics, the body is increasingly worn down. Many athletes are thus embroiled in a larger set of power relations inside and outside sport that are often exploitative and lead to physical entropy rather than health (Messner & Sabo, 1995). White, Young, and McTeer offer readers critical feminist insights that stretch understanding of sports injury beyond the biomedical explanations of allied health professionals, who generally have seen sports injury and pain as strictly bodily processes.

In Chapter 9, Thomas Gerschick and Adam Stephen Miller report on in-depth interviews with men who have incurred physical disabilities. The lives of men with physical disabilities are situated on the margins of mainstream society. In that strength and physical ability are key components of hegemonic masculinity, they show how men with physical disabilities experience considerable difficulties constructing a workable masculine identity. On the one hand, they struggle to cope with stigma and feelings of inferiority, whereas, on the other hand, they strive to redefine masculinity in ways that circumvent, transform, or reject dominant cultural definitions of manhood.

Modifying Feminist Theories

Gender scholars are attempting to modify feminist theory to accommodate the analysis of differential privilege and power *among* male subgroups within the intermale dominance hierarchies that constitute the larger gender order. If feminist theory is to grow, it needs to continue to change. Feminist theory has demonstrated the capacity to change in relation to women of color. Feminism in industrialized societies has been essentially a movement of and by white, middle-class women who have tended to falsely universalize their own issues and interests as "women's" issues and interests. This contributed to the marginalization and alienation of working-class women and women of color from feminism (Davis, 1981; hooks, 1984). As Messner and Sabo (1990) write, the initial response of feminist scholars to the criticism of their class and race biases was to conduct more studies of working-class women and women of color. Yet many of these studies still used a theoretical framework that *a priori* privileged gender oppression over other forms of oppression. As a result, as Baca Zinn, Weber Cannon, Higginbotthen, and Thornton-Dill (1986) pointed out in an influential *Signs* article, women of color still felt that their experiences and needs were being falsely subsumed under the rubric of a middle-class feminist agenda.

Some critical feminist approaches are attempting to fill the need for a conceptual scheme that theorizes the varied and shifting manifestations of male domination as they interact with other forms of social domination. The term *multiple systems of domination analysis* has been used to describe these efforts. What we are suggesting is that the adaptation of feminist theory to the study of men's health and illness needs to somehow address the differential exploitation of lesser-status, marginalized male subgroups (e.g., men of color, gay men, underclass men) in the changing gender order. The life chances of prison inmates and college students, congressmen and inner-city black and Hispanic men, straight and gay men, and professional men and homeless men are clearly different, and yet in the political and economic webworks of the contemporary gender order, their respective destinies and opportunities are inexorably interrelated. Analyses of men's health, therefore, need to be highly nuanced and sensitive to differences in men's lives.

Psychosocial Aspects
of Men's Health and Illness

Research on the psychosocial aspects of health and illness has expanded during the past two decades. Though modern medicine acknowledges the integrity of the whole person, the emotional and intellectual uniqueness of the individual is sometimes lost amid the highly bureaucratized, technological, and sterile environments of contemporary medicine (Shontz, 1975). Critics of the biomedical model of illness charge that it ignores the social contexts of meaning that individuals attach to health and illness (Mishler, 1989).

The experience of illness, for both the ill person and those who care for him or her, is infused with meaning and emotional struggle. For researchers concerned about how gender infiltrates the social and psychological dimensions of illness, there is no shortage of questions. How do women and men account for illness, respond to illness, or define themselves following recovery from illness? What kinds of meanings do men and women bring to the experiences of illness, death, or dying? Do men and women respond differently to their own illness? Do women and men function differently as caregivers or, conversely, does the caregiver role somehow exact similar reactions and feelings that are independent of sex or gender? Does *health* mean different things to men and women (Kristiansen, 1989)? How does the concept of health vary across male or female subgroups by class, race, ethnicity, or sexual preference?

The chapters in Part III explore a variety of psychosocial and clinical aspects of men's health and illness. In Chapter 10, Lenard W. Kaye and Jeffrey Applegate chronicle the experiences of male caregivers of ill older persons. Cultural stereotypes surrounding the caregiver role tinge it with feminine qualities. Indeed, it is fair to speculate that if asked to envision a caregiver, most individuals will picture a woman in their mind's eye. Kaye and Applegate not only present statistics that challenge this stereotypical assumption but they also show how male caregivers are adopting emotionally expressive ways of being men that stretch beyond the traditional role of provider and protector. They see men's increasing involvement with caregiving as part and parcel of larger changes in family relations and transformation in the social meaning of gender itself.

The social, cultural, and political dimensions of illness have been strikingly evident in the AIDS epidemic (Shilts, 1988). As Jeffrey Weeks (1991) observes, "AIDS has become the symbolic bearer of a host of meanings about our contemporary culture: about its social composition, its racial boundaries, its attitudes to social marginality; and above all, its moral configurations and its sexual mores" (p. 115). For men, especially gay and bisexual men, who are infected by the HIV virus, the myriad meanings associated with AIDS steep into their gender and sexual identities. In Chapter 11, Richard Tewksbury examines the psychosexual adjustments of gay men to being HIV positive. His analysis of interviews with 45 HIV+ (positive) gay men provides insights into how masculinity, sexuality, social stigmatization, and interpersonal commitment mesh in the decision making around risky sexual behavior.

Tewksbury's findings show that researchers need to learn more about how HIV+ men think, feel, and behave, particularly in the realm of sexual behavior, which is such a central vehicle for the transmission of the HIV virus. Survey researchers have been generating useful information about how men's sexual practices, attitudes, and risk behaviors are linked to the growing AIDS epidemic.[5] Some critics of quantitative approaches to the study of AIDS claim that they fall short of producing highly nuanced understandings of human sexual behavior, in which irrationality, physical urges, and complex gender identity dynamics play such a crucial role in shaping people's perceptions and actions (Bolton, 1992; Leap, 1993). Tewksbury's findings and interpretations of HIV+ men's dilemmas and decisions illustrate the relevance of qualitative methods for generating a more complete study and prevention of AIDS.

David Gordon explores men's psychosocial reactions and adjustments to testicular cancer in Chapter 12. The epidemiological data on testicular cancer is sobering. Though relatively rare in the general population, it is the fourth most common cause of death among 15- to 35-year-old males, accounting for 14% of all cancer deaths for this age group. It is the most common form of cancer affecting 20- to 34-year-old white males. The incidence of testicular cancer is increasing, and about 5,900 new American cases were diagnosed in 1990. If detected early, the cure rate is high; delayed diagnosis is life-threatening. Regular testicular self-examination (TSE), therefore, is an effective preventive means for ensuring early detection and successful treatment.

Despite the growing prevalence of testicular cancer, little is known about how men perceive and adjust to its diagnosis and treatment. Gordon interviewed former testicular cancer patients and found they employed one of two general coping strategies to reconstruct their identities to deal with the threat of illness and surgical loss of a testicle. Whereas some men coped in a traditionally masculine fashion, others found meaning and emotional health by formulating new conceptions of manhood. Gordon's findings vividly demonstrate the potential benefits of more flexible conceptions of manhood for men themselves.

In Chapter 13, Kathy Charmaz discusses the identity dilemmas of men faced with chronic, life-threatening illness. How do men come to grips with the specter of death and dying, or what Charmaz calls "awakening to death"? How does chronic illness alter the self-concept? Does the experience of chronic illness bring with it a reformulation of male identity and relationships? Charmaz's research shows that traditional masculine identity functions as a two-edged sword for men, facilitating positive coping in some respects, but setting men up for greater risk for depression as well.

Several of the authors in this book presented epidemiological data on male suicide. (See the chapters by Waldron, Stillion, and Staples.) In Chapter 14, Silvia Sara Canetto reviews the literature on nonfatal suicides among males; that is, men who have survived a suicide attempt. Although she recognizes that men's psychosocial reactions and adjustments to nonfatal suicide vary by race or ethnicity, socioeconomic status, and age, she also finds that gender identity is an important factor in men's experiences. Suicide data show that men attempt suicide less often than women but are more likely to die than women. Canetto indicates that men's comparative success rate points toward a tragic irony in that, consonant with gender stereotypes, men's failure even at suicide undercuts the cultural mandate that men are supposed to succeed at everything. A lack of embroilment in traditionally masculine expectations, she suggests, may actually increase the likelihood of surviving a suicide attempt for some men.

Conclusion: Toward Men's Health Studies

This book is a collaborative effort to define and develop an emerging area of theory and research we call men's health studies. In pursuing this vision, we find ourselves walking a rather difficult theoretical line. How can men's health studies position itself in relation to women's health studies, women's studies, gender studies, or the feminist paradigm?

Unraveling Masculinities

Sex role theorists and critical feminist theorists agree that the social construction of masculinity in the American gender order produces negative impacts on men's health. If this premise is legitimate, then it follows that men in the 1990s have a vested interest in challenging the traditional gender roles and timeworn notions of masculinity that have proven dangerous to their health (Harrison et al., 1992). Stated another way, if aspects of hegemonic masculinity are dangerous to men's health, then they ought to be changed, abandoned, or resisted. For purposes of self-preservation and the public health, to use John Stoltenberg's (1989) words, more men ought to refuse to be men.

Transforming Gender Order

If sex role theory puts us on the scent of the symptoms for some of men's illnesses, critical feminist perspectives help us understand their broader etiology. The sources of men's malaise and risk for many diseases are not inside men's psyches or gender identities or the roles that they enact in daily life. Men's roles, routines, and relations with others are fixed in the larger historical and structural relations that constitute the gender order. Critical feminist perspectives remind us that any realistic agenda for the transformation of the self and gender relations has got to go beyond therapeutic vision and practice. Yes, men need personal change, but without changing the political, economic, and ideological structures of the gender order, the subjective gains and insights forged within individuals will erode and fade away (Lorber, 1994).

Personal change needs to be rooted in structure and buoyed by institutional realities. Without a raft or boat or some structure to hang on to, even the best swimmer will tire and slip beneath the waves. Whether couched in the feminist dictum that the "personal is political" or C. Wright Mills's contention that personal issues are rooted in social problems, the message is the same. If men are going to embark upon the grand mission of self-healing, they need to set their course along a profeminist tack that seeks to redress the oppression of women by men and the oppression of lesser-status men by privileged males within the intermale dominance hierarchy.

Men's Health Studies
and Preventive Health Care

The study of how gender relations influence men's health and illness is at an early stage of development. How can we continue to mobilize a broad spectrum of social scientists, medical researchers, public health advocates, and men themselves to decide to think about and "do masculinity" differently. Health seems to be one of the most clear-cut areas in which the damaging impacts of traditional masculinity are evident (Sabo, 1995). Part of the mission of men's health studies, therefore, is to carefully research these linkages and to discuss them with professional audiences and the general public.

Proponents of men's health studies might reflect on these guidelines. First, make an effort to link descriptive studies to analytical studies. Descriptive epidemiology is not enough. Patterns not only need to be identified but also interpreted within the total context of the gender order. This wider contextualization calls for an acknowledgment and analysis of the multiple systems of inequality that constitute the postmodern disorder. Second, as many of the writings in this book indicate, the sociocultural model for understanding men's health and illness needs to be politicized. Politicization in this context does not call for the abandonment of commitment to rigorous research methods and logic. It means lending credence to feminist theoretical insights that social inequality irrevocably influences women's and men's health and that differences in political and economic power yield differential health effects.

Third, researchers working in the area of men's health studies can profit from the study of feminist theory and dialogue with women scholars and researchers. We must be wary of creating a new cannon of men's studies; that is, of becoming a fresh set of choir boys (or girls) singing new arrangements of timeworn patriarchal scores. Familiarity with profeminist values and objectives such as self-care or male aggression can also help men's studies practitioners envision useful public health reforms. And finally, men's studies practitioners will need to continue to struggle to formulate theories that take into account forms of men's collective exploitation of women as well as the victimization of marginalized, lesser-status men by male elites within the larger gender order.

Notes

1. The knowledge and spirit generated by the women's health movement is illustrated by the work of the Boston Women's Health Collective. Their book, *Our Bodies, Ourselves: A Book by and for Women,* first published in 1969, was a feminist entreaty for women to learn more about their bodies, medical practices and beliefs, and the politics of the medical system. Expanded editions of this ground-breaking self-help book were published throughout the 1970s, 1980s, and 1990s. See *The New Our Bodies, Ourselves* (1993), New York: Simon & Schuster.

2. There were not tens of thousands of men signing up to join the men's movement in the early 1970s. The first national conference of the men's movement was held in the summer of 1973 in Louisville, Kentucky, and annual "men and masculinity" conferences have occurred since then. The 1980s saw the growth of men's movements in the United States. The followers of Robert Bly "mythopoetic men's movement," for example, use chants and drumming to help men get in touch with the cultural roots of masculinity. The National Organization for Men against Sexism (NOMAS) struggles against sexism and explores gender issues as varied as men's violence against women, men and spirituality, reproductive rights, men and pornography, homophobia, bisexuality, gay rights, and men's health. There are also organizations that advocate for fathers' rights. Religious denominations have begun sponsoring men's weekends and support groups.

3. For introductions to the emerging area of men's studies, see Brod (1987) and Kimmel and Messner (1994). There are two interdisciplinary journals that publish scholarly work on men and masculinity: *Masculinities,* c/o Michael Kimmel, Department of Sociology, S.U.N.Y. at Stony Brook, Stony Brook, NY, 11794-4396; and *The Journal of Men's Studies,* c/o James Doyle, P.O. Box 32, Harriman, TN 37748-0032.

4. The concept of hegemony refers to the influence of certain beliefs that overshadow public awareness in social and political situations and, in the process, help dominant groups to maintain their power over subordinate groups (Sage, 1990). The prevailing model of masculinity in our culture (i.e., hegemonic masculinity) emphasizes aggressiveness, striving for dominance, competition, size, physical strength, and phallocentrism. Hegemonic femininity, in contrast, stresses passivity, physical frailty, dependence (on men), nurturance, cooperation, and sexual submissiveness. The maintenance of hegemonic masculinity and femininity helps men collectively to maintain their control and domination of women.

5. For an example of effective survey research in which researchers worked closely with members of lesbian and gay communities, see *Men's survey '90, AIDS: Knowledge, attitudes, behaviours. A study of gay and bisexual men in Toronto.* (1991). Toronto, Ontario: City of Toronto Department of Public Health and the Toronto Lesbian and Gay Community Appeal.

References

Anderson, M. (1988). *Thinking about women: Sociological perspectives on sex and gender.* New York: Macmillan.

Baca Zinn, M., Weber Cannon, L., Higginbotthen, E., & Thornton-Dill, B. (1986). The costs of exclusionary practices in women's studies. *Signs: Journal of Women in Culture and Society, 11,* 290-303.

Bem, S. L. (1974). The measurement of psychological androgyny. *Journal of Consulting and Clinical Psychology, 42,* 155-162.

Bolton, R. (1992). AIDS and promiscuity: Muddles in the models of HIV prevention. *Medical Anthropology, 14,* 145-224.

Brannon, R. (1976). The male sex role: Our culture's blueprint of manhood, and what it's done for us lately. In D. David & R. Brannon (Eds.), *The forty-nine percent majority* (pp. 1-45). Reading, MA: Addison-Wesley.

Brod, H. (Ed.). (1987). *The making of masculinities: The new men's studies.* Boston: Allen and Unwin.

Castlerman, M. (1980). *Sexual solutions: An informative guide.* New York: Simon & Schuster.

Chodorow, N. (1978). *The reproduction of mothering: Psychoanalysis and the sociology of gender.* Berkeley: University of California Press.

Cockerham, W. C. (1986). *Medical sociology.* Englewood Cliffs, NJ: Prentice Hall.

Connell, R. W. (1987). *Gender and power: Society, the person, and sexual politics.* Stanford, CA: Stanford University Press.

Conrad, P., & Kern, R. (Eds.). (1994). *The sociology of health and illness* (4th ed.). New York: St. Martin's.

Coopersmith, R. (1978). Sex differences in psychotropic drug use. *Social Science in Medicine, 12*(38), 179-186.

Corea, G. (1977). *The hidden malpractice: How American medicine treats women as patients and professionals.* New York: Morrow.

Daly, M. (1978). *Gyn/Ecology: The metaethics of radical feminism.* Boston: Beacon.

Davis, A. (1981). *Women, race and class.* New York: Vantage.

Dubos, R. (1959). *Mirage of health.* New York: Doubleday.

Dutton, D. B. (1989). Social class, health, and illness. In P. Brown (Ed.), *Perspectives in medical sociology* (pp. 23-46). Belmont, CA: Wadsworth.

Ehrenreich, B., & English, D. (1973). *Complaints and disorders: The sexual politics of sickness.* Old Westbury, NY: The Feminist Press.

Ehrenreich, B., & English, D. (1974). *Witches, midwives, and nurses: A history of women healers.* Old Westbury, NY: The Feminist Press.

Farrell, W. (1975). *The liberated man.* New York: Random House.

Fasteau, M. F. (1974). *The male machine.* New York: McGraw-Hill.

Filene, P. (1974). *Him/Her/Self: Sex roles in modern America.* New York: Harcourt, Brace, Jovanovich.

Frank, A. (1991). For a sociology of the body: An analytical review. In M. Featherstone, M. Hepworth, & B. Turner (Eds.), *The body: Social process and cultural theory* (pp. 36-102). London: Sage.

Freund, P. (1982). *The civilized body: Social domination, control and health.* Philadelphia: Temple University Press.

Gibbs, J. T. (1988). *Young, black, and male in America: An endangered species.* Dover, MA: Auburn House.

Glassner, B. (1989). Men and muscles. In M. S. Kimmel & M. A. Messner (Eds.), *Men's lives* (pp. 287-298). New York: Macmillan.

Gramsci, A. (1971). *Selections from the prison notebooks.* London: Lawrence & Wishart.

Harrison, J., Chin, J., & Ficarrotto, T. (1992). Warning: Masculinity may be dangerous to your health. In M. Kimmel & M. Messner (Eds.), *Men's lives* (pp. 296-309). New York: Macmillan.

Hartman, H. (1981). The unhappy marriage of Marxism and feminism. In L. Sargent (Ed.), *Women and revolution* (pp. 1-42). Boston: South End.

hooks, b. (1984). *Feminist theory: From margin to center.* Boston: South End.

Kimmel, M. S., & Messner, M. (Eds.). (1993). *Men's lives.* New York: Macmillan.

Kimmel, M. S., & Mosmiller, T. E. (Eds.). (1992). *Against the tide: Pro-feminist men in the United States, 1776-1990, A documentary history.* Boston: Beacon.

Kristiansen, C. (1989). Gender differences in the meaning of health. *Social Behavior, 4*(3), 185-188.

Leap, W. L. (1993, March). Condom avoidance in a health club locker room: Elites, erotics and the ethnography of AIDS. In *AIDS and the Political Economy of Risk.* Symposium conducted at the annual meeting of the Society for Applied Anthropology, San Antonio, TX.

Lerner, G. (1986). *Creation of patriarchy.* New York: Oxford University Press.

Lorber, J. (1994). *Paradoxes of gender.* New Haven, CT: Yale University Press.

Messner, M. A., & Sabo, D. (Eds.). (1990). *Sport, men and the gender order: Critical feminist perspectives.* Champaign, IL: Human Kinetics.

Messner, M. A., & Sabo, D. (1995). *Sex, violence and power in sports: Rethinking masculinity.* Freedom, CA: Crossing Press.

Mishler, E. G. (1989). Critical perspectives of the biomedical model. In P. Brown, (Ed.), *Perspectives in medical sociology* (pp. 153-166). Belmont, CA: Wadsworth.

Muff, J. (1982). *Socialization, sexism, and sterotyping: Women's issues in nursing.* St. Louis, MO: C. V. Mosby.

Pleck, J. H., & Sonenstein, F. L. (1991). Problem behaviors and masculinity ideology in adolescent males. *Adolescent Problem Behaviors.* Hillsdale, NJ: Lawrence Erlbaum.

Rubin, G. (1975). The traffic in women: Notes on the "political economy" of sex. In R. R. Reiter (Ed.), *Toward an anthropology of women* (pp. 157-210). New York: Monthly Review Press.

Sabo, D. F. (1984). Sharing some of the pain: Men's response to mastectomy. In A. Shostak & G. McLouth (Eds.), *Men and abortion: Lessons, losses, and love.* New York: Praeger.

Sabo, D. F. (1990). Men, death anxiety, and denial: Critical feminist interpretations of adjustment to mastectomy. In E. J. Clark (Ed.), *Clinical sociological perspectives of illness and loss: The linkage of theory and practice* (pp. 71-84). Philadelphia: Charles Press.

Sabo, D. F. (1994, June). *The body politics of sports injury: Culture, power, and the pain principle.* An address presented to National Athletic Trainers Association, Dallas, TX.

Sabo, D. F. (1995). Caring for men. In J. M. Cookfair (Ed.), *Nursing care in the community* (2nd ed.). St. Louis, MO: C. V. Mosby.

Sabo, D. F., Brown, J., & Smith, C. (1986). The male role and mastectomy: Support groups and men's adjustment. *Journal of Psychosocial Oncology, 3*(2), 19-31.

Sabo, D. F., & London, W. (1992). Understanding men in prison: The relevance of gender studies. *Men's Studies Review, 9*(1), 4-9.

Sabo, D. F., & Runfola, R. (1980). *Jock: Sports and male identity.* Englewood Cliffs, NJ: Prentice Hall.

Sage, G. (1990). *Power and ideology in American sport.* Champaign, IL: Human Kinetics.

Scully, D., & Bart, P. (1973). A funny thing happened on the way to the orifice: Women in gynecology textbooks. *American Journal of Sociology, 78*(4), 1045-1050.

Shilts, R. (1988). *And the band played on: Politics, people, and the AIDS epidemic.* New York: Harmondsworth, Penguin.

Shontz, F. C. (1975). *The psychological aspects of physical illness and disability.* New York: Macmillan.

Spence, J. T., Helmreich, R. L., & Stapp, J. (1974). The personal attributes questionnaire: A measure of sex-role stereotypes and masculinity-femininity. *JSAS Catalog of Selected Documents in Psychology, 4,* 127.

Stillion, J. (1985). *Death and the sexes: An examination of differential longevity, attitudes, behaviors, and coping skills.* New York: Hemisphere Publishing.

Stoltenberg, J. (1989). *Refusing to be a man: Essays on sex and justice.* Portland, OR: Breitenbush.

Verbrugge, L. M. (1985). Gender and health: An update on hypotheses and evidence. *Journal of Health and Social Behavior, 26,* 156-182.

Waldron, I. (1983). Sex differences in illness incidence, prognosis and mortality. *Social Science and Medicine, 17,* 1107-1123.

Walkowitz, J. R. (1980). *Prostitution and Victorian society: Women, class, and the state.* Cambridge, UK: Cambridge University Press.

Weeks, J. (1991). *Against nature: Essays on history, sexuality and identity.* London: Rivers Oram Press.

West, C., & Zimmerman, D. (1987). Doing gender. *Gender and Society, 1,* 125-151.

Wolinsky, F. D. (1980). *The sociology of health: Principles, professions, and issues.* Boston: Little, Brown.

2

Contributions of Changing Gender Differences in Behavior and Social Roles to Changing Gender Differences in Mortality

INGRID WALDRON

In the United States and other developed countries males have had higher mortality than females for many decades, but the magnitude of this gender difference in mortality has varied over time (Lopez, 1983; United Nations Secretariat [UNS], 1988; Waldron, 1986b, 1993). During the mid-20th century the male mortality disadvantage increased substantially. In contrast, the male mortality disadvantage has begun to decrease recently in the United States and some other developed countries.

This chapter discusses the contributions of changing gender differences in behavior and social roles to changing gender differences in mortality. Other factors that influence gender differences in mortality are also discussed briefly. The first section summarizes evidence concerning the causes of contemporary gender differences in mortality, and the second section briefly discusses the causes of the mid-20th century increases in gender differences in mortality. These two sections provide the context for a more detailed analysis of recent trends in the United States. This analysis uses U.S. data for 1979 to 1989 to describe recent trends in gender differences in mortality and to address several important questions. Have

AUTHOR'S NOTE: It is a pleasure to thank Tracy Brooks and Katie Eyer for their help in obtaining information used in preparing this chapter.

gender differences in behavior and social roles decreased recently, and have these trends contributed to recent trends in gender differences in mortality? Have trends been similar for different types of behavior and for different causes of death? What other factors have contributed to recent trends in gender differences in mortality? The chapter concludes with a brief discussion of some possible causes of recent trends in gender differences in health-related behavior.

In this chapter gender differences are assessed by means of sex ratios. For example, a sex mortality ratio is the ratio of male to female death rates. Sex mortality ratios are presented rather than difference measures (male minus female death rates), because a difference measure generally decreases as the level of mortality decreases. A sex mortality ratio decreases if there is a greater proportionate decrease in mortality for males than for females (Waldron, 1993). The terms *men* and *women* are used in discussing causes of death or behaviors observed exclusively or almost exclusively among adults, whereas the terms *males* and *females* are generally used to refer to a broader age range, including teenagers and in some cases children.

Causes of Males' Higher Mortality

In the United States and other contemporary developed countries, males have higher mortality than females at all ages (Lopez, 1983; UNS, 1988; Waldron, 1986b). The largest single contributor to males' higher mortality is ischemic heart disease (also called coronary heart disease), which includes myocardial infarctions (commonly known as heart attacks). Other major causes of males' higher mortality are lung cancer, chronic obstructive pulmonary disease (including conditions such as emphysema), accidents, suicide, homicide, chronic liver disease and cirrhosis, and HIV infection or AIDS (see Table 2.1). Gender differences in behavior are a major cause of males' higher mortality for each of these causes of death. The following paragraphs summarize evidence for the importance of behavioral causes of males' higher mortality, based primarily on data for the United States.

More males than females smoke cigarettes and, in general, males have more risky smoking habits (Waldron, 1991b). Gender differences in smoking have been a major cause of men's higher mortality, including men's higher mortality due to lung cancer, chronic obstructive pulmonary disease, and ischemic heart disease (U.S. Department of Health and Human Services [USDHHS], 1989; Waldron, 1986a). It has been estimated that, in the United States, men's higher smoking-related mortality has accounted for as much as half of gender differences in adult mortality, including

Table 2.1 Trends in Gender Differences in Mortality, United States, 1979-1989

Cause of Death	1979			1989		
	Male	Female	Sex Ratio	Male	Female	Sex Ratio
Ischemic heart disease	219.0	99.9	2.19	146.3	72.4	2.02
Lung cancer	59.3	17.3	3.43	59.3	25.4	2.33
Chronic obstructive pulmonary disease	24.7	7.9	3.13	26.4	14.7	1.80
Motor vehicle accidents	35.8	12.1	2.96	26.8	11.2	2.39
Other accidents	30.4	10.2	2.98	22.7	7.6	2.99
Suicide	18.3	6.0	3.05	18.6	4.5	4.13
Homicide	16.7	4.3	3.88	14.7	4.1	3.59
Chronic liver disease and cirrhosis	17.1	7.8	2.19	12.8	5.5	2.33
Human immunodeficiency virus (HIV)	NA[a]	NA	NA	15.7	1.8	8.72
Breast cancer	0.2	22.8	.01	0.2	23.0	.01
All causes	780.3	433.5	1.80	678.7	395.3	1.72

SOURCE: National Center for Health Statistics (1984, 1992a).
NOTE: Data shown are age-adjusted male and female death rates per 100,000 population and sex mortality ratios. Data are given for all specific causes of death that were responsible for at least 1% of mortality and had a sex mortality ratio of greater than 2.0 or less than 0.5. *Lung cancer* is the common name for malignant neoplasms of respiratory and intrathoracic organs.
a. NA = Not Available.

approximately 90% of gender differences in lung cancer mortality and roughly a third of gender differences in ischemic heart disease mortality (Waldron, 1986a, 1995).

More males than females drink heavily, and this contributes to males' higher mortality due to liver disease, accidents, suicide, and homicide (Waldron, 1986b). Male drivers are considerably more likely than female drivers to have high blood alcohol levels, which substantially increases the risk of fatal motor vehicle accidents. In addition, males have less safe driving habits than females, and this also contributes to males' higher rates of fatal accidents per mile driven. Males also use guns more and take more physical risks, for example, in swimming and other types of recreation, and these behaviors contribute to males' higher mortality due to accidents and other violence (Waldron, 1986b). More males inject drugs, which contributes to males' higher rates of HIV infection and resultant mortality (National Institute on Drug Abuse, 1990).

More males than females are employed, and males' jobs are more physically hazardous on the average (Waldron, 1991a). Males' greater exposure to occupational hazards contributes to their higher rates of lung cancer and accident mortality. Evidence for the United States suggests that males' greater exposure to occupational hazards is responsible for roughly 5% to 10% of the gender difference in mortality (Waldron, 1991a).

Additional gender differences in behavior and psychological character- istics appear to influence gender differences in ischemic heart disease mortality. Men have higher scores on measures of hostility and mistrust of others, psychological characteristics that are associated with increased risk of ischemic heart disease (Barefoot et al., 1991; Matthews et al., 1992; Scherwitz et al., 1991). Thus, men's greater hostility and mistrust appear to contribute to men's higher ischemic heart disease mortality. Gender differences in diet may also play a role. For example, data for the United States indicate that men's diets have had somewhat higher ratios of saturated to polyunsaturated fat and men have had lower vitamin C intake on a per calorie or per body weight basis, and these gender differences in diet would be expected to contribute to higher ischemic heart disease mortality for men (Block, Rosenberger, & Patterson, 1988; Enstrom, Kanim, & Klein, 1992; Ulbricht & Southgate, 1991; U.S. Department of Health, Education, and Welfare, 1977; Van Horn et al., 1991; Waldron, 1995). On the other hand, some gender differences in behavior would be expected to contrib- ute to lower mortality for men. For example, men are more involved in vigorous physical exercise than women, and this would be expected to reduce men's ischemic heart disease mortality (Berlin & Colditz, 1990; Blair et al., 1992; Piani & Schoenborn, 1993; Schoenborn, 1988; Stephens, 1987; White et al., 1987).

It should also be noted that some hypotheses concerning contributions of gender differences in behavior to gender differences in mortality have not been confirmed. For example, one hypothesis has been that women obtain more medical care than men, and this results in better prognosis for women for various illnesses and thus contributes to women's lower mor- tality. Women do visit physicians more often than men, but this difference is observed primarily for conditions that are not major causes of death (Waldron, 1983). In the United States, women visit physicians more often than men for conditions related to the reproductive system, general exams, and problems such as weight gain and psychological symptoms. In con- trast, for most types of cancer and ischemic heart disease, women delay as long or longer than men before seeking medical care (Turi et al., 1986; Waldron, 1983, 1995). Correspondingly, for most types of cancer and for myocardial infarctions, women do not have a better prognosis than men. Thus, although women visit physicians more often than men, this appears to make relatively little contribution to women's lower mortality (Waldron, 1983, 1986b, 1995).

Biological differences between the sexes also contribute to gender differences in mortality. For example, gender differences in ischemic heart disease mortality appear to be due in part to protective effects of female sex hormones and risks due to men's tendency to accumulate fat in the upper abdomen (Kalin & Zumoff, 1990; Larsson et al., 1992; Stampfer, Colditz, & Willett, 1990; Waldron, 1995). In summary, contemporary gender differences in mortality are caused by the interacting effects of sex differences in biology and gender differences in behavior and roles.

Mid-20th-Century Trends

The male mortality disadvantage was relatively small in Western countries at the beginning of the 20th century. During the mid-20th century, female mortality fell more rapidly than male mortality and consequently the male mortality disadvantage increased (Lopez, 1983; UNS, 1988; Waldron, 1986b). For example, in the United States, the sex mortality ratio (the ratio of male to female mortality) increased from 1.29 in 1940 to 1.80 in 1979 (calculated from data in National Center for Health Statistics [NCHS], 1984, 1992a). (Similarly, the sex difference in life expectancy increased from a female advantage of 4.4 years in 1940 to 7.8 years in 1979.)

A variety of causes of death contributed to the more favorable mortality trends for females (Anderson, 1973; Enterline, 1961; Gee & Veevers, 1983; UNS, 1988; Waldron, 1986b). Females benefited more from decreases in certain causes of death, such as the decrease in maternal mortality. At the same time, decreases in male mortality were slowed because males experienced increased mortality for certain causes of death, particularly lung cancer and ischemic heart disease. The increases in male lung cancer and ischemic heart disease mortality were due in large part to males' early and widespread adoption of cigarette smoking (Burbank, 1972; Preston, 1970; Retherford, 1975; Waldron, 1991b). Thus, changing gender differences in cigarette smoking were one major cause of the mid-20th century increase in the male mortality disadvantage.

Recent Trends

In the United States, the trend to increasing gender differences in mortality reversed during the late 1970s, and gender differences in mortality decreased during the 1980s. From 1979 to 1989 the sex mortality ratio decreased from 1.80 to 1.72, as male mortality decreased more than female mortality (Table 2.1). (Similarly, the sex difference in life expectancy decreased from a peak female advantage of 7.8 years in 1979 to a female advantage of 6.8 years in 1989; NCHS, 1992a.)

Several causes of death contributed to more favorable mortality trends for males than for females during the 1980s in the United States (Table 2.1). Males had greater proportionate decreases than females for ischemic heart disease and motor vehicle accident mortality. In addition, mortality for lung cancer and chronic obstructive pulmonary disease increased substantially for females, but not for males.

In contrast to these trends that favored males, trends for some other major causes of death favored females or were similar for males and females (Table 2.1). Suicide rates tended to increase for males, but decreased for females. Mortality due to HIV infection or AIDS increased particularly for males. For accidents other than motor vehicle accidents, males and females had similar proportionate decreases in mortality.

The following sections discuss possible causes of these varied trends in gender differences in mortality. Evidence is presented concerning trends in several types of health-related behavior and social roles and the possible contributions of these behavioral and social trends to the mortality trends in the United States in the 1980s. Other possible causes of recent mortality trends are also discussed briefly.

Smoking, Diet, and Exercise

Gender differences in the prevalence of cigarette smoking have been decreasing for decades (Fiore et al., 1989; Waldron, 1991b). The male excess in the prevalence of smoking decreased at first because an increasing proportion of females adopted smoking and in recent decades because the prevalence of smoking has decreased more rapidly for males than for females. Table 2.2 illustrates these trends for the 1980s and from 1955 to 1965, 2.5 decades earlier. The earlier trends in smoking are relevant for mortality trends in the 1980s because there appears to be a considerable lag time between the adoption of smoking and the occurrence of mortality due to lung cancer and chronic obstructive pulmonary disease (Brown & Kessler, 1988; Burbank, 1972; Lee, Fry, & Forey, 1990; USDHHS, 1989, 1990). As would be expected on the basis of the earlier trends in smoking, female mortality for lung cancer and chronic obstructive pulmonary disease increased during the 1980s and sex mortality ratios for these causes of death decreased (Tables 2.1 and 2.2). Ischemic heart disease mortality is

Table 2.2 Trends in Gender Differences in Smoking, Diet, and
Exercise, United States, 1979-1989

Behavior Measure	Circa 1979			Circa 1989		
	Male	Female	Sex Ratio	Male	Female	Sex Ratio
Percent of adults who smoked cigarettes	37.2	30.3	1.23	29.1	24.6	1.18
Percent of adults who smoked cigarettes 24 years earlier	52.6	24.5	2.15	51.1	33.3	1.53
Index of atherogenicity for fats in diet	0.713	0.685	1.04	0.645	0.645	1.00
Vitamin C (mg per 1000 calories)	40.4	56.7	0.71	43.7	52.0	0.84
Percent of adults who were very physically active	27.0	16.4	1.65	36.6	22.6	1.62

NOTE: All data are for national samples. The smoking data are age-adjusted rates for adults aged 17 and above or 18 and above. The rates given for 1989 are averages of 1988 and 1990 data; the rates given for 24 years earlier are for 1955 and 1965 (National Center for Health Statistics, 1992b). The index of atherogenicity is saturated fat intake divided by polyunsaturated plus monounsaturated fat intake (adapted from Ulbricht & Southgate, 1991). Dietary data are for 20 to 49 year olds in 1976 to 1980 and 1985 to 1986 (Life Sciences Research Office, 1989). Very physically active adults were those who expended at least 3 kcal. of energy per kilogram body weight per day in leisure-time exercise. Slightly different methods were used to obtain the data for 1981 to 1983 (White et al., 1987) and for 1990 (Piani & Schoenborn, 1993).

influenced more by current and recent smoking, as well as by a number of other major risk factors (USDHHS, 1989, 1990; Waldron, 1995). Corresponding to recent trends in smoking, ischemic heart disease mortality showed a greater decrease for males than for females and the sex mortality ratio for ischemic heart disease decreased during the 1980s (Tables 2.1 and 2.2).

Limited data suggest that gender differences in diet may have decreased during the 1980s. For example, national data indicate that men's diets contained less vitamin C per calorie than women's diets, on average, and this gender difference appears to have decreased during the early 1980s (Table 2.2). Decreasing gender differences in vitamin C intake may have contributed to decreasing gender differences in mortality, because higher intake of vitamin C appears to reduce the risk of cardiovascular disease, cancer, and total mortality (Enstrom et al., 1992).

The index of atherogenicity is a measure of the expected contribution of dietary fats to atherosclerosis, the buildup of plaque that plays a major role in the development of ischemic heart disease (Ulbricht & Southgate, 1991). The index of atherogenicity is assessed here as the ratio of saturated fat intake to polyunsaturated plus monounsaturated fat intake. Data for a national sample of 20 to 49 year olds suggest that men's diets had a slightly higher index of atherogenicity than women's diets in the late 1970s (Table 2.2). The index of atherogenicity appears to have decreased more for men than for women during the early 1980s, and consequently no gender difference was observed by the mid-1980s. However, two additional observations do not support the suggestion that gender differences in the atherogenicity of dietary fats decreased and disappeared by the mid-1980s. First, data for a large sample of 18 to 30 year olds in four U.S. cities suggest that males still consumed more atherogenic diets than females in the mid-1980s (Van Horn et al., 1991). Second, national data indicate that serum cholesterol and LDL cholesterol fell slightly faster for women than for men during the 1980s (Johnson et al., 1993), and this suggests that the atherogenicity of dietary fats fell at least as rapidly for women as for men (Waldron, 1995). Thus, a variety of evidence suggests improvement in fat composition of diets during the 1980s, but gender differences in this trend are uncertain.

Levels of exercise participation appear to have increased for both men and women during the 1980s, but it is unclear whether gender differences in exercise participation changed during this period. National data suggest differing trends, depending on the time period and the exercise measure considered. More women than men were sedentary in the late 1970s, and this gender difference decreased during the early 1980s as the proportion sedentary decreased more rapidly for women than for men (Stephens, 1987). In contrast, more men than women are very physically active in leisure time, and this gender difference appears to have remained relatively stable during the 1980s (Table 2.2). (The sex ratio for this measure of exercise participation appears to have decreased slightly during the first half of the decade and increased slightly during the second half of the decade [calculated from data in Piani & Schoenborn, 1993; Schoenborn, 1988; White et al., 1987].) With respect to physical activity in job or housework, men's main daily activity is more likely than women's to require at least a moderate amount of hard physical work, and this gender difference was stable during the late 1980s. Thus, the available evidence indicates that exercise participation increased during the 1980s and this probably contributed to decreased ischemic heart disease and total mortality, but it is unclear whether there were gender differences in the exercise trends.

In summary, gender differences in smoking have decreased and this has contributed to decreasing gender differences in lung cancer, chronic obstructive pulmonary disease, and ischemic heart disease mortality. Diet and exercise habits have improved, but gender differences in these trends are uncertain.

Driving and Drinking

Gender differences in driving-related behavior show differing trends, depending on the specific behavior considered (Table 2.3). Overall, the data indicate decreasing gender differences in amount of driving but increasing gender differences in driving-related safety during the 1980s. At the beginning of the decade, a higher proportion of males than females were licensed drivers, and male drivers drove over twice as many miles per year as female drivers. These gender differences decreased during the 1980s, due to substantial increases in female driving. As miles driven by the average female driver increased, females experienced increased rates of fatal crashes per driver, and gender differences in fatal crashes per driver decreased. In contrast, rates of fatal crashes per mile driven decreased substantially for females. In fact, rates of fatal crashes per mile driven decreased more for females than for males, and the sex ratio for fatal crashes per mile driven increased during the 1980s. These trends suggest that females had greater improvements than males in driving-related safety habits. Additional evidence that females had greater improvements in safety habits is provided by the finding that females increased seat belt use more than males during the 1980s. In 1979 males and females had similar rates of seat belt use, but by the mid- and late 1980s, more females than males used seat belts (Table 2.3; NCHS, 1988; Piani & Schoenborn, 1993).

In summary, gender differences in driving decreased during the 1980s as more females were driving more miles. In contrast, the available evidence suggests that gender differences in safety habits related to driving tended to increase. These results suggest that the decrease in the sex mortality ratio for motor vehicle accident fatalities (Table 2.1) was not due to decreased gender differences in driving-related safety, but may have been due in part to decreased gender differences in driving and exposure to accidents.

In contrast to the decreasing gender differences in smoking and amount of driving, gender differences in alcohol consumption appear to have increased during the 1980s. National survey data indicate that drinking, especially heavy drinking, has been more common among males than

Table 2.3 Trends in Gender Differences in Driving and Drinking, United States, 1979-1989

Behavior Measure	Circa 1979			Circa 1989		
	Male	Female	Sex Ratio	Male	Female	Sex Ratio
Percent of adults who were licensed drivers	88.8	73.3	1.21	92.9	85.8	1.08
Thousands of miles driven per licensed driver	13.4	5.9	2.26	16.5	9.5	1.74
Drivers involved in fatal crashes per 100,000 licensed drivers	56.5	14.9	3.79	53.2	17.5	3.04
Drivers involved in fatal crashes per billion miles driven	52.0	25.0	2.10	45.0	17.0	2.60
Percent of adults who usually used seat belts	19.8	19.5	1.02	34.7	38.7	0.90
Percent of fatal crashes in which driver was intoxicated	32.4	18.8	1.72	27.1	14.3	1.90
Percent of adults who drank alcohol	75.0	60.0	1.25	68.0	47.0	1.45
Percent of adults who were heavy drinkers	14.0	4.0	3.50	13.0	3.0	4.30

NOTE: The data concerning the percent who were drivers and miles driven are for people aged 16 and above in 1977 and 1990 (U.S. Department of Transportation, 1992). For drivers involved in fatal crashes, the rates per billion miles driven are for 1979 and 1988, whereas the rates per driver and proportion intoxicated (blood alcohol levels of 0.10 g/dl and above) are for 1982 and 1989 (Centers for Disease Control, 1992; National Safety Council, 1980, 1990). Seat belt use data are for adults aged 20 to 64 in 1979 and 1985 (National Center for Health Statistics, 1988). Drinking data are for adults aged 18 and above in 1979 and 1988; heavy drinking is the consumption of 1.00 ounce or more of ethanol per day (National Center for Health Statistics, 1992b). All data are for national samples or estimates for the U.S. population as a whole.

females, and this gender difference increased during the 1980s (Table 2.3). The male excess in the prevalence of drinking increased because the prevalence of drinking decreased more rapidly for females than for males. Similarly, survey results for heavy drinking (consumption of one ounce or more of ethanol per day or about two drinks or more per day) indicate that the sex ratio for heavy drinking increased as heavy drinking decreased proportionately more for females than for males during the 1980s. This conclusion is supported by suggestive data for 1979 to 1988 (Table 2.3) and more detailed data for 1985 to 1990, which show increases in sex ratios for the prevalence of heavy drinking in each of four adult age groups (calculated from data in Piani & Schoenborn, 1993; Schoenborn, 1988).

Decreased prevalance and increased sex ratios for drinking and heavy drinking could account for the trends observed for several measures of alcohol-related mortality. For example, decreasing rates and increasing sex ratios were observed for the percentage of fatal crashes in which the driver was intoxicated (Table 2.3) and for mortality due to chronic liver disease and cirrhosis (Table 2.1). Similar trends were also observed for a measure of alcohol-induced mortality that includes deaths due to physiological damage resulting from chronic alcohol consumption and accidental poisoning by alcohol but does not include motor vehicle accidents, homicide, and so forth in which alcohol was a contributory cause. For this index of alcohol-induced mortality, females had a greater proportionate decrease than males during the 1980s and, as a result, the sex mortality ratio increased from 2.9 in 1979 to 3.4 in 1989 (calculated from data in NCHS, 1992a).

In summary, gender differences in amount of driving appear to have decreased during the 1980s due to increased driving by females. In contrast, gender differences in driving-related safety and alcohol use appear to have increased during the 1980s because females had greater improvement in driving-related safety and greater decreases in drinking than males. These varied behavioral trends appear to have made significant contributions to recent trends in death rates and sex mortality ratios for motor vehicle accidents and alcohol-induced mortality.

Employment and Marital Status

During the 1980s, as in previous decades, women's employment increased and gender differences in employment rates decreased (see Table 2.4). Trends in blue-collar employment are of particular interest here because the major proven mortality effects of employment are due to occupational hazards that are more common in blue-collar occupations than in white-collar occupations. In contrast to the trends for total employment, the proportion of women who had blue-collar jobs tended to decrease during the 1980s, and the sex ratio for blue-collar employment remained unchanged (Table 2.4).

Because the trends in blue-collar employment were similar for males and females, it would be expected that trends in mortality due to work-related accidents were similar for males and females. Most work-related accidents are included in the cause of death category, "all other accidents," which showed similar proportionate decreases for males and females and

Table 2.4 Trends in Social Roles, United States, 1979-1989

Measure of Social Roles	1979			1989		
	Male	Female	Sex Ratio	Male	Female	Sex Ratio
Labor force						
participation rate (%)	78.2	51.0	1.53	76.8	57.5	1.34
Blue-collar workers (%)	37.4	7.4	5.10	33.0	6.5	5.10
Married (%)	72.3	72.1	1.00	65.5	66.5	0.98

NOTE: Labor force participation includes both those who were employed and those who were unemployed but looking for a job; labor force participation rates are for the U.S. population aged 16 and above (U.S. Department of Labor, 1990). The proportion who were blue-collar workers has been estimated by multiplying the proportion who were employed by the proportion of civilian workers who were employed in blue-collar occupations (calculated from data in U.S. Department of Commerce, 1981, 1991; U.S. Department of Labor, 1990). The percent married is for adults in the United States aged 20 to 64 (calculated from data in U.S. Department of Commerce, 1980, 1990).

no change in sex mortality ratio from 1979 to 1989 (Table 2.1). Within the category of other accidents, a crude estimate of fatal work accidents is provided by the proportion of accidental deaths that occurred in industrial places, mines, quarries, or farms for those aged 15 to 69 (calculated from data in NCHS, 1984, 1991). From 1979 to 1988 this proportion decreased from 14.7% to 10.6% for males and from 2.0% to 1.5% for females. Taken together, these data suggest that males and females had similar proportionate decreases in fatal work accidents during the 1980s, as would be expected based on the trends in blue-collar employment. Occupational hazards also contribute to gender differences in lung cancer mortality (Waldron, 1991a), but limited evidence suggests that recent trends in occupational exposures have made only minor contributions to trends in lung cancer mortality (Brown & Kessler, 1988; Swerdlow, 1990).

Employment affects health not only via exposures to occupational hazards but also via the multiple psychosocial and economic effects of employment (Repetti, Matthews, & Waldron, 1989; Waldron, 1991a). Given the multiple hypothesized effects of employment on health and the changing gender differences in employment, it is of interest to evaluate the total health effects of employment. Due to substantial methodological problems, useful evidence is limited, but evidence from several well-designed longitudinal studies suggests the following conclusions.

It appears that the health effects of employment vary, depending on job characteristics, family situation, attitudes toward employment, and other factors (Repetti et al., 1989). However, for middle-aged and older women as a whole, harmful and beneficial effects of employment appear to be roughly balanced, resulting in little or no net effect of employment on total mortality, on average (Waldron, 1991a). Similarly, it appears that for middle-aged and older women and men, employment has little or no effect on general morbidity, on average. Additional longitudinal evidence suggests that on average women's employment does not affect their risk of ischemic heart disease or their husband's risk of ischemic heart disease (Waldron, 1991a). Relationships between women's employment and suicide risk have been inconsistent in different studies (Austin, Bologna, & Dodge, 1992; Ornstein, 1983). These findings, together with additional evidence summarized in a previous review, suggest that increases in women's employment have had relatively little effect on trends in gender differences in mortality (Waldron, 1991a).

Trends in marital status have been generally similar for both sexes during the 1980s. The proportion married has decreased as the proportion never married has increased at younger ages and the proportion divorced has increased at older ages (Table 2.4 and data in U.S. Department of Commerce, 1980, 1990). Epidemiological evidence indicates that not being married increases mortality more for men than for women, both for total mortality and for specific causes of death such as suicide (Gove, 1973; Hu & Goldman, 1990; Smith, Mercy, & Conn, 1988). Thus, the decrease in proportion married during the 1980s would be expected to result in relatively unfavorable mortality trends for men. Quantitative calculations indicate that if mortality rates within each marital status category had remained unchanged and the proportion in each marital status category had changed as observed from 1979 to 1989, then the expected effect of the marital status trends would have been to increase sex mortality ratios for total mortality and for suicide by somewhat less than 5% (calculated from data in Smith et al., 1988; United Nations, 1987; U.S. Department of Commerce, 1980, 1990). This suggests that trends in marriage and divorce made a modest contribution to the increase in the sex mortality ratio for suicide during the 1980s (Table 2.1). For total mortality, the sex mortality ratio did not show the predicted increase, but rather decreased (Table 2.1). Thus, for total mortality, any disadvantage for males due to trends in marital status was presumably more than counterbalanced by other trends that favored males.

External Causes of Death

During the 1980s, different external causes of death showed very different trends in gender differences in mortality. Specifically, sex mortality ratios decreased for motor vehicle accidents, remained unchanged for other accidents, and increased for suicide (Table 2.1).

As discussed earlier, it appears that sex mortality ratios decreased for motor vehicle accidents, in part because gender differences in exposure to risk of motor vehicle accidents decreased as a result of increased driving by females. In contrast, gender differences in driving-related safety appear to have increased during the 1980s. The other accidents category includes diverse types of accidents that are related to a wide variety of risky behaviors. For most major categories of other accidents it appears that gender differences have been stable or have increased during the 1980s. Evidence presented previously suggests quite stable sex ratios for fatal work accidents and for the proportion employed in blue-collar occupations in which the risk of fatal work accidents is highest. In addition, sex mortality ratios were stable or increased for drownings (7.6 in 1979 vs. 7.9 in 1988), firearm accidents (6.4 vs. 7.1), fatal falls (6.0 vs. 6.3), and accidental poisonings (2.5 vs. 3.5) (calculated from mortality data for 15 to 44 year olds in World Health Organization, 1983, 1991).

In summary, it appears that gender differences in amount of driving decreased during the 1980s, but gender differences persisted or even increased for many other behaviors related to accident fatality risk, including seat belt use, blue-collar employment, and the types of behavior that contribute to drownings, fatal gun accidents, fatal falls, and accidental poisonings.

Several hypotheses have been proposed to explain why male suicide rates tended to increase whereas female suicide rates tended to decrease during the 1980s. As discussed in the previous section, the decrease in the proportion married and increase in the proportion divorced probably had a more adverse effect on men and this may have made a modest contribution to men's more unfavorable suicide trends. It has also been suggested that women's suicide rates had increased during the 1960s due to anomie resulting from uncertainty concerning women's changing roles and then decreased during the late 1970s and 1980s in part due to decreased anomie as women's new roles were more widely accepted (Austin et al., 1992). Another hypothesis has been that trends in unemployment might contribute to gender differences in suicide trends, but no consistent gender differences were found in trends in unemployment or in the relationship between unemployment and suicide rates (Pritchard, 1990). Finally, in the context of this volume, it is of interest to speculate concerning possible effects of changes in earnings. Decreased earnings might be expected to have particularly adverse effects on men's mental health, in that earnings appear to be closely linked to American conceptions of masculinity. National poll data have repeatedly shown that being a "good provider for his family" is considered one of the most important characteristics that defines masculinity (Faludi, 1991; Susan Hayward, personal communication, July 1992). From 1979 to 1987, the inflation-adjusted earnings of males employed full-time year-round showed a small net decrease (an overall 2.4% decrease due to unfavorable trends in the late 1970s and early 1980s) (England & Browne, 1992). In contrast, this measure of earnings increased for females (an overall 6.9% increase due to favorable trends from 1981 on). Could males' unfavorable suicide trends be due in part to the increasing difficulty of satisfying a major criterion of masculinity, being a good provider? It will be of interest to explore this hypothesis and other possible influences on gender differences in suicide trends in future research.

Sex Differences in the Mortality Effects of Certain Behavioral and Environmental Trends

Previous sections of this chapter have discussed changing gender differences in behavior that have contributed to changing gender differences in mortality during the 1980s. It should also be noted that even when males and females have experienced similar behavioral or environmental trends these trends can contribute to changing gender differences in mortality if a given change in behavior or environment has a greater impact on male or female mortality. For example, as discussed previously, marital status may influence male mortality more than female mortality, so recent decreases in the proportion married may have contributed to males' more unfavorable suicide trends. Several additional examples illustrate the potential importance of the differential impact on male and female mortality of certain behavioral or environmental trends.

A variety of evidence suggests that a given decrease in the atherogenicity of dietary fats may decrease ischemic heart disease risk more for men than for women (Clifton & Nestel, 1992; Waldron, 1995). Thus, the decreases in the atherogenicity of dietary fats during the 1980s would be expected to benefit men more, and this appears to be one reason why ischemic heart disease mortality decreased more for men than for women during the 1980s (Tables 2.1 and 2.2). Given the long time span for the development of atherosclerosis, dietary trends during the 1970s may also be relevant to ischemic heart disease mortality trends during the 1980s. It appears that men and women had similar decreases in atherogenicity of dietary fats during the 1970s (calculated from data in Life Sciences

Research Office, 1989). Because men appear to be more responsive to dietary change, these earlier dietary trends may also have contributed to the greater decrease in ischemic heart disease mortality for men than for women during the 1980s (Waldron, 1995). Additional evidence suggests that recent advances in medical treatment of ischemic heart disease may have benefited men more than women, in part because men may seek medical treatment more promptly than women and in part because the extent and efficacy of medical treatment may be greater for male ischemic heart disease patients (Maynard et al., 1992; Turi et al., 1986; Waldron, 1995). Thus, men may have benefited more from recent improvements in diet and medical treatment, and this may be one reason why ischemic heart disease mortality decreased more for men.

The spread of a major new infectious disease, AIDS or HIV, has thus far had a much greater impact on male than female mortality (Table 2.1). Males have been more vulnerable to HIV infection than females in part because males have been more likely to engage in behaviors that increase the risk of HIV infection and in part because sex differences in anatomy and physiology contribute to greater vulnerability of male, as opposed to female, homosexuals (National Institute on Drug Abuse, 1990; Smith, 1991). For both behavioral and anatomical reasons, then, the spread of the AIDS epidemic increased male mortality more than female mortality.

Discussion

Previous research has established that gender differences in behavior are a major cause of gender differences in mortality. Behavioral causes of males' higher mortality include males' higher rates of smoking, heavy drinking, employment in hazardous occupations, and physical risk taking, including less safe driving habits. Historically, males' earlier and more widespread adoption of cigarette smoking was a major cause of the increase in the male mortality disadvantage during the mid-20th century.

Data for the United States indicate that the long-term trend to an increasing male mortality disadvantage has been reversed recently. Specifically, the male mortality disadvantage decreased during the 1980s primarily because males had more favorable mortality trends than females for ischemic heart disease, lung cancer, chronic obstructive pulmonary disease, and motor vehicle accidents. These decreasing gender differences in mortality are linked to decreasing gender differences in certain types of health-related behavior. For example, decreasing gender differences in smoking have been an important cause of decreasing gender differences in mortality due to lung cancer, chronic obstructive pulmonary diseases, and ischemic heart disease. Gender differences in amount of driving decreased, and this appears to have been one important cause of the decreasing gender difference in motor vehicle accident mortality.

However, trends during the 1980s do not present a uniform picture of decreasing gender differences in behavior resulting in decreasing gender differences in mortality. Gender differences in some types of health-related behavior did not decrease. For example, it appears that gender differences in driving-related safety habits increased during the 1980s. Also, no clear trends were observed for gender differences in exercise or dietary fat intake. Although the trends in dietary fats may have been similar for both sexes, decreased consumption of atherogenic fats appears to benefit men more than women, so the dietary trends may have contributed to decreasing gender differences in ischemic heart disease mortality. Similarly, improvements in medical care for ischemic heart disease may have benefited men more and thus may have contributed to decreasing gender differences in ischemic heart disease mortality.

It should also be noted that although gender differences decreased for total mortality and several major causes of death during the 1980s, gender differences did not decrease for several other categories of mortality. For example, sex mortality ratios remained unchanged or increased slightly for mortality due to other accidents and alcohol-related mortality. Correspondingly, gender differences in underlying behaviors such as blue-collar employment and heavy drinking remained unchanged or increased somewhat. The sex mortality ratio for suicide increased during the 1980s because male suicide rates tended to increase while female suicide rates decreased. The causes of the trends in suicide are uncertain but may include a greater male vulnerability to decreases in the proportion married during the 1980s. Males have also been more vulnerable to HIV infection or AIDS, for both biological and behavioral reasons, so the spread of AIDS increased mortality more for males than for females during the 1980s.

In summary, decreasing gender differences in smoking and driving, together with differential effects of dietary and medical improvements, appear to have been major causes of decreasing gender differences in mortality during the 1980s. Several other behavioral and mortality trends did not show decreasing gender differences during the 1980s. It should also be noted that one major trend toward converging gender roles, that is, the decreasing gender difference in employment rates, appears not to have contributed to decreases in gender differences in mortality during the 1980s.

Mortality data for other economically developed countries suggest that several of the trends observed in the United States have been very widespread during the 1980s (Waldron, 1993). For example, sex mortality ratios for lung cancer decreased due to increases in women's lung cancer mortality in most Western European and Anglophone developed countries during the 1980s. Also similar to the United States, males tended to have more favorable trends than females for motor vehicle accident mortality, but not for other accident mortality. Also, males had more unfavorable suicide trends than females, resulting in increasing sex mortality ratios for suicide in most developed countries during the 1980s. One exception to the pattern of similar trends in the United States and other developed countries was ischemic heart disease mortality; in the United States men had a greater proportionate decrease in ischemic heart disease mortality than women, but in many Western European countries this gender difference in ischemic heart disease mortality trends was not observed. Nevertheless, the widespread occurrence of similar recent trends in gender differences in mortality due to lung cancer, accidents, and suicide is noteworthy and suggests that there have been widespread similarities in the underlying behavioral and social trends in developed countries during the 1980s.

One of the most interesting conclusions from the evidence concerning behavioral trends in the United States is that trends in gender differences in behavior have differed for different types of behavior. During the 1980s, gender differences in smoking and amount of driving decreased, but gender differences in driving-related safety and alcohol consumption appear to have increased somewhat. In addition, mortality data suggest stable or increasing gender differences in behavior related to firearm accidents, drownings, falls, and accidental poisonings. These observations run counter to the popular impression that females are adopting a broad range of typically male risky behaviors as part of a general convergence in female and male behavior. For example, contrary to this expectation, it appears that during the 1980s females did not adopt male drinking habits, but rather females reduced their drinking more than males did. Similarly, there were increasing gender differences in some types of preventive behavior. For example, males and females have had similar rates of seat belt use in the past, but during the 1980s more females than males began regular seat belt use, and by the late 1980s, seat belt use was more common among females than males. Thus, gender differences have increased for some types of health-related behavior while gender differences have decreased for other types of health-related behavior.

It is beyond the scope of this chapter to present a full analysis of the reasons why gender differences decreased for certain types of health-related behavior but not for others during the 1980s. However, the following paragraphs briefly discuss possible reasons why gender differences in smoking have decreased, but gender differences in drinking did not decrease during the 1980s.

Gender differences in smoking decreased during the 1980s in part due to a cohort phenomenon as older cohorts with larger gender differences in smoking were gradually replaced by younger cohorts with smaller gender differences in smoking (Waldron, 1991b). The differences between cohorts were due in part to increased smoking adoption by successive cohorts of women as social disapproval of women's smoking decreased during the mid-20th century. Since the mid-1970s, there have been only small gender differences in smoking adoption (Moss, Allen, & Giovino, 1992). Gender differences in smoking adoption have been small because factors that tend to increase males' smoking adoption have been counter-balanced by factors that tend to increase females' smoking adoption (Waldron, Lye, & Brandon, 1991). Factors that increase females' smoking and decrease males' smoking include two gender-typed concerns—athletic ability and weight control. Males' smoking adoption is reduced by males' greater involvement in sports and concern that smoking may harm their athletic ability. In contrast, females have been more concerned than males about attractive appearance and maintaining low body weight, and females may more often use smoking as an aid in weight control.

Social acceptance of women's drinking has not followed the same trend as social acceptance of women's smoking. Recently, levels of social disapproval of girls' and women's smoking have been relatively similar to levels of social disapproval of boys' and men's smoking, but there still is considerably more social disapproval of girls' and women's drinking than of boys' and men's drinking. This contrast is illustrated by the proportions of high school seniors who reported that their close friends would strongly disapprove if they smoked one or more packs of cigarettes per day (43% of females vs. 37% of males) compared to the proportions of high school seniors who reported that their close friends would strongly disapprove if they took one or two drinks nearly every day (51% of females vs. 31% of males) (Johnston, Bachman, & O'Malley, 1986). Continuing social disapproval of heavy drinking by females appears to be linked to concerns that heavy drinking may interfere with a woman's responsibilities for child care and may leave a women vulnerable to seduction or rape (George, Gournic, & McAfee, 1988; Klee & Ames,

1987; Waldron, 1988). Thus, it appears that traditional roles and expectations for women, namely, responsibility for child care and restrictions on sexual behavior, may contribute to stronger social disapproval of women's drinking, which in turn contributes to the persistence of substantial gender differences in alcohol consumption.

These observations suggest that trends in gender differences in health-related behavior have been influenced by the perceived compatibility of these behaviors with fundamental aspects of traditional male and female roles. It appears that gender differences in smoking have decreased more than gender differences in heavy drinking at least in part because smoking is perceived as more compatible than heavy drinking with traditional female roles and responsibilities. It is interesting to speculate that compatibility with fundamental aspects of traditional female roles may also explain why gender differences decreased for amount of driving and employment rates, but apparently not for driving-related safety habits, risk-taking in recreation, or gun use. Increased driving and wage-earning by women may have been more socially acceptable, because women's driving and wage-earning frequently served the needs of families and thus were compatible with women's role as family caretakers. These arguments suggest that fundamental aspects of traditional gender roles continue to exert an influence on trends in health-related behavior, even while major changes have occurred in some aspects of gender roles and expectations concerning gender-appropriate behavior.

In future research, it will be of interest to explore these issues further and to investigate other factors that may have influenced trends in gender differences in health-related behavior. For example, the trend data suggest that public health campaigns concerning the hazards of smoking may have influenced male behavior more than female behavior, whereas public health campaigns concerning the benefits of using seat belts may have influenced female behavior more than male behavior. It would be of interest to investigate this issue (Waldron, 1991b).

In conclusion, decreasing gender differences in certain types of health-related behavior contributed to decreasing gender differences in mortality in the United States in the 1980s. However, for some types of health-related behavior and certain causes of death, gender differences were stable or even increased during the 1980s. Also, recent trends in gender differences in mortality have been influenced by additional factors, such as gender differences in the mortality effects of certain behavioral and environmental changes.

References

Anderson, T. W. (1973). The changing pattern of ischemic heart disease. *Canadian Medical Association Journal, 108,* 1500-1504.

Austin, R. L., Bologna, M., & Dodge, H. H. (1992). Sex-role change, anomie and female suicide. *Suicide and Life-Threatening Behavior, 22,* 197-225.

Barefoot, J. C., Peterson, B. L., Dahlstrom, W. G., Siegler, I. C., Anderson, N. B., & Williams, R. B., Jr. (1991). Hostility patterns and health implications. *Health Psychology, 10,* 18-24.

Berlin, J. A., & Colditz, G. A. (1990). A meta-analysis of physical activity in the prevention of coronary heart disease. *American Journal of Epidemiology, 132,* 612-628.

Blair, S. N., Kohl, H. W., Gordon, N. F., & Paffenbarger, R. S., Jr. (1992). How much physical activity is good for your health? *Annual Review of Public Health, 13,* 99-126.

Block, G., Rosenberger, W. F., & Patterson, B. H. (1988). Calories, fat and cholesterol. *American Journal of Public Health, 78,* 1150-1155.

Brown, C. B., & Kessler, L. G. (1988). Projections of lung cancer mortality in the United States. *Journal of National Cancer Institute, 80,* 43-51.

Burbank, F. (1972). U.S. lung cancer death rates begin to rise proportionately more rapidly for females than for males: A dose-response effect? *Journal of Chronic Diseases, 25,* 473-479.

Centers for Disease Control. (1992). Trends in alcohol-related traffic fatalities, by sex— United States. *Journal of American Medical Association, 268,* 313-314.

Clifton, P. M., & Nestel, P. J. (1992). Influence of gender, body mass index, and age on response of plasma lipids to dietary fat plus cholesterol. *Arteriosclerosis and Thrombosis, 12,* 955-962.

England, P., & Browne, I. (1992). Trends in women's economic status. *Sociological Perspectives, 35,* 17-51.

Enstrom, J. E., Kanim, L. E., & Klein, M. A. (1992). Vitamin C intake and mortality among a sample of the United States population. *Epidemiology, 3,* 194-202.

Enterline, P. E. (1961). Causes of death responsible for recent increases in sex mortality differentials in the United States. *Milbank Memorial Fund Quarterly, 39,* 312-338.

Faludi, S. (1991). *Backlash—The undeclared war against American women.* New York: Crown Publishers.

Fiore, M. C., Novotny, T. E., Pierce, J. P., Hatziandreu, E. J., Patel, K. M. & Davis, R. M. (1989). Trends in cigarette smoking in the United States. *Journal of American Medical Association, 261,* 49-55.

Gee, E. M., & Veevers, J. E. (1983). Accelerating sex differentials in mortality. *Social Biology, 30,* 75-85.

George, W. H., Gournic, S. J., & McAfee, M. P. (1988). Perceptions of postdrinking female sexuality. *Journal of Applied Social Psychology, 18,* 1295-1317.

Gove, W. R. (1973). Sex, marital status and mortality. *American Journal of Sociology, 79,* 45-67.

Hu, Y., & Goldman, N. (1990). Mortality differentials by marital status. *Demography, 27,* 233-250.

Johnson, C. L., Rifkind, B. M., Sempos, C. T., Carroll, M. D., Bachorik, P. S., Briefel, R. R., Gordon, D. J., Burt, V. L., Brown, C. D., Lippel, K., & Cleeman, J. I. (1993). Declining serum total cholesterol levels among U.S. adults. *Journal of American Medical Association, 269,* 3002-3008.

Johnston, L. D., Bachman, J. G., & O'Malley, P. M. (1986). *Monitoring the future—Questionnaire responses from the nation's high school seniors.* Ann Arbor: University of Michigan, Institute for Social Research.

Kalin, M. F., & Zumoff, B. (1990). Sex hormones and coronary disease. *Steroids, 55,* 331-352.

Klee, L., & Ames, G. (1987). Reevaluating risk factors for women's drinking. *American Journal of Preventive Medicine, 3,* 31-41.

Larsson, B., Bengtsson, C., Björntorp, P., Lapidus, L., Sjöström, L., Svördsudd, K., Tibblin, G., Wedel, H., Welin, L., & Wilhelmsen, L. (1992). Is abdominal body fat distribution a major explanation for the sex difference in the incidence of myocardial infarction? *American Journal of Epidemiology, 135,* 266-273.

Lee, P. N., Fry, J. S., & Forey, B. A. (1990). Trends in lung cancer, chronic obstructive lung disease, and emphysema death rates for England and Wales 1941-85 and their relation to trends in cigarette smoking. *Thorax, 45,* 657-665.

Life Sciences Research Office, Federation of American Societies for Experimental Biology. (1989). *Nutrition Monitoring in the United States* (DHHS Pub. No. 89-1255). Hyattsville, MD: Department of Health and Human Services.

Lopez, A. D. (1983). The sex mortality differential in developed countries. In A. D. Lopez & L. T. Ruzicka (Eds.), *Sex differentials in mortality* (pp. 53-120). Canberra: Australian National University, Department of Demography.

Matthews, K. A., Woodall, K. L., Engebretson, T. O., McCann, B. S., Stoney, C. M., Manuck, S. B., & Saab, P. G. (1992). Influence of age, sex, and family on Type A and hostile attitudes and behaviors. *Health Psychology, 11,* 317-323.

Maynard, C., Litwin, P. E., Martin, J. S., & Weaver, W. D. (1992). Gender differences in the treatment and outcome of acute myocardial infarction. *Archives of Internal Medicine, 152,* 972-976.

Moss, A. J., Allen, K. F., & Giovino, G. A. (1992). Recent trends in adolescent smoking, smoking-uptake correlates, and expectations about the future. *Advance Data from Vital and Health Statistics,* No. 221, 1-28.

National Center for Health Statistics. (1984). *Vital Statistics of the United States, 1979, Vol. 2, Mortality, Part A* (DHHS Pub. No. 84-1101). Washington, DC: Government Printing Office.

National Center for Health Statistics. (1988). Adult health practices in the United States and Canada. *Vital and Health Statistics, Series 5, no. 3* (DHHS Pub. No. 88-1479). Washington, DC: Public Health Service.

National Center for Health Statistics. (1991). *Vital Statistics of the United States, 1988, Vol. II, Mortality, Part A* (DHHS Pub. No. 91-1101). Washington, DC: Public Health Service.

National Center for Health Statistics. (1992a). Advance report of final mortality statistics, 1989. *Monthly Vital Statistics Report, Vol. 40, no. 8, suppl. 2.* (DHHS Pub. No. 92-1120). Washington, DC: Public Health Service.

National Center for Health Statistics. (1992b). *Health United States 1991* (DHHS Pub. No. 92-1232). Hyattsville, MD: Department of Health and Human Services.

National Institute on Drug Abuse. (1990). *National Household Survey on Drug Abuse: Main Findings 1988* (DHHS Pub. No. 90-1682). Rockville, MD: NIDA, Department of Health and Human Services.

National Safety Council. (1980). *Accident Facts, 1980 Edition.* Chicago: National Safety Council.

National Safety Council. (1990). *Accident Facts, 1990 Edition.* Chicago: National Safety Council.

Ornstein, M. D. (1983). The impact of marital status, age and employment on female suicide in British Columbia. *Canadian Review of Social Anthropology, 20,* 96-100.

Piani, A., & Schoenborn, C. (1993). Health promotion and disease prevention, United States, 1990. *Vital and Health Statistics, Series 10, No. 185* (DHHS Pub. No. 93-1513). Hyattsville, MD: U.S. Department of Health and Human Services.

Preston, S. H. (1970). *Older male mortality and cigarette smoking.* Berkeley: University of California, Institute of International Studies.

Pritchard, C. (1990). Suicide, unemployment and gender variations in the Western world 1964-1986. *Social Psychiatry and Psychiatric Epidemiology, 25,* 73-80.

Repetti, R. L., Matthews, K. A., & Waldron, I. (1989). Employment and women's health. *American Psychologist, 44,* 1394-1401.

Retherford, R. D. (1975). *The changing sex differential in mortality.* Westport, CT: Greenwood.

Scherwitz, L., Perkins, L., Chesney, M., & Hughes, G. (1991). Cook-Medley Hostility scale and subsets: Relationship to demographic and psychosocial characteristics in young adults in the CARDIA study. *Psychosomatic Medicine, 53,* 36-49.

Schoenborn, C. A. (1988). Health promotion and disease prevention: United States, 1985. *Vital and Health Statistics, Series 10, No. 163* (DHHS Pub. No. 88-1591). Hyattsville, MD: U.S. Department of Health and Human Services.

Smith, J. C., Mercy, J. A., & Conn, J. M. (1988). Marital status and the risk of suicide. *American Journal of Public Health, 78,* 78-80.

Smith, T. W. (1991). Adult sexual behavior in 1989: Number of partners, frequency of intercourse and risk of AIDS. *Family Planning Perspectives, 23,* 102-107.

Stampfer, M. J., Colditz, G. A., & Willett, W. C. (1990). Menopause and heart disease. *Annals N.Y. Academy of Sciences, 592,* 193-203.

Stephens, T. (1987). Secular trends in adult physical activity. *Research Quarterly for Exercise and Sport, 58,* 94-105.

Swerdlow, A. J. (1990). Effectiveness of primary prevention of occupational exposures on cancer risk. In M. Hakama, V. Beral, J. W. Cullen, et al. (Eds.), *Evaluating effectiveness of primary prevention of cancer* (No. 103, pp. 23-56). Lyon: IARC Scientific Publications.

Turi, A. G., Stone, P. H., Muller, J. E., Parker, C., Rude, R. E., Raabe, D. E., Jaffe, A. S., Hartwell, T. D., Robertson, T. L., Braunwald, E., & the MILIS Study Group. (1986). Implications for acute intervention related to time of hospital arrival in acute myocardial infarction. *American Journal of Cardiology, 58,* 203-209.

Ulbricht, T. L. V., & Southgate, D. A. T. (1991). Coronary heart disease: Seven dietary factors. *Lancet, 338,* 985-992.

U.S. Department of Commerce, Bureau of the Census. (1980, 1990). Marital status and living arrangements. *Current Population Reports,* Series P-20, No. 349, 445. Washington, DC: Government Printing Office.

U.S. Department of Commerce, Bureau of the Census. (1981). Money income of families and persons in the U.S., 1979. *Current Population Reports, Series P-60, No. 129.* Washington, DC: Government Printing Office.

U.S. Department of Commerce, Bureau of the Census. (1991). Consumer income. *Current Population Reports, Series P-60, No. 172.* Washington, DC: Government Printing Office.

U.S. Department of Health, Education and Welfare (1977). Dietary intake findings. *Vital and Health Statistics, Series 11, No. 202.* Washington, DC: Government Printing Office.

U.S. Department of Health and Human Services. (1989). *Reducing the Health Consequences of Smoking, A Report of the Surgeon General* (DHHS Pub. No. 89-8411). Rockville, MD: DHHS, Centers for Disease Control, Office on Smoking and Health.

U.S. Department of Health and Human Services. (1990). *The Health Benefits of Smoking Cessation, A Report of the Surgeon General* (DHHS Pub. No. 90-8416). Rockville, MD: DHHS, Centers for Disease Control, Office on Smoking and Health.

U.S. Department of Labor. (1990). Employment status of the noninstitutional population 16 years and over by sex, 1979 to date. *Employment and Earnings, 37*(12), 7.

U.S. Department of Transportation. (1992). *Nationwide Personal Transportation Survey, Summary of Travel Trends* (Pub. No. FHWA-PL-92-027). Washington, DC: Department of Transportation, Federal Highway Administration.

United Nations. (1987). *1985 Demographic Yearbook.* New York: Author.

United Nations Secretariat. (1988). Sex differentials in life expectancy and mortality in developed countries. *Population Bulletin of the U.N., 25,* 65-106.

Van Horn, L. V., Ballew, C., Liu, K., Ruth, K., McDonald, A., Hilner, J. E., Burke, G. L., Savage, P. J., Bragg, C., Caan, B., Jacobs, D., Jr., Slattery, M., & Sidney, S. (1991). Diet, body size and plasma lipids-lipoproteins in young adults. *American Journal of Epidemiology, 133,* 9-23.

Waldron, I. (1983). Sex differences in illness incidence, prognosis and mortality. *Social Science & Medicine, 17,* 1107-1123.

Waldron, I. (1986a). The contribution of smoking to sex differences in mortality. *Public Health Reports, 101,* 163-173.

Waldron, I. (1986b). What do we know about causes of sex differences in mortality? *Population Bulletin of the U.N., No. 18-1985,* 59-76.

Waldron, I. (1988). Gender and health-related behavior. In D. S. Gochman (Ed.), *Health Behavior* (pp. 193-208). New York: Plenum.

Waldron, I. (1991a). Effects of labor force participation on sex differences in mortality and morbidity. In M. Frankenhaeuser, U. Lundberg, & M. Chesney (Eds.), *Women, Work, and Health* (pp. 17-38). New York: Plenum.

Waldron, I. (1991b). Patterns and causes of gender differences in smoking. *Social Science & Medicine, 32,* 989-1005.

Waldron, I. (1993). Recent trends in sex mortality ratios for adults in developed countries. *Social Science & Medicine, 36,* 451-462.

Waldron, I. (1995). Contributions of biological and behavioural factors to changing sex differences in ischemic heart disease mortality. In A. Lopez, G. Caselli, & T. Valkonen (Eds.), *Adult Mortality in Developed Countries* (pp. 161-178). New York: Oxford University Press.

Waldron, I., Lye, D., & Brandon, A. (1991). Gender differences in teenage smoking. *Women & Health, 17,* 65-90.

White, C. C., Powell, K. E., Hogelin, G. C., Gentry, E. M., & Forman, M. R. (1987). The Behavioral Risk Factor Surveys. *American Journal of Preventive Medicine, 3,* 304-310.

World Health Organization. (1983, 1991). *World Health Statistics Annual, 1983, 1990.* Geneva: World Health Organization.

3

Premature Death Among Males

Extending the Bottom Line of Men's Health

JUDITH M. STILLION

Perhaps, as writers have suggested across the ages, the inevitability of death is the common tie binding all humans together. Certainly, it is the stuff of philosophy, drama, and religion—the theme that all humans must die and that no matter how long we may live, life is over all too soon. Death has been called the "Great Equalizer" because it comes to rich and poor alike, to the powerful and the powerless, to people of all nations, creeds, and religions. However, there is one inequity that remains a constant: the sex differential in death. On average, men die nearly 7 years earlier than women.

Common wisdom holds that men, particularly those in the business world, are concerned with the bottom line. When the fiscal year is over and all accounts are tallied, the bottom line shows whether the company has had a profitable or an unprofitable year. Throughout the year, most business actions are planned and carried out with an eye to that bottom line. If one regards life as a business, the bottom line would be longevity. Putting aside for the moment the debate about quantity versus quality of life, most would agree that death represents the greatest of all losses because it represents the loss of personality, worldly possessions, friends and family, potential for growth, and loss of self.

In spite of the enormity of the loss, policymakers and health promoters have not paid adequate attention to the likelihood that males are significantly more apt to die at earlier ages than their female counterparts. In this chapter, causes of premature death among males are identified and analyzed. A hierarchy of causes of death that is increasingly open to human influence at the higher stages is also suggested. The chapter concludes by calling for a redefinition of masculinity that may in fact increase the bottom line for males in the business of life.

A distinction is made throughout the chapter between sex and gender. Sex refers to genetically determined and biologically maintained physical differences between the sexes. Gender, on the other hand, is a cultural artifact. Gender identity is learned behavior that reflects the meanings that individuals come to understand regarding being a male or female in a given culture.

The Statistical Picture

Where do the sex differences in mortality begin and how great are they? A historical examination of bottom-line life expectancy figures should shed some light on these questions. Table 3.1 shows that male life expectancy has historically been lower than that of females. For example, males born in the state of Massachusetts in 1850 could expect to live to be 38.3 years old, whereas females, even in an age of heavy maternal mortality, could expect more than 2 years of additional life. A century later, males born in 1950 could expect to live almost 5 years fewer than females. During the next 40 years, in part due to improvements in nutrition, technology, and medicine, life expectancy increased for both sexes and all races in the United States. However, the sex differential in death continued to widen so that by 1987, it reached approximately 8 years. By 1989, however, as Waldron has pointed out in another chapter in this volume, the rate of increase for females had leveled off, possibly because of increased cigarette smoking or increased stress in the workplace. In that year, white males could expect to live 6.8 years fewer than white females, and males of all other races combined could expect to live 8.4 years fewer than females of all other races.

Is the pattern of life expectancy in the United States uncommon, or do males universally have lower life expectancies at birth than do females? Table 3.2 speaks to that question. It shows current life expectancy figures by sex for 18 countries.

Two things are obvious from Table 3.2. First, life expectancy is correlated with the economic status of the country. Citizens, both males and females, in notably poor countries like Pakistan and Kenya have lower

Table 3.1 Life Expectancy by Sex and Year

	Whites			All Others		
Year	Both Sexes	Male	Female	Both Sexes	Male	Female
1850[a]	NA	38.30	40.50	—	NA	NA
1900	NA	48.23	51.08	—	32.54	35.04
1910	NA	50.23	53.62	—	34.05	37.67
1920	NA	56.34	58.53	—	47.14	46.92
1930	NA	59.12	62.67	—	47.55	49.51
1940	64.20	62.10	66.60	53.10	51.50	54.90
1950	69.10	66.50	72.20	60.80	59.10	62.90
1960	70.60	67.40	74.10	63.60	61.10	66.30
1970	71.70	68.00	75.60	65.30	61.30	69.40
1980	74.40	70.70	78.10	69.50	65.30	73.60
1989	76.00	72.70	79.20	71.20	67.10	75.50

SOURCE: Adapted from the 1992 *Information Please Almanac* (45th ed.).
a. Massachusetts only.

life expectancies than those in more developed countries like Japan and Switzerland. Second, males in all the countries cited in the Table 3.2 have lower life expectancies than do females given the same economic conditions. Lower male life expectancy appears to be the rule rather than the exception across nations and cultures. This has led at least one author to conclude that the "world of the very old is a world of women, both in society and within families" (Hagestad, 1986, p. 125). Indeed, as longevity has increased, it has caused the family to become top-heavy with elderly females. Hagestad cites a German study that found that many five-generation families contained three generations of widows.

Lower life expectancy is only one way to express the sex differential in death. To make the point more clearly, Table 3.3 shows death rates by age and sex for the years 1960 to 1991. It is clear that at all ages male deaths have outnumbered female deaths for the past 20 years.

Another question helps clarify the extent of the sex differences in death: When does the sex differential in death first appear? The evidence shows that male mortality exceeds female mortality from conception throughout the life span. We only have estimates of the rate of male to female deaths in utero. The most generally accepted figure is that 120 to 160 males are conceived for every 100 females (Ounsted, 1972; Tricomi, Serr, & Solish, 1960). By birth, however, the sex differential has dropped to approximately 106 to 100 (Tricomi et al., 1960). Moving to infancy, defined as

Table 3.2 Life Expectancy at Birth by Sex for Selected Countries

Country	Date Born	Males	Females
Australia	1987	73.03	79.46
Canada	1985-1987	73.02	79.33
Egypt	1985-1990	59.29	61.46
Germany (East)	1987-1988	69.81	75.91
Germany (West)	1985-1987	71.81	78.37
Greece	1980	72.15	76.35
Ireland	1980-1982	70.14	75.62
Israel	1987	73.60	77.00
Italy	1985	72.01	78.61
Japan	1988	75.54	81.30
Kenya	1985-1990	56.50	60.46
Mexico	1979	62.10	66.00
Pakistan	1976-1978	59.04	59.20
Spain	1980-1982	72.01	78.61
Sweden	1987	74.16	80.15
Switzerland	1987-1989	73.90	80.70
United Kingdom	1985-1987	71.90	77.27
United States	1986	71.30	78.30

SOURCE: Adapted from the 1992 *Information Please Almanac* (45th ed., p. 138).
NOTE: Figures are the latest as of August 1991.

under 1 year of age, Table 3.4 shows that there is a minimum of 20% more male deaths than female deaths during the first year of life.

Having documented that males are at higher risk than females both prenatally and across the life span, perhaps a more detailed examination of causes of death for each sex would be instructive. Table 3.5 shows age-adjusted death rates for 10 of the most prevalent causes of death. The final column in the Table 3.4 indicates the sex differential in death. A figure of 1.00 would mean that when age is factored out, one male died for every female who died in that year for that cause of death. The data reveal that for each of those causes of death, males were more likely to die than females. After reviewing figures for an even longer list of causes of death, the U.S. Bureau of the Census concluded that,

> mortality levels for each of the 15 leading causes of death were higher for males than for females. The largest differentials were for HIV infection, Suicide, Homicide and Legal Intervention. Specifically, the age-adjusted death rate for HIV infection was 8.7 times as high for males as for females; for Suicide, 4.1

Table 3.3 Death Rates per 100,00, by Age and Sex: 1960-1991

Age		1960	1970	1980	1990	1991
Under 1:	Male	3,059.3	2,410.0	1,428.5	1,037.5	1,007.2
	Female	2,321.3	1,863.7	1,141.7	831.2	790.5
1-4	Male	119.5	93.2	72.6	48.7	48.9
	Female	98.4	75.4	54.7	39.4	44.5
5-14	Male	55.7	50.5	36.7	29.1	28.8
	Female	37.3	31.8	24.2	18.8	19.0
15-24	Male	152.1	188.5	172.3	156.1	160.8
	Female	61.3	68.1	57.5	50.8	52.2
25-34	Male	187.9	215.3	196.1	205.6	201.1
	Female	106.6	101.6	75.9	73.4	73.6
35-44	Male	372.8	402.6	299.2	306.1	311.3
	Female	229.4	231.1	159.3	138.1	135.8
45-54	Male	992.2	958.5	767.3	600.9	598.2
	Female	526.7	517.2	412.9	332.6	325.6
55-64	Male	2,309.5	2,282.7	1,815.1	1,507.5	1,503.6
	Female	1,196.4	1,098.9	934.3	877.5	854.7
65-74	Male	4,914.4	4,873.8	4,105.2	3,358.5	3,307.3
	Female	2,871.8	2,579.7	2,144.7	2,002.1	1,971.7
75-84	Male	10,178.4	10,010.2	8,816.7	7,950.2	7,663.1
	Female	7,633.1	6,677.6	5,440.1	4,941.7	4,862.2
Over 85	Male	21,286.3	17,821.5	18,801.1	17,521.6	17,150.9
	Female	19,008.4	15,518.0	14,746.9	13,727.5	13,328.4

SOURCE: Adapted from NCHS (1992).

times as high; for Homicide and legal intervention, 3.6 times as high; and for Accidents and adverse effects the rate was 2.6 times as high for males as for females. (National Center for Health Statistics [NCHS], 1992, p. 7)

In summary, the evidence shows that males are more predisposed to early death than females. A more careful examination of the social worlds of many males yields additional insights into the causes of their early demise.

The Violent World of Males

There can be no question that males live in a much more dangerous world than do females. A finer examination of just three violent causes of death—accidents, suicide, and homicide—makes this point. Table 3.6 shows that males are nearly three times as likely to die from motor vehicle

Table 3.4 Infant Mortality Rate

	All Races			White			Black		
Year	Both Sexes	Male	Female	Both Sexes	Male	Female	Both Sexes	Male	Female
1940	47.0	52.5	41.3	43.2	48.3	37.8	72.9	81.1	64.6
1950	29.2	32.8	25.5	26.8	30.2	23.1	43.9	48.3	39.4
1960	26.0	29.3	22.6	22.9	26.0	19.6	44.3	49.1	39.4
1970	20.0	22.4	17.5	17.8	20.0	15.4	32.6	36.2	—
1980	12.6	13.9	11.2	11.0	12.3	9.6	21.4	23.3	19.4
1989	9.8	10.8	8.8	8.2	9.2	7.2	17.7	19.0	16.3

SOURCE: Adapted from NCHS (1992).
NOTE: Rates are for infant (under 1 year) deaths per 1,000 live births.

Table 3.5 Death Rates by Sex and 10 Leading Causes: 1989

	Age-Adjusted Death Rate per 100,000 Population			
Cause of Death	Total	Male	Female	Sex Differential
Diseases of the heart	155.9	210.2	112.3	1.87
Malignant neoplasms	133.0	162.4	111.7	1.45
Accidents and adverse effects	33.8	49.5	18.9	2.62
Cerebrovascular disease	28.0	30.4	26.2	1.16
Chronic liver disease, cirrhosis	8.9	12.8	5.5	2.33
Diabetes	11.5	2.0	11.0	1.09
Suicide	11.3	18.6	4.5	4.13
Homicide and legal intervention	9.4	14.7	4.1	3.59

SOURCE: Adapted from the U.S. Bureau of the Census, *Statistical Abstract of the United States: 1992* (112th ed., p. 84). Washington, DC.

accidents as females and over twice as likely to die from accidents of all other kinds. It further shows that although the direction of the change for all groups is downward the relative status of the sexes remains nearly constant. Males continue to die from all types of accidents far more often than do females.

Typically we think of accidents as occurring outside of our control. This idea is evident in two synonyms for accidents—mischance and misfortune. In reality, however, there are at least two variables operating in any accident situation. The first is the external situation itself and the second is the individual's internal readiness, willingness, and skill to deal with it. For example, we can clean up a workplace to reduce the probability of

Table 3.6 Death Rates per 100,00 From Accidents by Sex and Race:
1970-1989

	Motor Vehicle Accidents				Other Accidents			
	Male		Female		Male		Female	
Year	White	Black	White	Black	White	Black	White	Black
1970	39.1	44.3	14.8	13.4	38.2	63.3	18.3	22.5
1980	35.9	31.1	12.8	8.3	30.4	46.0	14.4	8.6
1989	27.0	28.3	12.1	9.3	24.5	37.0	12.7	15.0

SOURCE: Adapted from the U.S. Bureau of the Census, *Statistical Abstract of the United States: 1992* (112th ed., p. 828). Washington, DC.

mishaps. We can also educate male workers that ignoring safety guidelines on the job is not a sign of toughness. Likewise, we can make automobiles safer as well by teaching males that speeding and taking unnecessary risks on the road are not a badge of manly courage. In short, the prevalence of accidents can be decreased both by attending to the external causes and by significantly revising the socialization of males.

A close examination of the figures for suicide contained in Table 3.7 shows that both black and white males have increased their rates of death by suicide across the time period whereas both white and black females have decreased their rates. Much has been written about sex differences in suicide (Linehan, 1971, 1973; Marks, 1989; Rosenthal, 1981; Stillion, 1985, in press; Stillion, McDowell, & May, 1984, 1989; Stillion, White, McDowell, & Edwards, 1989). For our purposes here, we need only note that from middle childhood until old age males, particularly white males, are at significantly higher risk for self-murder than are females. In that more females report suffering from depression than males (Nolen-Hoeksema, 1987; Weissman & Klerman, 1977), males who kill themselves may be responding to some gender role signals rather than to some internal illness. That is, suicidal females may make attempts, cry for help, expect to be rescued, and receive social and emotional support. Suicidal males, in contrast, may see attempting suicide as evidence of weakness and, moreover, surviving a suicide attempt may be regarded as yet another failure, a mark against their masculine adequacy as it were.

Research has also found that both males and females regard completed suicide as an indication of strength and attempted suicide as weakness (Linehan, 1971, 1973). In addition, males view males who attempt suicide more negatively than they view males in the same problem situation who

Table 3.7 Suicide Rates by Sex, Race, and Age Group: 1970-1989

| | Total[a] | | | Male | | | | | | Female | | | | | |
| | | | | White | | | Black | | | White | | | Black | | |
Age	1970	1980	1989	1970	1980	1989	1970	1980	1989	1970	1980	1989	1970	1980	1989
All Ages[b]	11.6	11.9	12.2	18.0	19.9	21.4	8.0	10.3	12.2	7.1	5.9	5.2	2.6	2.2	2.4
10-14	0.6	0.8	1.4	1.1	1.4	2.2	0.3	0.5	1.7	0.3	0.3	0.7	0.4	0.1	(B)
15-19	5.9	8.5	11.3	9.4	15.0	19.4	4.7	5.6	10.3	2.9	3.3	4.5	2.9	1.6	2.3
20-24	12.2	16.1	15.3	19.3	27.8	26.8	18.7	20.0	23.7	5.7	5.9	4.3	4.9	3.1	3.4
25-34	14.1	16.0	15.0	19.9	25.6	24.9	19.2	21.8	22.0	9.0	7.5	5.9	5.7	4.1	3.7
35-44	16.9	15.4	14.6	23.3	23.5	23.8	12.6	15.6	18.1	13.0	9.1	7.1	3.7	4.6	3.9
45-54	20.0	15.9	14.6	29.5	24.2	24.2	13.8	12.0	10.9	13.5	10.2	8.0	3.7	2.8	3.0
55-65	21.4	15.9	15.5	35.0	25.8	26.6	10.6	11.7	10.4	12.3	9.1	7.9	2.0	2.3	2.5
65-Up	20.8	17.8	20.1	41.1	37.5	43.5	8.7	11.4	15.7	8.5	6.5	6.3	2.6	1.4	1.8
65-74-Up	20.8	16.9	18.0	38.7	32.5	35.1	8.7	11.1	15.4	9.6	7.0	6.4	2.9	1.7	(B)
75-84-Up	21.2	19.1	23.1	45.5	45.5	55.3	8.9	10.5	14.7	7.2	5.7	6.3	1.7	1.4	(B)
85-Up	19.0	19.2	22.8	45.8	52.8	71.9	8.7	18.9	(B)	5.8	5.8	6.2	2.8	—	(B)

SOURCE: Adapted from the National Center for Health Statistics, *Vital Statistics of the United States* (annual); *Monthly Vital Statistics Report;* and unpublished data.
NOTE: — represents or rounds to zero; (B) represents a base figure too small to meet statistical standards for reliability of derived figure.
a. Includes other races not shown separately.
b. Includes other age groups not shown separately.

5

do not attempt suicide (White & Stillion, 1988). Other researchers have maintained that more men than women intend to commit suicide. They point to males' greater frequency of substance abuse, subjection to more psychosocial stressors than women, and their use of more violent, immediately lethal means of taking their lives when compared to females. These researchers concluded, "We believe our data favor the conclusion that the major reason more men than women in the United States commit suicide is that more men intend to do it" (Rich, Ricketts, Fowler, & Young, 1988, p. 721).

When homicide is examined, another indicator of the toll of masculinity on men's health and longevity becomes apparent. Table 3.8 presents the rate of homicide by sex and race for the years 1970 to 1989. If homicide is considered a major indicator of the level of violence, then one conclusion that can be drawn from Table 3.8 is that the world of white males is over three times as violent as the world of white females. The data also show that the world of black males is over five times as violent as the world of black females. Socialization messages, particularly to males, seem to remain remarkably constant in this area; "You must be ready to defend yourself," "Get him before he gets you." The media reinforce these stereotypes, which are conveyed in myriad settings ranging from the American Old West to the star wars in other galaxies. The cultural message is kill or be killed, and the statistics show that the this violent moral is being heard, internalized, and to some extent, grafted to men's gender identities.

Perspectives on Causes
of Early Death Among Males

There are at least three nonexclusive schools of thought attempting to explain the gender differential in death. The first school suggests that male biology is influenced by genetic messages that mitigate against male survival (for discussion, see Pleck, 1983; Stillion, 1985; Verbrugge, 1985; Waldron, 1983). Proponents of this view point to the intricacy of male sex differentiation in utero as a factor influencing increased prenatal male death. They assert that increased levels of testosterone contribute to men's violence proneness, and they point to lower levels of immunoglobulin M as a source of the heightened male vulnerability to disease. Further, they call attention to the protection that female hormones seem to give young and middle-aged women against heart diseases (Markides, 1990; Waldron,

Table 3.8 Death Rates From Homicide by Sex and Race, 1970-1989

	Male		Female	
Year	White	Black	White	Black
1970	6.8	67.6	2.1	13.3
1980	10.9	66.6	3.2	13.5
1989	8.2	61.1	2.8	12.9

SOURCE: Adapted from the U.S. Bureau of the Census, *Statistical Abstract of the United States: 1992* (112th ed., p. 89). Washington, DC.

1976, 1983). In addition, Verbrugge (1985) notes that women have "greater resistance to infectious diseases and also to some rare X-chromosome linked diseases" (p. 164).

Because we are biological creatures, these and other factors, no doubt do contribute to the sex differential in death in complex and subtle ways. Markides (1990) has summarized the situation, saying that "although a great deal of debate regarding specific factors continues, it is generally agreed that both psychosocial and biological (genetic or hormonal) factors are involved" (p. 19).

The second school of thought uses historical or anthropological frameworks for understanding links between patterns of gender relations and susceptibility to early death. According to this perspective, differential gender roles represent a division between men and women that is based on power differences. What we now regard as traditional gender roles—that is, those that reflect male dominance and female submission—are said to have originated in antiquity when physical power largely determined dominance hierarchies that had species survival value (Engels, 1942; Friedl, 1978; Wilson, 1978). According to this line of reasoning, socialization pressures continue along traditional lines to assure the continuation of male dominance over females. Doyle (1983) identified six types of social power that are typically found in male-female relations; that is, coercive, reward, legitimate, referent, expert, and informational (p. 261). In each of these, gender relations have been structured in ways that privilege males over females.

In recent years, feminist theorists have added their insights to this line of reasoning. They maintain that gender differences are a product of the entire social structure and so infuse that structure that they come to be accepted as the "natural order of things" (Hare-Mustin & Mareck, 1990). They also point out that because of the separate physical and psychological worlds that males and females inhabit from conception onward, it is impossible to tease out the relative contributions of nature and nurture (Bernard, 1981; Hare-Mustin & Mareck, 1990). What has received less attention, however, are the negative impacts on men's health and longevity that flow from men's immersion in and pursuit of masculine identity and roles and their accompanying power and privileges.

The third framework for understanding the gender differential in death emphasizes the influence of gender socialization on male development. According to this line of reasoning, males are socialized to conform to existing gender expectations and behaviors. The gendered worlds into which small boys are socialized emphasize emotional inhibition (Big boys don't cry), demands for independence (If he hits you, hit him back. Handle it yourself!), and above all, prohibitions against any behavior that smacks of femininity (Don't be a sissy!). Especially in American culture, boys are socialized into competitive games at an early age, often learning to endure physical punishment and pain as part of "having fun" or as a prerequisite to becoming a man (Sabo, 1989, 1993). Sabo (1989) describes it well:

> Male supremacists are not born, they are made, and traditional athletic socialization is a fundamental contribution to this complex social-psychological and political process. Through sport, many males, indeed, learn to "take it"—that is, to internalize patriarchal values which, in turn, become part of their gender identity and conception of women and society. (p. 183)

The bottom line of the developmental perspective of male socialization and its later consequences on health has been captured by Komisar (1976):

> The differences between boys and girls are defined in terms of violence. Boys are encouraged to rough-house; girls are taught to be gentle ("ladylike"). Boys are expected to get into fights, but admonished not to hit girls. (It is not "manly" to assault females except, of course, sexually, but that comes later.) Boys who run away from fights are "sissies," with the implication that they are homosexual or "queer." As little boys become big boys, their education for violence continues. The leadership in this country today consists of such little boys who attained "manhood" in the approved and heroic violence of World War II. They returned to a society in which street and motorcycle gangs, fast cars, and fraternity hazing confirmed the lessons of war—one must be tough and ready to inflict pain in order to get ahead. (p. 203)

Although the context of this quote may be dated, the substance remains accurate.

Girls, on the other hand, are freer to engage in cooperative and imaginative play (e.g., playing house or mothering dolls). Tolerance for emotional expressiveness and for dependence on parents and other authority figures may be acceptably maintained longer by girls than by boys. There are, of course, negative consequences to female socialization, including acceptance of standards of passivity and dependency that impede the full development of females. Hare-Mustin and Mareck (1990) have pointed out that traditional sex role socialization results in marginality, denial of opportunity, and continuing conflict between personal attachments and career autonomy for women. Such conflicts create stress that has negative effects on women's psychological and physical health. Some research also points to females' more frequent report of morbidity across the life span than males'. One report (Kaplan, Anderson, & Wingard, 1991) estimated that when quality of life as well as sheer longevity was taken into account females' advantage over males decreased from about 7 to about 3 years. Nevertheless, it is clear that current socialization pressures disadvantage males more than females regarding years of life.

Cognitive psychologists have added to our understanding of socialization pressures by providing support for the idea that babies as well as children take an active role in shaping their own understandings of the world (Gilligan, 1982; Kohlberg, 1966). Thus, middle-class boy children actively work to create their own conception of their gender role from the sports-studded wallpapers and the car-shaped beds in their rooms as well as the rough-and-tumble way in which they are treated by the male adults in their world (Rheingold & Cook, 1975). Girls, in their pink, flowered rooms, surrounded by adults who treat them more gently and talk with them more and in more subdued tones, supply the conditions for female babies to create an understanding of their gender identity, which is far different from their male counterparts. Gender socialization is much more subtle than we have surmised. It penetrates our thinking so substantially that it is one of the first understandings that babies attain about themselves. By age 3, children of both sexes have developed their core gender identities as well as their understanding that gender is constant and they can competently classify gender-related characteristics (Bernard, 1981; Green, 1987). From that time onward, unless specific questions are raised, males and females tend to actively construct their worlds along different lines according to their understanding of what it means to be male or female. Those constructions have negative as well as positive consequences. For males, one of those consequences is the predisposition for death at an earlier age.

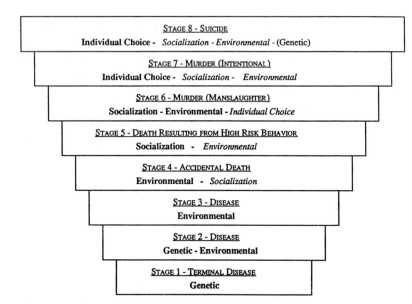

Figure 3.1. Hierarchy of Influence in Types of Causes of Death

NOTE: **Bold** indicates the primary sources of influence; *italics* indicates the secondary sources of influence. Each level reflects increasing susceptibility to social, environmental, and/or individual influence.

A Hierarchy of Risks and Choices

All humans must die and there are inevitably causes of death. Yet it is possible to conceptualize causes of death as existing in a hierarchy that is susceptible to human influence. Figure 3.1 presents an eight-stage hierarchy of causes of death. This classification system suggests that causes of death may range from the totally inescapable to the totally controllable; that is, there are varying degrees of human influence and intervention possible at each level.[1]

Stage 1 diseases are those that are inherited and that inevitably lead to premature death. For example, at least at present, children born with the dominant gene for Huntington's disease will develop symptoms of the disease some time in midlife and it will be fatal. Neither the people who inherit the disease nor the society into which they are born can intervene to change that fate.

Stage 2 disease, however, is a disease such as diabetes, which, although genetically foreordained, can be treated and ameliorated by drugs and lifestyle considerations, thus increasing longevity. Because of society's recent advances in medical treatments of diabetes and the changing behavior of individuals suffering from diabetes, the age-adjusted rate of death from diabetes has gone from 14.1 deaths per 100,000 population in 1970 to 8.9 such deaths in 1989.

Stage 3 diseases are those that are environmentally based. The best examples of these are black lung disease of coal miners and asbestosis of those working in industries exposing them to asbestos. These diseases are highly controllable. If we no longer needed coal, if we banned asbestos from the environment, these diseases would disappear.

Stage 4 causes of death are also highly amenable to external influences. This is why, as parents, we caution our adolescent children to be careful in driving or our young children to be wary in crossing the street. We urge them to be aware of their surroundings; to avoid courting disaster. We even teach them old superstitions about not walking under ladders. Humans seem to operate from a basic belief that the world is full of dangers but we can affect the safety of our world through education and through changes we make to the environment. Good illustrations of such changes are the introduction of driver's training programs to the schools and of seat belts and air bags in cars. Evidence that we can make a difference in deaths from this cause can be seen in that the rate of age-adjusted deaths from "accidents and adverse effects" has decreased from 53.7 per 100,000 in 1970 to 33.8 per 100,000 in 1989.

Stage 5 causes of death are even more subject to human influence than those of Stage 4. No one is required to sky dive or to ride motorcycles or to go bungee jumping. There are no requirements to play chicken in automobiles or to take up high-risk habits such as smoking that will lead to earlier death. Thus, death rates from this type of death appear to be almost totally under human control, at least to an observer not familiar with the power of sex role socialization to shape and psychosocial forces to maintain behavior.

Stage 6 deaths could generally be averted by making wiser choices. For example, people committing vehicular manslaughter could choose not to drive while under the influence of alcohol or drugs and to keep their automobiles in better repair. People striking out in a rage at others could have been taught a different reaction leading to a different type of response or at least the use of less violence in their response. Simple measures, such as restricting the availability of handguns, could help decrease this cause of death.

Stage 7 deaths are entirely controllable. People do not have to choose to murder others, with the possible exception of those who are under orders in the military. People can choose to build the type of culture and teach the types of responses that make murder a rare event.

Stage 8 deaths are also entirely controllable. Although people in all ages have chosen to take their own lives (Stillion, McDowell, & May, 1989), suicide is a deliberately self-selected act by all except the most seriously mentally disturbed. Without debating the rights of individuals to end their lives as they choose, it is apparent that suicide is, by its very nature, a selection or choice to die.

The interesting thing about this hierarchy, from the point of view of this chapter, is that as one moves upwards in the hierarchy, the sex differential in death increases. It is almost as though our society has chosen to exert control where it is possible with the aim of increasing the sex differential in death by ensuring that males inhabit a much more dangerous world than do females. Blum (1987) has observed that violence has replaced disease as the most prevalent cause of death among young people in the United States across the past 30 years and Lore and Schultz (1993) have indicated that "interpersonal violence is obviously not limited to young adults. Even at the ripe old age of 36, assault rates are 50% of those at age 21, and appreciable numbers of men at age 50 are still at it" (p. 16). Goldberg (1977) has described the male socialization process as a prescription for early death and suicide.

Toward a Multidimensional Model for Understanding Early Death Among Males

The model that follows (Figure 3.2) summarizes what has been discussed thus far. The model can best be conceptualized as a set of concentric circles of influences, each of which adds to the sex differential in mortality. The first sphere, genetic factors, is the smallest because it probably contributes the least amount of variance to differential longevity. Under the influence of the XY chromosome, masculinization of the fetus begins. As has been shown, this process may contribute to the higher death rates of males in utero. In addition, X-linked diseases add their part to the variance surrounding differential longevity. This core of genetic traits is

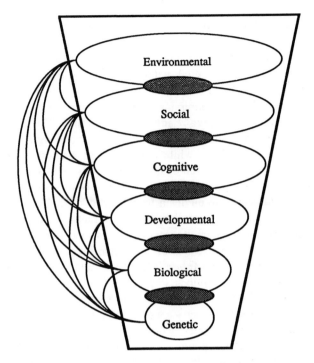

Figure 3.2. Factors Influencing Early Death Among Males

important not because it contributes greatly to the number of years of decreased life that males experience but because it sets in motion other types of genetically based influences that contribute to the growing sex differential in death.

The next sphere consists of biological factors that add their variance to the sex differential in death. Under the influence of genetics, males produce increased levels of testosterone that contribute to aggressive behavior. Aggressive behavior is undeniably a part of the sex differential in homicide and suicide and probably also plays a role in the differential in death by accident. In addition, males do not have the protection of higher levels of estrogen that help to guard premenopausal females from heart disease or the presence of higher levels of protective substances such as immunoglobulin M, which help females experience lower levels of serious infectious diseases.

Moving upward in the figure, males and females experience differential socialization as they develop from infants through maturity. Thus, gender socialization, especially during the preschool years, lends a developmental dimension to the sex differential in death as boys come to understand that their sex role requires emotional inexpressiveness, use of denial of feelings of pain and suffering, permission to be more aggressive and violent, aspiration for success or winning at any cost, and so forth. The result of these messages is behavior that cuts males off from acknowledging bodily problems, even to themselves, while it requires constant striving for success and constant pitting of self against other males in every arena of life. The combination can literally be deadly and is best reflected in the statistics on violent death and on death from heart disease. "In men, the Type A personality is clearly established as a risk factor for myocardial infarction" (Haalstrom, Lapidus, Bengtsson, & Edstrom, 1986, p. 547).

As males develop cognitive structures or schemas for masculine behavior, they begin to structure their future interactions in the world in such a way as to maintain those perceptions. Phenomenologists have long maintained that human beings attend and respond to those stimuli in the environment that agree with their concept of self as it is developing (Lecky, 1945; Rogers, 1980). Thus, males, whose basic orientation toward the world is more active and aggressive than females, find those tendencies sharpened by their cognitive understanding and acceptance of the emphasis on competition and success inherent in traditional male socialization.

The final sphere represents those forces in the external environment that provide pressure for males to maintain current sex role qualities. Such forces include society's emphasis on material success and constant reinforcement of traditional sex-role socialization through the media.

The interconnecting lines on the left of the model indicate that each of the factors included may influence all of the other factors. For example, the presence of the XY chromosome may predispose a given male to a higher physical aggression level. As the higher aggression level is expressed, male adults who believe their child is showing characteristics of becoming a "real man" may reinforce these behaviors. At puberty, under the biological influence of increased testosterone, and operating from his cognitive understandings of appropriate male behavior, this male may enter a social world where aggression, domination, and conflict are realities. Reinforced through every type of media outlet in his environment, by his everyday experience of surviving in a world where he is more likely to witness or experience accidents, murders, and suicide than are his female peers, the young male has little reason to question the validity of his perceptions and socialization. The spiral in the model suggests that the interaction of each of these spheres provides strong ongoing support for maintaining the status quo in socialization as the more violent world of males becomes a self-fulfilling prophecy.

Conclusion: Nurturing Men's Health by Redefining Masculinity

There is little, if anything, we can do about the biological factors that influence longevity. We must, however, recognize that when an organism, plant or animal, appears to be at biological risk, rational caregivers will attempt to create an environment that will nurture that organism and provide it the safest and most fertile climate in which to grow and flourish. Furthermore, we need to realize that the type of socialization we have put in place to date in American culture builds on many existing genetic predispositions that make males prone to early death, especially violent death and death from heart disease.

We do not have to continue to socialize males to premature death. Masculinity and male socialization are malleable. As Bernard (1981) observed over a decade ago,

Presented only as food for thought . . . is the idea that just as the primordial fetal stuff would remain female if not prodded by the male hormone, so the "real" nature of humanity or "human nature" would probably be more like "female" human nature than like the "nature" that has to be achieved with so much effort as "male" nature is, if it were not prodded from infancy on to be aggressive, competitive, dominant.(p. 544)[2]

More recently, Lore and Schultz (1993), in a comparative analysis of aggression, maintained that although males of most mammalian species are clearly more aggressive than are females, aggression is a malleable behavior that can either be expressed or inhibited depending upon the conditions and expectations dominant in the environment. These authors point to relatively simple changes that could be made to decrease violent death in our society, including adopting a national policy that discourages the expression of individual aggression, adopting more stringent gun control, and limiting "the almost continuous exposure to glorified, unrealistic violence in the entertainment media" (p. 23).

To change existing gender socialization practices, however, there must be widespread acceptance of such change as beneficial. One starting point would be for the leaders and policymakers to reach some consensus about what characteristics we expect of adult males. These characteristics can be conceptualized as goals for healthy adults. Some goals have been suggested by past theorists. For example, Erikson (1959) argued that healthy adults were able to work effectively (industry), to form and maintain intimate human relationships (intimacy), to find positive ways to give back to the society that had nurtured them (generativity), and to come to old age with a feeling that their lives had been lived according to a sense of values that were positive for them at this time in history (ego integrity).

Maslow (1968) suggested that healthy humans have an innate urge to move toward self-actualization, that is, to become all they can become. Doyle (1983), in a comment on how psychology could address the question of gender roles, highlighted the Maslowian tradition:

> As more and more contemporary women and men begin to question and challenge their respective sex roles, psychology can best assist them by systematically debunking those persistent myths that have grown up and supported the unrealistic, contradictory, and, often times, debilitating aspects of sex roles. Rather than helping people to adjust to or fit into outmoded sex roles, clinical psychologists, counselors, and psychiatrists would do better to assist people in their strivings for self-actualization. (p. 142)

This list of goals might not be a bad starting place for redefining masculinity and transforming the process of male socialization. Nowhere on the list do you find dominance, aggression, brutal competitiveness, or emotional inexpressiveness as ideals for healthy adult males.

What is needed at this time in history is a thorough reexamination of the cumulative costs of the male gender role as well as a widely accepted redefinition of what constitutes healthy masculine adulthood. Such a definition should lead to a change in the socialization practices of young boys and in time might result in increased longevity that in turn would produce a more favorable bottom line in the business of life.

Notes

1. There are some causes of death that are outside the ability of human beings to alter, whereas other risks for early mortality can be reduced by individual choice, shifts in social policy, or changes in the environment. Figure 3.1 presents a hierarchy of risk and influence in relation to causes of death. Figure 3.1 shows how the opportunity for human beings to avoid risking early death increases as you move up the hierarchy from Stage 1 to Stage 8.

2. *The Female World* by Jessie Bernard. copyright © 1981 by The Free Press, a division of Simon & Schuster, Inc. Reprinted with permission of the publisher.

References

Bernard, J. (1981). *The female world.* New York: Free Press.

Blum, R. (1987). Contemporary threats to adolescent health in the United States. *Journal of the American Medical Association, 257,* 3390-3395.

Doyle, J. S. (1983). *The male experience.* Dubuque, IA: William C. Brown.

Engels, F. (1942). *The origin of the family, private property, and the state.* New York: International Publishing. (Original work published 1884)

Erikson, E. H. (1959). *Identity and the life cycle.* New York: Norton.

Friedl, E. (1978, April). Society and sex roles. *Human Nature, 4,* 68-75.

Gilligan, C. (1982). *In a different voice: Psychological theory and women's development.* Cambridge, MA: Harvard University Press.

Goldberg, P. (1977). *The hazards of being male: Surviving the myth of masculine privilege.* New York: New American Library.

Green, R. (1987). *The "sissy boy syndrome" and the development of homosexuality.* New Haven, CT: Yale University Press.

Haalstrom, T., Lapidus, L., Bengtsson, C., & Edstrom, K. (1986). Psychosocial factors and risk of ischemic heart disease and death in women: A twelve-year follow-up of participants in the population study of women in Gothenburg, Sweden. *Journal of Psychosomatic Research, 30,* 451-459.

Hagestad, G. O. (1986). The aging society as a context for family life. *Daedalus, 115,* 119-139.

Hare-Mustin, R. T., & Mareck, J. (1990). *Making a difference.* New Haven, CT: Yale University Press.

Kaplan, R. M., Anderson, J. P., & Wingard, D. L. (1991). Gender differences in health-related quality of life. *Health Psychology, 10,* 86-93.

Kohlberg, L. (1966). A cognitive-developmental analysis of children's sex-role concepts and attitudes. In E. Maccoby (Ed.), *The development of sex differences.* Stanford, CA: Stanford University Press.

Komisar, L. (1976). Violence and the masculine mystique. In D. David & R. Brannon (Eds.), *The forty-nine percent majority* (pp. 201-215). Reading, MA: Addison-Wesley.

Lecky, D. (1945). *Self-consistency: A theory of personality.* Seattle, WA: Shoestring Press.

Linehan, M. M. (1971). Toward a theory of sex differences in suicidal behavior. *Crisis Intervention, 3,* 93-101.

Linehan, M. M. (1973). Suicide and attempted suicide: Study of perceived sex differences. *Perceptual and Motor Skills, 37,* 31-34.

Lore, R. K., & Schultz, L. A. (1993). Control of human aggression: A comparative perspective. *American Psychologist, 48,* 16-25.

Markides, K. S. (1990). Risk factors, gender, and health. *Generations: Gender and Aging,* 17-21.

Marks, A. (1989). Structural parameters of sex, race, age, and education and their influence on attitudes toward suicide. *Omega, 19,* 327-336.

Maslow, A. H. (1968). *Toward a psychology of being* (2nd ed.). New York: Van Nostrand Rienhold.

National Center for Health Statistics. (1992). Advance report of final mortality statistics, 1989. *Monthly Vital Statistics Report* (Vol. 40). Hyattsville, MD: Public Health Service.

Nolen-Hoeksema, S. (1987). Sex differences in unipolar depression: Evidence and theory. *Psychological Bulletin, 101,* 259-282.

Ounsted, M. (1972). Gender and intrauterine growth with a note on the sex proband as a research tool. In C. Ounsted & D. C. Taylor (Eds.), *Gender differences: Their ontogeny and significance* (pp. 177-201). London: Churchill Livingston.

Pleck, J. H. (1983). *The myth of masculinity.* Cambridge: MIT Press.

Rheingold, H., & Cook, K. (1975). The contents of boys' and girls' rooms as an index of parents' behavior. *Child Development, 46,* 459-463.

Rich, C. L., Ricketts, J. E., Fowler, R. C., & Young, D. (1988). Some differences between men and women who commit suicide. *American Journal of Psychiatry, 145,* 718-722.

Rogers, C. (1980). *On becoming a person.* Boston: Houghton Mifflin.

Rosenthal, M. J. (1981). Sexual differences in the suicidal behavior of young people. *Adolescent Psychiatry, 9,* 422-442.

Sabo, D. (1989). Pigskin, patriarchy and pain. In M. S. Kimmel & M. A. Messner (Eds.), *Men's lives* (2nd ed., pp. 184-187). New York: Macmillan.

Sabo, D. (1993). Understanding men. In G. Kimball (Ed.), *Everything you need to know to succeed after college* (pp. 71-94). Chico, CA: Equality Press.

Stillion, J. M. (1985). *Death and the sexes: An examination of differential longevity, attitudes, behaviors, and coping skills.* Washington, DC: Hemisphere.

Stillion, J. M. (In press). Through a glass darkly: Women and attitudes toward suicidal behavior. In S. Canetto & D. Lester (Eds.), *Women and suicide.* New York: Springer.

Stillion, J. M., McDowell, E. E., & May, J. H. (1984). Developmental trends and sex differences in adolescent attitudes toward suicide. *Death Education, 8*(Suppl.), 81-90.

Stillion, J. M., McDowell, E. E., & May, J. H. (1989). *Suicide across the life span: Premature exits.* New York: Hemisphere.

Stillion, J. M., White, H., McDowell, E. E., & Edwards, P. (1989). Ageism and sexism in suicide attitudes. *Death Studies, 13,* 247-261.

Tricomi, U., Serr, D., & Solish, G. (1960). The ratio of male to female embryos as determined by the sex chromatin. *American Journal of Obstetrics and Gynecology, 79,* 504-509.

Verbrugge, L. M. (1985). Gender and health: An update on hypotheses and evidence. *Journal of Health and Social Behavior, 26,* 156-182.

Waldron, I. (1976). Why do women live longer than men? *Social Science and Medicine, 10,* 349-362.

Waldron, I. (1983). Sex differences in illness incidence, prognosis and mortality. *Social Science and Medicine, 17,* 1107-1123.

Weissman, M. M., & Klerman, G. L. (1977). Sex differences and the epidemiology of depression. *Arch Gen Psychiatry, 34,* 98-111.

White, H., & Stillion, J. M. (1988). Sex differences in attitudes toward suicide: Do males stigmatize males? *Psychology of Women Quarterly, 12,* 235-259.

Wilson, E. (1978). *On human nature.* Cambridge, MA: Harvard University Press.

4

Masculinity, Men's Roles, and Coronary Heart Disease

VICKI S. HELGESON

As the leading causes of death in the United States shifted from infectious disease during the first half of the 20th century to chronic disease (e.g., cancer, heart disease) during the last half of the 20th century, the sex differential in mortality widened. In 1920, men lived to be 54 and women lived to be 56. In 1990, men lived to be 72 and women lived to be 79. It is unlikely that the increase in the sex differential in mortality can be attributed to changes in biology (Johnson, 1977). Men are more likely than women to die of the four leading causes of death in the United States: (a) heart disease, (b) cancer, (c) cerebrovascular disease, and (d) accidents (Verbrugge, 1985). As the preceding chapters by Ingrid Waldron and Judith Stillion have demonstrated, these leading causes of death are ones in which psychological, social, and behavioral factors contribute to men's substantially higher mortality rates compared to women. They argue that a sizable portion of men's excess mortality over women is linked to masculine identity, men's roles, and gendered patterns of socialization.

There is emerging evidence that aspects of masculine identity and male socialization are related to men's risk for coronary heart disease. Strickland (1988) suggests that men cope with stress by independent and aggressive behavior, which results in a higher rate of male-to-female heart disease. For example, traditionally masculine behaviors such as smoking and drinking have been linked to heart disease. Aspects of masculinity also overlap with the Type A behavior pattern, which has been linked to coronary heart disease. Traditional masculinity not only may place men at greater risk for disease but also may shape men's personal reactions and subsequent adjustment to heart disease. Specifically, men's unwillingness to rely on others for assistance and inability to express emotions may pose obstacles for successful adjustment to heart disease.

Although scholars have made good progress with unraveling the theoretical links between masculinity, men's roles, and coronary heart disease, their efforts have been hampered by a shortage of empirical research. This chapter reports on an array of research studies that shed light on whether aspects of the traditional male gender role are associated with psychological, social, and behavioral risk factors for the onset of coronary heart disease as well as poor psychological and physical adjustment to the disease. Specific pathways by which masculinity may be linked to the onset of heart disease as well as poor adjustment to heart disease are examined. The chapter concludes with some future directions for research on masculinity, health, and illness.

Before discussing the empirical research, it is necessary to examine how researchers have conceptualized and measured masculinity in their studies of men's health.

Measuring Masculinity in Studies of Health and Illness

Researchers have taken several approaches to studying the male gender role. Personality theorists and social psychologists have developed several trait inventories to measure masculinity, the most common of which are the Bem Sex Role Inventory (BSRI; Bem, 1974) and the Personal Attributes Questionnaire (PAQ; Spence, Helmreich, & Stapp, 1974). The masculinity scales on these instruments reflect an instrumental (Parsons & Bales, 1955) or agenetic (Bakan, 1966) orientation. Items on these scales were developed by having people rate the extent to which they considered characteristics to be desirable in men and in women (BSRI) or the extent to which characteristics applied to men and women (PAQ).

The authors of the PAQ recognized that one limitation of these instruments was that they assessed only the socially desirable features of masculinity. In 1979, Spence, Helmreich, and Holahan developed the Extended Version of the Personal Attributes Questionnaire (EPAQ) that contained an additional masculinity scale to reflect the socially undesirable features of this construct. This "negative masculinity" scale also was developed to reflect the extreme masculine orientation or the extreme agenetic orientation. The scale is referred to as *unmitigated agency*—meaning agency unmitigated by (i.e., in the absence of) communion, or focus on self to the exclusion of others (Helgeson, 1994b). For example, *self-confident* is an item on the positive masculinity scale of the PAQ and *arrogant* is an item on the negative masculinity scale of the EPAQ. The positive and negative masculinity scales are positively correlated, suggesting that the scales reflect an underlying dimension (agency) and do *not* reflect a socially desirability response bias.

A second approach to studying masculinity has been to study the aspects of the male gender role that are sources of conflict or stress for men. For example, Eisler and Skidmore (1987) have developed a Masculine Gender Role Stress Scale that reflects situations that are a source of stress for men because they conflict with the male gender role. The scale contains five factors: (a) physical inadequacy, (b) emotional inexpressiveness, (c) subordination to women, (d) intellectual inferiority, and (e) performance failure. Another set of researchers developed two gender-role conflict scales, one to reflect men's thoughts and feelings about their behavior and one to reflect men's degree of conflict in certain situations (O'Neil, Helms, Gable, David, & Wrightsman, 1986). Items on these two scales reflect four themes: (a) success, power, and competition, (b) restrictive emotionality, (c) restrictive affectionate behavior between men, and (d) conflicts between work and family relations. These four sources of gender-role conflict are considered to have "fear of femininity" as their basis. That the primary motivator of men's behavior is something negative (avoiding the appearance of anything feminine) rather than something positive (power, control) has been suggested by other researchers (Thompson, Grisanti, & Pleck, 1985).

Third, scales have been developed to measure one's attitude toward the traditional male gender role. These scales reflect beliefs about the way men should be rather than beliefs about the way men are. For example, Pleck, Sonenstein, and Ku (1993) developed a Masculine Ideology Scale that reflects endorsement of traditional attitudes toward the male gender role. It includes items such as "It bothers me when a guy acts like a girl," and "A young man should be physically tough, even if he's not big." Brannon and Juni (1984) also have developed a scale to measure attitudes about masculinity. This instrument is composed of seven subscales: (a) avoiding femininity, (b) concealing emotions, (c) the breadwinner, (d) admired and respected, (e) toughness, (f) the male machine, and (g) violence and adventure. Each of these scales reflects a way that men ought to appear or ought to behave.

Thus, there are at least three distinct ways to examine the male gender role: possession of a distinct set of personality traits, feelings of conflict stemming from being socialized male, and an attitude toward the appropriate behavior for men. Evidence for the distinctiveness of these measures stems from the finding that trait masculinity is not correlated with either of the other two measurement strategies (Eisler, Skidmore, & Ward, 1988). Although the relation of gender-role conflict to traditional attitudes toward men's roles has not been examined, the two are likely to be positively correlated; that is, someone who endorses more traditional beliefs about the male role (e.g., men should not express emotions) will have that as a source of gender-role conflict (e.g., inability to express emotions).

Now I turn to the evidence that the male gender role, conceptualized in any of the previously described ways (trait masculinity, male gender-role conflict, traditional beliefs about the male role), poses health hazards. Paradoxically, the evidence reveals a positive link between trait masculinity and psychological well-being but a negative relation between trait masculinity and health behavior or physical health. There is less research on the health implications of gender-role conflict or traditional beliefs about men, but existing evidence suggests that they are related to worse psychological health and poor health behavior.

Male Gender Role and Psychological Well-Being

Trait masculinity has a pervasive and positive effect on psychological well-being among both men and women (see Bassoff & Glass, 1982; Whitley, 1984, for reviews). Specifically, trait masculinity has been related to reduced depression (Holahan & Spence, 1980; Roos & Cohen, 1987; see Whitley, 1984, for a review), reduced anxiety (Holahan & Spence, 1980; Nezu & Nezu, 1987; Nezu, Nezu, & Peterson, 1986; Roos & Cohen, 1987), and enhanced self-esteem (Carlson & Baxter, 1984; see Whitley, 1983, for a review). When subject sex is statistically controlled, trait masculinity continues to be related to reduced distress (Nezu et al., 1986; Nezu & Nezu, 1987).

Studies that have used the EPAQ to distinguish negative masculinity from positive masculinity (or the extreme from the nonextreme masculine dimension) reveal divergent effects on psychological well-being. In a study of college students, some of whom were seeking counseling, nonextreme masculinity was related to better mental health and extreme masculinity was related to worse mental health (Holahan & Spence, 1980). In a study of male psychiatric inpatients, nonextreme masculinity was related to less pathology and extreme masculinity was related to more pathology (Evans & Dinning, 1982).

Scales that measure male gender-role conflict have been related to lower psychological well-being. The Masculine Gender Role Stress Scale has been related to increased anxiety (Eisler et al., 1988) and the Gender Role Conflict Scale (O'Neil et al., 1986) has been related to depression in one study (Good & Mintz, 1990) and to low self-esteem, anxiety, and depression in another study (Sharpe & Heppner, 1991).

Male Gender Role, Behavioral
Risk Factors, and Physical Well-Being

The PAQ and EPAQ have been used in several studies of health promoting or health risk behavior. Two studies of college students have shown that the nonextreme version of masculinity is related to health-enhancing behaviors (e.g., exercise; Eisler et al., 1988; Robbins, Spence, & Clark, 1991). Studies that have distinguished between positive and negative masculinity have found negative masculinity to be related to risky behavior. In one study of college students, negative or extreme masculinity was related to using alcohol, mind-altering drugs, tranquilizers, and sedatives (Snell, Belk, & Hawkins, 1987), and in another study of college students, negative masculinity was associated with acting out behavior (e.g., drug use, school misbehavior, and misdemeanors; Spence et al., 1979).

Gender-role conflict and traditional attitudes about the male gender role also appear to be related to risk-producing behavior. The Masculine Gender Role Stress Scale was related to poor health habits among college students (e.g., exercise, diet, seat belt use, tobacco, alcohol; Eisler et al., 1988). Traditional beliefs about masculinity, as assessed by the Masculine Ideology Scale, have been identified as a risk factor for problems such as using alcohol and drugs, sexual promiscuity, and school suspension among adolescent males (Pleck et al., 1993).

Few studies have attempted to link aspects of the male gender role to physical health outcomes. In two studies of college students, trait masculinity was associated with the self-report of fewer physical symptoms (Heiser & Gannon, 1984; Robbins et al., 1991). Results from a longitudinal study of patients being treated for chronic pain either through an anesthesiology or psychiatry department revealed that higher masculinity MMPI scores at the beginning of treatment were associated with better subjective outcomes (e.g., pain relief) an average of 20.5 months later, when subject sex, levels of pain prior to treatment, years of pain, and time in treatment were statistically controlled (Strassberg, Reimher, Ward, Russell, & Cole, 1981). These data are limited, however, in their implications for the experience of physical symptoms because self-reports of physical symptoms are as likely to be correlated with psychological well-being as physical well-being and may be influenced by self-presentation concerns.

Although many men have written books describing characteristics of the traditional male gender role and the hazardous health implications of these characteristics (e.g., Goldberg, 1976; Naifeh & Smith, 1984; Nichols, 1975), empirical evidence on the association of the male gender role with physical health outcomes is lacking. This observation led me to develop a program of research that would determine whether there was a link between aspects of the traditional male gender role and coronary heart disease (CHD). I focused on CHD for two reasons. First, coronary heart disease is the leading cause of death in the United States among both men and women. Thus, it is an important health problem. Second, rates of heart disease are higher for men than women at all ages. Because men in our nation die much younger than women and their shorter life expectancy is primarily attributable to heart disease, the study of heart disease was a good candidate for exploring links between masculinity and men's health and illness.

Trait Masculinity and Coronary Heart Disease

As the incidence of CHD increased during the first half of the 20th century, the sex differential in CHD mortality also increased (Johnson, 1977). In fact, CHD accounts for the major portion of the sex differential in longevity (Nathanson, 1977; Waldron, 1976, Chapter 2, this volume). Men suffer more than two times the incidence of CHD compared to women, with rates only approaching equality at the age of 70 (Kannel, Hjortland, McNamara, & Gordon, 1976).

Jenkins noted in 1971 that the standard biological risk factors did not adequately identify new cases of CHD and that psychological, social, and behavioral factors made significant contributions to CHD risk. Studies that have controlled for physical aspects of lifestyle reveal that psychosocial factors are among the remaining culprits (Cooper, Faragher, Bray, & Ramsdale, 1985; Liljefors & Rahe, 1972; see Rosenman, 1980, for a review). According to Lynch (1977), this set of factors is not just *a* risk; it is the most important risk factor (see Haynes, Levine, Scotch, Feinleib, & Kannel, 1978, for an opposite view).

Research has ruled out the possibility that sex differences in the primary CHD risk factors (e.g., hypertension, high cholesterol) explain sex differences in CHD mortality (Johnson, 1977; Wingard, Suarez, & Barrett-Connor, 1983). Social scientists have suggested that cultural and economic pressures related to the role of men in our society account for men's shorter life expectancy, in general (Harrison, 1978), and encourage the development of coronary prone behavior, in particular, resulting in excess mortality from CHD (Waldron, 1976). In fact, in a study of life expectancy on a kibbutz where men's and women's roles are more similar than they are in the United States, gender differences in life expectancy were reduced (Leviatan & Cohen, 1985).

Theoretical Links of Masculinity to CHD

The aspect of the male gender role that I examined in studies of coronary heart disease was trait masculinity. I suggest that trait masculinity consists of a set of psychosocial characteristics that place men at risk for heart disease. A model of how masculinity might be related to CHD is displayed in Figure 4.1. First, there is a set of traditional coronary risk factors, including smoking, hypertension, diabetes, alcohol abuse, and high cholesterol, that place one at risk for CHD. Some of these risk factors may be related to masculinity, for example, smoking. Second, independent of this biological pathway, masculinity may place one at risk for heart disease by leading to the development of (a) impaired social networks, (b) Type A behavior, and (c) poor health care. All three of these psychosocial characteristics place one at risk for CHD.

Type A Behavior. Extensive research, mostly with men, has shown a relation between the Type A behavior pattern and CHD (see Matthews & Haynes, 1986, for a review), but researchers have failed to recognize that characteristics of the traditional masculine role overlap with characteristics of Type A behavior. The Type A behavior pattern includes extreme

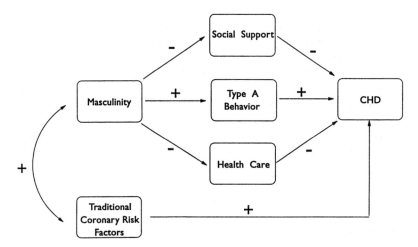

Figure 4.1. Psychosocial Components of Men's Risk for Coronary Heart Disease (CHD)

aggressiveness, easily aroused hostility, sense of time urgency, and competitive achievement striving (Friedman & Rosenman, 1974). It also is characterized by an intense focus on central rather than peripheral information. This full allocation to central events or tasks (such as job-related activities) has been suggested to decrease awareness of symptoms (Carver & Humphries, 1982; Jennings, 1983). Research has shown that Type As report fewer symptoms than Type Bs (Hart, 1983), particularly symptoms associated with fatigue (Carver, Coleman, & Glass, 1976; Weidner & Matthews, 1978). And fatigue is one of the warning signs of an impending heart attack (Carver & Humphries, 1982; Greene, Moss, & Goldstein, 1974).

Interestingly, many of these components—competitiveness, hostility, symptom suppression, and attentional style—are similar to trait masculinity as defined by personality theorists and social psychologists (Bem, 1974; Spence et al., 1974). The BSRI and the PAQ include traits such as aggressive, competitive, never gives up, hostile, dictatorial, arrogant, not being excitable in a major crisis, not crying, standing up well under pressure, and looking out for oneself. Research has shown that both males and females who score high on masculinity also score higher on measures of Type A behavior (Batlis & Small, 1982; DeGregorio & Carver, 1980; Nix & Lohr, 1981; Payne, 1987). Those who endorse the traditional male gender role (as measured by the Brannon Masculinity Scale) also endorse

Type A behavior (Thompson et al., 1985). All of these studies were conducted, however, with college students—who are unlikely to show symptoms of CHD.

The characteristics of the coronary-prone individual described by List (1967) are strikingly similar to the characteristics of the traditional male gender role. List suggests that coronary-prone persons hide weaknesses, inhibit emotional expression, lack empathy, fear homosexuality, and fail to reveal their true selves partly from a lack of self-knowledge and partly from a desire to conform to others' expectations. The overlap between trait masculinity and coronary-prone behavior, or Type A behavior, is shown in Table 4.1.

Social Support. The lack of an adequate social support network is associated with mortality (Berkman & Syme, 1979; Blazer, 1982; House, Robbins, & Metzner, 1982), including mortality from CHD (Berkman & Syme, 1979; Ruberman, Weinblatt, Goldberg, & Chaudhary, 1984). The social networks of coronary-prone persons are impoverished (see Jennings, 1983, for a review), and men, in general, are at a support disadvantage compared to women (Belle, 1987; Burda, Vaux, & Schill, 1984; Hirsch, 1979; Roos & Cohen, 1987; see Shumaker & Hill, 1991, for a review). Men provide and receive less social support than women (Belle, 1987; Burda et al., 1984; Roos & Cohen, 1987; Stokes & Wilson, 1984). Men also are less likely than women to seek social support (Butler, Giordano, & Neren, 1985), presumably because asking for help implies weakness and dependence. Social support may act as a buffer against stress and an aid to recovery, and masculinity plays a role in the nature of a person's social supports.

One study demonstrated that sex differences in social support (women greater than men) were reduced when gender role (trait femininity) was statistically controlled (Burda et al., 1984). This finding suggests that men's support disadvantage is partly due to a lack of feminine traits. The characteristics of the traditional male gender role are inconsistent with the provision, activation, and receipt of social support, particularly emotional support (i.e., comfort, caring, understanding, reassurance). The provision and receipt of support is more likely to occur in a relationship characterized by emotional expressiveness, mutual self-disclosure, and empathy. The traditional male gender role poses difficulties for enacting each of these behaviors.

First, men experience and express less *emotion* than women in close relationships (Sprecher & Sedikides, 1993). The male emphasis on self-control, toughness, and autonomy prevents the expression of emotions

Table 4.1 Comparison of Coronary Prone Behavior and Trait Masculinity

Characteristics of the Coronary-Prone Individual	Sample of Trait Masculinity Features
Fails to attend to others' feelings[a]	
Lacks self-knowledge	*Independent*
Isolated	*Active*
Hides weaknesses	*Never cries*
Rigid performance at work	Never gives up
Self-control	*Self-confident*
Inhibited expression	Hostile
Fears homosexuality	*Not excitable in a major crisis*
Lacks empathy[a]	*Competitive*
	Arrogant, egotistical
	Looks out for self
	Greedy
	Dictatorial
Impatient	Cynical
Hostile	
Preoccupied with self	
Guilty if relax	
Achievement-oriented	*Ambitious*
Appears *self-confident*	Athletic
Active	Assertive
Independent	Willingness to take risks
Competitive drive	*Dominant*
Hyperaggressiveness	*Aggressive*
Dominant	Leader

SOURCE: Bem (1974); Friedman & Rosenman (1974); Friedman & Ulmer (1984); List (1967); Spence, Helmreich, & Stapp (1974); and Spence, Helmreich, & Holahan (1979).
NOTE: Italicized words are those that are common to both columns.
a. The counterpart of these characteristics are features of trait femininity.

and feelings (Kilmartin, 1994). Men are socialized to believe that expressiveness is inconsistent with masculinity (Balswick & Peek, 1971), and, in fact, trait masculinity has been related to less emotional expression (Ganong & Coleman, 1984). O'Neil and colleagues (1986) believe that men's fears of appearing feminine underlie their inability to express emotion. In a study in which college men were asked to role play different emotions, subjects high in masculine gender-role stress were rated by observers as less verbally and nonverbally expressive (Saurer & Eisler, 1990). Men's inability to express emotions may make them uncomfortable asking for support and less capable of eliciting it nonverbally (Saurer & Eisler, 1990).

Men's cool detachment, which is intended to convey strength and objectivity, unfortunately, may inhibit the development of close relationships and lead to misunderstandings (Nichols, 1975). One reason that men's relationships suffer is because they are more concerned with maintaining objectivity and proving themselves than with being expressive (Keith, 1974). According to Naifeh and Smith (1984), the more a man becomes confused about his emotions, the more he will retreat into the safer realm of rationality and objectivity. Unfortunately, avoiding feelings may result in the inability to feel (Nichols, 1975). Rubin (1983) has said that some men simply do not know how to respond to the question, How do you feel?, and that feelings consciously available to women are not always available to men who have learned to repress them.

Research has indirectly substantiated the belief that repression of emotions has adverse health consequences. Pennebaker, Kiecolt-Glaser, and Glaser (1988) randomly assigned college students to write about either a traumatic event or a superficial event that they had experienced. A comparison of the two groups revealed that those who wrote about traumatic experiences had better immune function and visited the health center less frequently than those who wrote about superficial events. The conclusion drawn from this study is that expressing emotions is good for one's health.

Second, a way to develop close relationships and a support network is through revealing personal information about oneself, *self-disclosure.* According to Jourard (1971), men are difficult to love because they do not disclose their needs. Men do not self-disclose to the extent that women do (Notarius & Johnson, 1982) for three reasons. First, men's "restricted emotionality" inhibits self-disclosure (Snell, 1986). Second, self-disclosure implies revealing weaknesses or vulnerabilities, which is inconsistent with the masculine image of strength and control. Third, revealing vulnerabilities provides the recipient with a source of power over the discloser. Self-disclosure is inversely related to trait masculinity (Winstead, Derlega, & Wong, 1984) and endorsement of the traditional male gender role (Thompson et al., 1985). In a study of college students who were asked to become acquainted by discussing intimate topics, half of the males in this study refused to initiate this type of discussion (Walker & Wright, 1976).

Third, *empathy,* a useful skill used to maintain a support network, is not as available to men as it is to women (see Hoffman, 1977, for a review). Empathy is inversely related to trait masculinity (Hansson, Jones, & Carpenter, 1984). A recent study of empathy and social support showed that sex differences in social support can be accounted for by women's greater empathy compared to men (Trobst, Collins, & Embree, 1994). A lack of empathy also has been described as a feature of the coronary-prone individual. The coronary-prone individual has been described as paying less attention to the feelings and emotions of others (List, 1967) and failing to notice important social cues.

Each of these features of the male gender role—restricted emotionality, unwillingness to self-disclose, and lack of empathy—appears to influence men's relationships. Friendships among men are often restricted by competitiveness (Garfinkel, 1985; Goldberg, 1976; Komarovsky, 1974, 1976; Lewis, 1978; Tognoli, 1980) and homophobia (Garfinkel, 1985; Lewis, 1978; McGill, 1985; Tognoli, 1980). Competition inhibits the disclosure of vulnerabilities, and fear of being labeled a homosexual keeps men from showing affection to one another (Naifeh & Smith, 1984; Nichols, 1975). Our culture promotes negative affect and inhibits positive affect among men (Lewis, 1978).

Men's relationships with other men are often activity focused rather than emotion focused—"doing" instead of "being" (Rubin, 1985; Wright, 1982). Men emphasize same sex friends who do the same things, whereas women emphasize same sex friends who feel the same about things (Caldwell & Peplau, 1982). Men tend to compartmentalize their relationships with other men, having different friends for different functions, whereas women tend to have friends with whom they share all aspects of their lives (McGill, 1985; Wright, 1982).

The limits on male-male friendships may cause men to rely too heavily on women for intimacy and emotional support (Pleck, 1976; Rubin, 1983). Men often find it easier to show emotion and self-disclose to women than to other men. Komarovsky's male college students revealed that their primary confidant was their closest female, rather than male, friend. In a study of college students, Wheeler, Reis, and Nezlek (1983) found that the amount of time men spent with men was associated with more loneliness and the amount of time men spent with women was associated with less loneliness. The authors also showed that male-male interactions were less intimate than any interaction involving a female. Further evidence for the positive effects of relationships with women on men's psychological well-being comes from a recent study of college student long-distance romantic relationships (Helgeson, 1994). Men whose relationships had dissolved were more distressed than men whose relationships remained intact, whereas the converse occurred for women (i.e., women whose relationships had dissolved were less distressed than women whose relationships remained intact). This finding among dating couples parallels that found among married couples. Most studies find that men benefit more psychologically and physically from marriage compared to women (Belle, 1987; Berkman & Syme, 1979; Gove, 1973), and suffer more upon divorce and widowhood compared to women (Bloom, White, & Asher, 1979; Stroebe & Stroebe, 1983; Umberson, Wortman, & Kessler, 1992; Wallerstein & Kelly, 1980). One reason for these findings is that men rely almost solely on their wives for support, whereas wives retain family and friends as members of their network (Fischer & Phillips, 1982; Lowenthal & Haven, 1968; Veroff, Douvan, & Kukla, 1981).

Just because men are at a support disadvantage compared to women does not mean that the presence of support will not have a positive effect on men's health. There is some evidence that support has a stronger impact on men's health than women's health. Seeman and Syme (1987) studied men and women undergoing coronary angiography and found that social support was related to less severe disease among men but not women. In a study of heart attack survivors, inability to disclose to one's spouse was associated with a cardiac-related rehospitalization during the next year for men but not women (Helgeson, 1991).

Jourard (1971) suggests that being loved and loving gives value to a man's life. If this is true, he concludes that the male handicap in love is lethal for men. Men are prone to what Jourard (1971) calls *dispiritation;* that is, the loss of a sense of meaning in life. Instead of investing in intimate relationships, men depend on their jobs, status, and sexual potency for their identities, none of which are immutable. When all of these things are gone—for example, when men retire or become chronically ill—much of life's meaning is lost. Thus, Jourard (1971) suggests that men become susceptible to illness and Naifeh and Smith (1984) conclude that men die earlier.

Having outlined the features of the male gender role that leave men vulnerable to a lack of support, it must be noted that there are some aspects of the male gender role that are quite consistent with social support. The kind of social support described above was more of an emotional nature. Among the kinds of support, researchers consider emotional support to be the primary function (Cohen & Hoberman, 1983; House, 1981; Schaefer, Coyne, & Lazarus, 1981). There are other kinds of support, however, such as instrumental support and informational support that may be more consistent with masculinity. Men who have an instrumental orientation may find it easier to provide advice or guidance (informational support) and tangible assistance (instrumental support).

Health Care. A third way that the male gender role may be linked to CHD is through health practices. Men have shown a greater failure to follow standard health practices, report symptoms, and visit physicians compared to women (Lewis & Lewis, 1977; Nathanson, 1977; Verbrugge, 1985; Waldron, 1976). In a survey of Dayton residents, redivorced men cited depression twice as often as redivorced women, but did not seek therapy for it to the extent that women did (Balk, 1985).

Men's lack of desire to seek help for problems may be due, in part, to society's response to men with problems. For example, other people view depressed men more negatively than depressed women (Hammen & Peters, 1977, 1978). Others may encourage men to solve their own problems or to overcome symptoms of illness (Goldberg, 1976). The extent to which other people adhere to or endorse the male gender role is likely to influence the kind of support given to men. For example, a study of male counselors showed that counselors who held traditional attitudes toward men emphasized vocational concerns (rather than emotional or psychological concerns) among their clients (Thoreson, Shaughnessy, Cook, & Moore, 1993).

Researchers have suggested that sex differences in illness behavior are due to differences between male and female role expectations (Nathanson, 1975; Verbrugge, 1985). The male gender role, and people who endorse it, discourages men from admitting vulnerabilities and from seeking help when they first realize they may need it. These beliefs are instilled during men's childhood (Lewis & Lewis, 1977). Men learn to avoid or refuse to admit pain, to not ask for help, and to try to appear strong. It is even possible that socialization has taught men not to experience feelings and symptoms that they perceive as signs of weakness (Rubin, 1983). The individual who adheres to the male gender role may practice poor health care and fail to respond to symptoms because he or she either believes help is not warranted or it is inappropriate to seek help. Seeking help is inconsistent with self-reliance and restricting emotions, and it may signify weakness. Traditional attitudes toward men and male gender-role conflict have been related to negative attitudes toward seeking psychological help and to a history of not having sought help for personal or vocational problems (Good, Dell, & Mintz, 1989).

The potential harmfulness of this component of the male gender role becomes especially clear when considering the consequences of a delay in seeking treatment for an acute myocardial infarction (MI). Failure to notice symptoms and respond to them will affect health behavior that may be critical to survival from an MI (e.g., seeking needed rest, altering eating and smoking habits, seeking medical attention; Jennings, 1983). Sixty percent of those who die from myocardial infarction do so before reaching the hospital (Wright, 1980). Noticing and reporting symptoms at an early stage of the disease might reduce the 55% to 80% of deaths that occur within 4 hours of the onset of symptoms (Hackett & Rosenbaum, 1980). The recent development of thrombolytic agents (e.g., streptokinase, tissue plasminogen activator) to halt heart damage during a heart attack makes a timely response to symptoms even more critical.

A 1991 episode of "20/20" illustrated the association of traditional masculinity with the failure to seek help for symptoms of a heart attack in one instance and colon cancer in the other instance. The man who had the heart attack said he had felt symptoms but refused to admit or report them because symptoms signified weakness that contradicted the masculine role. He also refused to seek help for symptoms because it would have interfered with his business, which was his primary route to affirming his masculine identity. Ironically, his failure to adhere to good health behavior after the first MI led to a second, more debilitating, MI that resulted in the loss of the business he was striving to maintain.

Summary. I have suggested three pathways by which the male gender role, specifically trait masculinity, might be linked to coronary heart disease: Type A behavior, impoverished social networks, and poor health care. Trait masculinity may have positive as well as negative implications for each of the three pathways. For example, the overlap between the features of trait masculinity and Type A behavior might be responsible for a high-achievement orientation and a successful career as well as a risk factor for heart disease. Some features of trait masculinity (e.g., restricted emotionality) may inhibit the availability of social support, whereas other features of trait masculinity (e.g., self-confidence) may attract potential supporters. Finally, trait masculinity has been linked with both good health habits (e.g., exercise) and poor health behaviors (e.g., smoking).

The male gender role is a multifaceted construct, and even trait masculinity has been found to have different components. An important distinction has been made between positive trait masculinity (nonextreme version) and negative trait masculinity (extreme version) or between agency and unmitigated agency. Nonextreme masculinity (positive masculinity) consists of characteristics such as self-confident, independent, and stands up well under pressure; whereas extreme masculinity (negative masculinity) consists of characteristics such as hostile, arrogant, and selfish. There is a common dimension underlying these two constructs, as evidenced by their positive correlation. Yet the two scales have divergent effects on well-being and mediators of well-being. The distinction between positive masculinity and negative masculinity, therefore, may account for some of the paradoxical findings relating trait masculinity to health or risk factors for health.

Empirical Links Between
Trait Masculinity and CHD

The theoretical model discussed above was used to develop a study that would test for relations between aspects of the male gender role and CHD. The aspect of the male gender role studied is trait masculinity. Three hypotheses were formulated to examine the extent to which trait masculinity was indirectly linked to CHD through increased Type A behavior, reduced social support, and poor health behavior.

To test this hypothesis, 70 men and 20 women who were admitted to the hospital for an acute myocardial infarction during the years 1986 and 1987 were interviewed. Patients were enrolled consecutively in the study and were eligible to participate if they were age 70 and under and had no history of another major chronic illness such as cancer or mental illness. Ages ranged from 37 to 70, with a median of 61. The majority of patients were married (82.2%). The majority of subjects were Catholic (62.2%), 18.9% were Jewish, 17.8% were Protestant, and 1 person was an atheist (1.1%). Twenty percent did not graduate from high school, 37.8% completed high school only, 25.6% completed some college, 8.9% graduated from college, and 7.8% reported some postgraduate training. The major findings of this study are reported in Helgeson (1990), and detailed results are provided in Helgeson (1987).

Interviews lasted 90 minutes and were conducted shortly before discharge. The CHD outcome chosen for study was not the incidence or development of heart disease (for practical reasons and economic constraints) but the severity of heart disease. The rationale of why trait masculinity would be linked to the development of heart disease should hold for the severity of heart disease. CHD does not develop over several hours or days as an infection but develops over a period of years. In fact, most everyone has some atherosclerotic plaque in their arteries, but the severity is not such that all people suffer heart attacks. I reasoned that the lethal effects of traditional masculinity should have cumulative effects over the life span leading to more severe coronary artery disease and, thus, more severe heart attacks.

Multiple regression analysis was used to examine the links of trait masculinity to the proposed mediating variables (Type A behavior, social support, health care), and the links of trait masculinity as well as the mediators to heart attack severity. Subject sex was statistically controlled in all analyses so that the effects of trait masculinity independent of biological sex could be examined.

Link to Type A Behavior. The most lethal components of the Type A behavior pattern were measured—that is, hostility and time urgency (impatience). Negative or extreme masculinity predicted increased Type A behavior. There was no relation of positive masculinity to Type A behavior. This was the first study of adults to demonstrate the overlap between trait masculinity and Type A behavior and to distinguish which aspects of masculinity are associated with the most lethal components of Type A behavior.

Link to Social Support. Negative masculinity did not predict the quantity of social support (i.e., number of social contacts) or the presence of a confidant. Instead, positive masculinity predicted a greater quantity of social support. Empathy and lack of homophobia predicted the presence of a confidant.

Link to Health Care. The relation of masculinity to health care in the context of heart disease is of particular interest. Two measures of cardiac-related health care were developed. First, having sustained the heart attack, patients were asked to recall their first warning signs of a heart problem. The time between the initial awareness of symptoms and the development of an acute myocardial infarction is referred to as the *prodromal period.* Second, patients were asked how long they waited before going to the hospital after having symptoms of the heart attack. This is referred to as the *acute delay period.*

Patients who scored high on negative masculinity had longer prodromal periods; that is, they delayed longer before seeking help after their first warning signs of a heart problem. These men either noticed symptoms and failed to act, noticed symptoms but did not interpret them as symptoms of a heart problem, or did not notice symptoms at the time but could now recollect them. For example, one 56-year-old man with a history of hypertension and coronary artery disease noticed symptoms but failed to act. He had been aware of shortness of breath and fatigue for 6 months before his heart attack and had been actively seeking newspaper articles on insurance policies. He had refilled his prescription for nitroglycerine tablets because the old one had expired. "I knew it was coming on," he said. Several men found it difficult to recollect symptoms because they were focused on the task at hand. A 40-year-old man said, "Who knows if I've had symptoms? Sometimes I feel achy and I don't feel good, but I just keep going because I have things to do."

Although neither of the masculinity variables predicted the acute delay period, the number of work-related stressors did. Among men only, more work-related stressors were associated with longer delays before seeking help for acute symptoms of a heart attack. One man who had experienced grave financial difficulties was aware that something was seriously wrong for 12 hours before calling the doctor. He stayed up the entire night thinking about ongoing changes at work instead of important changes in his body. For some men, seeking help for acute symptoms would have disrupted work. An auto mechanic was working with a grinder machine when he was forced to stop due to severe chest pain. He waited until the pain subsided and then pushed himself to finish the task while experiencing a second, third, and fourth pain before calling the emergency medical service.

A number of men spontaneously revealed negative, if not hostile, attitudes toward doctors, hospitals, and having to ask for help. One man who initially refused all medications because he did not "need" them said, "If I had it my way, I would've called a cab 2 days ago and got out of here." Two days prior to our conversation he had been in the Coronary Care Unit with congestive heart failure, and several weeks after discharge he was rehospitalized for coronary artery bypass surgery. Several men insisted that they had a high tolerance for pain and could take care of themselves. One said, "If I had a choice of going to a doctor now or in 3 days, I'd go in 3 days. I'd overcome it myself." Another said he simply did not believe in fatigue: "It's mind over matter—tired is what you tell yourself. If you rest there's a good chance you'll end up lazy." Such men have difficulty interpreting fatigue as a warning signal of future heart problems.

Links to Heart Attack Severity. Multiple regression analysis was used to predict the index of heart attack severity. None of the traditional coronary risk factors (e.g., smoking) predicted heart attack severity. Controlling for subject sex, age, and socioeconomic status, negative masculinity significantly predicted more severe heart attacks and positive masculinity marginally predicted less severe heart attacks. The hypothesized mediating variables—Type A behavior, social support, health care—did not predict heart attack severity. Thus, negative masculinity was directly related to CHD. That aspects of trait masculinity were linked to the three hypothesized mediators is still important, however, because these variables may have other health consequences or cardiac consequences in the years to come.

Masculinity and Adjustment
to Coronary Heart Disease

Having interviewed these 70 men and 20 women in the hospital and spoken with them informally about their intentions upon leaving the hospital, the next question that arose was, What implications does traditional masculinity have for adjustment to heart disease? First, this question is examined from the perspective of previous research and theory. Then, I present empirical data from my own work to address this question.

The onset of a chronic illness such as CHD can be construed as a victimization experience. Victimization involves the shattering of basic assumptions about the self and the world; for example, discovering that one is vulnerable, that the world is not a meaningful and comprehensible place (Janoff-Bulman & Frieze, 1983). Heart disease, in particular, poses a threat to self-esteem and feelings of invulnerability that may be particularly severe for the traditionally masculine individual.

Power, control, achievement at work, and physical strength are integral aspects of the traditional male gender role (Garfinkel, 1985; Gross, 1978; Tolson, 1977) that are challenged by heart disease. For example, heart disease may lead to forced retirement. Because work is a primary means of validating masculinity for many men, this consequence of chronic illness may be extremely upsetting. If not retirement, coronary heart disease leads one to restrict activities, to take time off from work, and to refrain from driving for some period of time. That is, the cardiac patient is placed in a dependent role, possibly for the first time in his or her life, which may be perceived as being inconsistent with masculinity. Recovery from an initial cardiac event also involves a loss of physical strength. In some instances the loss is permanent, as patients are told not to lift heavy objects or shovel snow. Physical strength also is a characteristic of traditional masculinity (Eisler & Skidmore, 1987). One patient from the previous study reported dismay at the loss of physical strength: "Until a couple of years ago, I used to believe my body was indestructible. I could drive my body as hard as possible—now I go faster and faster, but I feel tired and exhausted."

Theoretical Links of
Masculinity to Adjustment to CHD

To understand how traditionally masculine individuals might adjust to heart disease, consider how men cope with other stressful events. One way of coping is to seek out social support either from one's network or from others who have a similar kind of problem. Recent studies have shown that men are less likely than women to cope with stressful events by seeking support. In a study of adolescents, males were less likely than females to seek social support in response to their current most important problem (Frydenberg & Lewis, 1991). Among medical residents, men reported seeking support as a way of coping less than women did (Archer, Keever, Gordon, & Archer, 1991). In a diary study in which married couples were asked to indicate how they coped with the most bothersome event of the day for each of 21 days, husbands reported seeking support less often than wives (Stone & Neale, 1984).

Men—especially traditionally masculine ones—may be less likely to be comforted by people facing the same stressor. In a study of patients who attended a cardiac rehabilitation program, 46 of the 60 (77%) patients were men (Helgeson & Taylor, 1993). Although there were three times as many men as women in the program, women reported feeling more similar to other patients than did men. When given the choice between exercising with other cardiac patients or with healthy people, women were more likely than men to prefer to exercise with other heart patients. Men are less interested than women in sharing their experiences with others to establish a common bond (Helgeson & Mickelson, in press), and men are less likely than women to attend support groups (e.g., Taylor, Falke, Mazel, & Hilsberg, 1988).

A second way of coping with a stressful event is to avoid, deny, or distract oneself from the problem. This way of coping is common among cardiac patients (Croog & Levine, 1977). There is some evidence that men are more likely than women to engage in distraction (Nolen-Hoeksema, 1987). Among cardiac patients, there are positive and negative consequences associated with distraction or denial. On the positive side, denial has been associated with reduced psychological distress (Levine et al.,

1987), return to work, resumption of sexual activity, better medical outcomes during hospitalization, and less mortality in the coronary care unit (Croog, Shapiro, & Levine, 1971; Granger, 1974; Hackett, Cassem, & Wishnie, 1968; Levenson, Mishra, Hamer, & Hastillo, 1989; Stern, Pascale, & McLoone, 1975). On the negative side, denial has been associated with noncompliance (e.g., smoking in the hospital, failure to follow prescribed medical regimen in and out of the hospital; Croog et al., 1971; Granger, 1974; Stern et al., 1975). One explanation for these diverse findings is that there are multiple facets of denial. Havik and Maeland (1986) distinguished between denial of illness (i.e., denying one is ill and needs treatment) and denial of impact (i.e., admitting one is ill but minimizing the severity of the problem). They found that denial of illness was related to less optimism and denial of impact was related to more optimism. It is expected that denial of impact would reduce anxiety, lead patients to resume a normal life, and restore self-esteem, whereas denial of illness would lead patients to reject or fail to attend to information necessary for compliance. Which aspect of denial, if any, characterizes men more than women or is associated with trait masculinity is not clear.

A third way of coping is to take direct action, or what is often referred to as problem-focused coping. Men have been shown to engage in more problem-focused coping compared to women (Stone & Neale, 1984), and trait masculinity has been linked to problem-focused coping among both men and women (Nezu & Nezu, 1987). In fact, men's greater use of problem-focused coping compared to women partially accounts for men's lower rates of psychological distress (Nezu & Nezu, 1987). To the extent that heart disease is construed as a problem that men can conquer or overcome, men's achievement orientation may be an advantage, if channeled in a positive direction. The "task focus" aspect of masculinity may facilitate adjustment to heart disease if the task is construed as recovery. A parallel finding exists in the Type A literature. Although Type As are at greater risk for the onset of heart disease, they may recover faster and be at less risk for subsequent coronary events (Ragland & Brand, 1988). Researchers have theorized that some Type A individuals shift task focus from work to recovery.

A traditionally masculine individual could respond to a heart attack by developing a recovery plan and enacting it. A cardiac rehabilitation program is one recovery plan traditionally masculine patients may pursue with vigor. The concern arises, however, that a shift from work achievement to physical achievement will occur at the expense of other aspects of recovery (e.g., time for relationships with family and friends, relaxation). There is some support for this concern from a study of cardiac rehabilitation patients (Helgeson & Taylor, 1993). The cardiac patients' evaluations of their recovery were positively correlated with the level of physical performance achieved during rehabilitation (i.e., MET level achieved). Unfortunately, the level of physical performance achieved was uncorrelated with the nurse's rating of the patient's physical recovery. This suggests that the patients base their recovery on physical performance but nurses do not. Some nurses expressed concern that patients were "overdoing it" and "trying to prove themselves"; that is, overinvesting in exercise at the expense of other aspects of recovery (e.g., relaxation). These men may be exercising at a level higher than they should be, placing themselves at additional risk for another acute coronary event.

Some of the variables thought to mediate the link between masculinity and onset or severity of heart disease also might have implications for adjustment to heart disease. Lack of social support is not only a risk factor for heart disease but it also has been linked to recovery from MI (Mumford, Schlesinger, & Glass, 1982; Trelawney-Ross & Russell, 1987; Winefield & Martin, 1981). If male coronary patients' social networks are impoverished, they face an additional risk during recovery.

Health care following MI also is important to recovery. Patients are typically told by physicians to make a number of lifestyle changes (e.g., quit smoking, start exercising, alter diet). These instructions may threaten a patient's (particularly a masculine patient's) need to feel in control. Threats to control can induce psychological reactance, a state of arousal that is remedied by reassertions of control. One way to restore control is noncompliance. Thus, trait masculinity may be linked to noncompliance.

Empirical Links of Trait Masculinity to Adjustment to CHD

Three studies have been conducted to examine the implications of trait masculinity for adjustment to heart disease as well as the pathways by which trait masculinity might influence adjustment. These studies began in 1987 and one is ongoing.

Study 1

The first study consisted of phone follow-up interviews of the 90 patients enrolled in the previously described study on heart attack severity. Patients were contacted 1 year following hospital discharge. Information on three measures of recovery were obtained: rehospitalization for or death from a cardiac event, severity of chest pain, and health perception. These indices ranged from completely objective to completely subjective. The extent to which masculinity, Type A behavior, health care, and social support predicted these outcomes was examined through multiple regression analysis. Statistical controls were implemented for subject sex, heart attack severity, psychological distress during the initial hospitalization, and significant coronary risk factors. Thus, the extent to which masculinity and mediators posed a threat to recovery could be examined independent of the severity of the initial coronary event. More detail is contained in Helgeson (1991).

The single greatest predictor of all indexes of recovery was not masculinity but a social support indicator—the extent to which patients self-disclosed to spouses. Patients who reported in the hospital that they could talk with their spouse about whatever was on their mind and feel comfortable with him or her evidenced better recovery on all three indexes. This finding is particularly compelling when one considers that the three recovery indexes were weakly correlated. Because a substantial number of the patients were unmarried, I investigated whether being married and unable to disclose to one's spouse was better than, worse than, or equal to not being married at all regarding its impact on recovery. The rehospitalization rates of unmarried persons were similar to the rehospitalization rates of married high-disclosure persons but significantly lower than the rehospitalization rates of married low-disclosure persons. These results demonstrate not so much that having a good marital relationship is health protective but that having a poor marital relationship is a health hazard. The variable that reflects a poor relationship is inability to confide in or talk comfortably with a spouse. Thus, it may be that the health benefits derived from marriage are not grounded in marriage per se, but stem from good communication practices in the relationship.[1]

Study 2

A second study was conducted that focused on adjustment to heart disease in more detail. Patients aged 70 and under, who had sustained a first coronary event (myocardial infarction, unstable angina), and had no previous history of other major chronic illnesses were eligible to participate in the study. Patients were enrolled consecutively ($N = 96$, 77 men, 19 women), interviewed in the hospital shortly before discharge (Time 1 [T1]), interviewed in their homes along with spouses 3 months later (Time 2 [T2]), and contacted by phone 1 year later (Time 3 [T3]). Ages ranged from 31 to 69, with a mean of 57. The majority of patients were Caucasian (82%) and fairly well-educated. Only 17% did not attend college. Slightly more than half of the sample was Jewish (55%) because one of the hospitals had a Jewish affiliation. More information about this study can be found in Helgeson (1993a) and Helgeson (1993b).

Trait masculinity, social support, and health behavior were measured in this study. Changes in social support and health behavior over the year were examined. The goal of the study was to determine the implications of trait masculinity for psychological and physical adjustment to heart disease and to examine whether changes in social support or health behavior accounted for such relations.

Social Support. The negative as well as the positive aspects of social interactions were measured in this study. Researchers have noted that negative interactions often have a greater impact than positive interactions on well-being (Fiore, Becker, & Coppel, 1983; Rook, 1984). Patients reported an increase in support (positive social interactions) from spouses from T1 to T2, but then a decrease in support from T2 to T3. Similarly, patients reported a decrease in negative interactions with spouses from T1 to T2, but then an increase from T2 to T3. These results are consistent with those found in a previous study of male heart attack victims, showing that spouses made efforts to avoid conflict immediately after the patient's heart attack but that such efforts ceased during the later stages of recovery (Michela, 1986).

In this study, positive masculinity was related to an increase in support received from all network members from T1 to T2, and a decrease in negative support with the spouse from T1 to T2. Thus, support was activated in the short term for the person characterized by positive masculine traits. By contrast, negative masculinity was associated with a decrease in perceived availability of social support from T1 to T2.

Negative and positive masculinity also were measured among spouses. Spouses who were characterized by negative masculinity reported more negative interactions with the patient at both times of measurement. In addition, negative masculinity in spouses was related to less self-disclosure to the patient.

Health Behavior. At T1 and T2, patients were asked about health behaviors, such as smoking, exercise, and level of stress. Controlling for subject sex, positive masculinity was related to making greater lifestyle changes during the 3 months following hospital discharge, and negative masculinity was related to smoking status 3 months later (still smoking). A particularly vivid example of noncompliance with physician instructions is the high negative masculinity cardiac patient who admitted to me during a discussion of health behavior that the only change he had made in his diet was to increase his intake of eggs!

Negative masculinity also was related to reports of greater stress 3 months later, with and without controls for stress prior to hospitalization (T1). Thus, the negative masculine individual not only reports more stress at a given time but also was less likely than others to have reduced daily stress after the coronary event.

One 38-year-old man, who scored high on negative masculinity, viewed his heart attack and subsequent bypass surgery as signs of an early death to which he should respond by attempting to accomplish more instead of less. By T2, he had expanded his workload from 50 hours a week to 70 hours a week, increased the amount of cigarettes he smoked, and spent less instead of more time with his wife and young children. He believed that his death was impending and that he should make the most of the time left by ensuring that his wife and children would be provided for after his death. It is unlikely that his wife and children agreed that this is how he should spend his time.

Patients also were asked to reduce household and work activities after the coronary event. Thus, at both T1 and T2 patients were asked to indicate the extent to which they or their spouse performed a list of household and work activities. By comparing T1 and T2 reports of "who did what," activity restriction could be examined. Men who scored high on negative masculinity during hospitalization were less likely to have decreased the stereotypical masculine household tasks they performed (e.g., taking out the garbage, driving, working outside the home) during the first 3 months following discharge. This behavior runs counter to physician instructions.

Coping. Scales were administered that measured the tendency to seek help for health problems and discussion of heart problem with family members. Among men, positive masculinity was related to higher scores on the help-seeking index, whereas negative masculinity was related to less frequent discussions of heart problems in the family.

Psychological Adjustment. Three months after hospital discharge, patients were asked to what extent they had noticed any changes in their personality and behavior and if these changes were good or bad. Positive masculinity was related to the perception that more positive changes in the self had taken place. Controlling for sex and the nature of the coronary event, positive masculinity also was related to better adjustment to the illness. For men only, negative masculinity was related to greater psychological distress (e.g., anxiety, hostility).

Physical Health. For men only, positive masculinity was related to less likelihood of a cardiac-related rehospitalization during the year following the initial coronary event.

Mediation. One pathway by which negative masculinity was found to affect well-being among spouses was through impaired social networks. The relation of negative masculinity to greater psychological distress was reduced when negative social interactions were statistically controlled. That is, one reason that negative masculine individuals evidence psychological distress is that they are more likely to be involved in negative interactions with network members. Hostility is a feature of negative masculinity (as well as Type A behavior), and it has been suggested that the relation of hostility to poor health outcomes is mediated by stressful social interactions (see Smith, 1992, for a review). Stressful social interactions may ultimately drive network members away. For example, the negative masculine individual who snaps at an offer of help may find the potential supporter unavailable the next time help is needed. To the extent that support is available, the negative masculine person may suffer further because he or she lacks the inclination to activate it. In the present study, patients who scored high on negative masculinity had spouses who said that the patients withdrew from them.

Study 3

A third study of adjustment to heart disease is currently being conducted. Patients are eligible to participate in this study if they have no history of heart disease, are admitted for a first coronary event, and are treated with percutaneous transluminal coronary angioplasty (PTCA). Angioplasty is a less invasive, less costly, less physically and emotionally traumatic procedure compared to coronary bypass surgery. Because none of this research has been published, greater statistical detail is provided. Data on the first 100 patients are presented.

The majority of patients are male (70%), white (95%), and married (76%). Ages range from 34 to 75, with a median of 54. Slightly over half are Catholic (52%), 38% are Protestant, 3% are Jewish, and 7% are classified as "other." Half have not attended college, 29% have some college or vocational training, 12% have graduated from college, and 9% have had postgraduate training.

In this study, patients' cognitions surrounding their illness before and after recovery are more fully assessed, as well as trait masculinity, social support, health behavior, and coping styles.

Social Support. Although men reported receiving less support from family compared to women, neither aspect of masculinity was related to the receipt of support. Negative masculinity, however, was related to more negative interactions with spouse ($r = .26$, $p < .05$) and family ($r = .28$, $p < .01$), and less satisfaction with the relationship with spouse ($r = -.25$, $p < .05$).

Cognitions. Positive masculinity was related to a number of "healthy" cognitions: mastery ($r = .22$, $p < .05$), perceptions of personal control over heart problem ($r = .19$, $p < .05$), optimism ($r = .32$, $p < .001$), and self-esteem ($r = .50$, $p < .001$). Negative masculinity was not related to these cognitions.

Coping Styles. Negative masculinity was not related to any of the coping styles. Positive masculinity, however, was related to problem-focused coping ($r = .29$, $p < .05$).

Psychological Distress. Negative masculinity was related to greater hostility ($r = .28$, $p < .01$), greater depression ($r = .27$, $p < .01$), less life satisfaction ($r = -.33$, $p < .01$) and lower psychological well-being ($r = -.38$, $p < .001$). Positive masculinity was not related to any of these measures of psychological health.

Health Behavior. Positive masculinity was related to eating a healthier diet ($r = .30$, $p < .05$), whereas negative masculinity was related to smoking ($r = .19$, $p = .06$).

Treatment Outcome. Between 30% and 40% of angioplasties restenose within 6 months, meaning the blockage reappears. Preliminary follow-up on 41 patients showed that 16 or 39% have restenosed. Although trait masculinity did not predict restenosis, most of the support variables and several of the "healthy cognitions" (e.g., personal control over illness, optimism) did. Correlational analyses (controlling for subject sex and age) revealed that patients who received more support prior to hospitalization had fewer negative interactions prior to hospitalization, and more healthy cognitions were more likely to have arteries that remained open at 6 months. It must be noted, however, that physiological data from medical records (e.g., site of blockage) have not yet been considered in these analyses.

Summary

Taken collectively, these studies suggest that trait masculinity has implications for adjustment to heart disease. The distinction between the negative and positive features of masculinity is an important one. Negative masculinity, in particular, seems to be related to impaired social networks and poor health behavior—both of which appear to be health hazards during recovery from heart disease. Positive masculinity, by contrast, seems to enable men to adjust more successfully to their illness, possibly by creating positive beliefs about their self-concepts and recovery.

Conclusions

Sex differences in health and illness are pervasive. Although theoretical links between gender roles and well-being have been made, there is less empirical research on this issue. The present chapter explored the theoretical and empirical links of the male gender role to coronary heart disease. Although the theoretical links are still in the early stages of development, empirical research shows that there are connections between trait masculinity and more severe heart disease as well as trait masculinity and poor adjustment to heart disease.

There are several directions that future research should take to elaborate on the implications of the male gender role for coronary heart disease. First, the male gender role is a multidimensional construct, consisting of traits, attitudes and beliefs, and behaviors. In the empirical research on coronary heart disease reported in this chapter, only one aspect of the male gender role was studied—trait masculinity. Even for this one aspect of the male gender role, it was important to separate the extreme version of trait masculinity (negative masculinity) from the nonextreme version of trait masculinity (positive masculinity). Future work with cardiac patients should incorporate measures of gender-role conflict and attitudes toward the male gender role so that the constellation of traits, attitudes, and behaviors that are harmful for men can be distinguished from those that are helpful.

Second, future work should continue to examine the theory of how the male gender role might be linked to heart disease. In this chapter, three primary pathways are proposed: increased Type A behavior, impaired social support, and poor health behavior (see Figure 4.1). Theoretical and empirical evidence for the relation of trait masculinity to each of these variables and the link of these "mediators" to risk for heart disease and adjustment to heart disease was provided. A fourth pathway that was discussed in an exploratory manner was coping styles. Two coping styles that characterize the male gender role are denial/distraction and problem-focused coping. The first was considered to be unhealthy, and the second was considered to be healthy. There was some evidence that positive masculinity was related to problem-focused coping.

Another plausible pathway by which the male gender role might be related to heart disease that was not discussed in this chapter but should be investigated in future research is cardiovascular reactivity (i.e., elevated blood pressure). Men show greater cardiovascular reactivity than women (see Polefrone & Manuck, 1987, for a review), which may account for men's greater rate of heart disease. Only a couple of studies have examined whether aspects of the male gender role are related to cardiovascular reactivity. One study showed that men exhibited greater cardiovascular reactivity than women when the task was described as masculine but not when the task was described in gender-neutral terms (Lash, Gillespie, Eisler, & Southard, 1991). Another study showed that men who scored high on masculine gender-role stress exhibited greater cardiovascular reactivity than men low in masculine gender-role stress but only when the stressor was presented as a challenge to the male gender role (Lash, Eisler, & Schulman, 1990). These studies suggest that men who experience threats to their masculinity may respond with heightened cardiovascular reactivity.

Third, future researchers should begin to develop interventions that address the unhealthy components of the male gender role. Just because men do not seek support to the extent that women do does not mean that men may not benefit from the provision of support. Few support interventions exist for men. The rationale for the lack of male supportive services is that men will not take advantage of them. This hypothesis or potential "myth" remains untested. One way to embark on an intervention is to take advantage of some of the healthy components of the male gender role. For example, men's desire for information, need for control, and problem-focused coping style may make them more amenable to an intervention that appears to have an educational focus. Through education, aspects of the male gender role that inhibit health care could be addressed and an environment of emotional support created. Cardiac rehabilitation programs may be an example of such an intervention. Patients come to these programs to exercise but have the opportunity to socialize with other patients. Studies that have tested the effectiveness of cardiac rehabilitation programs on health find little evidence that the program reduces mortality but greater evidence for a positive impact on psychological well-being and physical symptoms. It is not clear whether exercise or socialization with other patients accounts for these positive effects. Indeed, men—especially traditionally masculine ones—may benefit from both informational and emotional support because features of their gender role make these kinds of support less available.

Note

1. Previous research has demonstrated the effects of communication on the cardiovascular system (Thaler Singer, 1974; Weiner, 1979). In *The Language of the Heart*, James Lynch (1985) says, "The response of our hearts, blood vessels, and muscles when we communicate with spouse, children, friends, colleagues, and the larger community has as much to do with our cardiovascular health as do factors such as exercise and diet" (p. 10).

References

Archer, L. R., Keever, R. R., Gordon, R. A., & Archer, R. P. (1991). The relationship between residents' characteristics, their stress experiences, and their psychosocial adjustment at one medical school. *Academic Medicine, 66*(5), 301-303.

Bakan, D. (1966). *The duality of human existence.* Chicago: Rand McNally.

Balk, D. M. (1985, March 30). Divorced males' plight cited in study. *Denver Post.*

Balswick, J., & Peek, C. (1971). The inexpressive male: A tragedy of American society. *The Family Coordinator, 20,* 363-368.

Bassoff, E., & Glass, G. (1982). The relationship between sex roles and mental health: A meta-analysis of 26 studies. *Counseling Psychologist, 10*(4), 105-112.

Batlis, N., & Small, A. (1982). Sex roles and Type A behavior. *Journal of Clinical Psychology, 38*(2), 315-316.

Belle, D. (1987). Gender differences in the social moderators of stress. In R. C. Barnett, L. Biener, & G. K. Baruch (Eds.), *Gender and stress* (pp. 257-277). New York: Free Press.

Bem, S. L. (1974). The measurement of psychological androgyny. *Journal of Consulting and Clinical Psychology, 42,* 155-162.

Berkman, L. F., & Syme, S. L. (1979). Social networks, host resistance, and mortality: A nine-year follow-up of Alameda County residents. *American Journal of Epidemiology, 109,* 186-204.

Blazer, D. (1982). Social support and mortality in an elderly community population. *American Journal of Epidemiology, 115,* 684-694.

Bloom, B. L., White, S. W., & Asher, S. J. (1979). Marital disruption as a stressful life event. In G. Levinger & O. C. Moles (Eds.), *Divorce and separation* (pp. 184-200). New York: Basic Books.

Brannon, R., & Juni, S. (1984). A scale for measuring attitudes about masculinity. *Psychological Documents, 14*(1), ms. 2612.

Burda, P. C., Vaux, A., & Schill, T. (1984). Social support resources: Variation across sex and sex role. *Personality and Social Psychology Bulletin, 10,* 119-126.

Butler, T., Giordano, S., & Neren, S. (1985). Gender and sex-role attributes as predictors of utilization of natural support systems during personal stress events. *Sex Roles, 13,* 515-524.

Caldwell, M. A., & Peplau, L. A. (1982). Sex differences in same-sex friendship. *Sex Roles, 8,* 721-732.

Carlson, H. M., & Baxter, L. A. (1984). Androgyny, depression, and self-esteem in Irish homosexual and heterosexual males and females. *Sex Roles, 10,* 457-467.

Carver, C. S., Coleman, A. E., & Glass, D. C. (1976). The coronary-prone behavior pattern and the suppression of fatigue on a treadmill test. *Journal of Personality and Social Psychology, 33,* 460-466.

Carver, C. S., & Humphries, C. (1982). Social psychology of the Type A coronary-prone behavior pattern. In G. S. Sanders & J. Suls (Eds.), *Social psychology of health and illness.* Hillsdale, NJ: Lawrence Erlbaum.

Cohen, S., & Hoberman, H. M. (1983). Positive events and social supports as buffers of life change stress. *Journal of Applied Social Psychology, 13*(2), 99-125.

Cooper, C. L., Faragher, E. B., Bray, C. L., & Ramsdale, D. R. (1985). The significance of psychosocial factors in predicting coronary disease in patients with valvular heart disease. *Social Science and Medicine, 20,* 315-318.

Croog, S. H., & Levine, S. (1977). *The heart patient recovers.* New York: Human Sciences Press.

Croog, S. H., Shapiro, D. S., & Levine, S. (1971). Denial among male heart patients. *Psychosomatic Medicine, 33*(5), 385-397.

DeGregorio, E., & Carver, C. S. (1980). Type A behavior pattern, sex role orientation, and psychological adjustment. *Journal of Personality and Social Psychology, 39,* 286-293.

Eisler, R. M., & Skidmore, J. R. (1987). Masculine gender role stress: Scale development and component factors in the appraisal of stressful situations. *Behavior Modification, 11*(2), 123-136.

Eisler, R. M., Skidmore, J. R., & Ward, C. H. (1988). Masculine gender-role stress: Predictor of anger, anxiety, and health-risk behaviors. *Journal of Personality Assessment, 52,* 133-141.

Evans, R. G., & Dinning, W. D. (1982). MMPI correlates of the Bem Sex Role Inventory and Extended Personal Attributes Questionnaire in a male psychiatric sample. *Journal of Clinical Psychology, 38,* 811-815.

Fiore, J., Becker, J., & Coppel, D. B. (1983). Social network interactions: A buffer or a stress. *American Journal of Community Psychology, 11,* 423-439.

Fischer, C. S., & Phillips, S. L. (1982). Who is alone? Social characteristics of people with small networks. In L. A. Peplau & D. Perlman (Eds.), *Loneliness: A sourcebook of current theory, research and therapy*. New York: John Wiley.

Friedman M., & Rosenman, R. H. (1974). *Type A behavior and your heart*. New York: Knopf.

Friedman, M., & Ulmer, D. (1984). *Treating Type A behavior and your heart*. New York: Fawcett Crest.

Frydenberg, E., & Lewis, R. (1991). Adolescent coping: The different ways in which boys and girls cope. *Journal of Adolescence, 14,* 119-133.

Ganong, L. H., & Coleman, M. (1984). Sex, sex roles, and emotional expressiveness. *Journal of Genetic Psychology, 146*(3), 405-411.

Garfinkel, P. (1985). *In a man's world: Father, son, brother, friend, and other roles men play*. New York: New American Library.

Goldberg, H. (1976). *The hazards of being male*. New York: New American Library.

Good, G. E., Dell, D. M., & Mintz, L. B. (1989). Male role and gender role conflict: Relations to help seeking in men. *Journal of Counseling Psychology, 36*(3), 295-300.

Good, G. E., & Mintz, L. B. (1990). Gender role conflict and depression in college men: Evidence for compounded risk. *Journal of Counseling and Development, 69,* 17-21.

Gove, W. R. (1973). Sex, marital status, and mortality. *American Journal of Sociology, 79,* 45-67.

Granger, J. W. (1974). Full recovery from myocardial infarction: Psychosocial factors. *Heart and Lung, 3,* 600-609.

Greene, W. A., Moss, A. J., & Goldstein, S. (1974). Delay, denial, and death in coronary heart disease. In R. S. Eliot (Ed.), *Stress and the heart*. New York: Futura.

Gross, A. E. (1978). The male role and heterosexual behavior. *Journal of Social Issues, 34*(1), 87-107.

Hackett, T. P., Cassem, N. H., & Wishnie, H. A. (1968). The coronary care unit: An appraisal of its psychological hazards. *New England Journal of Medicine, 279,* 1365-1370.

Hackett, T. P., & Rosenbaum, J. F. (1980). Emotion, psychiatric disorders, and the heart. In E. Braunwald (Ed.), *Heart disease: A textbook of cardiovascular medicine*. Philadelphia: W. B. Saunders.

Hammen, C. L., & Peters, S. D. (1977). Differential responses to male and female depressive reactions. *Journal of Consulting and Clinical Psychology, 45,* 994-1001.

Hammen, C. L., & Peters, S. D. (1978). Interpersonal consequences of depression: Responses to men and women enacting a depressed role. *Journal of Abnormal Psychology, 87,* 322-332.

Hansson, R. O., Jones, W. H., & Carpenter, B. N. (1984). Relationship competence and social support. In P. Shaver (Ed.), *Review of personality and social psychology* (Vol. 5). Beverly Hills, CA: Sage.

Harrison, J. (1978). Warning: The male sex role may be dangerous to your health. *Journal of Social Issues, 34*(1), 65-86.

Hart, K. E. (1983). Physical symptom reporting and health perception among Type A and B college males. *Journal of Human Stress, 9*(4), 17-22.

Havik, O. E., & Maeland, J. G. (1986). Dimensions of verbal denial in myocardial infarction. *Scandinavian Journal of Psychology, 27,* 326-339.

Haynes, S. G., Levine, S., Scotch, N., Feinleib, M., & Kannel, W. B. (1978). The relationship of psychosocial factors to coronary heart disease in the Framingham Study. *American Journal of Epidemiology, 5,* 362-383.

Heiser, P., & Gannon, L. R. (1984). The relationship of sex role stereotype to anger expression and the report of psychosomatic symptoms. *Sex Roles, 10*(7/8), 601-611.

Helgeson, V. S. (1987). *The role of masculinity in coronary heart disease.* Unpublished doctoral dissertation, University of Denver.

Helgeson, V. S. (1990). The role of masculinity in a prognostic predictor of heart attack severity. *Sex Roles, 22*(11/12), 755-774.

Helgeson, V. S. (1991). The effects of masculinity and social support on recovery from myocardial infarction. *Psychosomatic Medicine, 53*, 621-633.

Helgeson, V. S. (1993a). Implications of agency and communion for patient and spouse adjustment to a first coronary event. *Journal of Personality and Social Psychology, 64*, 807-816.

Helgeson, V. S. (1993b). Two important distinctions in social support: Kind of support and perceived versus received. *Journal of Applied Social Psychology, 23*(10), 825-845.

Helgeson, V. S. (1994a). Long-distance romantic relationships: Sex differences in adjustment and breakup. *Personality and Social Psychology Bulletin, 20*, 254-265.

Helgeson, V. S. (1994b). The relation of agency and communion to well-being: Evidence and potential explanations. *Psychological Bulletin.*

Helgeson, V. S., & Mickelson, K. D. (in press). Motives for social comparison. *Personality and Social Psychology Bulletin.*

Helgeson, V. S., & Taylor, S. E. (1993). Evaluative and affiliative comparisons and coping among cardiac patients. *Journal of Applied Social Psychology, 23*, 825-845.

Hirsch, B. J. (1979). Psychological dimensions of social networks: A multimethod analysis. *American Journal of Community Psychology, 7*, 263-277.

Hoffman, M. L. (1977). Sex differences in empathy and related behaviors. *Psychological Bulletin, 84*, 712-722.

Holahan, C. K., & Spence, J. T. (1980). Desirable and undesirable masculine and feminine traits in counseling clients and unselected students. *Journal of Consulting and Clinical Psychology, 48*(2), 300-302.

House, J. S. (1981). *Work stress and social support.* Reading, MA: Addison-Wesley.

House, J. S., Robbins, C., & Metzner, H. L. (1982). The association of social relationships and activities with mortality: Prospective evidence from the Tecumseh Community Health Study. *American Journal of Epidemiology, 116*, 123-140.

Janoff-Bulman, R., & Frieze, I. H. (1983). A theoretical perspective for understanding reactions to victimization. *Journal of Social Issues, 39*(2), 1-17.

Jenkins, C. D. (1971). Psychologic and social precursors of coronary disease. *New England Journal of Medicine, 284*, 244-255, 307-317.

Jennings, J. R. (1983). Attention and coronary heart disease. In D. S. Krantz, A. Baum & J. E. Singer (Eds.), *Handbook of psychology and health* (Vol. 3). Hillsdale, NJ: Lawrence Erlbaum.

Johnson, A. (1977). Sex differentials in coronary heart disease: The explanatory role of primary risk factors. *Journal of Health and Social Behavior, 18*, 46-54.

Jourard, S. M. (1971). *The transparent self* (Rev. ed.). New York: Van Nostrand Reinhold.

Kannel, W. B., Hjortland, M. C., McNamara, P. M., & Gordon, T. (1976). Menopause and the risk of cardiovascular disease. *Annals of Internal Medicine, 85*, 447-452.

Keith, J. (1974). My own men's liberation. In J. H. Pleck & J. Sawyer (Eds.), *Men and masculinity* (pp. 81-88). Englewood, NJ: Prentice Hall.

Kilmartin, C. T. (1994). *The masculine self.* New York: Macmillan.

Komarovsky, M. (1974). Patterns of self-disclosure of male undergraduates. *Journal of Marriage and Family, 36,* 677-686.
Komarovsky, M. (1976). *Dilemmas of masculinity: A study of college youth.* New York: Norton.
Lash, S. J., Eisler, R. M., & Schulman, R. S. (1990). Cardiovascular reactivity to stress in men: Effects of masculine gender role stress appraisal and masculine performance challenge. *Behavior Modification, 14*(1), 3-20.
Lash, S. J., Gillespie, B. L., Eisler, R. M., & Southard, D. R. (1991). Sex differences in cardiovascular reactivity: Effects of the gender relevance of the stressor. *Health Psychology, 10,* 392-398.
Levenson, J. L., Mishra, A., Hamer, R. M., & Hastillo, A. (1989). Denial and medical outcome in unstable angina. *Psychosomatic Medicine, 51,* 27-35.
Leviatan, U., & Cohen, J. (1985). Gender differences in life expectancy among kibbutz members. *Social Science and Medicine, 21,* 545-551.
Levine, J., Warrenburg, S., Kerns, R., Schwartz, G., Delaney, R., Fontana, A., Gradman, A., Smith, S., Allen, S., & Cascione, R. (1987). The role of denial in recovery from coronary heart disease. *Psychosomatic Medicine, 49,* 109-117.
Lewis, C. E., & Lewis, M. A. (1977). The potential impact of sexual equality on health. *New England Journal of Medicine, 297,* 863-868.
Lewis, R. A. (1978). Emotional intimacy among men. *Journal of Social Issues, 34*(1), 108-121.
Liljefors, E. A., & Rahe, R. H. (1972). An identical twin study of psychosocial factors in coronary heart disease in Sweden. *Psychosomatic Medicine, 32,* 523.
List, J. S. (1967). *A Psychological Approach to Heart Disease.* New York: Institute of Applied Psychology.
Lowenthal, M. F., & Haven, C. (1968). Interaction and adaptation: Intimacy as a critical variable. *American Sociological Review, 33,* 20-30.
Lynch, J. J. (1977). *The broken heart.* New York: Basic Books.
Lynch, J. J. (1985). *The language of the heart.* New York: Basic Books.
Matthews, K. A., & Haynes, S. G. (1986). Type A behavior pattern and coronary disease risk: Update and critical evaluation. *American Journal of Epidemiology, 123,* 923-960.
McGill, M. E. (1985). *The McGill report.* New York: Holt, Rinehart & Winston.
Michela, J. (1986). Interpersonal and individual impacts of a husband's heart attack. In A. Baum & J. E. Singer (Eds.), *Handbook of psychology and health: Vol 5. Stress and coping* (pp. 255-301). Hillsdale, NJ: Lawrence Erlbaum.
Mumford, E., Schlesinger, H. J., & Glass, G. V. (1982). The effects of psychological intervention on recovery from surgery and heart attacks: An analysis of the literature. *American Journal of Public Health, 72,* 141-151.
Naifeh, S., & Smith, G. (1984). *Why can't men open up? Overcoming men's fear of intimacy.* New York: Clarkson N. Potter.
Nathanson, C. (1975). Illness and the feminine role: A theoretical review. *Social Science and Medicine, 9,* 57-62.
Nathanson, C. A. (1977). Sex, illness and medical care: A review of data, theory, and method. *Social Science and Medicine, 11,* 13-25.
Nezu, A. M., & Nezu, C. M. (1987). Psychological distress, problem solving, and coping reactions: Sex role differences. *Sex Roles, 16,* 205-214.

102   Masculinity, Men's Roles, and CHD

Nezu, A. M., Nezu, C. M., & Peterson, M. A. (1986). Negative life stress, social support, and depressive symptoms: Sex roles as a moderator variable. *Journal of Social Behavior and Personality, 1,* 599-609.

Nichols, J. (1975). *Men's liberation: A new definition of masculinity.* New York: Penguin.

Nix, J., & Lohr, J. M. (1981). Relationship between sex, sex-role characteristics and coronary-prone behavior in college students. *Psychological Reports, 48,* 739-744.

Nolen-Hoeksema, S. (1987). Differences in unipolar depression: Evidence and theory. *Psychological Bulletin, 101,* 259-282.

Notarius, C., & Johnson, J. (1982). Emotional expression in husbands and wives. *Journal of Marriage and the Family, 44,* 483-489.

O'Neil, J. M., Helms, B. J., Gable, R. K., David, L., & Wrightsman, L. S. (1986). Gender-Role Conflict Scale: College men's fear of femininity. *Sex Roles, 14,* 335-350.

Parsons, T., & Bales, R. F. (Eds.). (1955). *Family: Socialization and interaction process.* Glencoe, IL: Free Press.

Payne, F. D. (1987). "Masculinity," "femininity," and the complex construct of adjustment. *Sex Roles, 17,* 359-374.

Pennebaker, J. W., Kiecolt-Glaser, J. K., & Glaser, R. (1988). Disclosure of traumas and immune function: Health implications for psychotherapy. *Journal of Consulting and Clinical Psychology, 56,* 239-245.

Pleck, J. H. (1976). The male sex role: Definitions, problems and sources of change. *Journal of Social Issues, 32*(3), 155-164.

Pleck, J. H., Sonenstein, F. L., & Ku, L. C. (1993). Masculinity ideology and its correlates. In S. Oskamp & M. Costanzo (Eds.), *Gender issues in contemporary society* (pp. 85-110). Newbury Park, CA: Sage.

Polefrone, J. M., & Manuck, S. B. (1987). Gender differences in cardiovascular and neuro-endocrine response to stressors. In R. C. Barnett, L. Biener, & G. K. Baruch (Eds.), *Genders and stress* (pp. 13-38). New York: Free Press.

Ragland, D. R., & Brand, R. J. (1988). Type A behavior and mortality from coronary heart disease. *The New England Journal of Medicine, 318*(2), 65-69.

Robbins, A. S., Spence, J. T., & Clark, H. (1991). Psychological determinants of health and performance: The tangled web of desirable and undesirable characteristics. *Journal of Personality and Social Psychology, 61,* 755-765.

Rook, K. S. (1984). The negative side of social interaction: Impact on psychological well-being. *Journal of Personality and Social Psychology, 46,* 1097-1108.

Roos, P. E., & Cohen, L. H. (1987). Sex roles and social support as moderators of life stress adjustment. *Journal of Personality and Social Psychology, 52,* 576-585.

Rosenman, R. H. (1980). The role of Type A behavior pattern in coronary heart disease. In J. Rieffel, R. Debellis, L. C. Mark, A. H. Kutscher, P. R. Patterson, & B. Schoenberg (Eds.), *Psychosocial aspects of cardiovascular disease* (pp. 71-80). New York: Columbia University Press.

Ruberman, W., Weinblatt, E., Goldberg, J. D., & Chaudhary, B. S. (1984). Psychosocial influences on mortality after myocardial infarction. *New England Journal of Medicine, 311,* 552-559.

Rubin, L. B. (1983). *Intimate strangers.* New York: Harper & Row.

Rubin, L. B. (1985). *Just friends.* New York: Harper & Row.

Saurer, M. K., & Eisler, R. M. (1990). The role of masculine gender role stress in expressivity and social support network factors. *Sex Roles, 23*(5/6), 261-271.

Schaefer, C., Coyne, J. C., & Lazarus, R. S. (1981). The health-related functions of social support. *Journal of Behavioral Medicine, 4,* 381-407.

Seeman, T. E., & Syme, S. L. (1987). Social networks and coronary artery disease: A comparison of the structure and function of social relationships as predictors of disease. *Psychosomatic Medicine, 49,* 340-353.

Sharpe, M. J., & Heppner, P. P. (1991). Gender role, gender-role conflict, and psychological well-being in men. *Journal of Counseling Psychology, 38,* 323-330.

Shumaker, S. A., & Hill, D. R. (1991). Gender differences in social support and physical health. *Health Psychology, 10*(2), 102-111.

Smith, T. W. (1992). Hostility and health: Current status of a psychosomatic hypothesis. *Health Psychology, 11*(3), 139-150.

Snell, W. E. (1986). The masculine role inventory: Components and correlates. *Sex Roles, 15*(7/8), 443-455.

Snell, W. E., Belk, S. S., & Hawkins II, R. C. (1987). Alcohol and drug use in stressful times: The influence of the masculine role and sex-related personality attributes. *Sex Roles, 16,* 359-373.

Spence, J. T., Helmreich, R. L., & Holahan, C. K. (1979). Negative and positive components of psychological masculinity and femininity and their relationship to self-reports of neurotic and acting out behaviors. *Journal of Personality and Social Psychology, 37,* 1673-1682.

Spence, J. T., Helmreich, R. L., & Stapp, J. (1974). The Personal Attributes Questionnaire: A measure of sex-role stereotypes and masculinity-femininity. *JSAS Catalog of Selected Documents in Psychology, 4,* 127.

Sprecher, S., & Sedikides, C. (1993). Gender differences in perceptions of emotionality: The case of close, heterosexual relationships. *Sex Roles, 28*(9/10), 511-530.

Stern, M. J., Pascale, L., & McLoone, J. B. (1975). Psychosocial adaptation following an acute myocardial infarction. *Journal of Chronic Disease, 29,* 513-526.

Stokes, J. P., & Wilson, D. G. (1984). The inventory of socially supportive behaviors: Dimensionality, prediction, and gender differences. *American Journal of Community Psychology, 12*(1), 53-69.

Stone, A. A., & Neale, J. M. (1984). New measure of daily coping: Development and preliminary results. *Journal of Personality and Social Psychology, 46*(4), 892-906.

Strassberg, D. S., Reimher, F., Ward, M., Russell, S., & Cole, A. (1981). The MMPI and chronic pain. *Journal of Consulting and Clinical Psychology, 49,* 220-226.

Strickland, B. R. (1988). Sex-related differences in health and illness. *Psychology of Women Quarterly, 12,* 381-399.

Stroebe, M. S., & Stroebe, W. (1983). Who suffers more? Sex differences in health risks of the widowed. *Psychological Bulletin, 93,* 279-301.

Taylor, S. E., Falke, R. L., Mazel, R. M., & Hilsberg, B. L. (1988). Sources of satisfaction and dissatisfaction among members of cancer support groups. In B. H. Gottlieb (Ed.), *Marshaling social support: Formats, processes, and effects* (pp. 187-208). Newbury Park, CA: Sage.

Thaler Singer, M. (1974). Presidential address-Engagement-involvement: A central phenomenon in psychophysiological research. *Psychosomatic Medicine, 36,* 1-17.

Thompson, Jr., E. H., Grisanti, C., & Pleck, J. H. (1985). Attitudes toward the male role and their correlates. *Sex Roles, 13*(7/8), 413-427.

Thoreson, R. W., Shaughnessy, P., Cook, S. W., & Moore, D. (1993). Behavioral and attitudinal correlates of masculinity: A national survey of male counselors. *Journal of Counseling and Development, 71,* 337-342.

Tognoli, J. (1980). Male friendship and intimacy across the life span. *Family Relations, 29,* 273-279.

Tolson, A. (1977). *The limits of masculinity.* New York: Harper & Row.

Trelawny-Ross, C., & Russell, O. (1987). Social and psychological responses to myocardial infarction: Multiple determinants of outcome at six months. *Journal of Psychonomic Resources, 31,* 125-130.

Trobst, K., Collins, R. L., & Embree, J. M. (1994). The role of emotion in social support provision: Gender, empathy and expressions of distress. *Journal of Social and Personal Relationships, 11,* 45-62.

Umberson, D., Wortman, C. B., & Kessler, R. C. (1992). Widowhood and depression: Explaining long-term gender differences in vulnerability. *Journal of Health and Social Behavior, 33,* 10-24.

Verbrugge, L. M. (1985). Gender and health: An update on hypotheses and evidence. *Journal of Health and Social Behavior, 26,* 156-182.

Veroff, J., Douvan, E., & Kukla, R. (1981). *The inner American: A self-portrait from 1957-1976.* New York: Basic Books.

Waldron, I. (1976). Why do women live longer than men? *Social Science and Medicine, 10,* 349-362.

Walker, L. S., & Wright, P. H. (1976). Self-disclosure in friendship. *Perceptual and Motor Skills, 42,* 735-742.

Wallerstein, J. S., & Kelly, J. B. (1980). *Surviving the breakup: How children and parents cope with divorce.* New York: Ticknor and Fields.

Weidner, G., & Matthews, K. A. (1978). Reported physical symptoms elicited by unpredictable events and the Type A coronary-prone behavior pattern. *Journal of Personality and Social Psychology, 36*(11), 1213-1220.

Weiner, H. (1979). *Psychobiology of essential hypertension.* New York: Elsevier North-Holland.

Wheeler, L., Reis, H., & Nezlek, J. (1983). Loneliness, social interaction, and sex roles. *Journal of Personality and Social Psychology, 45,* 765-778.

Whitley, B. E. (1983). Sex role orientation and self-esteem: A critical meta-analytic review. *Journal of Personality and Social Psychology, 44,* 765-778.

Whitley, B. E. (1984). Sex role orientation and psychological well-being: Two meta-analyses. *Sex Roles, 12,* 207-225.

Winefield, H. R., & Martin, C. J. (1981). Measurement and prediction of recovery after myocardial infarction. *International Journal of Psychiatry and Medicine, 11,* 145-154.

Wingard, D. I., Suarez, I., & Barrett-Connor, E. (1983). The sex differential in mortality from all causes and ischemic heart disease. *American Journal of Epidemiology, 117,* 165-172.

Winstead, B. A., Derlega, V. J., & Wong, P. T. P. (1984). Effect of sex-role orientation on behavioral self-disclosure. *Journal of Research in Personality, 18,* 541-553.

Wright, I. S. (1980). Care of the severely ill cardiovascular patient. In J. Reiffel, R. DeBellis, L. C. Mark, A. H. Kutscher, P. R. Patterson, & B. Schoenberg (Eds.), *Psychosocial aspects of cardiovascular disease.* New York: Columbia University Press.

Wright, P. H. (1982). Men's friendships, women's friendships, and the alleged inferiority of the latter. *Sex Roles, 8,* 1-20.

5

Life's Too Short to Die Small

Steroid Use Among Male Bodybuilders

ALAN M. KLEIN

The first time I witnessed a bodybuilder suffer a nosebleed while lifting weights it was triumphantly explained to me that the man in question was a true bodybuilder, paying dues, training in earnest and willing both to risk and to endure injury for his calling. Sometime later, when I watched another bodybuilder doubled over in pain from what would later be diagnosed as a symptom of hepatic tumors on the liver, it was again interpreted by the behemoths in the gym as testimony to his commitment to the subculture. In both cases I watched men reinterpret signs of clear and present danger to their health as ringing endorsements of character. This chapter attempts to examine how and, more important, why male bodybuilders engage in such health risks.

Sociologists have established a body of work that seeks to demonstrate how deviant behavior is socially labeled, but also how deviant subgroups interpret their behavior differently (Becker, 1972). Building on this view, social scientists using a cultural resistance model show how stigmatized groups view their behavior. This perspective claims that, in response to being marginalized, these groups intentionally subvert the stigmas (be-

AUTHOR'S NOTE: I would like to thank John Hoberman and Terry Todd for the many conversations and help in preparing this paper, and Don Sabo for his help in conceptualizing the issues of men's health and my research on bodybuilders.

haviorally or as objects) assigned to them, and in its stead wear it as an emblem of status or resistance rather than shame (Fiske, 1986; Hebdige, 1979). Hence, the Punk movement, Reggae or Rastafarian movements, and even Native American alcoholism have all been examined as intentional deviance, with a cultural resistance purpose in mind.

In sport sociology, Coakley (1989) has examined antinormative behavior more functionally as positive deviance (i.e., that the violation of norms in the first instance is carried out to adhere to a second and higher tier of norm, so, for instance, cheating is justified because it allows one to win). The following examination of the bodybuilding subculture uses both cultural resistance and positive deviance models, but it also seeks to add a critical dimension.

The two current venues for critical thinking in sport sociology are feminist analysis (Messner & Sabo, 1991) and political-economy (Gruneau, 1983; Klein, 1991). This chapter will concern itself with the former. As sport and subculture, bodybuilding is particularly suited to a critical-feminist analysis because, as a historically exclusive male domain, the sport (as is all sport) derived from a patriarchal premise. The male traits that are imbedded in this subculture constitute some of our society's most atavistic male traits and, hence, are amenable to and deserving of critical examination. For instance, because bodybuilding fetishizes muscles, it further exaggerates gender-based characteristics, characteristics that are also loaded with cultural meaning.

My research in the bodybuilding community began in 1979 at a gym in California that I will call Olympic Gym (Klein, 1993). Olympic Gym is one of the world's elite gyms, and as such is distinguished from all others by the profusion of competitors, both pros and amateurs, men and women. A large gym with over 1,500 members, Olympic's core of 200 to 300 represents an unusual social structure (relative to other gyms) because of a disproportionate number of competitors. Within this core one finds the penultimate bodybuilder, an individual who has subordinated all concerns (jobs, family, love interests) to the pursuit of titles and maximum muscularity. The preoccupation with amassing size borders on compulsion and, of necessity, calls for an examination of the psychosocial motives for this behavior. More precisely, the selection of apparently marginal or deviant lifestyle choices (e.g., hypermasculinity or steroid use) over normative one's (jobs, family, etc.) requires some sort of explanation.

Health Risks Associated
With Anabolic Steroid Use

Anabolic-androgenic steroids are synthetically produced testosterone (male sex hormone). In sports they enhance certain sports performances and constitute a banned substance. Moreover, steroids are injurious to health. Despite claims made of regular testing of contests by the International Federation of Bodybuilding (IFBB), the use of steroids is virtually universal. Whereas bodybuilders began using steroids only in the late 1950s, the athleticizing of male hormones is dated at least to 1894 when a young scientist-cum-cyclist-swimmer, Oskar Zoth, at the University of Graz (Austria) tested the effects of liquid extract of bulls testicles on himself (Hoberman, 1992).

Isolating human male hormones began in earnest in the 1920s as the modern field of endocrinology evolved. The extent of claims made of gains in strength and physical size that have been made of steroids are still debated but their ability to do so is not in question (Hoberman, 1992). The pioneering figure in synthesizing testosterone was Charles Kochakian who, in 1935, demonstrated the ways in which the metabolic properties of testosterone aided in the synthesis of protein (the anabolic aspect), thus showing how steroids are able to promote muscular gains (Tausk, 1984). It was Dr. John Ziegler, however, who introduced anabolic steroids to the weightlifting community after becoming attached to the American weightlifting team in 1954. In that they train in the same surroundings, bodybuilders quickly became aware of these steroids.

Most bodybuilders that I interviewed used combinations of injectable and oral steroids, a practice termed *stacking*. This practice involves patterned simultaneous use of high doses of several steroids. According to Arthur Siegel (1989), this is done to stimulate multiple androgen receptors and limit the "aggregate dose of side effects," accelerating physical gains derived from training. Another pattern of use involves using several steroids, each exclusively for 3 weeks, for a 6- to 12-week cycle.

The adverse health effects of steroid abuse are being increasingly documented and involve four primary areas: hepatic, cardiovascular, endocrinologic, and behavioral. The most clearly demonstrated area of health risk with steroid use is in the hepatic (or liver) area. Peliosis hepatitis and hepatoma (cysts and tumors of the liver), for example, are two irreversible liver conditions that are associated with prolonged steroid use (Siegel, 1989), whereas hepatic cholestasis (liver dysfunction) is an example of a reversible condition. Champion bodybuilder Steve Michalik came within a hair's breath of dying of liver cysts from his reckless use of steroids, but even as he was being diagnosed as having a liver disorder worse than he actually had (told of having liver cancer), he refused treatment that might scar his body and ruin it for competition (Solotaroff, 1991).

Although the results of studies done on the impact of steroid use on increased cardiovascular mortality is not definitively linked, there is enough evidence to show that cardiac disorders are disproportionately associated with steroid users (Siegel, 1989). One study of elite athletes and weight-lifters showed that those who use steroids have reduced HDL-C levels, which placed them at a significantly greater risk of ischemic heart disease (Peterson & Fahey, 1984). Elevated blood pressure is also a side effect of steroid use. Michalik reported that his blood pressure was so high he had to "pack his nose to stop the bleeding" (Solotaroff, 1991, p. 30). Fluid and water retention is another consequence of steroid use. There are enough cases related to cardiovascular dysfunctions within the powerlift-ing and bodybuilding communities to convince anyone who is capable of being convinced. Larry Pacifico, a world-class powerlifter and holder of several world records, was one such case. At the age of 36 he had a triple bypass operation performed on his heart, the arteries of which were severely blocked.

The use of steroids also negatively affects the body's endocrine system. Among the many side effects noted are suppression of gonadotropin levels, and the body's ability to produce its own testosterone, priapism, baldness, acne, gynecomastia, and suppressed sperm production. Used by teenagers not yet completely developed, steroids accelerate the masculini-zation process—deepening of the voice, male pattern baldness—but also cause them to cease growing.

Behavior associated with steroid use has only recently been studied. Increased aggression, or "roid rage," has been documented, but exagger-ated sense of self or grandiosity is also associated with steroid use. The autobiographical material on bodybuilder Steve Michalik and the late Lyle Alzado bear graphic testimony to the increased aggressiveness due to steroid abuse.

Unfortunately, many of the bodybuilders I studied tended to take other drugs along with steroids, thereby accelerating many of the effects and introducing others. Thyroid medication, for instance, was used to reduce the puffiness that occurred from water retention, but often resulted in hospitalization from hyperthyroidism (Klein, 1993). Others used hu-man growth hormones or, for particularly desperate and uninformed bodybuilders, horse hormones. Still others would use recreational drugs in conjunction with steroids. Taken as a whole, this dangerous use of drugs in the service of training could result in injury and death. A quote by Michalik in Solotaroff (1991) presents a particularly graphic portrait of the consequences of the overall drug abuse:

> See, we'd all of us [professional bodybuilders] been way over the line for years. . . . Victor Faizowitz took so much shit that his brain exploded. The Aldacta- zone [a diuretic] sent his body temperature up to 112 degrees, and he literally melted to death. . . . [A]n Egyptian bodybuilder . . . went the same way . . . a massive hemorrhage from head to toe. . . . And Tommy Sansone . . . blew out his immune system on Anadrol and D-ball, and died of tumors all over his body. As for me, I couldn't wait to join 'em.

By 1991, major newspapers published findings from the Department of Health that as many as 250,000 high school senior males were using steroids, all of which makes this a problem that extends beyond bodybuilders to men in general. Nevertheless, the root cause of this health risk and drug addiction is found in its purest form in the sport of bodybuilding.

The Steroid Dilemma

One would think that in the face of such overwhelming evidence of health risks associated with steroid use that bodybuilders would increas- ingly shun their use, but such is not the case. If anything, the use of steroids has spread to include significant sectors of the female competitors as well.

As bodybuilding became more culturally accepted through the 1970s, physiological criteria for a championship physique began to change. Where- as champions were once expected to become large and symmetrical, by 1975 they had to show maximum muscular striation as well. Attaining both maximum size and muscular striation normally do not go hand in hand. If one bulks up, one will (even with an excellent diet) maintain or increase his subcutaneous body fat content. Conversely, to become more striated one must diet, which necessitates losing size. Traditionally, com- petitors trained and dieted to gain maximum size during the first 6 to 7 months before a contest and dieted down for striation for the last 2. The use of steroids facilitated a path around this dilemma by increasing the size of the bodybuilder at the same time as he or she is training on a severely restricted calorie intake (e.g., 1,000 calories a day is common just prior to a contest).

Strategies for Taking Health Risks

The health risks attendant to steroid use that have been briefly discussed above are known to all athletes. Disquieting information about the health risks associated with steroid use is denied, obscured, and circumvented through combinations of compartmentalization, scientific fiction, and appeals to higher-order needs. These emotional and mental maneuvers unfold within individuals as well as inside the bodybuilding subculture itself.

A certain degree of hypocrisy is necessary to reconcile some of the contradictory value orientations that exist in the bodybuilding subculture as it is currently defined. First, in its headlong rush for cultural acceptance, bodybuilding aficionados have sought to promote the activity as part of the fitness boom, a position that obviously calls for an antisteroid stance. In the name of health and fitness, bodybuilding's ideologues publish medical findings linking steroid use to forms of cancer, cardiac damage, and a host of lesser health problems. At the same time, however, they informally prop up the need for steroids for maintaining competitive standards. The ideologues of bodybuilding, as many competitors, find themselves in the schizophrenic position of espousing antisteroid positions while indirectly supporting steroid use as a competitive practice. There exists a gnawing discrepancy between word and deed; that is, deeds are somehow compartmentalized as separate from the meanings assigned to the deeds (Klein, 1986).

How one crafts a personal world that involves a regular violation of norms and consciously risking one's health necessitates several strategies. First, compartmentalizing behavior so that the norms one upholds are not constantly at odds is critical. I have shown this in use the "hustling" among male bodybuilders, men who claim heterosexuality, yet systematically violate that norm by selling sex to gay men (Klein, 1989). This necessitates constructing distinct behavioral and psychological categories that are rigorously segregated so that no contamination is allowed.

Bodybuilders deploy a second strategy using a moral hierarchy that regards the normative trespass in light of accomplishing a higher good. Hence, one norm is more valued than another, canceling out a violation of the lower norm. As will be pointed out following, the bodybuilding subculture is based on achieving maximum size, and individuals in it are not only desperate to attain such size but also equally fearful of losing size. To make sure that the more highly valued norm is approximated, other, less valued norms (e.g., protecting one's health) are abandoned.

Two examples of risk strategies should suffice here. A former professional football player used steroids to maximize his performance on the field and found that it also increased his sexual appetite. He used cycling on and off of steroids as part of a strategy that allowed him to indulge in this risky behavior while maintaining the belief that he would remain healthy. His pseudoscientific belief is an elaboration (and medically not substantiated) that cycling (the use of steroids) will reverse all of the ill effects of steroid use. For this athlete, however, coming off of a steroid cycle to reverse some of the negative health effects not only meant a loss of size but also a loss of androgens (and reduced sexual performance). This particular player was "on" constantly for years and so compromised his cholesterol level that he had quadruple bypass surgery at age 40. Following his operation, he immediately asked his brother to get him more steroids, not to play football but because he had come to revere and depend on their sexual properties. In this case, the goals of athletic performance and enhanced sexual arousal were elevated over self-preservation (Todd, personal communication, December 1993).

The second case involves a former Mr. California title holder who had triple bypass heart surgery performed while in his early thirties. During his convalescence, he returned to the physician who had previously prescribed his steroids to get more, complaining of depression due to his loss of size and sexual appetite (Todd, personal communication, December 1993).

These cases dramatically illustrate how far some men will risk their health. For these two, the health risks associated with steroid use were no mere abstractions. They had both undergone heart surgery as a direct result of their steroid abuse, but were willing to attempt it again because their size and sexual performance meant more to them than their health. Something about the way these two men constructed a sense of masculinity caused both of them to link manliness with size and the ability to be sexually aroused. The quality of sexual experience was not a concern, no more than their apparent willingness to jeopardizes their health.

A third strategy used among bodybuilders includes the regularized mythmaking that allows and even promotes banned behavior in the gym. Most notably, this is fairly regular dissemination of scientific misinformation among bodybuilders that minimizes the health risks attendant to steroid use or other forms of drug use. Through what might be called a "scientific gossip network," word spreads around the gym of a new study showing that when the right combination of steroids is stacked in just the right manner, there will be no ill effects. Testimony might take the form of, "I've been taking it for 5 years and nothing's happened." News of other scientific breakthroughs spread that negative effects from steroid use that were previously thought to be irreversible can now be reversed. When questioned as to where the study was published or who learned of the findings, another bodybuilder would be identified. Eventually, after tracking down every source in the network, the "report" would invariably disappear into a corner of the gym somewhere. Even when confronted with the myth as myth and the possiblity of serious health compromise, one bodybuilder simply turned and said, "Shit! Life's too short to die small!"

What is so revealing and unsettling about this latter statement and the above examples is that basically the fears of reduced size and loss of sexual potency are more horrifying than concerns about death itself. Upon closer examination of the configuration of psychological traits that play an important role in the bodybuilder's makeup, we can see how his world and his ego structure are under constant attack from within and without. The male bodybuilder seeks to quell self-doubt by making a Faustian deal with steroids; that is, he trades the facade of invincibility now for sickness and potential death in the future.

Psychosocial Motives for Health Risks

To expand my ethnographic work at Olympic Gym, I gathered life history material on 25 men and 25 women in the core community. Among a wide range of issues discussed were early childhood, family relations, and initial entry into the lifestyle of bodybuilding. An effort was made to assess the general psychological health of these individuals. My primary interest was in determining the self-esteem of the subjects, their self-reliance, and the vitality of their social relations.

Clear patterns emerged almost immediately that indicated a widespread lack of self-esteem on the part of the men in the study. The lack of self-esteem was evident in discussions of problematic family relations, or the pain expressed over self-perceived shortcomings that had played such a powerful role in their taking on bodybuilding with single-minded intensity. Some of the men were quite clear about these motives:

These guys are drawn into bodybuilding for some reason, insecurities or whatever. Myself, it was cuz my brother got into it, and he was into it cuz his friend used to beat him up all the time. . . . Everybody's into it for some reason.

But, these guys [pointing around the gym] I think a lot of them are insecure; that's why they pump those lats out and walk around like that.

I got caught up in the sport because I was thin and I wanted to put on some size. And then, I set some size goals for myself, and so I was all hooked in and didn't want to give it [physical gains] up.

Some point to physical infirmities or handicaps:

In high school I was real bookish and not at all athletic. I was in real bad shape, I mean, I'd get up to walk across the room and black out . . . and one time in 1986 I was watching TV, and I just switched on the sports and there was Arnold Schwarzenegger. They had shots of him, and I thought, "God, I had never seen anything like this at all." Huge!! There was Arnold kicked back and sipping a daiquiri with a lion at his feet licking him, and he's going, "I am the greatest." And, I go, "Yeah." I had to find out about it.

The first 4 years of school I beat everybody up. See, I had dyslexia, so in school I didn't exactly excel. But in physical things I excelled, so we fought a lot.

Other men point to physical problems having to do with stuttering, or hearing impairment, or acne, or being too short or thin.

Some alluded to imperfect family relations (particularly with fathers):

My parents never gave me credit for anything, and that's where it [his insecurity] came from. We had a minor league team in town, and you know, fathers take their kids to the games, but mine never did. Mine never did nothin' for me.

I was small and weak, and my brother was big and graceful, and my old man made no bones about loving him and hating me. The minute I walked in from school, it was, "You worthless little shit, whadareyou doing home so early?" (Solotaroff, 1991, p. 31)

Social Relations

An examination of the social relations of bodybuilders also underscores the faulty ego structure of many male bodybuilders. Not only did male bodybuilders exhibit significantly more aggressive behavior around competitions than did women bodybuilders but they also evinced a lack of social bonding in general. It is precisely in relation to their life histories that one can question the individual bravado so quickly espoused. "Loner" was an epithet worn with pride, but made questionable in contrast to the life history material that dredged up serious wounds. The following are two of many responses pointing to brittle social relations, one phrased positively, the other negatively:

> Friends, I don't have. I don't believe in 'em. I'm a loner, and you have to be in bodybuilding. I don't believe in training partners either, because depending on them is no good.

> I don't think I have any friends. I don't make 'em easy. I'm friendly with people, but a friend is someone you can call up at two in the morning and get a ride home from the airport. I don't think these guys make friends. Bodybuilders are selfish, all they think about is themselves.

Some bodybuilders went one step further and, rather than argue that they exist in such an alienating world, they simply denigrated social bonding.

> I liked football and all, but there was too much sharing. I just didn't wanna depend on anyone. I wanted to do something totally by myself. Bodybuilding is it.

> I began developing a strong sense of individuality quite early. I was always turned off by team sports. I just didn't like being part of a team and the back-slapping and gropy sweating and all that shit.

There is a defensiveness in these statements, a proclamation that the world bodybuilders occupy is an alienating one requiring an alienated worldview. Defining friendship as something that exists outside of the subculture ("I don't think these guys make friends," or "You have to be a loner in bodybuilding") has the effect of objectifying their threadbare sense of social relations. In summary, the gym offered an excellent haven for men with a badly needed sense of intimacy and meaning without really revealing much of oneself.

Little Big Men

The social psychology of male bodybuilders is quite simple really, almost clichelike. The more insignificant he feels on the inside, the more significant the bodybuilder strives to appear on the outside. In bodybuilding terms this translates into an obsession with appearing large.

I want to revel in my size. I want to be wheeled out in a cage and look so awesome that everyone will just be terrified of me.

Another bodybuilder got at the lack of psychological fit between low self-esteem and the grandiose self in the following way:

Looking in the mirror I see strength, power, and size. Unfortunately, when I look in the mirror for any length of time I don't see exactly what I feel like. I feel big, powerful, but I don't see that power that I expect to see. If I didn't look in the mirror and just felt myself I'd think I was the most massive, chiseled dude in the world.

The extremely heavy psychological investment in grandiosity is institutionalized in bodybuilding subculture (Klein, 1992). Everything is larger than mortal man. Not only are bodybuilders considerably more muscular than ordinary people but also virtually everything having to do with the body is depicted as larger than life. The competition titles are of cosmic proportions—e.g., Mr. World, Mr. Universe, Mr. Olympia. The visual representations of bodybuilders in magazines and contests are staged to enhance the image of massive size (e.g., low-angle shots, costumes, and powerful music, and depilating and oiling the body). Bodybuilders, Fussell (1991) tells us, cultivate "the walk" that exaggerates their size as well—that is, strutting about with latissimus dorsi muscles extended as far as possible, arms tensed. Even the language of bodybuilding is designed to promote a body of superhuman proportions and power. One does not simply exercise or work a body part such as the chest or arms; one "rips," "blasts," or "chisels" as one would do to transform a mountainside into a superhighway.

Elsewhere (Klein, 1993) I have shown that the need to be perceived of as large fosters the creation of a psychological complex. Seeking to be large is, for the bodybuilder, a defense against the thing he fears most of all, his smallness. This has clear implications not only for his fragile ego structure but also for his gender identity structure, which is also shaky. In short, for those bodybuilders who are muscling up as a psychological defense, the construction and maintenance of masculine identity is a crucial issue.

How this is played out for bodybuilders and nonbodybuilders alike is that the icons of masculinity (which is bound up with sense of self) become exaggerated. In our culture masculinity is inscribed on the body (as well as the body politic) through power. Hence, as Sabo (1986), Messner (1992), and others have pointed out, men prove themselves by achieving success in the society's dominant institutions, or at the very least through the ideologies and icons that suggest this power (dangerous professions, sports, military).

I argue that, though a muscled body is a significant emblem or symbol of masculine achievement or excellence, in contemporary society, bodybuilding has become an end in itself. There is no longer a need of demonstrating masculinity through danger or sport. As such, the cultural equations between masculinity and muscle in bodybuilding have therefore become mute statements, symbols without a basis in reality. Now, one can seek only the trappings of masculinity and claim a toehold in the masculine hierarchy. Or at least bodybuilders would like to think so. In reality, this has proven problematic in that the sport world, not to mention other areas of society, have historically viewed anything less than functional physicality as suspect. In short, bodybuilding is devoid of function and so still seems like mere posturing. The separation between form and function is crystallized in the following:

> Big strong people have always fascinated me. I grew up revering Wilton Norman Chamberlain, not for netting 100 points or snaring 55 boards, but for the strength rumors surrounding him . . . Sonny Liston may have pulverized Floyd Patterson a second time, but I was more intrigued by his unusual 18-inch bicep.

The headlong pursuit of large size spills over into related areas. Narcissism is a psychological complex that is particularly close to the bodybuilder's condition (Klein, 1989). Typically perceived as pathological, narcissism runs along a psychological continuum from necessary to pathological. Bodybuilding subculture plays an ambivalent role in all of this. On the one hand, because of the widespread lack of self-esteem among bodybuilding males, the institutionalized forms of narcissism found in the sport actually work to bolster a flagging sense of self. The universal use of mirrors and constant visual examination of self and the preoccupation with bodily appearance have a potentially positive windfall in that they create at least a veneer of self-esteem. Similarly, preparation for a competition improves one's condition significantly, and in a social world that reinforces self-preoccupation, flagging self-esteem can receive a boost.

However, other aspects of the narcissistic complex are more problematic. The bodybuilder's brittle social relations seem to reflect the self-absorbed and empty object relations of the narcissist who views anything short of praise for himself as betrayal. Narcissism is also present in the preoccupation with celebrity and grandiosity that is so central to the sub-culture and its practitioners. Males I studied were not simply trying to win grandiose contests but were busily engaged in the fashioning of an image of themselves as grandiose. Magazines, videos, contests, photos all were employed to present the bodybuilder to himself and others as superhuman. If this could not be done, then the bodybuilder was busy getting as close to those on the up side of their careers as possible. What makes this narcissistic is that the need to present themselves in exaggerated terms to themselves and to have others reflect this back to them is excessive.

The narcissistic complex also fuels another somewhat dysfunctional psychological condition, that is, authoritarianism. Drawing upon the work of Adorno, Frenkel, Levenson, and Sanford (1975) and Theweleit (1989), it is possible to trace the parallels between the authoritarian behavior in fascism and the social-psychology of the bodybuilder. Adorno character-izes authoritarian personalities as

> exploitative parent-child relationship(s) apt to carry over into power-oriented, exploitatively dependent attitudes toward one's sex partner and one's God, and may well culminate in a political philosophy and social outlook which has no room for anything but a desperate clinging to what appears to be strong and a disdainful rejection of whatever is relegated to the bottom. (p. 235)

This characterization seems to mark the social, political, and psycho-logical outlook of many of the bodybuilders with whom I worked. The rigidity Adorno points to is manifest in the bodybuilder's ascetic lifestyle and view of the body. Of particular importance, however, is the potential obsession with power—that is, either appearing to possess it or being surrounded with people and things that do possess it. At times this shows up in the apolitical views of bodybuilders as when Schwarzenegger listed both dictators and Christ as role models. Unable to distinguish on the basis of morality or politics, and confounding celebrity and heroism, the bor-derline narcissist bodybuilder notes only people recognized historically. Parenthetically, Lasch (1979) has pointed out that the fusing of celebrity with heroism is a hallmark of narcissism as well. In other work, I have linked the authoritarianism of bodybuilding with its cultural and political expression in fascism. Suffice it to say that authoritarianism is but a psychological disposition of the latter and that bodybuilding as a system of cultural expressions unwittingly gives credence to fascism in its wor-ship of hierarchy, dominance-submission, atavistic notions of aesthetics, and its subordination and altering of science to the service of the subjec-tive condition (the heart over the head).

Other aspects of the bodybuilding complex include homophobia and femiphobia. Described by Harlow (1951), Pleck (1982), and Thune (1949) as insecure, the bodybuilder's shortcoming spills over into gender issues. Bodybuilders simultaneously revere the masculinity that proves troublesome and despise the presence in them (and in the world) of groups and forms that symbolize or suggest femininity (opposite of masculinity). And, in that they tend to exaggerate what masculinity is to make it more simple to attain, they paint gender with a broad brush: Men are strong, women are weak; men are stoic, women are emotional; and so forth. Both women and gays (who are one-dimensionally portrayed as effeminate) are in this context the negation of masculinity. As such, they and what they symbolize are feared and, ultimately, disdained. By "buffing out," by maximizing their musculature, these men feel that they can safely distance themselves from the fear that haunts them. Ironically, this denies that gays or women can exhibit the muscularity that classically masculine men can, a position that proves increasingly hollow and difficult to express.

Conclusion

This psychological complex depicts an insecure man, one filled with self-doubts about himself: his gender, his ability to be valued and loved by friends and family. And hiding behind a formidable looking fortress that he fashioned he can simultaneously hope to feel impervious to slights and doubts as well as take pride in something accomplished. Moreover, as a member of a community of like-minded questers, he has a coherent and established community that underwrites his accomplishments, while it helps obscure his insecurities through institutionalized hypermasculinity and narcissism. Small wonder then that health risks associated with steroid abuse should be reinterpreted or otherwise subordinated to allow an unhampered quest for maximum size.

The use of steroids by male bodybuilders is essential because it enhances their quest for physical massiveness—for the look of the powerful male who is in control and master of his destiny and all that is around him. The very exaggerated nature of this look and what it is supposed to suggest indicates a fundamental vulnerability, for most people have long since given up the grandiose fantasies of comic book male heroes. Those who still require some sort of validation through social membership in such a world suggest that their mortality and vulnerability are more than they can cope with effectively. And so they strive to look the opposite of what they truly feel inside. Steroids promote aggressiveness, strength, size, and feelings of empowerment, all of which are valued by male bodybuilders. That steroids also enhance sexual appetite only fuels the ties between masculinity and bodybuilding.

Bodybuilders are an exaggerated form of a societal masculine malaise. Boys are taught to desire the emblems of our gender and the behavioral traits that society attached to them—for example, aggressiveness, power, mastery of self and others, bravery in the face of pain. We are socialized to equate physical daring with bravery. The detrimental consequences of steroid use are more or less factored into the equation, risk = masculinity, and for male bodybuilders, the presumed benefits outweigh the health risks. More important, for these men the fear of being small, of appearing less than fully masculine is so frightening that anything, including death, is preferable.

Although most men would stop short of such behavior, there are watered-down versions of this complex that affect significant numbers of men in our society. Consider the lengths to which men go to appear manly to others: for example, suppressing emotion in public, affecting denial or bravado in the face of physical or mental health problems, reckless driving, binge drinking, or displaying aggression in normal workaday lives. Steroid use may be understood as a more extreme version of proving one's masculinity, but it is still part of a cultural legacy that is dangerous to men's well-being.

References

Adorno, T., Frenkel, E., Levenson, D., & Sanford, R. N. (1975). *The authoritarian personality.* New York: Norton.

Becker, H. (Ed.). (1972). *The outsiders: Studies in the sociology of deviance.* Encino, CA: Glencoe.

Coakley, J. (1989). *Sport in society* (4th ed.). St. Louis, MO: Times Mirror/Mosby College Publishing.

Fiske, J. (1986). *Understanding popular culture.* London: Allen Unwin.

Fussell, S. (1991). *Muscle: Confessions of an unlikely bodybuilder.* New York: Poseidon Press.

Gruneau, R. (1983). *Class, sport, and social development.* Amherst: University of Massachusetts Press.

Harlow, R. (1951). Masculine inadequacy and compensatory development of physique. *Journal of Personality, 19,* 312-333.

Hebdige, D. (1979). *Subculture: The meaning of style.* London: Verso.

Hoberman, J. (1992). *Mortal engines: The science of performance and the dehumanization of sport.* New York: Free Press.

Klein, A. M. (1989). Fear and self-loathing in bodybuilding. *Deviant Behavior, 10*(1), 11-27.

Klein, A. M. (1986). Pumping irony: Crisis and contradiction in bodybuilding. *Sociology of Sport Journal, 3*(1), 3-23.

Klein, A. M. (1989). Managing deviance: Hustling, homophobia, and bodybuilding subculture. *Deviant Behavior, 10*(1), 11-29.

Klein, A. M. (1991). *Sugarball: The American game, the Dominican dream.* New Haven, CT: Yale University Press.

Klein, A. M. (1992). "Man makes himself": Alienation and self-objectification in bodybuilding. *Play and Culture, 5*(4), 323-336.

Klein, A. M. (1993). *Little big men: Bodybuilding subculture and gender construction.* Albany: State University of New York Press.

Lasch, C. (1979). *The culture of narcissism.* New York: Norton.

Messner, M. (1992). *Power at play.* Boston: Beacon.

Messner, M., & Sabo, D. (Eds.). (1991). *Sport, men, and the gender order: Critical feminist perspectives.* Champaign, IL: Human Kinetics.

Peterson, G. E., & Fahey, T. D. (1984). HDL-C in five elite athletes using anabolic androgenic steroids. *Physician Sportsmedicine, 121*(6), 120-130.

Pleck, J. (1982). *The myth of masculinity.* Cambridge: MIT Press.

Sabo, D. (1986). Pigskin, patriarchy, and pain: New questions about men and sport. *Arena Review, 9*(1), pp. 1-24.

Siegel, A. J. (1989). The effects of anabolic steroids. *Your Patient's Fitness, 2*(3), 7-12.

Solotaroff, P. (1991, October 29). The power and the gory. *Village Voice Supplement,* pp. 29-31.

Tausk, M. (1984). Androgens and anabolic steroids. In M. J. Parnham & J. Bruinvels (Eds.), *Discoveries in pharmacology* (Vol. 2, pp. 307-320). The Netherlands: Elsevier Science Publishers.

Theweleit, K. (1989). *Male fantasies: Male bodies* (Vol. 2). Minneapolis: University of Minnesota Press.

Thune, J. (1949). Personality of weightlifters. *Research Quarterly, 20,* 296-306.

6

Health Among
Afro-American Males

ROBERT STAPLES

Newsweek magazine ("Brothers," 1987) began a cover story on black men with the following statement:

> Black men are six times as likely as white men to be murder victims. They are two and a half times as likely to be unemployed. They finish last in practically every socio-economic measure from infant mortality to life expectancy . . . black men in America seem almost an endangered species. (p. 55)

Time magazine ("A New Generation," 1986, pp. 34-35) had largely reached the same conclusion when it noted that more than half of young black males in most cities are isolated from the average working man and seem incapable, sometimes unwilling, to assimilate into mainstream society.

If the white controlled news magazines can make such apocalyptic claims about the status of black men in North America, the alarm in the black community is considerably greater. According to Reverend Floyd Rose (Herbers, 1987), a former president of the Toledo Chapter of the NAACP, the children have been lost. By the time they reach age 16, they have left school, are unemployed, and are out on the streets. By the turn of the century, as many as 70% will be incarcerated, dead, addicted to drugs, or victims of alcohol abuse.

Echoing the same concern, a black newspaper columnist (Robertson, 1987) quotes a black medical doctor as saying that based on current statistical data, if no cure is discovered for AIDS and there is no reduction in drug abuse, worrying about desegregation and racial parity is futile. The black race will no longer be a viable entity in the next 100 years. Blacks will not be around to celebrate the 200th anniversary of their freedom from slavery.

Although it is obvious that biogenic factors play a large part in black men's health, it is equally true that a larger percentage of black men are becoming ill and dying prematurely because of environmental forces. The fragility of the black male's existence in this country is illustrated, for example, by the fact that his life expectancy rate is actually declining while other sex-race groups are on the increase (U.S. Bureau of the Census, 1992). In this chapter, we assess the etiology of black male mortality by examining his overall lifestyle, his concentration in hazardous occupations, income factors, the availability of health care, education, diet, and personal hygiene. We theorize black men's health as positioned amid a wider configuration of class, race, and gender relations. We explore some of the ways black men's pursuit of the masculine mystique shapes their health and life chances.

Black Men's Health
and the Masculine Mystique

The major causes of death among black males (homicide, suicide, acquired immune deficiency syndrome or AIDS, drug and alcohol abuse) are related to sociopsychological factors. In that the death rate among black females is considerably lower, we need to consider stress situations peculiarly related to black masculinity and its expression or lack of expression in American life. Along with the low sex ratio of black births, the high mortality rate of black males serves to create a male shortage in the black community that creates a number of problems in that group. Among these difficulties are the decreased opportunities for many black women to form a monogamous family. There are also tensions and conflicts produced by the intense competition for the available males, and the ego expansion among the black males who find themselves in short supply and higher demand.

Men who fall victim to the masculine mystique often pay a high penalty. The low life expectancy of black males is known, but its causes are not merely related to their greater susceptibility to illness. In American society, men generally have a lower life expectancy than women, but black men have the lowest life expectancy of all racial and ethnic groups (except Native Americans). In addition, the sex differential is greater for black men and women. One reason is that the black woman is more likely to visit a doctor and receive the treatment that is prescribed. The masculine mystique often indoctrinates men into ignoring an illness until it becomes disabling. The masculine mystique can also deter men from following prescribed treatments. When one considers the high mortality rate among young black men (20 to 35 years), it too is obviously related to the operative effects of the masculine mystique. With homicide, accidents, and suicide ranked as the three leading causes of death in that age group, it seems that the price of proving one's manhood can be deadly as well as costly (Reed, 1991).

Black men suffer a disproportionate burden of illness. The drug and alcoholism rate for blacks, for example, is about four times higher than whites. Whereas black men suffer higher rates of diabetes, strokes, and a variety of chronic illnesses, they are also at the mercy of public hospitals, and, therefore, are the first victims of government cutbacks. When they do go to a hospital, they are more likely to receive inadequate treatment. One study revealed that for two routine types of surgery, blacks were two to four times more likely than whites to get a less experienced surgeon who was less informed about medical and surgical treatment ("Operation Room," 1977).

Living in cities has become a hazard to black health. A report by Congressman John Conyers, Jr. (1984) documented a doubling of cancer among blacks vis-à-vis whites. Prostate and colon cancer were also doubled for black men compared to white men. Black men were also found to have a 37% higher risk of occupationally induced diseases and a 20% higher mortality rate from occupationally related diseases than their white counterparts. Black male children suffer from lead poisoning at a rate three times higher than that of white children. These mortality rates are rooted in the structure of racial inequality. Over 75% of hazardous waste sites studied were located in predominantly black communities. The higher cancer rates are also often a result of job patterns. About 89% of black steel workers labor at coke ovens—the most dangerous part of the steel industry—compared to 32% of white workers. Along with disparate exposure to toxic substances in their living and work environments, blacks have a significantly lower survival rate from cancer, a result of the generally inferior health care available to them (Bullard, 1992).

Race, Violence, and Masculinity

Based on the high rate of homicide in the United States, violence might be seen as normative. The birth of the United States as a free nation was rooted in the violent overthrow of a dictatorial regime, and this tradition of violence has permeated the social fabric of North America from that time to this day. By any statistical measure, it outranks all countries in the world in the prevalence of violent acts. Its homicide rate is double that of all other industrialized nations. A number of its public officials have been victims of assassination or assassination attempts. Each hour of the day at least two Americans are homicide victims. Such a pattern of violence led Sartre (1963) to label "that super-European monstrosity, North America, as a bastard child or satanic mutation of degraded Europe" (p. 10).

Hence, black violence in the United States may be viewed as an exaggerated form of the normative pattern of violence in this cultural context. Although violent crime in this country is associated in the public mind with the presence of blacks, any review of history shows violence to be an institutionalized part of America's social structure. Beginning with the war against the Native Americans, this country has rarely experienced a period without violent strife of some kind. Its wars alone have accounted for over 4 million American deaths, with even larger casualties for the enemy country. Labor violence, lynchings, riots, assassinations, and mob violence are all part of this country's violent history (Curtis, 1985).

Homicide and Black Males

In light of the way in which violent crimes are defined, the amount of violence by blacks is disproportionately high. The Department of Justice reports that although blacks make up 12% of the total population, they constitute 48% percent of all murder victims. The homicide rate for black males, aged 15 to 24, in 1987 was 85.6 deaths per 100,000 population compared to 11.2 for white males of the same age. In 1990, a black male's chance of becoming a homicide victim was 1 in 21, whereas it was 1 in 131 for white males (DHHS, 1992).

This high rate of intragroup violence has a significant impact on the Afro-American's life chances. A black male between the ages of 15 and 34 years is seven times more likely to be a homicide victim than his white cohort. In fact, homicide is the leading cause of death among black males aged 15 to 34. Between the ages of 25 and 44, a black man's chances of being murdered are greater than the probability of a white male dying from the number one cause of death among whites of the same age—accidents. In the country with the highest homicide rate, a white male can look forward to 6 more years of an average life expectancy rate than black males. About 20% of that difference is attributed to the high homicide rate (Reed, 1991).

Theories of Black Violence

Various theories attempt to explain the reason for the high rate of black violence. In an earlier period, criminologists leaned toward a genetic explanation. Using a social Darwinist approach, Lombroso (1911) asserted that criminality was an atavistic throwback to an earlier evolutionary stage. Thus, primitive people (or those originally from primitive societies) possessed a predisposition toward criminal tendencies. This theory is largely discredited in most scientific circles today. The history of violence throughout the world reveals a pattern of the violent subjugation of nonwhite peoples by white settlers. Moreover, centuries-old patterns of miscegenation and amalgamation tend to violate any assumption of racially defined groups as biologically unique.

A more prominent theory is that of Wolfgang and Ferracuti (1967), who believe that differences in attitudes toward the use of violence exist in specific populations and are organized into a set of culturally transmitted norms. Undergirding this theory is the assumption that lower-class black males have a culturally transmitted value system that approves the use of violence for conflict resolution more so than is found in other American groups. The problem with this theory is its failure to account for social structural factors, especially measures of poverty (Reed, 1991).

Another theory of black violence is the regional tradition explanation of Pettigrew and Spier (1962). They noted that Afro-Americans were primarily descendants of the Southern region of the United States and that this area has a markedly higher degree of violence than other parts of the country. This tradition of violence found in the South was, they asserted, responsible for the greater proclivity to commit homicide among blacks. Although the highest murder rates exist in large Northern cities, they think this can be explained by the large number of black migrants from the South in those locations. In their migration to the North, Southern blacks carried values related to violence that they had learned as long ago as the era of slavery. Elkins (1959) also argued that the slave's only source of value derived from the slavemaster. By identifying with the slaveholder's beatings, torture, and rape of the bondsmen, these values were internalized by

Afro-Americans who bring a predilection toward violence with them to the Northern states.

Another theory of black violence argues that violent acts are associated with relative deprivation. Rates of violence will be highest in areas where the occupational and income gap between blacks and whites is the greatest (Everts & Schwirian, 1968). In that the economic means to achieve the social earmarks of masculinity are often denied to Afro-American males, some rechannel these needs and aspirations into violent forms. An additional major explanation of black men's need to prove manhood through violence is the lack of a male role model in the family. Uncertain of his masculinity, he adopts a tough, violent life that is closely associated with the dominant culture's definition of maleness (Miller, 1958). Using ecological analysis as a model, Reed (1991) suggests that homicides are the product of poverty, unemployment, substandard housing, and stressful life events and conditions, which may render individuals more vulnerable to violent assault and death. When these forces are added to the rise in the supply of handguns, it is possible to explain the rise in black homicide.

Although some of these theories seem to offer some insight into black violence, they fail to acknowledge the political economy of violence. Violence in America is concentrated in urban ghettos, not the South. Only 3 Southern cities are represented of the 10 with the highest homicide rate, and the majority of black violence in the North is not committed by Southern immigrants. To contend that black violence in the North is a reflection of Southern ethos presumes a tenacity of the norms of violence that is transmitted intergenerationally (Hawkins, 1986).

Likewise, the argument that black males enact violence to compensate for a lack of male role models in their lives is simply not plausible. This theory is part and parcel of the matriarchy myth, which attempts to blame blacks for their own social condition. Almost all black males have masculine role models, even if there is no legal husband or biological father within the nuclear family context. Men from broken homes dominate the violence statistics simply because fatherless black families represent the poorest of the poor, the most oppressed of the oppressed. It is the relationship between racial inequality and black violence that should be examined (Staples & Johnson, 1993).

The disproportionate share of black male casualties from social causes is what led Secretary of Health and Human Services Louis W. Sullivan to declare the plight of the black male a major public health problem. He has lamented the generation of young black men who measure their manhood by the caliber of their guns (Lacey, 1992). However, his political superiors in the White House have allowed easy access to handguns, and they are the favored weapon for most teenage murders by black males (Hilts, 1992). Along with the lethality of firearms, urban poverty, and other social forces is the use of crack cocaine among young black men. Black street gangs are engaged in constant battles over who will reign as drug entrepreneurs, and this accounts for much of the increase in black homicides. Drug related homicides range from less than 10% in 1988 in Chicago to 80% in the same year in Washington, D.C. (Bell & Jenkins, 1990). The role drugs play in contributing to black homicide is symptomatic of an array of social and economic problems that America refuses to address.

Suicide

The practice of suicide has been of considerable interest to researchers, theologians, and mental health personnel in recent years. As societies become more complex, suicide frequently becomes a way out for the individual torn between the will to live and emotional struggles that create an urge to die. Despite the increase in suicidal attempts, suicide remains an act committed by few members of American society. This raises the question of who commits suicide and what motivates them to seek this resolution of their emotional turmoil, which other individuals facing the same problem handle in other ways.

A huge suicide rate would be expected for members of the black population in the United States. In a society that admittedly is racist, blacks have been subjected to a host of problems that create a constant state of rage and frustration in individual members of this group. However, the black suicide rate has, historically, been lower than that of whites. A popular explanation for this unexpected racial difference in suicide rates has been the stronger social ties in the black community that sustain individuals in the face of adversity. The black church, particularly, has been a buffer institution that provided many blacks with an outlet for their frustration in a society that penalized them daily for their racial membership (Davis, 1980a).

In recent years, however, there has been a pronounced increase in black suicide vis-à-vis white suicide. At one point, the national black suicide rate was less than half that of whites (4.6 vs. 11.0 per 100,000 population per year). The latest available mortality data show a white male to black male suicide ratio of 1.75, 1 higher than it has been in half a century. In fact, the national suicide rate among black males aged 25 to 29 is greater than that of their white peers of the same age. Of course, in certain cities such as Washington, D.C., and New York, the suicide rate for black males under age 35 has long exceeded their white counterpart. Data show that whereas the suicide rate among blacks reaches a peak in the early years, among whites it increases in direct relationship to advancing chronological age (DHHS, 1992).

Before examining the rates and causes of suicide among black youth, it is necessary to note that this problem should be put into proper perspective. Self-destruction among blacks has definitely increased, but it still involves a small number of Afro-Americans. Although suicide as the cause of death increased, it still ranks considerably below the death rates for hypertension, cancer, and strokes. The peculiar nature of suicidal deaths tends to create a greater concern about its prevalence, and each suicidal death dramatically impacts the public consciousness.

However, suicide is a particularly serious problem among black youth. Death records since 1960 show that blacks aged 15 to 20 commit suicide at a rate higher than that of the total population of all ages. The increase in black suicides has been highest in this group. Moreover, it is claimed by some behavioral scientists that if many of the black deaths that are labeled homicide were more seriously investigated, they would be revealed as suicides because the victim arranged or demanded to be killed (Seiden, 1970). At any rate, among black males in the age range 15 to 24, suicide is the third leading cause of death after accidents and homicides. It ranks sixth among black females in the same age range (DHHS, 1992).

When we consider the causes of black youth suicide, the reasons vary by sex and educational level. The basic demographic data on black suicide victims are very sparse and generalizations must be made on the basis of the limited evidence available. First, it appears that most black youth suicides occur among noncollege students. This characteristic is related to the forces responsible for many black youth suicides. Whereas many whites commit suicide during their middle and later years because they did not achieve success according to their expectations, a large number of blacks kill themselves at very early ages because they believe there is no incentive for trying to achieve anything in a racist society. These low expectations will be somewhat more common to black youth who have dropped out of high school and see little future for themselves in this country. With the unemployment rate as high as 65% among black teen-agers, this is not a totally unrealistic perspective (Gibbs, 1988).

The motives for black suicide have not been thoroughly investigated. Most research on black suicide has focused on the black male. Several reasons have been proposed to account for black male suicide. Among them is the theory that most black suicide is of the fatalistic type. Fatalistic suicide was a typology originally developed by Durkheim (1952), which refers to the individual whose suicidal actions are a result of overregulation by authority figures such as the police. Other explanations include the following: (a) The stresses associated with urbanization expose blacks to new and unfamiliar problems that tend to increase suicide rates; (b) as conditions for some blacks improve, aspirations rise that when left unfulfilled create individual dissatisfaction with low status and a greater likelihood for self-destruction; and (c) maternal rejection creates in the black male emotions of rage, self-hate, worthlessness, and depression, which can result in suicide attempts (Davis, 1980b).

In a study of black male suicides in New Orleans, a sociologist found that the majority of blacks who committed suicide had recently had difficulties with the police or law courts, whereas 10% of the white suicide victims had had such problems. Many of these black suicide victims had expressed fear of the police and a few stated they would kill themselves before going to jail. The point to be emphasized here is that these black men saw the police as the operant enforcer and as the symbol of white authority over institutions in the black community (Breed, 1970).

What is significant to the black community is that most black male suicide victims are killing themselves before the age of 35, when they should be reaching the flower of manhood. Young black men find themselves locked in a life-and-death struggle with a massive and basically oppressive system of laws, customs, procedures, and enforcement. In the words of James Baldwin (1963), "To be a Negro in this country and to be relatively conscious is to be in a rage almost all the time" (p. 36). To be black in this country, young, uneducated, and unskilled is to be confined to the ranks of the unemployed, a permanent member of the American underclass. It means being unable to establish a home or family or maintain one. The lack of family and occupational ties leads to further alienation and frustration. Such a situation, which is becoming more and more common, generates suicide because it creates despair and apathy in the individual. And it is this sense of despair, the feeling that life will never be satisfying, that blacks must face at a much younger age than whites.

The Politics of AIDS

There can be hardly a person in the world who has not heard of the AIDS "epidemic." Surprisingly, the reason for its widespread fame lies as much in the media blitz this disease has received as in its importance. Rarely, if ever, has one particular subject—including wars, race riots, poverty, governmental scandals, or nuclear fallout—received such media exposure. Statisticians began keeping records on AIDS cases in early 1981 and, by April 1991, there were 171,876 cases of full-blown AIDS infection in the United States, 30% of them black. During this 10-year period the disease had killed 108,731 persons. On the basis of those known figures, one poll showed that Americans rated AIDS, over all other diseases, as the nation's number one health problem ("Poll Calls," 1987).

The extensive media publicity around the largely sexual disease known as AIDS ran headlong into the rising tide of sexual conservatism that outcropped during the 1980s. Although originally thought of as a white male's disease, the Centers for Disease Control (1991) reported that black and Latino males constituted 25% of those diagnosed with AIDS, 70% of the heterosexual cases, 70% of the female cases, and 75% of all pediatric cases in 1988. It seems to be women who appear to be most frightened of acquiring the disease. Such a fear is disproportionate to the risks they face. According to the Centers for Disease Control (1991), of the documented AIDS cases as of April 1991, heterosexual transmission of AIDS is the cause of but 5% (9,191) of the cases and these heterosexual transmissions include sexual partners from the high-risk pool—that is, intravenous drug users constitute 4,868 such infections, and partners born in Pattern 2 high-risk countries of Central Africa, South America, and the Caribbean, where transmission is predominantly heterosexual, constitute another 2,143 cases. Thus, of the 5% portion of Americans who have acquired the disease through heterosexual contact, 76% of such infections come from high-risk partners; another 6% of this group, or 540 cases, come from a sexual partner who also has had homosexual experiences, and about 3% or 260 cases come from blood transfusion activity. Thirteen percent of infections are from other causes. About 93% of the AIDS victims are men. When the other high-risk group of intravenous drug users is excluded, the Centers for Disease Control (1991) found that fewer than 1,000 heterosexual Americans in 1987 had acquired the AIDS disease by intercourse with others who do not belong to one of the high-risk groups (Selik, 1988).

Emphasis on the very small portion of infections occurring through heterosexual contact among low-risk partners should not trivialize the seriousness of this disease—it is always fatal—nor discourage respect and care for one's self and others in sexual matters. However, the media emphasis on the risk for HIV transmission from heterosexual contact reveals an underlying politics of AIDS that orchestrates racism, homophobia, and sexual anxiety. Interest groups inadvertently arise in response to the AIDS hysteria—or at least it appears so on the surface. Gays believe that society will treat AIDS as a serious threat only if the disease is considered a risk to heterosexuals. Many people of color feel the government will make a serious effort to deal with the presence of drugs among their group if they regard drug addicts as a serious source of AIDS propagation. The politicians exploit the issue of AIDS to appeal to their constituencies. Liberals demand money for education, research, and treatment of AIDS. Conservative politicians are demanding mandatory testing and recommending sexual abstinence and confinement of infected individuals. For selected businesses, such as condom and blood-testing kit manufacturers, the AIDS hysteria has provided a number of commercial opportunities (Staples, 1991b).

One has to be struck by the anomaly of white middle-class women being the most frightened of acquiring AIDS. Not only are 93% of the AIDS victims men but also, of the heterosexual women with AIDS, 70% are women of color from inner-city neighborhoods. Yet the fear and the campaigns for safe sex and education efforts seem to target a group of middle-class white women who probably number fewer than 1% of the 107,000 AIDS deaths in the United States. Understandably racial attitudes in this country would make it difficult to promote safe sex practices if the educational programs were aimed primarily at lower-income black and Hispanic women. The conventional wisdom is that sexual promiscuity and drug use are strongly ingrained parts of those cultures. This begs the question of why the condom commercials are not aimed at the white male population.

The AIDS hysteria has and will continue to have a negative impact on other groups. The number of incidents of physical or verbal violence against homosexuals more than doubled from 1985 to 1986 (Gordon, 1987). Various forms of discrimination against gay men are on the increase. And yet at least white male homosexuals have the option of hiding their sexual preference. If the number of AIDS cases among blacks and Latino males continues to grow, and they become more strongly associated with the disease, their high visibility will add to the discriminatory treatment they already face in American society. The AIDS cases of Magic Johnson and Arthur Ashe have provided a strong association of black male heterosexuals with the disease. Worst of all may be the treatment of AIDS victims themselves. The hysteria surrounding this disease has led to the denial of civil liberties for many persons with AIDS, and proposals are circulating that would quarantine them from the rest of society. Other vulnerable groups, such as foreigners, many of them people of color, are being earmarked for mandatory testing procedures.

AIDS certainly lends itself to a divide-and-conquer strategy. It pits major groups in the society against each other. The homosexual victims of AIDS find themselves scorned, isolated, and discriminated against by a heterosexual majority. In this country, the relatively higher prevalence of AIDS among people of color and the growing visibility of black and Latinos among AIDS victims are inflaming the racial hostilities that lie just below the surface for black and white Americans. The politics of AIDS, therefore, is only adding to racial polarization in America.

Drug Use

Recent studies indicate an increase in hard drug use and a decline in alcohol consumption among American youth. This incipient trend is hardly cause for celebration. Although alcohol is legally sold, it is hardly a benign beverage when used to excess. Indeed, considering the alcohol related deaths from drunken driving, cirrhosis of the liver, homicides, some suicides, and family violence, alcohol is probably a more destructive drug than heroin and cocaine combined. Its impact on black communities is particularly negative. The combination of economic, social, and psychological problems faced by black youth renders them vulnerable to the enticement of alcohol so readily available in their communities. Because those problems so easily interface with the patterns of alcohol consumption, alcohol abuse must be seen as more than a legal or medical problem: It is also a political problem.

Throughout America, black male youth must struggle merely to survive. Their forms of coping with Euro-American rule are often nothing more than a slow death for many of them. One of these coping mechanisms is simply to become so narcotized that their subjugation under Euro-American rule is tolerable. Although alcohol consumption has become pervasive throughout the United States, the abusers still come from the least educated and poorest segment of the black community. Alcohol abuse is pure and simple a way of coping with a society in which young black men see themselves as powerless and without any kind of future.

Institutional racism and economic marginality have forced black males to disproportionately experience the ravages of inner-city life. Bereft of any income from legitimate sources, only a limited number of options are available to them. Many are living with their parents. Some of them may find temporary shelter with a woman who is eligible for public assistance (if no adult male is living with her). After those two options, all that is left is homelessness and public begging or participation in the underground economy. Increasingly, the sale of drugs to alienated and powerless young black men has produced an alternative economy that can provide high wages and self-esteem to young men denied both in mainstream America. With the lack of successful role models in the inner city, drug dealers often become heroes to ghetto youth (Gibbs, 1988).

A combination of the above named forces threatens to institutionally decimate much of the black male population. The public schools fail to provide them with marketable skills in today's economy, and increasing competition among a variety of cultural groups for the scarce jobs available place them among the most vulnerable groups to unemployment status. For those with no jobs, hence no income, commission of street crimes leads to a lifelong career in prison. Those who survive by other means are still left with nothing meaningful to do in a society where money and work define masculinity. Instead, they will define their masculinity by siring children who they cannot support, and defend their masculinity by violently responding to any slight or provocation. Their time will be occupied by the use of alcohol and drugs to allow them to blot out the awareness of their superfluous existence in a country that devalues and fears them. The predictable consequences are fatherless families, homicides that occur at a rate seven times higher than among white men, and an early death from drug and alcohol related causes, including AIDS (DHHS, 1992).

Drug abuse is another medical problem that is defined as a crime. Although blacks make up only about 12% of those who regularly used illicit drugs in 1988, they accounted for some 38% of all drug arrests in 1988 (Meddis, 1989). A number of studies have found a strong relationship between heroin addiction and minority group status. In some parts of the inner city, addicts represent as much as 30% of its total population. The use of heroin by poor blacks can only be seen as an effort to cope with the stresses related to survival (Nobles & Goddard, 1989).

During the 1980s, public and governmental concern for social problems such as sexism, racism, poverty, and war was displaced by a focus on drugs, animal abuse, the destruction of the environment, and the lack of "family values." Although these latter problems merit attention and re-sources, it is clear that they pose little threat to the prevailing social order. Moreover, only one of those issues, drugs, directly impacts Afro-American communities as a salient concern. And even this issue has a cachet in the public consciousness as mostly a "black problem"; the bulk of media coverage of the drug problem focuses on blacks dealing drugs in a public area. As the government's efforts to control the distribution and consumption of illicit drugs such as cocaine has escalated, the percentage of blacks arrested and jailed for drug-related offenses has increased from 30% in 1984 to 38% in 1988. These statistics have led some public officials to declare that the war on drugs has, in effect, become a war on black people (Meddis, 1989).

The war on drugs may be doomed to failure because drugs are legally defined as the problem only due to the fact that their purchase and consumption is illegal. Alcohol, prescription drugs, and cigarettes combined may be more destructive of individuals and the social order than the illegal drugs. For instance, the health effects of alcohol consumption are alarmingly devastating to black people. In black males, the death rate for cirrhosis of the liver was 70% higher than in comparable white males in 1991; the black female death rate from the same cause was almost double that of white females (DHHS, 1992). In general, alcoholism is highly implicated in job absenteeism, motor vehicle fatalities, suicides, violent crimes, and homicides.

Whereas alcohol is legal, drugs such as cocaine and heroin are not. Hence, the government's efforts to control substance abuse are limited to the illicit drugs. Members and leaders of the Afro-American community certainly agree that drugs are the highest scourge of the black community. According to social psychologist Wade Nobles, the prevalence of drugs in the black community, with its concomitant violence, has seriously reduced the quantity and quality of black life. "Substance abuse," he says, "in many ways is becoming an American condition. However, in relation to the Afro-American community, substance abuse can be judged as an instrument of genocide" (Ball, 1989, p. A-9). At the Second Annual Conference on the Black Family and Crack Cocaine, a former drug dealer confessed, "I didn't know that I was selling death to my people when I was peddling crack. We need you to teach us to love the black culture because the drug culture has its arms wide open for young brothers" (White, 1990, p. A-18).

Certainly, the health implications, especially for young black men, from drug use are ominous. Between 1984 and 1987, the gap in life expectancy between blacks and whites increased from 5.6 years to 6.2 years. According to health statisticians, a white male child born in 1990 could expect to live about 75.6 years, whereas a black male child could expect to live about 64.8 years (DHHS, 1992). This trend is almost entirely the result of deaths from AIDS, drug abuse, alcoholism, and car accidents. The one thing these causes have in common is that they are all preventable. The causes of death that increased much more for blacks than whites that are mainly responsible for the widening life expectancy gap, were mostly drug related. Even the spread of AIDS, a mainly sexual disease, has been largely due to the incidence of drug use among Afro-Americans. The sharing of needles, common among heroin users, represents the primary mode of transmission of the virus in the black population. The number of blacks diagnosed with AIDS increased from 25% in 1984 to 29% of all AIDS cases in 1988. In September 1988, blacks composed about 55% of all AIDS cases among children under age 13 (Selik, 1988).

Amazingly, the devastating impact of drugs and alcohol consumption on black mortality rates is not reflected in the various surveys comparing whites and blacks on consumption patterns. Although the surveys are sparse in number, and inconsistent in their findings, they reveal blacks to have lower rates of mind altering substance levels. In a report by the Department of Health and Human Services (1985), researchers found that black youths tend to drink at slightly lower rates than white youths. They also found that the young black population has a lower rate of heavy drinkers and a larger proportion of abstainers. Byram and Fly (1984) also discovered that in contrast to white families there are fewer adult members who drink, fewer friends who drink, and a greater level of family closeness in disrupted black families than in intact families. Separate studies by the FBI and the National Institute for Drug Abuse concluded that blacks constitute only 12% of the United States' drug users. Studies of those who consume drugs reveal slightly lower percentages for blacks and Latinos than for whites (Meddis, 1989). The consensus of national research analyzing cocaine addiction by income and race is that cocaine use in all forms (snorted, injected, or smoked) is greatest among white single men in metropolitan areas of the Northeast and West. Drug therapy clinics consistently report that most of their patients are middle-class addicts with good jobs (Malcom, 1989).

Although drugs and alcohol are considered separate, the typical substance abuser uses both—known as polydrug use. Young people who start off using the less toxic beer graduate to hard liquor and eventually the more addictive drugs. Many black neighborhoods do not have grocery stores but they always contain liquor stores. Because alcohol and tobacco consumption has been declining faster among whites, blacks are increasingly the target of those products' advertising. Surveys across the United States show black communities have much more tobacco and alcohol advertising than white communities ("An Uproar," 1989). This marketing strategy is coming under fire. A cigarette company was forced to withdraw a cigarette aimed mostly at blacks. As alcohol sales have begun to decline, the liquor industry has been left with a disproportionate number of poor and uneducated people as their primary clients. And, they know that blacks are overrepresented among the poor and uneducated.

Conclusion

The statistics presented in this chapter seem to substantiate the contention that the situation of black men has deteriorated to the point where they can be called an endangered species. Problems confronting black men in the 1990s include the following: (a) Although black men account for only 6% of the population in the United States, they make up half of its male prisoners in local, state, and federal jails; (b) the majority of the 20,000 Americans killed in crime-related incidents each year are black men; (c) over 35% of all black men in American cities are drug and alcohol abusers; (d) 18% of black males drop out of high school; (e) 25% of the victims of the fatal disease, AIDS, are black men; (f) over 50% of black men under the age of 21 are unemployed; (g) 46% of black men between the ages of 16 and 62 are not in the labor force; (h) about 32% of black men have incomes below the officially defined poverty level (Staples, 1991a).

The theories that attempt to explain the aforementioned statistical trends range from change in the economy to the breakdown of the black family. Two older theories, however, seem most applicable to the understanding of what we can call black male genocide. One of them is W. E. B. Dubois's (1903) prediction that the problem of the 20th century would be the color line. A combination of social and cultural forces has brought about a social movement for black liberation in Africa, Asia, Latin America, and the Caribbean islands. Most important, the internationalization of the world's labor force has significant implications of color. The other theory was that of Sam Yette (1971), as articulated in his book *The Choice,* who predicted a choice between accommodation and extinction for the black population of the United States. Yette's prediction of genocide for the entire black population diverges from current trends in that it is black men who are most vulnerable to the ravages of an unbridled and dying American capitalism, and accommodation may no longer be an option for most of them.

References

An uproar over billboards in poor areas. (1989, May 1). *New York Times,* p. C-8.

Baldwin, J. (1963). *The fire next time.* New York: Dial.

Ball, J. (1989, June 11). Life span for blacks is getting shorter. *San Francisco Examiner,* p. A-9.

Bell, C. C., & Jenkins. (1990). Preventing black Homicide. In J. Deward (Ed.), *The state of black America 1990.* New York: National Urban League.

Breed, W. (1970). The Negro and fatalistic suicide. *Pacific Sociological Review, 13,* 156-162.

Brothers. (1987, March 23). *Newsweek,* p. 55.

Bullard, R. D. (1992). Urban infrastructure: Social, environmental, and health risks to African-Americans. In B. J. Tidwell (Ed.), *The state of black America 1992* (pp. 183-196). New York: National Urban League.

Byram, W., & Fly, J. W. (1984). Family structure, race and adolescents alcohol use: A research note. *American Journal of Drug and Alcohol Abuse, 10,* 467-478.

Centers for Disease Control. (1991, April). *HIV/AIDS Surveillance Report.* Atlanta, GA.

Conyers, J. (1984, February 23). Black health problems. Symptoms of social ills. *Synapse,* p. 3.

Curtis, L. (1985). *American violence and public policy.* New Haven, CT: Yale University Press.

Davis, R. (1980a). Black suicide and the relational system: Theoretical and empirical implications of communal and family ties. *Research in Race and Ethnic Relations, 2,* 43-71.

Davis, R. (1980b). Suicide among young blacks: Trends and perspective. *Phylon, 41,* 223-229.

Department of Health and Human Services [DHHS]. (1986). *Report of the Secretary's task force on black and minority health: Vol. 5. Homicide, suicide and unintentional injuries.* Washington, DC: Government Printing Office.

DuBois, W. E. B. (1903). *The soul of black folk.* Greenwich, CT: Fawcett.

Durkheim, E. (1952). *Suicide.* Glencoe, IL: Free Press.

Elkins, S. (1959). *Slavery.* New York: Grosset and Dunlap.

Everts, P., & Schwirian, K. (1968). Metropolitan crime rates and relative deprivation. *Criminologist, 5,* 43-52.

Gibbs, J. (1988). *Young, black and male in America.* Dover, MA: Auburn House.

Gordon, B. (1987, April 29). Rise seen in attacks on gays, survey shows. *San Francisco Chronicle,* p. 5.

Hawkins, D. F. (1986). *Homicide among black Americans.* Lanham, MD: University Press of America.

Herbers, J. (1987, January 28). More blacks slip into poverty. *San Francisco Chronicle,* p. 22.

Hilts, P. J. (1992, June 10). Gunshot wounds become second-leading cause of death for teenagers. *New York Times,* p. A-14.

Lacey, M. (1992, August 1). Solving the ills of black men. *Los Angeles Times,* p. A-1.

Lombroso, G. (1911). *Criminal man according to the classifications of Cesare Lombroso.* New York: Putnam.

Malcom, A. H. (1989, October 1). Crack, bane of inner city, is now gripping suburbs. *New York Times,* p. A-1.

Meddis, S. (1989, December 20). Drug arrest rate higher for blacks. *USA Today,* p. A-1.

Miller, W. (1958). Lower class culture as a generating milieu of gang delinquency. *Journal of Social Issues, 14,* 5-19.

A new generation of native sons. (1986, December 1). *Time,* pp. 34-35.

Nobles, W. W., & Goddard, L. (1989). Drugs in the African American community: A clear and present danger. In J. Deward (Ed.), *The state of black America 1989* (pp. 161-182). New York: National Urban League.

Operation room racism studies. (1977, November 24). *San Francisco Chronicle,* p. 75.

Pettigrew, T., & Spier, R. (1962). The ecological structure of Negro homicide. *American Journal of Sociology, 67,* 621-629.

Poll calls AIDS no. 1 health problem. (1987, June 6). *San Francisco Chronicle,* p. 6.

Reed, W. L. (1991). Trends in homicide among African Americans. *Trotter Institute Review, 5,* 11-16.

Robertson, S. G. (1989, April 2). Drugs, AIDS and blacks: A catastrophe. *Los Angeles Sentinel,* p. 6.

Sartre, J. P. (1963). Preface. In F. Fanon (Ed.), *The wretched of the earth* (p. 10). New York: Grove.

Seiden, R. (1970). We're driving young blacks to suicide. *Psychology Today, 4,* 24-28.

Selik, R. M. (1988). Distribution of AIDS cases by racial/ethnic group and exposure category United States June 1, 1981-July 4, 1988. *MMWR, 37,* 1-10.

Staples, R. E. (1991a). Black male genocide: A final solution to the race problem in America. In B. Bowser (Ed.), *Black male adolescents: Parenting and education in community context* (pp. 39-57). Lanham, MD: University Press of America.

Staples, R. E. (1991b). Social inequality and sexual pathology: The essential relationship. *The Black Scholar, 21,* 29-37.

Staples, R. E., & Johnson, L. B. (1993). *Black families at the crossroads: Challenges and prospects.* San Francisco: Jossey-Bass.

U.S. Bureau of the Census. (1992). *Statistical abstract of the United States* (112th ed.). Washington, DC: Government Printing Office.

White, E. C. (1990, April 27). Black family conference assails crack. *San Francisco Chronicle,* p. A-18.

Wolfgang, M., & Ferracuti, F. (1967). *The subculture of violence.* London: Tavistock.

Yette, S. (1971). *The choice: The issue of black survival in America.* New York: Putnam.

7

Gender Politics, Pain, and Illness

The AIDS Epidemic in North American Prisons

CAROL POLYCH
DONALD SABO

There is an "island" of 1.4 million men who are imprisoned in American jails and prisons (Nadelmann & Wenner, 1994). The United States has the highest rate of incarceration of any nation in the world, 426 per 100,000 (American College of Physicians, 1992), followed by South Africa and what was the Soviet Union (Mauer, 1992). Racial and ethnic minorities are overrepresented among those behind bars. Black and Hispanic males, for example, constitute 85% of prisoners in the New York State prison system. The estimated cost of incarceration for the United States is about $16 billion per year. The island has tripled in size since 1975 and, if the state prison population were to continue to grow at the same pace it did during 1989, that level of growth would require "building the equivalent of a 1000-bed prison every 6 days" (Langan, 1991, p. 1568).

The prison system acts as a pocket of risk, within which men already at greater risk of a preexisting acquired immune deficiency syndrome (AIDS) infection, are, because of prison conditions, yet again exposed to heightened risk of contracting human immunodeficiency virus (HIV) (Toepell, 1992) or other infections such as tuberculosis (TB) (Bellin, Fletcher, & Safyer, 1993) or hepatitis. The corrections system is part of an institutional chain that facilitates transmission of HIV and other infections in certain North American populations, particularly among poor, inner-city, minority males.

In this chapter, critical feminist perspectives are used to better understand the AIDS epidemic among men in prison. The prison system can be understood to reflect the larger sex-gender system or gender order. The prison system is not an isolated institutional element within American society, but is integrally melded to the social, political, and ideological landscape of the postindustrial gender order. Whereas the study of men *in* prisons can provide gender theorists with insights into men's lives and identities, the study of the prisons *of* men can forge understanding of the multiple systems of domination that constitute late 20th-century society.

Prisoners, who may be burdened not only with social disadvantage but also with high rates of physical illness, mental disorder, and substance use are entitled to protection from unacceptable conditions that may jeopardize their health ("Health Care for Prisoners," 1991). Although health care workers in corrections may flounder between the demands of the authorities, broad professional duties, and obligations to the individual under care, it is imperative that they learn to live with the tension of competing interests, rather than circumvent the issue of health care. *Health care* includes not just curative, tertiary aspects of care but also preventive, primary interventions. Health care workers have a shared responsibility to move the prison system into the 1990s through cooperation where possible, or challenge where blocked.

We begin by documenting the prevalence of HIV/AIDS in North American corrections. Next, the differential risk for HIV transmission among various subgroups of male prisoners is discussed. Next, some of the factors related to the spread of AIDS in prison populations are identified and discussed with reference to gender identity, men's relationships within the intermale dominance hierarchies of the prison, and gender politics. Finally, some reasons for the lack of comprehensive health care interventions to curb the AIDS epidemic in prisons are also presented.

The AIDS Epidemic:
Race, Class, and Urbanism

The HIV/AIDS epidemic in prisons is a multifactorial phenomenon, with origins and impacts that stretch far beyond the institutional confines of prisons themselves. To understand how the AIDS epidemic influences men inside prisons, therefore, it is necessary to present some initial data that describe the epidemic in American and Canadian societies in general.

Though homosexual white males are thought to be the primary risk group for HIV infection, the disproportionate impact of HIV on nondominant races was noted years ago. The cumulative incidence of AIDS among blacks and Hispanics is over 3 times the rate for whites, as is the rate of death from HIV (Centers for Disease Control, 1993, p. 898). Racial and ethnic minorities are also overrepresented among North American prison populations, especially in those states with a high prevalence of AIDS such as New York and California. The increasing risk for both HIV transmission and incarceration among racial-ethnic minorities is largely related to the growth in intravenous drug use, drug-related crime, and larger shifts in postindustrial capitalism toward widening social and economic inequality.

Since 1981, 339,250 persons with AIDS have been registered in the United States (World Health Organization [WHO], 1994) at a rate of 17.2 per 100,000 (Public Health Service [PHS], 1991). Canada has registered 8,640 persons with AIDS (WHO, 1994).

The proportion of American men with AIDS who are believed to have been infected through sex with men *decreased* from 70% in 1987 (PHS, 1989) to 46.6% in 1993 (PHS, 1994). This decline has been offset by an increase among men reporting a history of intravenous drug use, from 14% in 1987 to 20% in 1990 (PHS, 1989, 1991) to over one third by 1993 (Rogers & Osborne, 1993). Infection attributed to heterosexual contact has risen from 0.9% in 1983 to 5.3% in 1990 (PHS, 1990) and 9% by 1993 (PHS, 1994). Further, of the persons whose risk was believed to have been injection drug use, 14% also reported heterosexual contact with a person at risk.

Though blacks and Hispanics constituted only about 12% and 7% of the American population in 1980, they accounted for 33.8% and 17.6%, respectively, of persons diagnosed with AIDS in 1992 (PHS, 1993). Among people diagnosed with AIDS in 1993 reporting a risk of heterosexual sex only, the rate of AIDS was 20 times greater for blacks and 10 times greater for Hispanics than whites (PHS, 1994). New York City AIDS cases constitute 22% of all American cases (Chassin, 1993), most of which (44%) are related to intravenous drug use (New York City Department of Health, 1990). Of intravenous drug users with AIDS from New York City, 85% are black or Hispanic, whereas 75% are male (Drucker, 1990).

The aftereffects of HIV are experienced as AIDS a median of 10 to 11 years after infection (Fraser & Phillips, 1993; Hankins et al., 1990). The United States is estimated to have about one million HIV infected citizens (Novello, 1993) with about 45,000 to 80,000 additional cases expected each year (Osborn, 1993). Canada has about 30,000 persons infected with HIV (Remis & Sutherland, 1993). Judging from data collected from American hospitals in 1989, the general prevalence of HIV ranges from 0.1% to 7.8% (St. Louis et al., 1990). However pockets of extreme risk exist. Newark, a predominantly black city, experienced a growth rate in HIV of 45% in 1 year, from a rate of 39 per 100,000 in 1988 to 56.5 per 100,000 in 1989 (Fox, 1990). Of all Newark men between 25 and 44 years old admitted to hospital, 21% tested positive for HIV (Lombardo et al., 1990) and HIV was cited as the cause of death 45% of the time for men of this age who died (Selik, Chu, & Buehler, 1993). Meanwhile, in the same city, a separate study found that about 75% of sexually active adolescents were not consistently using condoms (Keller et al., 1991).

It is estimated that 6 million Americans have serious drug problems (Atkins, 1994). New York, with only 3% of the American population, is home to 22% of all Americans diagnosed with AIDS (Chassin, 1993) and 52% of all American intravenous drug users (Shadle & Ford, 1989), with 3% of all New Yorkers injecting drugs (Fraser & Phillips, 1993). Of New York City's intravenous drug users, 21% reside in the Bronx, which alone accounts for almost 15% of New York City's AIDS cases. Of Bronx AIDS cases, 62% occur among intravenous drug users, 80% among men, 87% among blacks and Hispanics (Drucker & Vermund, 1989). It is estimated that 65% of New York City drug injectors are seropositive for HIV (Fuller, 1993). Des Jarlais notes that 20% of injectors have shared equipment outside their own city within the past 2 years (Fraser & Phillips, 1993).

The province of Ontario has 41% of all Canadian AIDS cases, 53% of whom live in Toronto. Millson et al. (1990) found the seropositivity rate for HIV to be 6% among Toronto's intravenous drug users (Remis & Sutherland, 1993). In Quebec, which has 29% of Canadian AIDS cases, the seropositivity rate among Montreal intravenous drug users increased from 4.2% in 1988 to 20% by 1991 (Remis & Sutherland, 1993). Des Jarlais believes that a seroprevalence rate of 10% among the drug injecting population is a critical level that leads to explosive transmission (Fraser & Phillips, 1993).

The AIDS Epidemic
in North American Prisons

Olivero (1990) describes the prevalence of AIDS among American prisoners as a "special and mounting problem" (p. 113). Left unaddressed, the situation brewing in corrections has profound implications for all prisoners, corrections staff, and their families and people close to them.

In Canadian federal penitentiaries, it is believed that 1 in 20 inmates is HIV infected (Hankins, as cited in The Expert Committee on AIDS and Prison [Expert Commmittee], 1994). Similarly, AIDS prevalence is markedly higher among state and federal inmates than in the general United States population, with a known aggregate rate in 1992 of 202 per 100,000 (Brewer & Derrickson, 1992) compared to a total population prevalence of 14.65 per 100,000 (American College of Physicians, 1992). The disproportionate rate of HIV/AIDS in prison is believed to be due to the emphasis on incarceration as a strategy in the war on drugs.

It has been estimated by Canadian authorities that up to 50% of Canadian inmates may use drugs (Hankins, as cited in Expert Committee, 1994), and that only 5% of drugs entering Canadian prisons is apprehended by prison authorities (Coates, as cited in Expert Committee, 1994). It is expected that by 1995 70% of prisoners in the U.S. federal system will be drug offenders (American College of Physicians, 1992).

It is believed that 66% to 75% of inmates require substance abuse treatment, whereas about 5% receive it (American College of Physicians, 1992). More injection drug users are already in prison than are in treatment (Brewer & Derrickson, 1992). The cost for drug treatment for federal inmates is likely to be about $5,000 apiece. The cost for the National Drug Control Strategy planned for the expenditure of $2.1 billion from 1990 to 1992. The total amount allotted for drug treatment for inmates during that time was $39 million (American College of Physicians, 1992).

The cumulative total of American prisoners with AIDS in 1989 was estimated to be 5,411, a 72% increase over the previous year (Belbot & del Carmen, 1991). The total number of AIDS cases reported in U.S. corrections as of 1993 was 11,565 (a minimum estimate of the true cumulative incidence among U.S. inmates) (Hammett, as cited in Expert Committee, 1994). In New York State alone, at least 10,000 of the state's 55,000 prisoners are believed to be infected (Prisoners with AIDS/HIV Support Action Network [Prisoners], 1992).

The percentage of AIDS cases among inmates that is attributed to intravenous drug use (IDU) is highest in the mid-Atlantic states. In 1988, in New York State Corrections, 96% of AIDS cases were among persons reporting a risk of IDU, whereas the corresponding rate among the general New York State population was 34%. Of all deaths in New York State corrections due to AIDS, 95% were among IDUs, of whom 45% were Hispanic and 43% were black; 87% were New York City residents and

75% were between 25 and 39 years old. In 1991, New York State expected about 2,000 new cases of AIDS among its 50,000 prisoners, 60% of whom are admitted IDUs (Ron & Rogers, 1989).

The prevalence of HIV infection in 1991 among men in corrections ranged from 13.8% in New York to .2% in Kansas (Bureau of Justice, as cited in Expert Committee, 1994). In British Columbia, the seropositivity rate among injection drug using inmates was found to be 2.1% (Riley, 1993), whereas in 1989, Hankins et al. reported a rate of 3.6% among male inmates in Quebec, and 1% was reported at a federal institution for men in Ontario (Expert Committee, 1994). Of the Toronto IDUs found to have a seropositivity rate of 6% (Remis & Sutherland, 1993), Millson et al. (1990) reported that 82% of IDUs sampled had been jailed at least once; 25%, more than 10 times. Of these, 25% report having shared injection equipment while in custody (Prisoners, 1992).

HIV Transmission in Prison

The HIV virus is primarily transmitted between adults by unprotected penetrative sex, or needle sharing without bleaching with an infected partner. Sexual contacts between prisoners occur mainly through consensual unions and secondarily through sexual assault and rape (Vaid, as cited in Expert Committee, 1994). The amount of IV drug use behind prison walls is unknown, although it is known to be prevalent, and that the scarcity of needles often leads to needle and sharps sharing (Prisoners, 1992). In that needles are contraband, when IV drug use does occur, it is likely that needles are shared in haste and in secret. Needles are also shared through tattooing practices, which are a feature of prison subcultures.

The National Commission on AIDS stated that HIV disease is being concentrated in prisons (American College of Physicians, 1992). Researchers and health practitioners monitor rates of HIV transmission in prison populations directly (by counting confirmed cases) and indirectly (by observing markers for potential exposure to HIV such as the rates of sexually transmitted disease, hepatitis B virus, or TB). Upon reviewing information concerning sexual contact, IV drug use, and data on various markers for HIV exposure, the prison population appears to be at particular risk for AIDS.

Among Tennessee prisoners, Decker, Vaughn, Brodie, Hutcheson, and Schaffner (1984) found a seroprevalence rate of 29.5% of hepatitis B virus markers. Whereas 28% of these inmates reported intravenous drug use,

18% said they had sexual contact with other men. Van Hoeven, Rooney, and Joseph (1990) found that 10.3% of all gonorrhea cases among male inmates in New York corrections were acquired while in custody. (These data were later used to initiate condom distribution in the New York City jail system). The Federal Bureau of Prisons estimated that between 9% and 20% of prisoners became the victims of sexual assault. Lockwood (as cited in Expert Committee, 1994) found that 28% of inmates in two New York prisons had been targets of sexual aggression while in custody.

Of Toronto's IDUs currently not in custody, Millson et al. (1990) found that 31% of males reported intravenous drug use while in corrections, 63% had shared needles, and 6% reported having sex with men while inside. Shore (1991) estimated that 30% to 40% of federal inmates in Kingston, Ontario, engage in sex while imprisoned and that 60% of inmates use drugs while incarcerated. The prevalence of sexual contact among men in prison merits additional scrutiny.

The Hidden World of Prison Sexual Politics

We have discussed some of the ways that race and class hierarchies become infused in prison gender relations. Sexuality is yet another key locus through which domination and subordination are constructed in the prison. Sexual deviants such as openly gay men or transvestites, for example, are ridiculed and reduced to lower-status positions. Homophobia in prison is rampant. In addition, that men who rape other men in prison, for example, may often still think of themselves as "straight" and their victims as "fags" reveals the confounding malleability of constructions of masculinity and male sexuality in the service of power. The act of prison rape itself is clearly tied to the constitution of intermale dominance hierarchies within the larger system of homosocial relations. Blacks may rape whites to establish dominant status or vice versa. Older prisoners may use rape to enslave newcomers. Guards or prison administrators have been known to threaten to expose prisoners to a greater threat of rape to evoke good behavior, to punish, or to squeeze out information. As Cahill (1990) observes, there is usually little recourse for victims:

> Once "turned out"—prison parlance for raped—a survivor is caught in a bind. If an inmate reports a sexual assault, even without naming the assailant, he will be labeled a "snitch," a contract will automatically be placed on him, and his life expectancy will be measured in minutes from then. (p. 32)

It would be a mistake, however, to perceive prison rape mainly as a power dynamic of intermale dominance hierarchies. Men's struggles to weave webs of domination through rape in prison also reflect and reproduce men's domination of women in the heterosocial world beyond the walls. In the muscled, violent, and tattooed world of prison rape, woman is symbolically ever-present. The prison phrase "make a woman out of you" means that you will be raped. Rape-based relationships between prisoners are often described as relations between *men* and *women* are, in effect, conceptualized as *master* and *slave*.

There is yet another dimension of man-on-man prison rape that links it to heterosexual sexual politics. Despite its prevalence, the reality of prison rape is often overlooked by prison officials and unrecognized or denied by civilians. The failure to recognize man-on-man prison rape can be interpreted as a "socially structured silence" (Jansen, 1988) that in effect reconstitutes gender inequality by allowing heterosexual rape to remain defined as a sexual phenomenon rather than an act of personal and political domination.

And finally, the social construction of masculinity exerts myriad influences on men's sexual choices and practices. Kimmel and Levine (1989), for example, observe that many men perceive and define sexual behaviors through the prism of traditional masculinity, which, in turn, makes them unreceptive to condom use and safer sexual practices. The traditionally masculine tendencies to take sexual risks, to engage in sex without love, and to see sex as a game of conquest heightens the vulnerability to HIV infection. "To educate men about safe sex, then," they argue, "means to confront the issues of masculinity" (Kimmel & Levine, 1989, p. 352). In this light, AIDS education for prisoners will help them become more aware of risky sexual practices. Yet strict sex education or AIDS education alone may not be enough to change behavior. Educational interventions may also need to foster discussion and insight into the relationships between gender, masculinity, and sexuality.

The Lack of Systematic Interventions

Though epidemiologic evidence of the prevalence of AIDS and HIV in prison populations is ample, efforts to stem the epidemic through fundamental reform have been piecemeal and inadequate. The issues and political realities behind the sluggish response to the AIDS epidemic in prison populations are complex.

For example, proposals to distribute condoms to enable safer sex practices are criticized by moralists as decadent or sinful. Homophobia leads others to cringe at the idea of men having sex with one another. Guards are concerned that condoms will be used as weapons or receptacles for incendiary bombs. Tough-minded administrators worry about public outcries that they are being "soft" on criminals.

Persons with AIDS in prisons are often stigmatized and treated as pariahs by guards and noninfected prisoners. Olivero (1990) argues that poor treatment of prisoners with AIDS stems from their lack of social power in the prison community. Social and medical maltreatment might also be fueled by political conflicts within the intermale dominance hierarchies that constitute the gender order of the prison. A cult of toughness pervades relations between factions of male prisoners, guards, and the various levels of paramilitary administration and staff. There is much status and manly face to be paraded and maintained, and the potential for change to issue from these social psychological arrangements is mired in a politics of masculinity.

The lack of systematic interventions by governments, public health officials, and corrections officials to curb HIV transmission is, itself, serving to increase the prevalence of AIDS in prisons. Hankins's statement of 1990 is still true:

> In Canadian prisons right now, we are basically creating shooting galleries. If somebody has a drug and somebody has a needle, then 10 guys are going to take it on that one needle, and there is no bleach available, so we are setting them up. (Gray, 1990, p. 1100)

In the United States, condoms are conditionally available in a few corrections institutions, generally from health care workers. Included are New York City's Rikers Island, San Francisco, Philadelphia, Mississippi, Tennessee, and Vermont (Expert Committee, 1994). Although Canadian federal officials, as of 1992, have made provisions for condoms in prison, they are reluctant to consider needle exchange, and cite concerns about the dangers of needle availability. Despite a lack of supporting evidence from systems providing condoms, corrections officials express fears that condoms could potentially be used for drug packaging, firebombing, or as a strangulation weapon (Cummings, 1991).

The Politics of Neglect

The lack of a systematic and caring response to the AIDS epidemic in prisons is an expression of deeper problems within North American society;

that is, the failure to meaningfully address concurrent sociomedical and economic crises that contribute to drug abuse, homelessness, the collapse of families, and dire fiscal consequences. The absence of a strong political constituency clamoring for the needs of the underclass has resulted in a politics of neglect (Bayer, 1991).

The neglect of the public health in the United States is particularly pronounced in relation to poor racial and ethnic minorities. In Harlem, where 96% of the inhabitants are black and 41% live below the poverty line, the survival curve beyond the age of 40 for men is lower than that for men living in Bangladesh (McCord & Freeman, 1990). Murray (1990) states that the probability for African American men to die between 15 and 60 years of age is 30%, a figure in excess of that for men in such impoverished nations as Gambia, India, and El Salvador. It has actually been suggested that one seventh of New York City health areas, home to approximately 650,000 people, be declared disaster zones. Liebman and Axler (1990) document a similar pattern in poor Philadelphia neighborhoods.

Poverty and homelessness overlap with drug addiction, which, in turn, is linked to HIV infection. Of persons hospitalized with HIV in New York City, 9% to 18% have been found to be homeless. Of homeless men tested for HIV at a New York City shelter, 62% were seropositive (Ron & Rogers, 1989). Among run-away or homeless youth in New York City, 7% tested positive, while this rate rose to 15% among the 19- and 20-year-olds. Of homeless men in Baltimore, 85% admitted to substance use problems (Weinreb & Bassuk, 1990).

The benign neglect of the health of poor, minority people has been compounded by the destructive impact of the selective regard of the authorities. Mandatory minimum sentences for drug crimes were intended to equalize court proceedings across the nation, whether the locales have liberal or conservative standards. It has been noted that mandatory minimums for sentencing are invoked more often with black defendants than white. In an attempt to limit the impact of crack on inner cities, the amount of crack required to trigger a mandatory sentence was made 100 times smaller than powder cocaine. However, in that black defendants make up 90% of crack cases and only 25% in the less harshly enforced powder cocaine cases, the effect has been to selectively discriminate against black users (Steinberg, 1994).

The stressors that result in many young people having little stake in mainstream society include poverty, educational failure, unemployment, early parenthood, and suicide (Dembo et al., 1990). For many inner-city minority males, involvement in drugs is an occupational choice and career track (Cotts, 1994). Indeed, some underclass men see the roles of gangster and drug dealer as socially available routes for upward mobility. Messerschmidt (1993) discusses how certain forms of criminal activity help some poor males to develop their masculine identities and build a manly reputation on the street.[1] One person's manly success as a gangster or dealer, however, results in another person's drug addiction, HIV infection, or death by homicide. Gangsters and dealers are also frequently charged with crimes, convicted, and incarcerated. One result is that the prison health care system, already dangerously inadequate, is being swamped by two epidemics: one is that of AIDS, and the other is due to the mass imprisonment of poor black and Hispanic drug users (Hammett, 1990; also cited in Expert committee, 1994).

In response to these epidemics, the World Health Organization (WHO) has charged prison authorities with a special responsibility to educate prisoners who may have a history of behaviors that would expose them to HIV infection (Expert Committee, 1994). WHO stresses the need for prisons to support prisoners' health needs in a manner similar to that experienced by other citizens in the community, and particularly to provide for equal preventive measures. The Expert Committee on AIDS and Prisons (1994) also reminds Corrections in Canada that their mission has been declared to be rehabilitative in nature and calls for substantial changes in prison health services to come up to WHO standards.

The same population that is most affected by the "War on Drugs" is the same segment that is most heavily burdened by HIV infection and AIDS— that is, poor, inner-city, black and Hispanic intravenous drug users, their partners, and their children. The most common feature among prisoners is not intravenous drug use, but poverty (Dubler & Sidel, 1989). Wallace (1990) sardonically remarks that to address HIV/AIDS it is necessary to strengthen frayed domestic and community social networks as a public health measure, even at the "cost" of the political enfranchisement of the poor.

The Paucity of
Gender Studies Research on Men in Prisons

Gender studies practitioners have only recently begun to study men in prison. The paucity of systematic research on men's lives in prisons is itself, in part, an expression of the politics of neglect. There are several reasons why gender scholars need to devote more energy to understanding men in prisons.

First, the systematic study of men in prison will help expand feminist theory to include a critical analysis of men and masculinity. Men in prison, at first glance, present profound contradictions for much feminist theory. Within the sphere of sexual politics, for example, many men in prison are there because they have enacted the worst kinds of exploitation of women: for example, rape, child abuse, armed robbery, and homicide. It is, therefore, politically problematic to develop a profeminist theoretical framework that allows for understanding and reforming these men and yet, at the same time, holds them responsible for their complicity with the oppression of women.

Second, the study of and advocacy for men would help men's studies practitioners better recognize and grapple with intellectual biases that stem from their socioeconomic, racial, and cultural backgrounds. Intellectual movements are social constructions and, as such, they flow from and resonate with the cultural values, social backgrounds, and political agendas of their progenitors. Feminists have recently and self-critically begun to face the fact that the feminist chorus has been limited mainly to white, middle-to-upper-class female voices (Birrell, 1990; hooks, 1984). The "new man's studies" movement, like its forbear women's studies, has also been spearheaded mainly by white, middle-to-upper-class intellectuals and professionals. It is no surprise, therefore, that many of the main issues of men's studies should reflect the concerns of well-educated white men; for example, sexuality, marriage and divorce, fatherhood, regaining manly self-esteem, work and career, and men's health. In contrast, the male prison population is the demographic antithesis of men's studies practitioners; that is, prisoners are most often racial and ethnic minorities, poor and working class or underclass, uneducated, dislocated from work, anomic, and politically marginalized. Men's studies practitioners, therefore, might follow the lead of Birrell (1990), who entreats her colleagues in women's studies to develop more inclusive theories of gender inequality by viewing the world from the standpoint of oppressed peoples, especially people of color.

Finally, the study of men in prison provides a fruitful institutional site to study the politics of masculinities. At any given historical moment, there are competing masculinities—some hegemonic, some resistant, some marginalized, and some stigmatized (Connell, 1987). The prevailing cultural definition of masculinity within a political and economic social system is constructed in relation to various subordinated masculinities as well as in relation to femininities.

The "Otherness" of
Persons with HIV

As one traces cultural reactions to the development of the North American AIDS epidemic, a pattern of shifting stigmatization becomes discernible. The impacts of HIV infection have moved from the marginalized gay community, through marginalized intravenous drug users who are mainly poor racial and ethnic minorities, to women considered to be outside the limits of social respectability. By defining members of these groups as outsiders and inferior (via homophobia, racism, classism, sexism, or moralism), the general population somehow confirms its own health, sanity, and integrity through a process of separation from the diseased or the different. This process of distancing reflects and fosters discrimination against groups that may already be stigmatized (Crawford, 1994; Manderson, 1994; Ross, 1989).

Even the use of the term *risk group* exemplifies the process whereby a metaphor of "otherness" is generated. The connotation is that members of a particular minority group are a risk, as distinct from being potentially at risk. It is not membership in a particular group that confers risk, but performance of certain behaviors that expose the individual to risk (Schiller, Crystal, & Lewellen, 1994). The epidemiological fact is that HIV is a comparatively noncontagious illness behaviorally transmitted within geographically defined social network structures, and presently occurring most frequently among ghettoized and oppressed urban minorities—gay men, intravenous drug users, and persons of color living in predominantly white cities (Neaigus et al., 1993; Wallace, 1991).

Prisoners are often fitted into the political and cultural role of expendable scapegoats. The processes of scapegoating enable the dominant groups within a social order to develop a sense of goodness and control, while subordinate groups are devalued and maltreated. Prisoners are thus reduced to the role of other or outsider and, in the public imagination, the evils that lurk behind prison walls become self-contained. Nothing needs to change. Hence, the perception of the prisoner as other not only mitigates against the medical treatment of prisoners with AIDS but it also limits our ability to effectively reckon with the AIDS epidemic in society at large.

Links Between
Prisons and Communities

The failure to provide comprehensive health education and treatment interventions in prisons is not only putting more inmates at risk for HIV infections but also the public at large. Prisons are not hermetically sealed enclaves set apart from the community; they are an integral part of society ("Health Care for Prisoners," 1991). Each year, an estimated 22 million admissions and discharges occur in correctional facilities in the United States. In 1989, prisons in the United States admitted 467,227 persons and discharged 386,228 (American College of Physicians, 1992). The average age of inmates admitted to prison in 1989 was 29.6, with 75% between 18 and 34 years; 94.3% were male. These former inmates return to their communities after having served an average of 18 months inside (Dubler & Sidel, 1989). Within 3 years, 62.5% will be rearrested and jailed. Recidivism is highest among poor black and Hispanic men. The extent to which the drug-related social practices and sexual activities of released or paroled inmates who are HIV positive are putting others at risk upon return to their communities is unresearched and unknown.[2]

Conclusion

We have examined some of the complex social, structural, and psychological forces that come into play in men's lives within the criminal justice system, the prison system, and the larger gender order. At this time, a jail or prison sentence in current conditions may entail not just the loss of freedom but exposure to a heightened risk of infection by HIV or TB (Bellin et al., 1993; Snider & Hulton, 1989). However, just as prison acts as a pocket of risk for persons already exposed to a greater risk of infection by HIV while they are in their communities, prison can also act as a pocket of opportunity for interventions. The World Health Organization has observed that the rehabilitative and therapeutic aspects of prisons are not sufficiently utilized. As 85% to 90% of intravenous drug users do not go into treatment, counseling them while in prison is critical. As Millson et al. (1990) suggest, intravenous drug users who do not receive HIV prevention information while in corrections may not have access to counseling at all.

The increased risk of HIV infection posed by imprisonment, and attendant increase in TB infection, may ultimately be resolved as economic constraint drives the criminal justice system to consider nonincarcerative alternatives to corrections. It is apparent the prisons cure neither crime nor the social problems that are linked to crime (Lasker, 1991).

Although blacks and Hispanics are at the greatest risk of contracting HIV/AIDS infection in prisons, just as yellow fingers do not cause lung disease, it is not their race or ethnicity that confers risk but the behaviors they engage in, the social circumstances of their lives (PHS, 1993), and the regard of the authorities. HIV/AIDS is tied to a network of problems that includes community disintegration, unemployment, homelessness, eroding urban tax bases, mental illness, substance use, custom, criminalization, and poverty (Wallace, 1991). Inclusion of the other in our general society is critical to limiting the course of the HIV/AIDS epidemic among us.

The masculinity politics around AIDS in prisons stretch beyond linkages between education, gender identity construction, and sexual practices. Within the intermale dominance hierarchies that constitute the prison system, prisoners are being systematically deprived of comprehensive AIDS education, condom and needle promotion and provision, and drug counseling. The disproportionate death toll from AIDS in prisons among poor African American and Hispanic men, therefore, to some extent reflects structured race and class inequalities in public health priorities (Gilbert, 1991). Two net effects of the existing policies and structural conditions are (a) the systematic increase in the number of prisoners with HIV/AIDS, and (b) the ultimate spread of AIDS and TB by HIV-positive prisoners who are released and return to their own communities.

The lack of comprehensive health care interventions to deal with the AIDS epidemic in prisons, we feel, exposes the harshly punitive nature of modern corrections. Foucault's (1979) account of the historical transformation of the prison in Western society documents a trend away from overt torture to more covert forms of punishment. The new prison system is not really intended to be more humane than the primitive torture wheel or gallows, but "to punish better . . . to insert the power to punish more deeply into the social body" (Foucault, 1979, p. 82). The spread of the AIDS epidemic through prison populations, therefore, should be a prime phenomenon for future research and advocacy work by gender studies practitioners.

Notes

1. For discussion of the social construction of masculinity in prisons, see D. Sabo (1994), Doing time, doing masculinity. In M. A. Messner & D. Sabo (Eds.), *Sex, violence and power in sports: Rethinking masculinty* (pp. 161-170). Freedom, CA: Crossing Press.

2. One potential mode of transmission of HIV via sexual contact is unprotected sex during the conjugal visits that are allowed for in various prison systems. At Attica Correction Facility in New York State, some inmates use the expression "fuck trucks" to refer to the trailers that are used for conjugal visits.

References

American College of Physicians. (1992). The crisis in correctional health care: The impact of the national drug control strategy on correctional health services. *Annals of Internal Medicine, 117*(1), 71-77.

Atkins, N. (1994, May 5). The cost of living clean. *Rolling Stone,* pp. 41-42.

Bayer, R. (Spring, 1991). AIDS: The politics of prevention and neglect. *Health Affairs,* 87-97.

Belbot, B. A., & del Carmen, R. B. (1991). AIDS in prison: Legal issues. *Crime and Delinquency, 31*(1), 135-153.

Bellin, E. Y., Fletcher, D. D., & Safyer, S. M. (1993). Association of tuberculosis infection with increased time in or admission to the New York City jail system. *Journal of the American Medical Association, 269*(17), 2228-2231.

Birrell, S. (1990). Women of color: Critical autobiography and sport. In M. A. Messner & D. F. Sabo (Eds.), *Sport, men, and the gender order: Critical feminist perspectives.* Champaign, IL: Human Kinetics.

Brewer, T. F., & Derrickson, J. (1992). AIDS in prison: A review of epidemiology and preventive policy. *AIDS, 6*(7), 623-628.

Cahill, (1990). Prison rape: Torture in the American Gulag. In F. Abbott (Ed.), *Man and intimacy: Personal accounts exploring the dilemmas of modern male sexuality* (pp. 31-36). Freedom, CA: Crossing Press.

Centers for Disease Control. (1993). Update: Mortality attributable to HIV infection among persons aged 25-44 years—United States, 1991 and 1992. *Morbidity and Mortality Weekly, 42*(46), 891-900.

Chassin, M. R. (1993). Health challenges for the 1990s. *New York State Journal of Medicine, 93*(1), 1-4.

Connell, R. W. (1987). *Gender and power: Society, the person, and sexual politics.* Stanford, CA: Stanford University Press.

Cotts, C. (1994, May 5). Smart money. *Rolling Stone,* pp. 42-43.

Crawford, R. (1994). The boundaries of the self and the unhealthy other: Reflections on health, culture, and AIDS. *Social Science Medicine, 38*(10), 1347-1365.

Cummings, C. (1991). AIDS education in California prisons. *California AIDS Clearinghouse Reviewer, 3*(1), 1-3.

Decker, M. D., Vaughan, W. K., Brodie, J. S., Hutcheson, R. H., & Schaffner, W. (1984). Seroepidemiology of Hepatitis B in Tennessee prisoners. *Journal of Infectious Diseases, 150*(3), 450-459.

Dembo, R., Williams, L., Wothke, W., Schmeidler, J., Getreu, A., Berry, E., Wish, E. D., & Christiansen, C. (1990). The relationship between cocaine use, drug sales, and other delinquency among a cohort of high-risk youths over time. *Drugs and violence* (DHHS Pub. No. ADM 90-1721). Washington, DC: Government Printing Office.

Drucker, E. (1990). Epidemic in the war zone: AIDS and community survival in New York City. *International Journal of Health Services, 20*(4), 601-615.

Drucker, E., & Vermund, S. H. (1989). Estimating population prevalence of HIV infection in urban areas with high rates of intravenous drug use: A model of the Bronx in 1988. *American Journal of Epidemiology, 130*(1), 133-142.

Dubler, N. N., & Sidel, V. W. (1989). On research on HIV infection and AIDS in correctional institutions. *The Milbank Quarterly, 67*(1/2), 81-94.

The Expert Committee on AIDS and Prison. (1994). *HIV/AIDS in prisons: Summary report and recommendations of The Expert Committee on AIDS and Prisons* (Ministry of Supply and Services Canada Catalogue No. JS82-68/2-1994). Ottawa, Ontario: Correctional Service of Canada.

Foucault, M. (1979). *Discipline and punishment: The birth of the prison.* New York: Vintage.

Fox, D. M. (1990). Chronic disease and disadvantage: The new politics of HIV infection. *Journal of Health, Politics, Policy, and Law, 15*(2), 341-355.

Fraser, P. A., & Phillips, A. (1993). Conference report: Emerging patterns of heterosexual HIV infection and transmission. *International Journal of STD & AIDS, 4*(11/12), 348-352.

Fuller, J. D. (1993, February 25). *Reflections of a clinical bystander.* Plenary Presentation at the Third North American Syringe Exchange Convention, Boston, MA.

Gilbert, D. (1991). These criminals have no respect for human life. *Social Justice, 18*(3), 71-83.

Gray, C. (1990). Dr. Catherine Hankins: Fighting AIDS without mincing words. *Canadian Medical Association Journal, 143*(10), 1000-1001.

Hankins, C. A., Laberge, C., Lapointe, N., Lai Tung, M. T., Racine, L, & O'Shaughnessy, M. (1990). HIV infection among Quebec women giving birth to live infants. *Canadian Medical Association Journal, 143*(9), 885-893.

Health care for prisoners: Implications of "Kalk's refusal." (1991, March 16). *Lancet, 337,* 647-648.

hooks, b. (1984). *Feminist theory from margin to center.* Boston: South End.

Jansen, S. C. (1988). *Censorship: The knot that binds power and knowledge.* New York: Oxford University Press.

Lombardo, J. M., Kloser, P. C., Pawel, B. R., Trost, R. C., Kapila, R., & St. Louis, M. E. (1990). Anonymous HIV surveillance and clinically directed testing in a Newark, NJ hospital. *Archives of Internal Medicine, 151,* 965-968.

Keller, S. E., Bartlett, J. A., Schleifer, S. J., Johnson, R. L., Pinner, E., & Delaney, B. (1991). HIV-relevant sexual behavior among a healthy inner-city heterosexual adolescent population in an endemic area of HIV. *Journal of Adolescent Health, 12*(1), 44-48.

Kimmel, M., & Levine, M. P. (1989). Men and AIDS. In M. Kimmel & M. A. Messner (Eds.), *Men's lives* (pp. 344-354). New York: Macmillan.

Langan, P. A. (1991). America's soaring prison population. *Science, 251*(3), 1568-1573.

Lasker, M. E. (1991). American prisons and prisoners in 1990. *Proceedings of the American Philosophical Society, 135*(1), 30-40.

Manderson, D. (1994, April). *Drugs and aesthetics: The symbolic war.* Paper presented at the Fifth International Harm Reduction Conference, Toronto, Ontario, Canada.

Mauer, M. (1992). Men in American prisons: Trends, causes, and issues. *Men's Studies Review, 9*(1), 10-12. [A special issue on men in prison, edited by Don Sabo and Willie London.]

Messerschmidt, J. W. (1993). *Masculinities and crime: Critique and reconceptualization of theory.* Lanham, MD: Lanham and Littlefield.

Messner, M. A. & Sabo, D. (1994). *Sex, violence, and power in sports: Rethinking masculinity.* Freedom, CA: Crossing Press.

Millson, M. E., Coates, R., Myers, T., Rankin, J., Rigby, J., McLaughlin, B., Major, C., & Mindell, W. (1990). *Behavioural research in an AIDS prevention program for injection drug users in Toronto, Canada.* Unpublished manuscript, University of Toronto, Health and Welfare, Canada, Toronto.

Nadelmann, E., & Wenner, J. S. (1994, May 5). Toward a sane national drug policy [Editorial]. *Rolling Stone,* pp. 24-26.

Neaigus, A., Friedman, S. R., Curtis, R., Des Jarlais, D. C., Furst, R. T., Jose, B., Mota, P., Stepherson, B., Sufian, M., Ward, T., & Wright, J. W. (1993). The relevance of drug injectors' social and risk networks for understanding and preventing HIV infection. *Social Science Medicine, 38*(1), 67-78.

New York City Department of Health. (1990, July 25). *AIDS Surveillance update* (report). New York: Author.

Novello, A. C. (1993). The HIV/AIDS epidemic: A current picture. *Journal of Acquired Immune Deficiency Syndrome, 6*(6), 645-654.

Olivero, J. M. (1990). The treatment of AIDS behind the walls of correctional facilities. *Social Justice, 17*(1), 113-125.

Osborn, J. E. (1993). AIDS: Science, medicine, and metaphor. *Western Journal of Medicine, 158*(3), 304-307.

Prisoners with AIDS/HIV Support Action Network. (1992). *HIV/AIDS in prison systems: A comprehensive strategy* (Brief to the Minister of Correctional Services and the Minister of Health). Toronto, Ontario, Canada: Author.

Public Health Service. (1989). Update: Acquired immunodeficiency syndrome—United States, 1981-1988. *Morbidity and Mortality Weekly Report, 38*(14), 229-250.

Public Health Service. (1990). Update: Acquired immunodeficiency syndrome—United States, 1989. *Morbidity and Mortality Weekly, 39*(5), 81-86.

Public Health Service. (1991). The HIV/AIDS epidemic: The first ten years. *Morbidity and Mortality Weekly Report, 40*(22), 357-369.

Public Health Service. (1993). Current trends: Update—Acquired Immunodeficiency Syndrome—United States, 1992. *Morbidity and Mortality Weekly, 42*(28), 547-557.

Public Health Service. (1994). Current trends: Heterosexually acquired AIDS—United States, 1993. *Morbidity and Mortality Weekly, 43*(9), 155-160.

Remis, R. S., & Sutherland, W. D. (1993). The epidemiology of HIV and AIDS in Canada: Current perspectives and future needs. *Canadian Journal of Public Health 84*(Suppl. 1), S34-S37.

Riley, D. (1993). Harm reduction in prisons: Why we can't afford to wait. *Canadian Centre for Substance Abuse Action News,4*(6), 1-2.

Rogers, D. E., & Osborne, J. E. (1993). AIDS policy: Two divisive issues. *Journal of the American Medical Association, 270*(4), 494-495.

Ron, A., & Rogers, D. E. (1989). AIDS in New York City: The role of intravenous drug users. *Bulletin of the New York Academy of Medicine, 65*(7), 787-900.

Ross, M. W. (1989). Psychosocial ethical aspects of AIDS. *Journal of Medical Ethics, 15,* 74-81.

St. Louis, M. E., Rauch, K. J., Petersen, L. R., Anderson, J. E., Schable, C. A., Dondero, T. J., & the Sentinel Hospital Surveillance Group. (1990). Seroprevalence rates of HIV infection at sentinel hospitals in the United States. *New England Journal of Medicine, 323*(4), 213-218.

Schiller, N. G., Crystal, S., & Lewellen, D. (1994). Risky business: The cultural construction of AIDS risk groups. *Social Science Medicine, 38*(10), 1337-1346.

Selik, R. M., Chu, S. Y., & Buehler, J. W. (1993). HIV infection as a leading cause of death among young adults in U.S. cities and states. *Journal of the American Medical Association, 269*(23), 2991-2994.

Shadle, V., & Ford., J. L. (1989, Winter). AIDS from coast to coast: How San Francisco and New York differ in treating AIDS patients. *Human Ecology Forum,* pp. 2-9.

Shore, R. (Speaker). (1991, August 14). AIDS in Canadian corrections [Broadcast]. *Canada A.M.*: Canadian Broadcasting Corporation.

Snider, D. E., & Hulton, M. D. (1989). Tuberculosis is in correctional institutions. *Journal of the American Medical Association, 261*(3), 436-437.

Steinberg, N. (1994, May 5). The law of unintended consequences. *Rolling Stone,* pp. 33-34.

Toepell, A. R. (1992). *Prisoners and AIDS: AIDS education needs assessment.* John Howard Society of Metropolitan Toronto, Ontario, Canada.

van Hoeven, K. H., Rooney, W. C., & Joseph, S. C. (1990). Evidence for gonococcal transmission within a correctional system. *American Journal of Public Health, 80*(12), 1505-1506.

Wallace, R. (1991). Traveling waves of HIV infection on a low dimensional "socio-geographic" network. *Social Science Medicine, 32*(7), 847-852.

Weinreb, L. F., & Bassuk, E. L. (1990). Substance abuse: A growing problem among homeless families. *Family and Community Health, 13*(1), 55-64.

World Health Organization. (1994). AIDS global data: The current global situation of the HIV/AIDS pandemic. *Weekly Epidemiological Record, 69*(2), 5-12.

8

Sport, Masculinity, and the Injured Body

PHILIP G. WHITE
KEVIN YOUNG
WILLIAM G. McTEER

This chapter reports on how participation in violent sport, with its potential and actual injurious outcomes, reinforces and naturalizes notions of masculinity that value physical dominance. We begin with a discussion of how sport is intimately connected to gendering processes and argue that male involvement in physically hazardous sports is taken for granted, considered natural, and even appealing. Health-promoting and health-compromising aspects of men's sport are examined within a conceptual framework that focuses on how body awareness and orientations toward health are sometimes constructed through gendered physical activity. Our study uses data obtained from in-depth interviews with current and former male athletes with experiences of injury. We show how athletes learn to disregard risk of physical harm and to normalize pain and injury as part of the sport experience.

Recent research on sport and gendering processes has identified how sport is an institution through which certain types of masculinity are constructed and reconstructed (Bryson, 1987; Connell, 1983; Messner, 1990; Sabo & Panepinto, 1990; Theberge, 1987; White & Gillett, 1994; Young, 1993). In many male sport practices, the use of aggression and tolerance

AUTHORS' NOTE: The authors would like to thank Don Sabo, Peter Donnelly, Donald Hastings, and James Gillett for helpful comments on earlier drafts of this chapter.

of risk has been idealized and rationalized as part of the process of masculinization. As Messner (1990) has argued,

> in many of our most popular sports, the achievement of goals (scoring and winning) is predicated on the successful utilization of violence—that is, these are activities in which the human body is routinely turned into a weapon to be used against other bodies resulting in pain, serious injury, even death. (p. 203)

Disregard for health in violent sports helps reinforce a particular version of masculinity that is also valued in other social arenas. For example, contemporary film, video, and fashion culture embraces omnipotent male figures such as Arnold Schwarzenegger, Sylvester Stallone, Marky Mark, and Fabio, among others (Donald, 1992; Rutherford, 1992). Other sporting performances—of women, gay men, and men pursuing alternative versions of maleness—are, by contrast, trivialized. In the present chapter, we investigate how forceful types of masculinity become ascendant and ask what it is about these notions of masculinity that lead many men to ignore or deny the risk of physical harm.

Physical Prowess as a Sign of Masculinity

Our analysis begins with a discussion of the proposition that the declining significance of male physicality in the sphere of work is linked to the ascendance of the symbolic importance of strength and force in other social arenas, such as fitness and sport behavior (Gagnon, 1974). A starting point for this discussion is the paradox whereby male violence has met increasing resistance in general and yet within the world of sport, violence is taken for granted, considered natural, even appealing (Morse, 1983; Young, 1993). Violence, pain, and injury are frequently internalized and rationalized by players, coaches, and spectators at both amateur and professional levels of competition. Tolerance of risk and injury is, in fact, sometimes reframed and legitimated as a means of impressing coaches (Faulkner, 1973), or as a way of establishing kudos, prestige, and identity within the team setting (Colburn, 1985; Smith, 1975). Media coverage of these potentially health-compromising norms is reinforced by many well-known and respected sport figures who promote and defend violent play as a relatively harmless feature of sport. Television personalities such as John Madden in football and Don Cherry in ice hockey, for instance, have become well-known for prioritizing physical force over the execution of skill.

In this way, it has become "normal" for men to play sport in an intensely confrontational manner. As Connell (1983) suggests in his analysis of Australian Rules Football,

> A deft bit of passing, an accurate kick, is cheered by that side's supporters; but the jarring collision of two ruckmen at speed draws gasps and roars from the whole crowd. Among adolescent football players, pure brawn is respected, but not wholly admired. On the other hand, pure cleverness is admired, but slightly condescendingly. (p. 19)

Similarly, in ice hockey the journeyman grinder or the hard-nosed player who is enthusiastic about "going into the corners" commands a type of respect that ranks the player as more masculine than the less physical player who plays with finesse. For example, a scornful joke circulating in Canadian ice hockey circles a few years ago had Pierre Mondou, a small, skillful player as its target: Pierre's wife, it was said, wouldn't let him vacuum around the house because he wouldn't go into the corners. What this joke tells us is that men who do not conform to or celebrate forceful notions of masculinity are potentially subject to ridicule. A male athlete who does not relish the "heavy going" in many male sports renders himself vulnerable to derision.

The association of masculinity with violent sport practices has its historical roots in medieval folk games of societies that were more openly patriarchal and violent than modern societies (Dunning, 1986). When some of the more violent traditional popular recreations were repressed following the development of "muscular christianity" within a games tradition in the British private school system in the 18th and 19th centuries, the sport of rugby resisted civilizing trends and became a male preserve within which an essentially physical version of manliness was staunchly defended. The symbolic association of violence and manliness in 19th-century rugby has been interpreted as a response to the relative decline of male power in the face of a developing suffragette movement (Crosset, 1990; Dunning, 1986). This view is supported by broader historical evidence showing how gender relations tend to become more polarized during periods of contest and struggle over definitions of legitimate masculinity and femininity (Kimmel, 1987).

In a similar vein, it has been argued that male physicality has come over the course of the 20th century to represent "dramatic symbolic proof of the natural superiority of men over women" (Messner, 1990, p. 204). Through participation in and identification with contact sports, males have been able to demonstrate the physical basis of gender difference. The symbolic significance of the celebration of male violence through sport practices lies in the importance of strength and aggression for success. Within masculinist ideology, male physical superiority over women also signifies the physical domination of women by men (Theberge, 1987). This annexation of physical force by men rather than women is clearly socially constructed. Moreover, the monopolization of violence by males is reinforced by the sport-media nexus. The link between sport and male violence is strengthened by the type of male sport that is predominantly celebrated in the media (Bryson, 1987). The viewing audience is exposed primarily to male sporting practices that embody aggression and violence.

Sporting practices that do not involve violent contact are less highly valued for their potential for the reproduction of masculine hegemony or the idea of the "naturalness" of gender difference. Sports such as ice-skating or gymnastics are even devalued as male interests because their aesthetic components signify ambiguously masculine, even feminine, characteristics. More revered kinds of masculinity are produced through sports such as football, ice hockey, and rugby, all of which are physically confrontational. These sports are indeed consolidated as male territory largely through the exclusion of women or by the trivialization of their involvement (Lenskyj, 1986). Debates on the appropriateness of female involvement in the rougher contact sports remain common and are characterized by a number of specious premises, such as the argument that women lack the necessary physical and psychological requirements. The irony of such baseless arguments is exposed by Kaplan's (1979) description of how a Mexican cliff diver justified the exclusion of women by suggesting that diving is a death-defying activity. In his view, because male divers take a great gamble to prove their courage, there would be little point to the feat if everyone saw that a woman could do the same.

Having established the connection between masculinity and violent sport, we now turn to the implications of violence and injury for a sample of former and current male athletes. There are many areas to address concerning this issue: the risk of injury, the occurrence of injury, being injured, rehabilitation and recovery from injury, and the consequences of long-term debilitation from a sports injury. In exploring these issues, we proceed from the notion that the male body in sport is subject to powerful gendered forces the result of which can be physically hazardous, but which are nevertheless naturalized, idealized, and legitimized to the extent that health compromising outcomes are framed as relatively nonproblematic.

Damaged Athletic Bodies

In conforming to the naturalized, idealized, and legitimized ways in which "real" men are expected to play sport, participants routinely become injured. As Smith (1987) has indicated, "There is no shortage of research on injuries in sport" (p. 15). His collation of injury data from football and hockey is illuminating:

> In the Canadian Football League, 462 man-games were lost in the 1981 season owing to injury. . . . An estimated 318,000 football injuries annually require hospital emergency room treatment in the U.S. . . . 4,723 NHL man-games were lost in the 1984-85 season owing to injury. The estimated injury bill for a single NHL team is between $500,000 and $1 million a season. (1987, pp. 15-16)

No workplace matches professional football either for the regularity or severity of injury (Adams, Adrian, & Bayless, 1987). In a 4-month NFL season, almost every player can expect injuries (Underwood, 1979), with many sustaining more than one. Adams et al. (1987) use American data to show that football injuries include "turf toe," ligamental strain, concussion, fractures, and most catastrophically, paraplegia, quadriplegia, blindness, and death. In Australia, a million people, most of them males, are affected by sports injuries each year resulting in an annual cost to the health care system of approximately $1 billion (Connolly, 1990).

Ironically, within a culture that valorizes the concerns of heterosexual masculinity over femininity and nonhegemonic masculinity, male athletes learn to regard their bodies mechanistically. The constraints of hegemonic masculinity limit sport experiences for many males to a rationalized performance orientation that involves the demonstration of gameness and courage in the face of physical risk. But as Messner (1990) argues,

> Here is one of the ultimate paradoxes of organized combat sports: top athletes, who are often portrayed as the epitome of good physical conditioning and health, are likely to suffer from a very high incidence of permanent injuries, disabilities, alcoholism, drug abuse, obesity and heart problems. The instrumental rationality which teaches athletes to view their own bodies as machines

and weapons with which to annihilate an objectified opponent, ultimately comes back upon the athlete as an alien force. (p. 211)

There can also be no doubt that in the present athletic climate of anabolic androgenic steroids and other performance enhancing drugs, which have pushed human physiology beyond its natural frontiers, risk to player safety has increased significantly. A report appearing in *The Economist* ("Moriture te Salutamus," 1992) refers to an "evolution to hugeness" occurring in professional football, a trend linked to an unnatural genesis:

> Steroids (officially banned but probably still common) have made players larger and therefore able to injure one another more easily. Indeed, the number of NFL players weighing more than 300 lbs. increased from 23 to 370 between 1981 and 1991 . . . The Rose Bowl . . . featured 18 players weighing more than 280 lbs. Each wore 25 lbs. of protective gear. (p. 27)

Today, sport is simultaneously a site of medical mastery and of extraordinary medical neglect. In spite of their hypertrophy and often unnaturally developed hugeness, athletes' bodies, pummelled by nose-tackles and the like, are X-rayed, frozen, and splinted before being sent back into the fray. Don Strock, former quarterback with the Miami Dolphins, recounts how players would group around "injured teammates during a game to screen from spectators the use of pain-killing injections, then hide the needles under the carpetlike synthetic turf" ("Moriture te Salutamus," 1992, p. 27). Fractures and other injuries are so common in professional football that every stadium houses sophisticated X-ray equipment, as do many university level stadia.

Crucially, we must also speak of bodily *sights* here for, unlike other workplaces, this is a public and, in fact, celebrated world of disability. The roaming television lens captures and replays the writhing body in "super slo-mo," while color commentators respond using discourses of approval (Young, 1991). Combined, visual and oral commentaries serve to marginalize pain, to represent the commodified sports moment as artistic and even sensual (Morse, 1983). In recent seasons, television has allowed football viewers to watch several grotesque injuries happen live, most notably compound fractures to Tim Krumrie of the Cincinnati Bengals and Joe Thiesman of the Washington Redskins, whose legs were literally snapped in tackles during NFL games. Profoundly and unabashedly violent from antiquity to the present, masculinist spectator sport has in several key aspects, then, become even more violent and hazardous as a result of profit-centered media interests.

Data Source and Procedures

Sixteen current and former athletes from Southern Ontario and Southern Alberta were interviewed in the fall of 1992. The interviews, semi-structured and between 1 and 2 hours in length, were recorded and subsequently transcribed. The sample was based on a pool of personal acquaintances and contacts from which we recruited other respondents. Although this was a "snowball sample," we attempted, with limited success, to interview men from varying social backgrounds. Because our research objective was to gather fine-grained information, we did not manage to construct a sample large enough to allow us to explore class, race, or other demographic effects as thoroughly as we would have preferred. All but one subject was white, all could be broadly considered middle class, and approximately one quarter of the sample was over 40 years of age.

We recognize that as with other qualitative work, our findings represent our own interpretations of the meanings of sport injury expressed by the men we interviewed. Given the nature of the methodology, we cannot be certain that our interpretations are entirely reliable. However, we did check for consistency of interpretation in the ways each of the authors "read" the data and discovered very little variability. As three male, former varsity rugby and football players each having experienced the "very limiting, often painful downside" of sport (Messner & Sabo, 1990, p. 14), we feel confident that our decoding of the data is valid.

The objective of our analysis was to examine subjective experiences and meanings attached to sport injury by men. A number of issues were engaged in all of the interviews, although subjects were asked to talk freely about their experiences in general. Detailed information was gathered about early involvement in sport as children and how relationships with significant others had affected subjects' athletic experiences. Respondents were also asked about their earliest recollections of sport injury and about their bodies and health, their concepts of self, and their relationships with others.

Particular attention was paid to physical damage brought upon the body through sport. The respondents, all of whom had been injured seriously enough that their lives had been altered in some way, were asked to talk about the short- and long-term consequences of their injury experiences. We discovered that all respondents had experienced considerable pain and most had incurred multiple injuries. The types of injury were diverse. They included fractures to most bones, a ruptured spleen, concussions, a lacerated kidney, a punctured testicle, shoulder and other joint dislocations, torn ligaments, a heart attack, and a stroke. Many subjects experienced long-term consequences, including carpal tunnel syndrome, chronic pain variously located, a removed kidney, partial paralysis, tendinitis and arthritis, as well as body parts kept in place with braces, plates, pins, and other devices.

Although the interviews were guided by theoretical questions and propositions that emerged from our reading of the literature, we also wanted to remain open to unanticipated constructions of meaning by the respondents, and to new conceptual ideas. This mode of analysis of the transcribed interviews allowed a number of themes to emerge vis-à-vis the sense-making of an adjustment to injury.

Early Stages of Sport Involvement

Our analysis of the process of socialization into sport was guided by the understanding that sport is essentially *gendered*. This seemed important in that extant feminist writers have occasionally been guilty of assuming rather than showing a connection between sport and the gendering process. Our findings revealed that this connection was expressed in two ways.

First, reproduction of male privilege in sport across generations was evident in the manner in which early sport experiences were emphasized within the context of father-son relationships. The idea of sport as a rite of masculinization is, of course, a prominent theme in the sport literature in general. For example, in his 1913 book *Training the Boy,* which looks at traditional views on boyhood, McKeever argued that "no boy can grow to a perfectly normal manhood without the benefits of at least a small amount of baseball" (p. 91). Gagnon's (1974) more contemporary and critical work similarly conceives of sport as a "way to express male-to-male competitive physical behavior" (p. 145). And even more recently, Kimmel (1990) and Messner (1992) have probed male-to-male influence in the development of sports character.

In the present study, T——, for example, noted that his father "kind of pushed" him into football, and D—— spoke of his father's need for his son to participate at a very early age:

> Well, it really started . . . as sort of a trial-and-error thing. My father wanted me to get involved in sports at a fairly early age. Like, at 6 years old he was

trying to get me into soccer and I think I tried every sport there was for at least a couple of years. And then finally when I turned 12 I got involved in Bantam football and that's when I finally caught on with that. And finally there seemed to be something I was good at, so I continued on from there.

Yet although fathers had positive influences on sport participation that were taken for granted (as M—— said of his early sports experiences, "It was just something we did together"), other influences were negative, even coercive. In T——'s words,

My dad had a tough life coming from overseas. He's sort of a perfectionist, and if he came to watch and if I screwed up, then after the game he'd let you know about it. He didn't really think that you should be screwing up.

Here, we are reminded that early sport experiences clearly had a central role in boyhood masculinization. The legitimacy of male authority around sport appeared quite complete. For our subjects, early influences or initial contacts with sport were never associated with relationships with mothers or female significant others.

Second, we were struck by the degree to which physical strength was naturalized as an essentially masculine trait. From the interviews we discovered that sport experiences helped construct gender distinction by providing boys with the opportunity to establish an essentially robust and competent physical sense of self. For D——, now a university football player, this was a matter of connecting with forceful body work: "There's just not a lot of sports around where you can really use your whole body and, you know, engage in destroying another person."

At the same time, though, masculinity is not a monolithic construct. For example, J——'s anxieties over body size were ameliorated by the relatively less macho requirements of jogging: "I remember being in high school. I hated my skinny, slouched stature because I was interested in football and hockey, and only the big guys did well. I really [learned to] appreciate my slight stature in running."

Clearly, the notion of masculinity is flexible and incorporates a *range* of selves and identities whose definitions vary. In sports not requiring force and power, for instance, we discovered that masculinity may also be constructed through traits such as discipline and endurance.

Revealingly, however, M——'s long-standing career in semiprofessional kickboxing (one of the most violent of all sports) resulted from the rather excessive inducements of an overbearing father and his own insecurities vis-à-vis "not being able to look after" himself:

Being in London, England, during the 1960s and 1970s, being Indian, and being chubby and fat was not the best thing for a lot of reasons. We had problems with racial tensions in the neighborhood we lived in. So my father felt that a way of dealing with that was getting me involved in martial arts, especially since my older sister used to defend me on the street. In our culture, it was not a cool thing for your older sister to be defending you. But then I used to look at myself and look at my dad and say, "What do you want me to do?" So he signed me up in martial arts and it was terrible. Training was on Saturday mornings and I used to miss my cartoons. Didn't like it. But he used to drag me out of bed the first 3 or 4 years and forced me to go. I hated it. I didn't like it at all.

Similarly, many of our other respondents also espoused values and ideas about sport that were consistent with hegemonic forms of masculinity. This was evident in numerous ways, such as in their attitudes to male superiority ("Athletics is the key to the dominance of males," J——), to injury ("Take it like a man," J——), to players who demonstrate pain ("There's kind of a feeling that's put upon you by your peers; the expression is 'pussy,' " D——), to their sport's rituals ("It makes you more of a guy's guy to be involved in high risk," G——), to their impression of how the public sees players of violent sports ("They sort of look up to you because you're handling it," T——), and to what they desire most from sport ("I definitely wanted to get into the physical side of it," M——).

In sum, our findings revealed more about broader construction of masculine selves than simply insights into injury alone. The extent to which men's sport reproduces what Farr (1988) called *dominance bonding,* a system of peer group-based male privilege integrally based on gender *difference,* was also revealed. The intricacies of this process will be examined in detail by focusing on male athletes' perspectives on injury and pain.

Athletes Talk About Injury

In that only one of our respondents had played sport professionally, tolerance of risk could not be seen as an occupational imperative per se (cf. Young 1993). Nevertheless, sport participation was so key for our subjects' identities that they often voluntarily chose to play while severely injured and suffering from pain.

Normalized Pain

One of the ideals of hegemonic masculinity is the suppression of *affect.* In sport, playing with pain is viewed as appropriate and normal male behavior. For example, teammates or coaches or both may implore an athlete to "suck it up." Similarly, locker-room slogans such as "you don't make the club sitting in the tub," convey the message that tolerance of pain is normative, that it "shows character," and that it "separates the men from the boys," from women, and from men who are unwilling to pay the price of entry into the male world of sport. Sabo (1986) call this norm the *pain principle,* and identifies expectations in sport that priortize pain over pleasure. We found all subjects conformed to such a philosophy:

> Physical pain? Well, it's pretty constant. I have chronic tendinitis in my ankle and a little bit in my shoulder and it's a constant thing. You take a couple of Tylenol every day. For my leg, you take ice and put it in a bag and just put in on there. And it's on there for 20 minutes, you know. It seems to keep things, you know, sort of quiet in there. (D——)

> Lately, it's been not too bad. I train with more off days, which gives the wrists a rest. I also avoid activities (such as writing quickly or lots). Right now my fingers on the right hand tingle and occasionally go numb. I stop writing when it gets unbearable, drop my hand down, shake it a lot, and it's OK for another little bit. (I——)

> On the football team you expect your neck to hurt or your back to hurt and as long as you can keep playing things aren't that bad. I think that's your thinking. And plus after the season things get better. A few weeks later you can start to move your head again. (D——)

We identified in our data several strategies used by athletes to indulge injury and to comply with the "no pain, no gain" axiom of competitive sport. These strategies are articulated as rules of conduct, or norms, but they also include various techniques of neutralization (Sykes & Matza, 1989) and other linguistic justifications.

Hidden Pain

Denial of pain, as with coping mechanisms associated with illness more broadly, was reported by some athletes as a normal aspect of sport behavior. J——, for example, risked severe and possible fatal injury by playing football with internal bleeding caused by a ruptured spleen. As he explained, ignoring pain had always been a part of sport for him, even as a child athlete having badly injured his leg:

> Then, I responded the same way that I responded with the present injury because I would just try to hide it, and the doctors would tell you what not to do or not to play or whatever. And I remember playing hockey with the boys, you know, like after school or something, and that I was always goalie. And I remember playing with this broken leg. You know, taking shots off the leg and it would be, you know, right in the shin.

As an adult, J—— still speaks reluctantly of "giving in" to pain and disapprovingly of being "beaten" by it:

> I finished the practice and went home. At the game the next day, I just tried to eat something and it hurt a lot to eat because of the digestive system, all the gases and stuff inside the stomach didn't mix good. And so I just went to sleep and tried to forget about it and just hoped by morning it would be better. I couldn't really sleep because I couldn't lie on one side or any side and the pain was always really constant and numbing and dull. So the next day I tried to ignore it and tried to play but I just couldn't do it.

Similarly, D——'s career as a Canada West track-and-field athlete was one which, as he saw it, depended on constant pain suppression:

> I came straight down on my shoulders and one mat was a little higher than the other. So what happened then was I heard a pop. A very, very audible pop and it hurt like hell. And I thought, well, it might only hurt when I land so I'll give it another whirl. You know, see if it was something that just sort of clicked something here or there. I got up and I jumped again and I actually jumped another six or so times and I recall afterwards basically being doubled over and not being able to do anything because it didn't hurt until I hit the mat. And it was kind of bothering me. I generally would go through a real state of denial. And I was doing long jump the same way.

J——'s views on injury spoke both to a philosophy of hiding pain and to norms requiring that pain not be revealed to football teammates:

> I bite my tongue and sometimes, if it's really bad, I moan once or twice. But sometimes it gets pretty bad and hard to bear. If the guys were around it was a different story but if my girlfriend was there I kind of got more sympathy. When I was recuperating, it was hard. When I was starting to rehab, I would grin and bear it.

We note here that willingness to conceal pain was not restricted to players of contact or collision sports; it was also evident among participants of the over 20 sports represented by our other respondents, including high jump, squash, and downhill skiing. The general consensus seemed best summarized by M—— who, despite chronic foot pain aggravated by racquet sports, noted, "I sort of live with it. I block it out somehow."

Disrespected Pain

The athletes in our sample did not convert pain into pleasure, as some bodybuilders claim to be able to do (Smith, 1989). We found, instead, that they expressed a disrespect for what K—— called "everyday pain." This was especially evident in the manner several subjects (all football and hockey players) differentiated pain from injury. Whereas the former included, in T——'s words, "mostly soreness and aches" (but which nevertheless often required prescription drug treatment and even surgery), the latter implied either unbearable suffering or manifestly unplayable body conditions, such as a broken limb set in a cast.

As with many athletes in the study, D—— had spent several years on painkillers, even having to use them in the off-season to reduce his permanent pain:

> We have this term in football. People refer to it as a difference between pain and injury. If you can walk or you can run to any degree, you know, they look at your injury in terms of percentages. If you're at 70% and it's better than your second stringer's 100%, then you're playing. So, you tend to take a couple of painkillers and tape her up nice and tight and ice before you play, and away you go.

Almost a decade of playing football had led J—— to express similar indignation about the routine hazards of his sport:

> Last year I ripped my trap and separated my shoulder. . . . Every now and again it flares up and then I take a bunch of Tylenols and forget about that pain. That's probably the most pain I have. But is that injury?

Concealed Pain

The concealment of pain by athletes is also partly attributable to pain that is poorly received by teammates, coaches, and others. Our subjects were sometimes critical of the negative impact of injury on relationships with teammates and described the display of injury or pain as a "demoralizer":

In the dressing room before the game, you know, you're there an hour and a half before and if you know someone's hurt and they're showing that they're hurt, it kind of brings the other guys down, especially if they're a real leader on the team. If you're kind of whining and you've got the grimace on your face and other people are looking over while you're doing your stretches and stuff and they're going well, you know, what's with this? But you kind of bite the bullet, and you're pumped up and you're ready to go and it hurts but you can't show that it hurts. Then it kind of leads to a higher team morale and it shows that, you know, he's playing for us. (J——)

The rules of masculinist sports culture, then, seem to require that intense pain is controlled and masked. There were several accounts of this. J—— reported that after he broke his leg, the pressure to "play through it" came from peers, his coach, and even his father:

With my femur, I remember vividly just going up the wall and kind of having my head down and getting hit from the side. I know it was my left leg and all I felt was my left leg wrapping around my right leg. Then I fell down. I tried not to show pain and lay there on the ice. I was trying to get up and I remember just falling back down again. And then I remember the coach coming up and trying to help me up and he said, "Come on you can get up," "You're tough," or whatever, and just trying to stand on it, but there was no way. I remember my dad even giving me shit. Even going through the dressing room no one would help me take my equipment off. And we were in a small town and there was no stretcher, so I had to get put in the back of our van and taken to the nearest hospital.

When asked to explain the apparent negligence of those surrounding him, J—— hinted at the constraints of his "enforcer" role: "No one really thought it was anything serious because . . . of the tough guy label." Similarly, after tearing ligaments in his knee (subsequently requiring reconstructive surgery and a half year of physiotherapy), hockey player K—— recalled being told by teammates not to ice the swelling and not to "be a pussy."

Being hurt appears to be unwelcomed by many coaches even at the amateur level. D——, for instance, expressed concerns over his university football coaches' lack of support for his and others' suffering: "Really, they see it as more of an inconvenience." M—— came by this knowledge more explicitly and recalled several kickboxing coaches telling him not to display any physical distress to them. In the words of one of his coaches: "I'm not bringing a towel to your corner. So don't even bother thinking about stopping."

Depersonalized Pain

In that pain and injury are understood to be so poorly received by teammates, athletes often feel a need to rationalize their circumstances privately. This process entails a particular way of thinking and speaking about pain, including the use of certain discursive techniques that result in its depersonalization and objectification.

One technique is to view the local anatomical part, not the body as a whole, as (in D——'s words) "giving out." Given athletes' generally excellent health and their posture of physical invulnerability, injury is unsurprisingly often perceived by players as a form of bodily betrayal and often results in self-resentment. Injured body parts assume the status of "other." In K——'s words, "It's like it's not a part of you. Like it's a totally different portion or something." As further testimony to this depersonalization process, subjects frequently referred, for example, to an injury of *the* knee or *the* shoulder, and were often reluctant to explicitly acknowledge that the injured body part was their own. In general, we found that athletes were humbled, even embarrassed, by the vulnerability of their bodies.

To further distance themselves from personal bodily experience, body damage itself is often articulated by athletes through the use of impersonal and techno-rational discourse. Legs become "iced," knees "scoped," ankles "strapped," aches and pains "killed," and mechanical glitches (pulls, strains, tears, breaks) simply "fixed," often artificially. Remarkably, J—— noted that the pain from his ruptured spleen was "just like squeezing an orange," except rather than juice "a little bit of blood came out." Referring to a skiing accident that resulted in him "actually living on half a kidney . . . one kidney was totally ripped open and the other was lacerated," G—— described his injury as "the equivalent of dropping two eggs on the floor—one cracked, one smashed."

Injury and Masculinity

Because of the severity of injuries experienced, efforts by our respondents to suppress pain and injury were often limited in effectiveness. Seriously injured athletes ultimately have little choice but to deal with their problems in a practical way. Although at amateur and especially professional levels the structure of sport contains a medical infrastructure designed to accommodate the physiological and medical aspects of injury (sports medicine clinics, rehabilitation centers, physiotherapy), athletes seldom receive assistance in working through socio-emotional side effects, which, ironically, may be even more disempowering. However, although we found socio-emotional effects to be profound in the short term, all but two of the men we interviewed ultimately sought out and pursued alternative sports-related avenues for masculine reidentification. Our data suggest, then, that in assessing the relationship between sport, masculinity, and injury, we should distinguish between short-term and long-term adaptations. We do this next by discussing the initially disempowering impact of injury and pain, and the subsequent techniques men adopt to reframe, and recover from, compromised notions of self.

Disempowered Masculinity

Compromised health often confounds injured male athletes who are often dependent for their self-identity on physical power and fitness. Injury may involve, among other things, hospitalization, missing competition, social dislocation from the team, even retirement. But equally stupefying for men used to silence around health care and negative bodily change (Rutherford, 1992) are experiences such as unwanted weight gain or loss, feelings of ostracism, and depleted personal worth. In other words, athletes are forced to recognize, perhaps for the first time, that the physical body and its talents are integrally tied to self and to relationships. For men who conceive of sport in a principally gendered fashion, then, injury has consequences for the *masculine* self.

For both triathlete J—— and skier G——, niggling minor injuries had never been enough to detract from their feelings of invincibility. When asked about taking unnecessary risks, G——, for example, remembered that there "was a belief that you were bullet proof." So when G—— hurt his knee and lacerated a kidney in a bad fall and J—— suffered a heart attack during the biking leg of a triathlon event, reconceptualizing the place of sport in their lives and their self-image was unavoidable. As J—— put it, the process was a troubling one to his "inner self": "I've always prided myself on being healthy and strong and it was really confusing feeling weak." For others, coming to terms with injury was similarly demoralizing. K—— described his initial response to tearing knee ligaments as "pretty close to the biggest down of my life" and recalled the mental adjustment being "much tougher" than the leg pain. D——'s broken collarbone was reported as "a very big loss," and J——'s broken femur was "fully devastating."

The magnitude of adjustment problems is often determined by the nature and extent of injury. J——'s experiences with heart attack during a triathlon event and his subsequent stroke were highly traumatizing. Not only was he left partially paralyzed and without speech but also his medical difficulties were followed by family breakdown and what J—— described as a "downward spiral" personally:

> I was feeling less of a man. I was married. The doctors inserted a tube in my penis to control the urination and I couldn't control my bladder and I was pissing myself all the time. I felt just inadequate for maintaining my lifestyle with my wife and I suggested to her that we get separated and we did. For me, it was a nonverbal period. I couldn't explain my feelings. It was really frustrating. I felt like a baby. And in the hospital and the physio gym, I couldn't crawl because I'd get sore with my broken rib and my separated shoulder and I couldn't verbalize and I couldn't walk. I just felt like a baby.

Others also understood their injuries as demasculinizing in the short term. T——, for instance, saw his decreasing body mass as a betrayal rendering him "less attractive and less manly . . . you just feel incompetent . . . not being able to do things. You just feel helpless." M——'s diminished fitness level urged him to try other activities, even gingerly early on, "to try to maintain that image" of himself. For I——, simply having to adjust to a less rigorous bodybuilding routine because of carpal tunnel syndrome also affected his confidence, self-esteem, and mood. One crucial finding was that the difficulty brought on by adjusting to injury was strongly linked not only to the psychological reassessment anyone might face under similar circumstances but also to notions of truncated male adequacy and role performance.

In general, the short-term effects of injury required a series of physical and mental adjustments, all of them frustrating for men unaccustomed to conceiving of their bodies in any way as weak. These adaptations addressed problems associated with masculine self-image as well as with rehabilitation itself, disengagement from sport, lost training time, and the loss of camaraderie. All athletes lamented the latter. Importantly, J—— summarized his own despondency by hinting that whereas healthy athletes possess *active* bodies, injured athletes possess less potent or *passive* ones: "I can't relate to their physical activities anymore, and I felt the silences between us." Despite the fact that his illness occurred some 6 years earlier, J——'s mood when he made these comments remained extremely disconsolate.

Occasionally, extensive hospital stays and rehabilitation provided time for reflection, or what J—— called "soul searching," on the implications of the injury for future participation and lifestyle. Several subjects spoke of being bewildered by the ominous prognoses of doctors cautioning them against repeated risk taking. As previously mentioned, however, whereas concern for future health tended to be correlated with the type and severity of injury, the fears of all of our subjects of further injury quickly took second place to their desire to return to competition.

Masculinity Restored

A remarkable aspect of how injuries eroded feelings of invulnerability is that the erosion was extremely short-lived. Despite the severity of these athletes' injuries, all but two returned to essentially risky sports. The two not returning were physically unable to: At the time of this writing, one is still recovering from stroke-induced paralysis and the other is constrained by only having the use of one half kidney. It appears that the hegemonic model of sport with its emphasis on forceful male performance and its promise of "masculinity validation" (Sabo & Panepinto, 1990, p. 115) is so meaningful in the lives of some men that injury is as constituting as it is threatening. This may be demonstrated in several ways.

K——'s recovery from knee surgery depended on his overcoming the psychological hurdle of whether he "could take a hit again":

> I felt good after I came out of my surgery. I thought I'd worked hard in physio. I thought I could've done basically everything that I could've done to make myself better. People told me that the next year I skated with a limp. I still cross over one way better than the other. I still always turn to one side. That's just something that maybe came out of habit more than anything from being maybe timid on it for the first little while. The best thing that happened to me, I think, was that in the first game I played I just got hammered. I just got nailed. I got up and I felt great. I felt like nothing went wrong and after that I thought that was a big sort of camel's back to get over. It would've worked out better if I had maybe hit the guy, but all in all that was a big step for me.

With the knowledge that he could once more dole out and take pain, K—— returned to hockey more confident than ever. This was much the same for J——, for whom temporary disablement was a catalyst to a stronger, tougher self:

> I know that through hard work I can basically overcome anything and I proved that at a young age with my femur. You know, you've broken the biggest bone in your body and it's supposed to be a very serious injury and I've never had any, you know, complications with it since. So I knew that through hard work I would be able to come back, and at the end everything would be alright.

Finally, 6 weeks of recovering from his spleen injury had shaken J——'s confidence, but only temporarily. His main recollection was how rehabilitation "reenergizes" and provides an opportunity for "a brand new start." Paradoxically, and despite still having to use anti-inflammatory and painkilling drugs frequently, J—— saw his time away from sport as so "reviving" that he returned to football with an even more zealous commitment to the pain principle: "I could even learn to play with a little more pain."

Reframing injury as purposeful appears to result both from the machismo and fatalism of athletic culture, and from the persuasiveness of popular mythology about sport being a "character builder." J——'s belief that "everything happens for a reason" was tied to his and others' broader focus on the beneficial attributes of having to deal with the adversity of pain and disablement. When asked how he responded to injury in the short- and long-term, for instance, T—— noted how his initial feelings of anger and self-pity were ultimately superseded by a revelation that "in the long run it [injury] will make you a better person." Meanwhile, J—— saw his own "worthwhile" pain as consolidating the way he thought of himself as a man in and out of sport:

> I don't think it's really hurt the masculine side at all. If anything, in the long run, it's made me a better person because it's shown that through hard work and being positive you can get through those tough stages and, you know, each day is going to be better. And I think it's made me a better person just knowing that I can work through things like that.

Although not all athletes spoke directly of recovering masculinity from injured bodies and temporarily injured selves, all but one indicated that enduring pain while rehabilitating was linked to self-improvement. For some, this meant redefined philosophical postures (taking slightly less risk, being more prepared, living for more than the moment), but for most it meant regaining bulk, strength, confidence, and self-image—factors all demonstrably tied to reconstructed masculinity in the postinjury context.

The long-term inurement to injury is possible because the period of self-reflection following the injury is relatively brief and uncritical. Internal contradictions in the thought processes and discourses of the men returning to sport were evident in that having often reflected on future health immediately following injury, all subjects went on to say that they would change little if they could do it all again. At the time of the interviews, only one athlete had a totally clear bill of health, all but two had returned to competition in very demanding sports, and all of them continued to suffer from residual pain or irreparable physical damage. In sum, we found respondents' attitudes to be much less critical or reflexive than they were conciliatory toward the dominant code of hypermasculine competitive sport. The latter evidently allows for repeated disregard for physical well-being to be viewed, paradoxically, as constituting.

Discussion

Our findings suggest that acceptance of risk and tolerance of pain are connected to masculinizing experiences in sport. Failure to suppress affect around pain or to play with pain can lead to stigma and even ostracism. To be masculine is to conform to the so-called pain principle. Succumbing to injury, unless it is manifestly disabling, is a sign of weakness and an acknowledgement of willingness to deviate from norms of affect suppression. In gender terms, the athlete is perceived as having submitted to a side of himself that is soft or feminine. Norms of dominant masculinity require an emphasis on doing rather than being, activity rather than passivity. By not presenting the "performative" male body (Rutherford, 1992, p. 186), the athlete who withdraws from action becomes less physically forceful or competent than his teammates.

Different types of pressure may be brought to bear to encourage an athlete to play while injured or to play before an injury has fully healed. In extreme cases, an athlete may suffer degradation by having to sit in segregated meal areas, by being ostracized at team functions, or by being constantly questioned by coaches in public about the injury. All such measures mark the injured player as a deviant. Such pressures are powerfully insidious, however, because the fear of having one's masculinity questioned can threaten the long-term health of an athlete who might stop listening to pain signals from his body and return to the team.

It is paradoxical, of course, that the systematic destruction of the male body in sport is framed as empowering for masculinity. Ironically, the battle-worn athlete is subjectively hypermasculine when objectively he may be physically disabled. Injury and its consequences can be understood, indeed, as simultaneously empowering and disempowering for men. In the latter scenario, sport involvement intense enough to make injury a probability can be seen as part of a process of self-domination through body discipline. Foucault's (1979) ideas on objectification, which emerge principally in the form of discursive regimes, offer some insight into how men can become alienated from their bodies and from themselves through enmeshment with sport practices. For Foucault (1979), disciplined bodies are inescapably objects of power relations:

> The body is also directly involved in the political field; power relations have an immediate hold on it; they invest it; mark it, torture it, force it to carry out tasks, to perform ceremonies, to emit signs. (p. 25)

Here, the focus on sport as promising empowerment is cast in a different light as imposing regulatory forces of discipline and control—forces geared toward political, economic, and cultural profit: "the body becomes a useful force only if it is both a productive body and a subjected body" (Foucault, 1979, p. 26). In the context of the current study, this conceptualization raises important questions about the extent to which traditional sport structures can compromise men's health while promising to augment it, and in the process prevent many men from fully expressing themselves as humans. As Messner (1990) has suggested, the injured athlete represents the ultimate paradox of violent sport—the employment of one's body as a weapon inevitably results in violence against one's body.

Viewed in this way, self-domination is sufficiently internalized that whereas our respondents would acknowledge that their fathers and significant others may have applied too much pressure on them to conform to the pain principle, they would also quickly spring to their defense when tackled on this matter. Further, after suggesting that injury had caused them to reflect somewhat critically on their sport experiences, there was a wholesale return to action where rehabilitation allowed. As part of the latter process, the ready use of painkillers, anti-inflammatory medicine, and other drugs, lengthy ice treatments, physiotherapy, and other procedures were routinized uncritically. In brief, the athletes were for the most part unreflexive about their experiences with pain and disablement, yet their accounts were also full of internal contradictions.

The gendering of injury was brought into sharp relief by the ultramasculine gesture of returning to action following a very serious injury. This is accorded even higher status if the athlete risks permanent disablement if he is reinjured. Professional male sport, of course, offers numerous role models in this respect. Joe Montana, for example, who was with the Kansas City Chiefs in the NFL, assumed legendary status after returning to play against medical advice after a series of surgeries performed on his back and elbow.

Risky sport and injury experiences carry particular weight for adolescent and young men for whom the transition to adult masculinity is a primary concern. Sport is extraordinarily important for what Miles (1992, p. 85) calls "manhood training." As Connell (1983) has suggested: "Sport is, all considered, astonishingly important. It is the central experience of the school years for many boys, and something even the most determined swots have to work out their attitude to" (p. 18).

The masculinizing potential of sport is so potent that young males come to regard subjecting their bodies to violence as legitimate and natural, and debilitated ex-athletes tend to remain uncritical of the way much of male sport is organized. As Messner (1990) has suggested: "To question their decision to give up their bodies would ultimately mean to question the entire institutionalized system of rules through which they had successfully established relationships and a sense of identity" (p. 212).

The injury talk of our respondents demonstrates the significance of sport for the hegemonizing of a brand of masculinity based on physical dominance. Through sports violence young males can affirm a version of masculinity that remains widely revered and distance themselves from all that is weak or feminine (White & Vagi, 1990). Conversely, macho sport declines in importance as a source of masculinity validation during adulthood (Connell, 1983). In the present study, we found greater introspection about pain and injury and less tolerance of sport violence among the older respondents. Further evidence for this lies in the increasing numbers of former athletes from all levels of involvement who are resuming their sport careers but in less violent and competitive contexts. For example, "Master's" competitions and "Old-Timer's" leagues are imbued with different, less injury-inducing, values. Events are structured and bound by rules that make them safer. This is, of course, an ironic critique of the current structures that are often in place for sport for boys and young male adults.

In this chapter, we examined the idea that the social construction of sport injury is linked to the reproduction of male force, which in turn tends to be linked to the broader subjugation of alternative masculinities and femininities. For both its meaning for participants and its broader implications for health, the sport-injury nexus is best understood as part of a process whereby life tasks are assigned on the basis of gender. For male athletes, body mass, physical endurance, risk taking, and forms of body discipline, including pain denial, are integral features of culturally prescribed versions of masculinity. Learning to use the sporting body for boys and men implies also learning to detach oneself from it (Morgan, 1992, p. 168). As a result, sensitization to bodily well-being and matters of preventive health in general become viewed as the jurisdiction of women and "ambiguous" men. Cultural prohibitions on health orientations for men outside of sport are, of course, visible in the disproportionate numbers of women found in doctors' offices, clinics, nursing, and other venues of health care provision (Hearn, 1992, p. 44). In sum, health care interests tend to be conspicuously absent in the task orientation of men in general. In sport, this may be witnessed as a link between the gendering of injury and the gendering of men's health.

One of the main objectives of this anthology is to raise critical questions regarding the future of men's interests. As Sabo (1992) has written: "The task remaining for future scholars is to incorporate the insights yielded by both feminist and men's studies to reveal alternative possibilities for the construction of masculinities not yet realized" (p. 39).

Because our findings point to versions of male prowess that may be deleterious and even destructive, as well as to conspicuous silences around health care and identity formation for men (Rutherford, 1992), we suggest that sport is an important area for future inquiry. Exploring connections between sports culture, gender construction, and health will place students of men's lives in a more informed position to develop practical solutions to the abusive potential of traditional masculinity codes. Such students will no doubt discover within current male task orientations and ideologies a number of vulnerabilities and anxieties so far provided scarce opportunity for legitimate expression.

References

Adams, S., Adrian, M., & Bayless, M. (Eds.). (1987). Catastrophic injuries in sports: Avoidance strategies. Indianapolis, IN: Benchmark.

Bryson, L. (1987). Sport and the maintenance of masculine hegemony. Women's Studies International Forum, 10(4), 349-360.

Colburn, K. (1985). Honor, ritual and violence in ice hockey. Canadian Journal of Sociology, 10(2), 153-170.

Connell, R. (1983). Which way is up? Essays on sex, class and culture. Sidney: Allen and Unwin.

Connolly, A. (1990, November 15). Sport injuries cost $1 billion a year. The Australian, p. 4.

Crosset, T. W. (1990). Masculinity, sexuality and the development of early modern sport. In M. Messner & D. Sabo (Eds.), *Sport, men, and the gender order: Critical feminist perspectives* (pp. 45-55). Champaign, IL: Human Kinetics.

Donald, R. (1992). Masculinity and machismo in Hollywood war films. In S. Craig (Ed.), *Men, masculinity and the media* (pp. 124-137). Newbury Park, CA: Sage.

Dunning, E. (1986). Sport as a male preserve: Notes on the social sources of masculine identity and its transformations. In N. Elias & E. Dunning (Eds.), *Quest for excitement: Sport and leisure in the civilizing process* (pp. 267-284). New York: Blackwell.

Farr, K. A. (1988). Dominance bonding through the good old boys sociability group. *Sex Roles, 18*(5/6), 259-278.

Faulkner, R. R. (1973). On respect and retribution: Toward an ethnography of violence. *Sociological Symposium, 9*, 17-36.

Foucault, M. (1979). *Discipline and punish: The birth of the prison.* New York: Pantheon.

Gagnon, J. (1974). Physical strength, once of significance. In J. Pleck & J. Sawyer (Eds.), *Men and masculinity* (pp. 139-149). Englewood Cliffs, NJ: Prentice Hall.

Hearn, J. (1992). *Men in the public eye: The construction and deconstruction of public men and public patriarchies.* New York: Routledge.

Kaplan, J. (1979). *Women and sports.* New York: Avon.

Kimmel, M. (1987). The contemporary crisis of masculinity in historical perspective. In H. Brod (Ed.), *The making of masculinities* (pp. 55-67). Boston: Allen and Unwin.

Kimmel, M. (1990). Baseball and the reconstitution of American masculinity, 1880-1920. In M. Messner & D. Sabo (Eds.), *Sport, men, and the gender order: Critical feminist perspectives* (pp. 55-67). Champaign, IL: Human Kinetics.

Lenskyj, H. (1986). *Out of bounds: Women, sport and sexuality.* Toronto, ON: Women's Press.

McKeever, W. (1913). *Training the boy.* New York: Macmillan.

Messner, M. (1990). When bodies are weapons: Masculinity and violence in sport. *International Review for the Sociology of Sport, 25*(3), 203-218.

Messner, M. (1992). Boyhood, organized sports, and the construction of masculinity. In M. Kimmel & M. Messner (Eds.), *Men's lives* (pp. 161-176). New York: Macmillan.

Messner, M., & Sabo, D. (1990). *Sport, men, and the gender order: Critical feminist perspectives.* Champaign, IL: Human Kinetics.

Miles, R. (1992). *The rites of man: Love, sex, and death in the making of the male.* Hammersmith, UK: Paladin.

Morgan, D. (1992). *Discovering men.* New York: Routledge.

Moriture te salutamus. (1992, January, 18). *The Economist*, p. 27.

Morse, M. (1983). Sport on television: Replay and display. In E. Kaplan (Ed.), *Regarding television: Critical approaches—an anthology (pp. 44-66).* Los Angeles: University Publication of America.

Rutherford, J. (1992). *Men's silences: Predicaments in masculinity.* New York: Routledge.

Sabo, D. (1986, Summer). Pigskin, patriarchy and pain. *Changing men: Issues in gender, sex and politics, 16*, 24-25.

Sabo, D. (1992). Masculinity as signs: Poststructuralist feminist approaches to the study of gender. In S. Craig (Ed.), *Men, masculinity and the media.* Newbury Park, CA: Sage.

Sabo, D., & Panepinto, J. (1990). Football ritual and the social reproduction of masculinity. In M. Messner & D. Sabo (Eds.), *Sport, men, and the gender order: Critical feminist perspectives* (pp. 115-127). Champaign, IL: Human Kinetics.

Smith, E. (1989). *Not just pumping iron: On the psychology of lifting weights.* Springfield, IL: Charles C. Thomas.

Smith, M. (1975). The legitimation of violence: Hockey players' perceptions of their reference groups' sanctions for assault. *Canadian Review of Sociology and Anthropology, 12,* 72-80.

Smith, M. (1987). *Violence in Canadian amateur sport: A review of literature.* Report for the Commission for Fair Play, Government of Canada.

Sykes, G., & Matza, D. (1989). Techniques of neutralization: A theory of delinquency. In D. Kelly (Ed.), *Deviant behavior: A text-reader in the sociology of deviance* (pp. 104-111). New York: St. Martin's.

Theberge, N. (1987). Sport and women's empowerment. *Women's Studies International Forum, 10*(4), 387-393.

Underwood, J. (1979). *The death of an American game: The crisis in football.* Boston: Little, Brown.

White, P., & Gillett, J. (1994). Reading the muscular body: A critical decoding of advertisements in *Flex* magazine. *Sociology of Sport Journal, 11,* 18-39.

White, P., & Vagi, A. (1990). Rugby in the 19th century British boarding school system: A feminist psychoanalytic perspective. In M. Messner & D. Sabo (Eds.), *Sport, men and the gender order: Critical feminist perspectives* (pp. 67-79). Champaign, IL: Human Kinetics.

Young, K. (1991, November 6-9). *Writers, rimmers and slotters: Privileging violence in the construction of the sports page.* Paper presented at the North American Society for the Sociology of Sport, Milwaukee, WI.

Young, K. (1993). Violence, risk, and liability in male sports culture. *Sociology of Sport Journal, 10,* 373-396.

9

Coming to Terms

Masculinity and Physical Disability

THOMAS J. GERSCHICK
ADAM S. MILLER

Men with physical disabilities are marginalized and stigmatized in American society. The image and reality of men with disabilities undermines cultural beliefs about men's bodies and physicality. The body is a central foundation of how men define themselves and how they are defined by others. Bodies are vehicles for determining value, which in turn translates into status and prestige. Men's bodies allow them to demonstrate the socially valuable characteristics of toughness, competitiveness, and ability (Messner, 1992). Thus, one's body and relationship to it provide a way to apprehend the world and one's place in it. The bodies of men with disabilities serve as a continual reminder that they are at odds with the expectations of the dominant culture. As anthropologist Robert Murphy (1990) writes of his own experiences with disability: "Paralytic disability constitutes emasculation of a more direct and total nature. For the male, the weakening and atrophy of the body threaten all the cultural values of

AUTHORS' NOTE: We would like to thank our informants for sharing their time, experiences, and insights. Additionally, we would like to thank the following people for their comments on earlier drafts of this work: Sandra Cole, Harlan Hahn, Michael Kimmel, Michael Messner, Don Sabo, and Margaret Weigers. We, of course, remain responsible for its content. Finally, we are indebted to Kimberly Browne and Erika Gottfried for background research and interview transcriptions. This research was supported by a grant from the Undergraduate Research Opportunity Program at the University of Michigan.

masculinity: strength, activeness, speed, virility, stamina, and fortitude" (p. 94).

This chapter seeks to sharpen our understanding of the creation, maintenance, and recreation of gender identities by men who by birth, accident, or illness find themselves dealing with a physical disability. We examine two sets of social dynamics that converge and clash in the lives of men with physical disabilities. On the one side, these men must deal with the presence and pressures of hegemonic masculinity, which demand strength. On the other side, societal members perceive people with disabilities to be weak.

For the present study, we conducted in-depth interviews with 10 men with physical disabilities to gain insights into the psychosocial aspects of men's ability to come to terms with their physical and social condition. We wanted to know how men with physical disabilities respond to the demands of hegemonic masculinity and their marginalization. For instance, if men with disabilities need others to legitimate their gender identity during encounters, what happens when others deny them the opportunity? How do they reconcile the conflicting expectations associated with masculinity and disability? How do they define masculinity for themselves and what are the sources of these definitions? To what degree do their responses contest or perpetuate the current gender order? That is, what are the political implications of different gender identities and practices? In addressing these questions, we contribute to the growing body of literature on marginalized and alternative gender identities.

In this chapter, we first discuss the general relationship between physical disability and hegemonic masculinity. Second, we summarize the methods used in this study. Next, we present and discuss our central findings. Finally, we discuss how the gender identities and life practices of men with disabilities contribute to the politics of the gender order.

Hegemonic Masculinity
and Physical Disability

Recently, the literature has shifted toward understanding gender as an interactive process. Thus, it is presumed to be not only an aspect of what one is but also more fundamentally it is something that one does in interaction with others (West & Zimmerman, 1987). Whereas previously gender was thought to be strictly an individual phenomenon, this new understanding directs attention to the interpersonal and institutional levels as well. The lives of men with disabilities provide an instructive arena in which to study the interactional nature of gender and its effect on individual gender identities.

In the book *The Body Silent,* Murphy (1990) observes that men with physical disabilities experience "embattled identities" because of the conflicting expectations placed upon them as men and as people with disabilities. On the one side, contemporary masculinity privileges men who are strong, courageous, aggressive, independent, and self-reliant (Connell, 1987). On the other side, people with disabilities are perceived to be, and are treated as, weak, pitiful, passive, and dependent (Murphy, 1990). Thus, for men with physical disabilities, masculine gender identity and practice are created and maintained at the crossroads of the demands of contemporary masculinity and the stigmatization associated with disability. Thus, for men with physical disabilities, being recognized as masculine by others is especially difficult, if not impossible, to accomplish. Yet not being recognized as masculine is untenable because in our culture, everyone is expected to display an appropriate gender identity (West & Zimmerman, 1987).

Methods

This research was based on in-depth interviews with 10 men. Despite the acknowledged problem of identity management in interviews, we used this method because we were most interested in the subjective perceptions and experience of our informants. To mitigate this dynamic, we relied on probing questions and reinterviews. Informants were located through a snowball sample, using friends and connections within the community of people with disabilities. All of our informants were given pseudonyms, and we further protected their identity by deleting nonessential personal detail. The age range of respondents varied from 16 to 72. Eight of our respondents were white, two were African American. Geographically, they came from both coasts and the Midwest. All were "mobility-impaired" and most were para- or quadriplegics. Given the small sample size and the modicum of diversity within it, this work must necessarily be understood as exploratory.

We interviewed men with physical disabilities for three primary reasons. First, given the diversity of disabilities and our modest resources, we had to bound the sample. Second, mobility impairments tend to be more apparent than other disabilities, such as blindness or hearing loss, and people respond to these men using visual clues. Third, although the literature in this area is scant, much of it focuses on men with physical disabilities.

Due to issues of shared identities, Adam did all the interviews. Interviews were semistructured and tape-recorded. Initial interviews averaged approximately an hour in length. Additionally, we contacted all of our informants at least once with clarifying questions and, in some cases, to test ideas that we had. These follow-ups lasted approximately 30 minutes. Each informant received a copy of his interview transcript to ensure that we had captured his perspective accurately. We also shared draft copies of this chapter with them and incorporated their insights into the current version.

There were two primary reasons for the thorough follow-up. First, from a methodological standpoint, it was important for us to capture the experience of our informants as fully as possible. Second, we felt that we had an obligation to allow them to control, to a large extent, the representation of their experience.

Interviews were analyzed using an analytic induction approach (Denzin, 1989; Emerson, 1988; Katz, 1988). In determining major and minor patterns of masculine practice, we used the responses to a series of questions including: What is the most important aspect of masculinity to you? What would you say makes you feel most manly or masculine? Do you think your conception of masculinity is different from that of able-bodied men as a result of your disability? If so, how? If so, why? If not, why not? Additionally, we presented our informants with a list of characteristics associated with prevailing masculinity based on the work of R. W. Connell (1987, 1990a, 1990b, 1991) and asked them to rate their importance to their conception of self. Both positive and negative responses to this portion of our questionnaire guided our insight into how each man viewed his masculinity. To further support our discussion, we turned to the limited academic literature in this area. Much more helpful were the wide range of biographical and autobiographical accounts of men who have physical disabilities (see, for instance, Callahan, 1989; Hahn, 1989; Kriegel, 1991; Murphy, 1990; Zola, 1982).

Finally, in analyzing the data, we were sensitive to making judgments about our informants when grouping them into categories. People with disabilities are "shoehorned" into categories too much as it is. We sought to discover what was common among their responses and to highlight what we perceived to be the essence of their views. In doing so, we endeavored to provide a conceptual framework for understanding the responses of men with physical disabilities, while trying to be sensitive to their personal struggles.

Disability, Masculinity, and Coming to Terms

Although no two men constructed their sense of masculinity in exactly the same way, there appeared to be three dominant frameworks our informants used to cope with their situations. These patterns can be conceived of in relation to the standards inherent in dominant masculinity. We call them the three Rs: *reformulation,* which entailed men's redefinition of hegemonic characteristics on their own terms; *reliance,* reflected by sensitive or hypersensitive adoptions of particular predominant attributes; and *rejection,* characterized by the renunciation of these standards and either the creation of one's own principles and practices or the denial of masculinity's importance in one's life. However, one should note that none of our interviewees entirely followed any one of these frameworks in defining his sense of self. Rather, for heuristic reasons, it is best to speak of the major and minor ways each man used these three patterns. For example, some of our informants relied on dominant standards in their view of sexuality and occupation, but also reformulated the prevailing ideal of independence.

Therefore, we discuss the primary way in which these men with disabilities related to hegemonic masculinity's standards, while recognizing that their coping mechanisms reflected a more complex combination of strategies. In doing so, we avoid labeling men and assigning them to arbitrary categories.

Reformulation

Some of our informants responded to idealized masculinity by reformulating it, shaping it along the lines of their own abilities, perceptions, and strengths, thus defining their manhood along these new lines. These men tended not to overtly contest these standards but—either consciously or unconsciously—recognized in their own condition an inability to meet these ideals as they were culturally conceived. An example of this came from Damon, a 72-year-old quadriplegic who survived a spinal-cord injury in an automobile accident 10 years earlier. Damon said that he had always desired, and had, control of his life. Although Damon required round-the-clock personal care assistants (PCAs), he asserted that he was still a very independent person:

> I direct all of my activities around my home where people have to help me to maintain my apartment, my transportation which I own and direction in where I go. I direct people how to get there and I tell them what my needs will be when I am going and coming, and when to get where I am going.

Damon said that his sense of control was more than mere illusion; it was a reality others knew of as well. This reputation seemed important to him:

> People know from Jump Street that I have my own thing and I direct my own thing. And if they can't comply with my desire, they won't be around. . . . I don't see any reason why people with me can't take instructions and get my life on just as I was having it before, only thing I'm not doing it myself. I direct somebody else to do it. So, therefore, I don't miss out on very much.

Hegemonic masculinity's definition of independence privileges self-reliance and autonomy. Damon required substantial assistance: indeed, some might term him *dependent*. However, Damon's reformulation of the independence ideal, accomplished in part through a cognitive shift, allowed him to think otherwise.

Harold, a 46-year-old polio survivor, described a belief and practice akin to Damon's. Also a quadriplegic, Harold similarly required PCAs to help him handle daily necessities. Harold termed his reliance on and control of PCAs *acting through others:* "When I say independence can be achieved by acting through other people, I actually mean getting through life, liberty and the pursuit of happiness while utilizing high quality and dependable attendant care services."

As with Damon, Harold achieved his perceived sense of independence by controlling others. Harold stressed that he did not count on family or friends to do favors for him, but employed his PCAs in a business relationship he controlled. Alternatives to family and friends are used whenever possible because most people with disabilities do not want to burden or be dependent on their families any more than necessary (Murphy, 1990).

Social class plays an important role here. Damon and Harold had the economic means to afford round-the-clock assistance. Although none of our informants experienced economic hardship, many people with disabilities depend on the welfare system for their care, and the amount and quality of assistance they receive would make it much more difficult to conceive of themselves as independent.

A third man who reformulated predominant demands was Brent, a 45-year-old administrator. He told us that his paraplegic status, one that he had lived with since he was 5 years old, had often cast him as an "outsider" to society. This status was particularly painful in his late adolescence, a time when the "sexual revolution" was sweeping America's youth:

> A very important measure of somebody's personhood—manhood—was their sexual ability. . . . What bothers me more than anything else is the stereotypes, and even more so, in terms of sexual desirability. Because I had a disability, I was less desirable than able-bodied people. And that I found very frustrating.

His experiences led him to recast the hegemonic notion that man's relations with a partner should be predominantly physical. As a result, he stressed the importance of emotional relations and trust. This appeared key to Brent's definition of his manhood:

> For me that is my measure of who I am as an individual and who I am as a man—my ability to be able to be honest with my wife. Be able to be close with her, to be able to ask for help, provide help. To have a commitment, to follow through and to do all those things that I think are important.

As Connell (1990b) notes, this requires a capacity to not only be expressive but also to have feelings worth expressing. This clearly demonstrates a different form of masculine practice.

The final case of reformulation came from Robert, a 30-year-old survivor of a motorcycle accident. Able-bodied for much of his life, Robert's accident occurred when he was 24, leaving him paraplegic. Through 5 years of intensive physical therapy, he regained 95% of his original function, though certain effects linger to this day.

Before his accident, Robert had internalized many of the standards of dominant masculinity exemplified by frequenting bars, leading an active sex life, and riding a motorcycle. But, if our research, and the body of autobiographical works from men with physical disabilities, has shown anything, it is that coming to terms with a disability eventually changes a person. It appeared to have transformed Robert. He remarked that despite being generally "recovered," he had maintained his disability-influenced value system:

> I judge people on more of a personal and character level than I do on any physical, or I guess I did, but you know important things are guys that have integrity, guys that are honest about what they are doing that have some

direction in their life and know what, you know, peace of mind and what they stand for.

One of the areas that Robert said took the longest to recover was his sexuality—specifically, his confidence in his sexual ability. Although Robert said sexual relations were still important to him, like Brent he reformulated his previous, largely hegemonic notion of male sexuality into a more emotionally and physically egalitarian model:

> I've found a whole different side to having sex with a partner and looking at satisfying the partner rather than satisfying myself, and that has taken the focus off of satisfying myself and being the big manly stud and concentrating more on my partner and that has become just as satisfying.

However, reformulation did not yield complete severance from prevailing masculinity's standards as they were culturally conceived. For instance, despite his reformulative inclinations, Robert's self-described "macho" attitude continued in some realms during his recovery. He, and all others we interviewed, represented the complexity of gender identities and practices; no man's masculinity fell neatly into any one of the three patterns.

For instance, though told by most doctors that his physical condition was probably permanent, Robert's resolve was unyielding. "I put my blinders on to all negative insight into it and just totally focused on getting better," he said. "And I think that was, you know, a major factor on why I'm where I'm at today." This typified the second pattern we identified— reliance on hegemonic masculinity's standards. It was ironic, then, that Robert's tenacity, his never-ending work ethic, and his focused drive to succeed, were largely responsible for his almost complete recovery. While Robert reformulated much of his earlier sense of masculinity, he still relied on this drive.

Perhaps the area in which men who reformulate most closely paralleled dominant masculinity was the emphasis they placed on their occupation. Our sample was atypical in that most of our informants were professionally employed on a full-time basis and could therefore draw on class-based resources, whereas unemployment among people with disabilities is very high. Just as societal members privilege men who are accomplished in their occupation, Harold said he finds both purpose, and success, in his career: "No one is going to go through life without some kind of purpose. Everyone decides. I wanted to be a writer. So I became a writer and an observer, a trained observer."

Brent said that he drew much of his sense of self, his sense of self-esteem, and his sense of manhood from his occupational accomplishments. Initially, Brent denied the importance of the prevailing ideal that a man's occupational worth was derived from his "breadwinner" status:

> It is not so important to be the breadwinner as it is to be competent in the world, you know, to have a career, to have my name on the door. That is what is most important. It is that recognition that is very important to me.

However, he later admitted that being the breadwinner still was important to him, though he denied a link between his desires and the stereotypical conception of breadwinner status. He maintained that "it's still important to me, because I've always been able to make money." Independence, both economic and physical, were important to all of our informants.

Rejection of hegemonic ideals also occurred among men who primarily depended on a reformulative framework. Harold's view of relationships with a partner dismissed the sexually powerful ideal: "The fact of the matter is that I'm not all that upset by the fact that I'm disabled and I'm a male. I mean, I know what I can do." We will have more to say about the rejection of dominant conceptions of sexuality below.

In brief summary, the subset of our informants whose primary coping pattern involved reformulation of dominant standards recognized their inability to meet these ideals as they are culturally conceived. Confident in their own abilities and values, and drawing from previous experience, they confronted standards of masculinity on their own terms. In doing so, they distanced themselves from masculine ideals.

Reliance

However, not all of the men with physical disabilities we interviewed depended on a reformulative approach. We found that many of our informants were concerned with others' views of their masculinity and with meeting the demands of hegemonic masculinity. They primarily used the second pattern, reliance, which involved the internalization of many more of the ideals of predominant masculinity, including physical strength, athleticism, independence, and sexual prowess. Just as some men depended on reformulation for much of their masculine definition, others, despite their inability to meet many of these ideals, relied on them heavily. As such, these men did not seem to be as comfortable with their sense of manhood; indeed, their inability to meet society's standards bothered them very much.

This subset of our informants found themselves in a double bind that left them conflicted. They embraced dominant conceptions of masculinity as a way to gain acceptance from themselves and from others. Yet they were continuously reminded in their interactions with others that they were "incomplete." As a result, the identity behind the facade suffered; there were, then, major costs associated with this strategy.

The tension between societal expectations and the reality of men with physical disabilities was most clearly demonstrated by Jerry, a 16 year old who had juvenile rheumatoid arthritis. While Jerry was physically able to walk for limited distances, this required great effort on his part; consequently, he usually used a wheelchair. He was concerned with the appearance of his awkward walking. "I feel like I look a little, I don't know, more strange when I walk," he said.

The significance of appearance and external perception of manliness is symptomatic of the difficulty men with physical disabilities have in developing an identity and masculinity free of others' perceptions and expectations. Jerry said:

> I think [others' conception of what defines a man] is very important because if they don't think of you as one, it is hard to think of yourself as one or it doesn't really matter if you think of yourself as one if no one else does.

Jerry said that, particularly among his peers, he was not perceived as attractive as the able-bodied teenagers; consequently, he had difficulty in male-female relations, beyond landing an occasional date. "[The girls believe] I might be a 'really nice person,' but not like a guy per se," he said. "I think to some extent that you're sort of genderless to them." This clearly represents the emasculation and depersonalization inherent in social definitions of disability.

However, Jerry said that he faced a more persistent threat to his autonomy—his independence and his sense of control—from others being uncomfortable around him, and persisting in offering him assistance he often did not need. This made him angry, though he usually did not refuse the help out of politeness. Thus, with members of his social group, he participated in a "bargain": They would socialize with him as long as he remained in a dependent position where they could "help" him.

This forced, situational passivity led Jerry to emphasize his autonomy in other areas. For instance, Jerry avoided asking for help in nearly all situations. This was directly tied to reinforcing his embattled manhood by displaying outward strength and independence:

If I ever have to ask someone for help, it really makes me like feel like less of a man. I don't like asking for help at all. You know, like even if I could use some, I'll usually not ask just because I can't, I just hate asking . . . [a man is] fairly self-sufficient in that you can sort of handle just about any situation in that you can help other people and that you don't need a lot of help.

Jerry internalized the prevailing masculine ideal that a man should be independent; he relied on that ideal for his definition of manhood. His inability to meet this ideal—partly through his physical condition, and partly from how others treated him—threatened his identity and his sense of manhood, which had to be reinforced even at the expense of self-alienation.

One should not label Jerry a *relier* simply because of these struggles. Being only 16 years of age—and the youngest participant in our study—Jerry was still developing his sense of masculinity, and as with many teenagers, both able-bodied and disabled, he was trying to fit into his peer group. Furthermore, Jerry will continue to mature and develop his self-image and sense of masculinity. A follow-up interview in 5 years might show a degree of resolution to his struggles.

Such a resolution could be seen in Michael, a 33-year-old manager we interviewed, who also internalized many of the standards of hegemonic masculinity. A paraplegic from an auto accident in 1977, Michael struggled for many years after his accident to come to terms with his condition.

His struggles had several sources, all tied into his view of masculinity's importance. The first was that before his accident he accepted much of the dominant conception of masculinity. A high school student, farm hand, football and track star at the time, Michael said that independence, relations with the women he dated, and physical strength were central to his conception of self.

After his accident, Michael's doctors told him there was a 50-50 chance that he would regain the ability to walk, and he clung to the hope. "I guess I didn't understand it, and had hope that I would walk again," he said. However, he said he was "depressed" about his situation, "but not so much about my disability I guess. Because that wasn't real yet."

But coming home 3 months after his accident did not alleviate the depression. Instead, it heightened his anxiety and added a new component— vulnerability. In a span of 3 months, Michael had, in essence, his sense of masculinity and his security in himself completely stripped away. He was in an unfamiliar situation, and far from feeling strong, independent, and powerful, he felt vulnerable and afraid. "No one," he remarked, "can be prepared for a permanent disability."

His reliance on dominant masculinity, then, started with his predisabil-
ity past, and continued during his recovery as a coping mechanism to deal
with his fears. The hegemonic standard Michael strove most to achieve
was that of independence. It was central to his sense of masculinity before,
and at the time of our interview. Indeed, it was so important that it
frustrated him greatly when he needed assistance. Much like Jerry, he
refused to ask for it:

> I feel that I should be able to do everything for myself and I don't like. . . . I
> don't mind asking for things that I absolutely can't do, like hanging pictures
> or moving furniture or having my oil changed in my car, but there are things
> that I'm capable of doing in my chair like jumping up one step. That I feel like
> I should be able to do and I find it frustrating when I can't do that sometimes
> . . . I don't like asking for [help I don't think I need]. It kind of makes me mad.

When asked if needing assistance was unmanly, Michael replied, "There's
probably some of that in there." For both Michael and Jerry, the independence ideal often led to risk-taking behavior to prove to themselves
that they were more than their social definition.

Yet much like Robert, Michael had reformulated his view of sexuality.
He said that his physical sexuality made him "feel the most masculine"—
apparently another reliant response with a stereotypical emphasis on sexual
performance. However, it was more complicated. Michael said that he no
longer concentrated on pleasing himself, as he did when able-bodied, but
that he now had a more partner-oriented view of sexuality. "I think that
my compensation for my feeling of vulnerability is I've overcompensated
by trying to please my partner and leave little room to allow my partner
to please me . . . some of my greatest pleasure is exhausting my partner
while having sex." Ironically, whereas he focused more on his partner's
pleasure than ever before, he did so at his own expense; a sense of balancing
the needs of both partners was missing.

Thus, sex served multiple purposes for Michael: It gave him, and his
partner, pleasure; it reassured his fears and his feelings of vulnerability;
and it reconfirmed his masculinity. His sexuality, then, reflected both
reliance and reformulation.

Although independence and sexuality were both extremely important
to Scott, a 34-year-old rehabilitation engineer, he emphasized a third
area for his sense of manhood—athletics. Scott served in the Peace Corps
during his 20s, working in Central America. He described his lifestyle as
"rigorous" and "into the whole sports thing," and used a mountain bike

as his primary means of transportation and recreation. He was also an avid hockey player in his youth, and spent his summers in softball leagues.

Scott acquired a poliolike virus when he was 25 years old that left him permanently paraplegic, a situation that he did not initially accept. In an aggressive attempt to regain his physical ability, and similar to Robert, Scott obsessively attacked his rehabilitation:

> Thinking, that's always what I've done with all the sports. If I wasn't good enough I worked a little harder and I got better. So, I kept thinking my walking isn't very good now. If I push it, it will get better.

However, Scott's athletic drive led not to miraculous recovery but over-exertion. When ordered by his doctors to scale back his efforts, he realized he could not recover strictly through tenacity. At the time of our interview, he was ambivalent about his limitations. He clearly did not feel like a failure: "I think that if I wouldn't have made the effort, I always would have wondered could I have made a difference." Following the athlete's code of conduct, "always give 110%," Scott attacked his recovery. But when his efforts were not enough—when he did not emerge victorious— he accepted it, as an athlete would. Yet his limitations also frustrated him at times and in different areas.

For example, though his physical capacity was not what it was, Scott maintained a need for athletic competition. He played wheelchair basket-ball, and was the only wheelchair participant in a city softball league. However, he did not return to hockey, the sport he loved as a youngster; in fact, he refused to even try the sled-based equivalent.

Here was Scott's frustration. His spirit of athleticism was still alive, but he lamented the fact that he could not compete exactly as before:

> [I miss] the things that I had. I played hockey, that was my primary sport for so many years. Pretty much I did all the sports. But, like I never played basketball, I never liked basketball before. Which is why I think I can play now. See, it would be like the equivalent to wheelchair hockey. Some friends of mine have talked to me about it, [but] I'm not really interested in that. Because it wouldn't be real hockey. And it would make me feel worse, rather that better.

In this respect, Scott had not completely come to terms with his limita-tions. He still wanted to be a "real" athlete, competing in the same sports, in the same ways, with the same rules, with others who shared his desire for competition. Wheelchair hockey, which he derogatorily referred to as "gimp hockey," represented the antithesis of this for him.

Scott's other responses added to this emphasis. What he most disliked about having a disability was "that I can't do the things that I want to be able to do," meaning he could not ride his bike or motorcycle, he could not play real hockey, and he was unable to live a freewheeling, spontaneous lifestyle. Rather, he had to plan ahead of time where he went and how he got there. The frustration caused by having to plan nearly every move was apparent in almost all of our interviews.

However, on the subject of independence, Scott said, "I think I'm mostly independent," but complained that there were some situations in which he could not meet his expectations and had to depend on his wife. He said that usually this was not a "major issue," but "there's still times when, yeah, I feel bad about it, or you know it's the days where she doesn't feel like it, but she kind of has to, that's what bothers me the most I guess." Thus, he reflected the general desire among men with disabilities not to be a burden of any kind on family members.

Much of the time, Scott accepted being "mostly independent." His reliance on the ideals of athleticism and independence played a significant part in his conception of masculinity and self. However, Scott learned, though to a limited degree, to let go of some of his previous ideals and to accept a different, reformulated notion of independence and competition. Yet he could not entirely do so. His emphasis on athletics and independence was still strong, and there were many times when athletics and acceptance conflicted.

However, one should stop short of a blanket assessment of men with disabilities who rely on hegemonic masculinity standards. *Always* is a dangerous word, and stating that "men who rely on hegemonic standards are always troubled" is a dangerous statement. An apparent exceptional case among men who follow a reliant pattern came from Aaron, a 41-year-old paraplegic. Rather than experiencing inner turmoil and conflict, Aaron was one of the most upbeat individuals we interviewed. Aaron said that before his 1976 accident he was "on top of the world," with a successful business, a commitment to athletics that included basketball shoot-arounds with NBA prospects, and a wedding engagement. Indeed, from the time of his youth, Aaron relied on such hegemonic standards as sexuality, independence, athleticism, and occupational accomplishment.

For example, when asked what masculinity meant to him before his accident, Aaron said that it originally meant sexual conquest. As a teen, he viewed frequent sexual activity as a "rite of passage" into manhood.

Aaron said he had also enjoyed occupational success, and that this success was central to his definition of self, including being masculine.

Working a variety of jobs ranging from assembly line worker to white-collar professional, Aaron said, "I had been very fortunate to have good jobs which were an important part of who I was and how I defined myself."

Aaron said that much of his independence ideal came from his father. When his parents divorced, Aaron's father explained to him that, though he was only 5, he would have to be "the man of the house." Aaron took this lesson to heart, and strived to fulfill this role in both independence and providing for the family. "My image of manhood was that of a provider," he said, "one who was able to make a contribution to the financial stability of the family in addition to dealing with the problems and concerns that would come up."

His accident, a gunshot wound injuring his spinal cord, left him completely dependent. Predictably, Aaron could not immediately cope with this. "My whole self-image itself was real integrally tied up with the things I used to do," he said. "I found my desire for simple pleasures to be the greatest part of the pain I had to bear."

His pain increased when he left the hospital. His fiancee had left him, and within 2 years he lost "everything that was important to me"—his house, his business, his savings, most of his friends, even, for a while, his hope.

However, much as with Robert, Aaron's resiliency eventually turned his life around. Just as he hit bottom, he began telling himself that "if you hold on long enough, if you don't quit, you'll get through it." Additionally, he attacked his therapy with the vengeance he had always devoted to athletics. "I'd never been confronted with a situation in my entire life before that I was not able to overcome by the efforts of my own merit," he said. "I took the same attitude toward this."

Further, he reasserted his sexuality. Though he then wore a colostomy bag, he resumed frequent sexual intercourse, taking the attitude that "this is who I was and a woman was either going to have to accept me as I was, or she's got to leave me the —— alone."

However, he realized after those 5 years that his hard work would not be rewarded nor would he be miraculously healed. Figuring that "there's a whole lot of life that I need to live and this wasn't the most efficient way to live it," he bought a new sport wheelchair, found a job, and became involved in wheelchair athletics. In this sense, a complex combination of all three patterns emerged in Aaron, as reliance was mixed with reformulation and rejection.

Furthermore, his soul-searching led him to develop a sense of purpose in his life, and a reason for going on:

[During my recovery] I felt that I was left here to enrich the lives of as many people as I could before I left this earth, and it gave me a new purpose, a new vision, a new mission, new dreams.

Tenacity, the quest for independence, athletics, and sexual activity carried Aaron through his recovery. Many of these ideals, which had their source in his father's teachings, remained with him, as he continued to be active in athletics (everything from basketball to softball to scuba diving), to assert his sexuality, and to aim for complete autonomy. To Aaron, independence, both physical and financial, was more than just a personal ideal, it was one that should be shared by all people with disabilities. As such, he aspired to be a role model for others:

The work that I am involved in is to help people gain control over their lives and I think it's vitally important that I walk my talk. If . . . we hold ourselves out to be an organization that helps people gain control over their lives, I think it's vitally important for me as the CEO of that organization to live my life in a way that embodies everything that we say we're about.

Clearly, Aaron was not the same man he was before his disability. He said that his maturity and his experience with disability "made me stronger," and that manhood no longer simply meant independence and sexual conquest. Manhood also meant

being responsible for one's actions, being considerate of another's feelings, being sensitive to individuals who are more vulnerable than yourself to what their needs would be, standing up on behalf and fighting for those who cannot speak out for themselves, fight for themselves. It means being willing to take a position and be committed to a position even when it's inconvenient or costly to take that point of view and you do it only because of the principle involved.

This dovetailed significantly with his occupation, which was of great importance to him. But as alluded to above, Aaron's emphasis on occupation cannot be seen as mere reliance on the hegemonic conception of occupational achievement. It was more a reformulation of that ideal from self-achievement to facilitating the empowerment of others.

Nevertheless, Aaron's struggle to gain his current status, like the struggle of others who rely on hegemonic masculinity's standards, was immense. Constructing hegemonic masculinity from a subordinated position is almost always a sisyphean task. One's ability to do so is undermined continuously by physical, social, and cultural weakness. "Understandably, in an effort to cope with this stress [balancing the demands for strength and the societal perception of weakness]," writes political scientist Harlan Hahn, "many disabled men have tended to identify personally and politically with the supposed strength of prevalent concepts of masculinity rather than with their disability" (1989, p. 3). To relinquish masculinity under these circumstances is to court gender annihilation, which is untenable to some men. Consequently, relying on hegemonic masculinity becomes more understandable (Connell, 1990b, p. 471).

Rejection

Despite the difficulties it presents, hegemony, including that related to gender, is never complete (Janeway, 1980; Scott, 1985). For some of our informants, resistance took the form of creating alternative masculine identities and subcultures that provided them with a supportive environment. These men were reflected in the final pattern: rejection. Informants who followed this pattern did not so much share a common ideology or set of practices, rather they believed that the dominant conception of masculinity was wrong, either in its individual emphases or as a practice. One of these men developed new standards of masculinity in place of the ones he had rejected. Another, seemingly, chose to deny masculinity's importance, though he was neither effeminate or androgynous. Instead, they both emphasized their status as *persons,* under the motto of "people first." This philosophy reflected a key tenet of the disability rights movement.

Alex, a 23-year-old, first-year law student, survived an accident that left him an incomplete quadriplegic when he was 14. Before that time, he felt he was an outsider at his private school because he eschewed the superficial, athletically oriented, and materialistic atmosphere. Further, he said the timing of the accident, when many of his peers were defining their social roles, added to this outsider perspective in that it made him unable to participate in the highly social, role-forming process. "I didn't learn about the traditional roles of sexuality and whatever the rules are for such behavior in our society until later," he said. "Because of my physical characteristics, I had to learn a different set of rules."

Alex described himself as a "nonconformist." This simple moniker appeared to be central to his conception of selfhood and masculinity. Alex, unlike men who primarily reformulate these tenets, rejected the attitudinal and behavioral prescriptions of hegemonic masculinity. He maintained that his standards were his own—not society's—and he scoffed at commonly held views of masculinity.

For example, Alex blamed the media for the idea that men must be strong
and attractive, stating "the traditional conception is that everyone has to
be Arnold Schwarzenegger . . . [which] probably lead[s] to some violence,
unhappiness and things like that if they [men] don't meet the standards."

As for the importance of virility and sexual prowess, Alex said "there
is a part of me that, you know, has been conditioned and acculturated and
knows those [dominant] values," but he sarcastically laughed at the notion
of a man's sexual prowess being reflected in "making her pass out" and
summed up his feelings on the subject by adding "you have to be willing
to do things in a nontraditional way."

Alex's most profound rejection of a dominant ideal involved the importance of fathering, in its strictest sense of the man as impregnator:

> There's no reason why we [his fiancée and himself] couldn't use artificial
> insemination or adoption. Parenting doesn't necessarily involve being the male
> sire. It involves being a good parent . . . That's, that's not the sole definition
> of, parenting doesn't mean that it's your physical child. It involves responsi-
> bility and an emotional role as well. I don't think the link between parenthood
> is the primary link with sexuality. Maybe in terms of evolutionary purposes,
> but not in terms of a relationship.

Thus, Alex rejected the procreation imperative encouraged in hegemonic
masculinity. However, although Alex took pride at overtly rejecting prevailing masculinity as superficial and silly, even he relied on it at times.
Alex said he needed to support himself financially, and would not ever
want to be an emotional or economic burden in a relationship. On one
level, this is a common concern for most people, disabled or not. But on
another level, Alex admitted that it tied into his sense of masculinity:

> If I was in a relationship and I wasn't working, and my spouse was, what could
> be the possible reasons for my not working? I could have just been fired. I
> could be laid off. Who knows what happened? I guess, I can see an element of,
> but that's definitely an element of masculinity and I guess I am just as
> influenced by that as, oh, as I guess as other people, or as within my definition
> of masculinity. What do you know? I have been caught.

A different form of rejection was reflected in Leo, a 58-year-old polio
survivor. Leo, who had striven for occupational achievement since his youth,
seemed to value many hegemonic traits: independence, money-making
ability, and recognition by peers. But, he steadfastly denied masculinity's
role in shaping his outlook.

Leo said the most important trait to him was his mental capacity and intelligence, because that allowed him to achieve his occupational goals. Yet he claimed this was not related to the prevailing standard. Rather, it tied into his ambitions from before his disability and his willingness to do most anything to achieve his goals.

Before we label him a "rejector," however, note that Leo was a believer in adaptive technology and personal assistance, and he did not see a contradiction between using personal care assistants and being independent. This seemed to be a reformulation, just as with Damon and Harold, but when we asked Leo about this relation to masculinity, he flatly denied any connection.

Leo explained his renunciation of masculinity by saying "it doesn't mean a great deal . . . it's not how I think [of things]." He said that many of the qualities on our list of hegemonic characteristics were important to him on an individual level, but did not matter to his sense of manhood. Leo maintained that there were *external* and *internal* reasons for this.

The external factors Leo identified were the women's and disability rights movements. Both provided support and alternatives that allow a person with a disability the freedom to be a person, and not (to use Leo's words) a "strange bird." Indeed, Leo echoed the call of the Disability Rights Movement when he described himself as a "person first." In this way, his humanity took precedence and his gender and his disability became less significant.

Also, Leo identified his background as a contributing factor to his outlook. Since childhood, he held a group of friends that valued intellectual achievement over physical performance. In his youth, Leo said he was a member of a group "on the college route." He remained in academia.

Internally, his view of masculinity came from maturity. He dealt with masculinity and related issues for almost 60 years, and reached a point at which he was comfortable with his gender. According to him, his gender conceptions ranged across all three patterns. This was particularly evident in his sexuality. When younger, he relied on a culturally valued, genital sexuality and was concerned with his potency. He wanted to "be on top," despite the physical difficulties this presented him. At the time of our interview, he had a reformulated sexuality. The Women's Movement allowed him to remain sexually active without worrying about being on top. He even rejected the idea (but not necessarily the physical condition) of potency, noting that it was "even a funny word—*potent*—that's power."

Further, his age allowed Leo to let go of many of the expectations he had for himself when younger. For instance, he used to overcompensate with great physical activity to prove his manhood and to be "a good daddy." But, he said he gradually learned that such overcompensation was not necessary.

The practice of "letting go," as Leo and many of our other informants had done, was much like that described by essayist Leonard Kriegel (1991), who in a series of autobiographical essays discussed the metaphor of "falling into life" as a way of coping with a disability and masculinity. Kriegel described a common reaction to coping with disability, that is, attempting to overcome the results of polio, in his case, by building his upper body strength through endless hours of exercise. In the end, he experienced premature arthritis in his shoulders and arms. The metaphor of giving up or letting go of behavioral expectations and gender practices as a way to gain greater strength and control over one's life was prevalent among the men who primarily rejected dominant masculinity. As Hahn (1989) notes, this requires a cognitive shift as well as a change in reference group and a source of social support:

> I think, ironically, that men with disabilities can acquire strength by acknowledging weakness. Instead of attempting to construct a fragile and ultimately phony identity only as males, they might have more to gain, and little to lose, both individually and collectively by forging a self-concept about the concept of disability. Certainly this approach requires the exposure of a vulnerability that has been a primary reason for the elaborate defense mechanisms that disabled men have commonly employed to protect themselves. (p. 3)

Thus, men with disabilities who rejected or renounced masculinity did so as a process of deviance disavowal. They realized that it was societal conceptions of masculinity, rather than themselves, that were problematic. In doing so, they were able to create alternative gender practices. The role of the Disability Rights Movement in this framework is discussed following.

Conclusion

The experiences of men with physical disabilities are important because they illuminate both the insidious power and the limitations of contemporary masculinity. These men have insider knowledge of what the subordinated know about both the gender and social order (Janeway, 1980). Additionally, the gender practices of some of these men exemplify alternative visions of masculinity that are obscured, but available to men in our culture. Finally, they allow us to elucidate a process of paramount importance: how men with physical disabilities find happiness, fulfillment, and a sense of self-worth in a culture that has, in essence, denied them the right to their own identity, including their own masculinity.

Based on our interviews, then, we believe that men with physical disabilities depend on at least three patterns in their adjustment to the double bind associated with the demands of hegemonic masculinity and the stigmatization of being disabled. Although each of our informants used one pattern more than the others, none of them depended entirely on any one of the three.

To judge the patterns and practices associated with any form of masculinity, it is necessary to explore the implications for both the personal life of the individual and the effect on the reproduction of the societal gender order (Connell, 1990a). Different patterns will challenge, comply, or actively support gendered arrangements.

The reliance pattern is reflected by an emphasis on control, independence, strength, and concern for appearances. Men who rely on dominant conceptions of masculinity are much more likely to internalize their feelings of inadequacy and seek to compensate or overcompensate for them. Because the problem is perceived to be located within oneself, rather than within the social structure, this model does not challenge, but rather perpetuates, the current gender order.

A certain distancing from dominant ideals occurs in the reformulation pattern. But reformulation tends to be an independent project, and class-based resources play an important role. As such, it doesn't present a formidable challenge to the gender order. Connell (1990b, p. 474) argues that this response may even modernize patriarchy.

The rejection model, the least well represented in this chapter, offers the most hope for change. Linked closely to a sociopolitical approach that defines disability as a product of interactions between individuals and their environment, disability (and masculinity) is understood as socially constructed.

Members of the disability rights movement, as a result, seek to reconstruct masculinity through a three-prong strategy. First, they focus on changing the frame of reference regarding who defines disability and masculinity, thereby changing the dynamics of social construction of both. Second, they endeavor to help people with disabilities be more self-referent when defining their identities. To do that, a third component must be implemented: support structures, such as alternative subcultures, must exist. If the disability rights movement is successful in elevating this struggle to the level of collective practice, it will challenge the legitimacy of the institutional arrangements of the current gender order.

In closing, there is much fruitful work to be done in the area of masculinity and disability. For instance, we should expect men with disabilities to respond differently to the demands associated with disability and masculinity due to factors such as sexual orientation, social class, age of onset of one's disability, and race and ethnicity. However, *how* and *why* gender identity varies for men with disabilities merits further study. We hope that this work serves as an impetus for others to take up issues such as these.

References

Callahan, J. (1989). *Don't worry, he won't get far on foot.* New York: Vintage.

Connell, R. W. (1987). *Gender and power: Society, the person, and sexual politics.* Stanford, CA: Stanford University Press.

Connell, R. W. (1990a). An iron man: The body and some contradictions of hegemonic masculinity. In M. Messner & D. Sabo (Eds.), *Sport, men, and the gender order* (pp. 83-96). Champaign, IL: Human Kinetics.

Connell, R. W. (1990b). A whole new world: Remaking masculinity in the context of the environmental movement. *Gender & Society, 4*(4), 452-478.

Connell, R. W. (1991) Live fast and die young: The construction of masculinity among young working-class men on the margin of the labor market. *Australian and New Zealand Journal of Sociology, 27*(2), 141-171.

Denzin, N. (1989). *The research act: A theoretical introduction to sociological methods.* Englewood Cliffs, NJ: Prentice Hall.

Emerson, R. (1988). Introduction. In R. Emerson (Ed.), *Contemporary field research: A collection of readings* (pp. 93-107). Prospect Heights, IL: Waveland Press.

Hahn, H. (1989). Masculinity and disability. *Disability Studies Quarterly, 9*(3), 1-3.

Janeway, E. (1980). *Powers of the weak.* New York: Knopf.

Katz, J. (1988). A theory of qualitative methodology: The social system of analytic fieldwork. In R. Emerson (Ed.), *Contemporary field research: A collection of readings* (pp. 127-148). Prospect Heights, IL: Waveland Press.

Kriegel, L. (1991). *Falling into life.* San Francisco: North Point Press.

Messner, M. (1992). *Power at play: Sports and the problem of masculinity.* Boston: Beacon.

Murphy, R. F. (1990). *The body silent.* New York: Norton.

Scott, J. C. (1985). *Weapons of the weak: Everyday forms of peasant resistance.* New Haven, CT: Yale University Press.

West, C., & Zimmerman, D. H. (1987). Doing gender. *Gender and Society, 1*(2), 125-151.

Zola, I. K. (1982). *Missing pieces: A chronicle of living with a disability.* Philadelphia: Temple University Press.

10

Men's Style of Nurturing Elders

LENARD W. KAYE
JEFFREY S. APPLEGATE

Family structure and function have been subject to periodic reinterpretation. Recent discussion has been initiated that speaks to the emergence of a new orientation to the institution of family in American society. Coined the "new familism," America's cultural values are said to have entered a third cultural era. Proceeding from a period of traditional familism in the 1940s to the 1960s, to a period of individualism in the 1960s to the 1980s, we are now, it is argued, commencing a shift away from an ethos of expressive individualism and toward an ethos of family well-being, commitment, and obligation (Blankenhorn, 1991; Whitehead, 1992). This third cultural era is characterized by stabilizing divorce rates and family forms, increased fertility rates, engagement of the baby boomer cohort in parenthood, including recognition of the limitations of expressive self and a greater sense of being child centered, a shift from work to home as a source for fulfillment, shared responsibilities for work and home, and a renewed appreciation of the value of social norms. Put simply, this "new familism" represents "a shift away from a calculus of happiness based on individual fulfillment and toward a calculus of happiness based on the well-being of the family as a whole" (Whitehead, 1992, p. 1).

AUTHORS' NOTE: The research reported here was supported by a generous grant from the Andrus Foundation of the American Association of Retired Persons and conducted at Bryn Mawr Graduate School of Social Work & Social Research in Bryn Mawr, Pennsylvania.

The new familism framework provides an excellent backdrop against which to consider the contributions of men to the welfare of the family and in particular to the special needs of those frail and dependent elders who are included in the family constellation in ever increasing numbers. It leads naturally to a consideration of men's contributions in areas that extend beyond the traditional domains of breadwinner and protector. It affords an opportunity to inquire into men's capacity not only to provide instrumental and economic forms of support to the family unit but also to contribute as well to the integrity of the family by means of affective concern, personal care, and emotional intimacy. Such is the evolving scenario, then, that we use to explore the experiences generally, and the health-related issues in particular, that confront men as carers of older persons.

This chapter, in considering issues of men's health and well-being associated with their style of caring for elders, draws on research by the authors that inquired into the experiences of husbands, and to a lesser degree sons, serving as the predominant providers of care to older relatives. Although the new familism movement is said to reflect a turning by family members to children's needs, this chapter mounts the argument that a concurrent turn in attention, particularly by men, toward the needs of vulnerable family members at the other end of the life cycle is now underway. Thus, the third cultural era might be more accurately characterized in our view as including the notion of greater concern on the part of men expressed for others generally—regardless if they are young or old. Such a stance does not deny men's instrumental strivings but rather extends their capacity to substantial expressions of intimacy and affective concern as well. We hope that our data will serve to fuel the continuing evolution of the new familism paradigm by documenting the impressive contributions of men, even in the face of inevitably failing health, in the domain of elder family caregiving.

Gender and the Scope of Caregiving

Based on data from the 1984 National Long-Term Care Survey, a survey of a nationally representative sample of chronically disabled older persons, it is estimated that older adult caregiving is provided in the United States by some 7.3 million relatives, friends, and others who are not paid or associated with a formal service organization (Stone & Kemper, 1989). These individuals, commonly designated as informal caregivers in the United States, have also been characterized as "hidden providers" in the British literature (Olesen, 1989). Stone and Kemper (1989) calculate that there are actually a total of 13.3 million potential caregivers in this country who have disabled spouses or parents aged 65 and over. Spouses and children are known to represent the dominant providers of family care, comprising three fifths of all caregivers and almost three quarters of primary caregivers (those individuals who have assumed ongoing responsibility for the majority of daily living assistance to dependent elders).

Recent data serve to further affirm the substantial caregiving role being assumed by both men and women, which in turn may be seen as lending credence to the new familism argument. A recent survey conducted by Louis Harris and Associates for the Commonwealth Fund (1992) documents that more than 70% of all Americans age 55 and over (significantly more than thought previously) are actively contributing to society, their families, and communities through caring for sick and disabled persons. It is estimated that these Americans are contributing the equivalent of more than 20 million full-time workers as informal carers. Of particular significance for this discussion, the Commonwealth Fund research confirms that men are playing a larger role than expected as caregivers and volunteers. In total, 28% of men as compared to 29% of women age 55 and over are caring for sick and disabled parents, spouses, other relatives, friends, and neighbors. Similarly, 50% of men and 52% of older women who have children or grandchildren are helping or caring for them.

These data confirm that the caregiving role of family members and their nonrelative counterparts has emerged as a widespread phenomenon in American society. Montgomery and Datwyler (1990) argue that its emergence is due not only to the unprecedented growth of the aged population but also to the medical system's preoccupation with acute care and the consequent lack of attention to the chronic care needs of older Americans. This neglect of long-term care needs by the professional medical establishment has, by default, passed the responsibility down to low-paid workers (i.e., homemakers, home health aides, nurses aides) or in the case of families and friends, unpaid workers.

Widespread recognition of the scope of informal caregiving has led to the conduct of considerable research on the topic in the past 10 years. Unfortunately, the male carer experience has been, relatively speaking, neglected in the process (Carlson & Robertson, 1990; Harper & Lund, 1990; Kaye & Applegate, 1990b, 1990c; Pett, Caserta, Hutton, & Lund, 1988). Informal, family caregiving has been assumed to be a female dominated area of familial activity and in particular one dominated by the efforts of daughters. It is almost as if men are presumed to be incapable of adopting the caring role. Lack of knowledge of the caregiving experience of men has, according to Parker (1989), "undoubtedly led to some misunderstanding about the roles and motivations of male carers" (p. 552).

According to Arber and Gilbert (1989), men remain the "forgotten carers" because their considerable contributions to elder care often go unrecognized. They identify three assumptions that based on their research proved to be dubious but have nevertheless influenced our views dramatically. They are (a) that men are very unlikely to be primary caregivers of infirm older people, (b) that older men receive more support from formal and voluntary services than women carers, and (c) that when men do engage in the caregiving role they are more likely to obtain informal support from others than are women. If men are included in research samples they are often undifferentiated in data analyses, obscuring possible variations in their experiences (Aronson, 1985).

Although this chapter focuses much needed attention toward men's contributions and health-related challenges as carers of older adults, it can be argued similarly that fathers' contributions to the family generally have also been largely ignored. Cath, Gurwitt, and Gunsberg (1989) maintain that family science researchers have failed to study the multiple roles of fathers in child and family development. It seems clear that less is known of the filial behavior of men who have living parents or about the collection of roles assumed by middle-aged men and thus the extent to which they are caught "in the middle" in the same way that it is maintained women are (Spitze & Logan, 1990). Yet just as the current fatherhood literature documents significant contributions by men toward child and family development, this chapter aims to present evidence of the nature and significance of men's involvement in the caregiving of older persons.

Standardized definitions of what caregivers do, whether they be male or female, remain difficult to achieve. This is due in part in that descriptions of the caregiving function and what qualifies someone to be designated a caregiver vary considerably depending on the significance placed on such factors as the types and volume of care provided, the intensity and duration of care, the relationship of the caregiver to the care recipient, and the sociodemographic characteristics of the individuals that compose the caregiving dyad (i.e., the caregiver and the care recipient) (Stone, 1991). Depending on the needs of the frail elder and the inclinations of the carer, assistance may be provided in a multitude of personal domains, including the personal or physical, the environmental, the social, the emotional, and the financial. Furthermore, caregivers can engage in a wide range of specific activities such as the following: cooking meals; doing the laundry; household cleaning; going shopping; helping bathe, dress, and groom another person; handling bill paying and home repair requirements; and providing less tangible emotional support and affection. As can be surmised, this range of potential tasks encompasses both affective and instrumental aspects of caring.

The Research Project

The study of males and the elder caregiving experience was based on data collected from 148 primary caregivers throughout the United States and 30 such individuals and (when possible) their care recipients in the greater Philadelphia metropolitan area (Kaye & Applegate, 1989; Kaye & Applegate, 1990a). Data collected by means of mail questionnaires and intensive face-to-face interviews have served to document many extraordinary stories of men willing to assume elder care responsibilities. The men participating in our research, all of whom were or had recently been associated with caregiver support groups, provided richly detailed scenarios depicting the substantial demands required of someone bearing major responsibility for the well-being of a loved one suffering from the disabling consequences of Alzheimer's disease, stroke, arthritis, cancer, and other age-related diseases. The professional leaders and facilitators of 152 caregiver support groups throughout the United States, also surveyed during the course of this research, served only to further confirm that these men may well be the unsung heroes in family elder caregiving.

Findings presented in this chapter focus primarily on data derived from the national survey of male carers. These men ranged in age from 36 to 84 years with the majority (82%) 60 years of age and older. Their average age was almost 68 years. Seventy percent of these men were married and living with their spouses and the overwhelming majority were white (96%). Approximately 72% of these men were retired. The majority had at least a high school education (94%), whereas almost 40% had achieved a college education. More than three fifths of these men (65%) lived with the person to whom they were providing care and they had resided with them for many years (20 years or more in some cases).

Those receiving these men's help were most likely to be spouses over 70 years of age. Approximately two of every three males were caring for spouses. An additional 12% were sons caring for their mothers. Only half as many men (6%) were caring for their fathers. These men less frequently cared for parents-in-law, siblings, and friends. It is noteworthy that 81%

of the men surveyed believed their wives were suffering from Alzheimer's disease or a related disorder and thus exhibited varying degrees of mental and behavioral dysfunction.

Physical and Emotional
Health of Male Carers

Profiles of the men in our research affirm a troubling health profile of the man who engages in family caregiving. Our data document a cohort of carers whose health status, while not unduly poor, appears to be on the decline. In general, the men surveyed perceived themselves to be in fair health. However, when asked if their health in any way limited the care that they provided to their impaired elders, more than 40% of the men said it did. This suggests that the physical demands of caring can be exceedingly demanding even for men who are relatively healthy. As one gentleman put it, "When you're old, you get tired. If you were feeling good and wanted to do it, you'd be OK."

These men registered only midrange assessments of their emotional health. These same men also reported only fair assessments of their personal satisfaction with life regarding feelings of loneliness, frequency of worrying, general perceptions of life, and overall satisfaction with life. One older man caring for his brain damaged wife expressed the sentiments of many: "[My life] could be worse; could be a whole lot better also."

The caregiving experience for men and women is known to be associated with elevated risk of depression. Estimates of depressive symptomatology among caregivers of frail older persons have been as high as 43% to 46% (Tennstedt, Cafferata, & Sullivan, 1992). Rates of depression are elevated among caregivers whether care is being provided to cognitively or physically impaired elders. However, rates are highest for those providing assistance to cognitively impaired persons, such as those suffering from Alzheimer's disease. Recent evidence has emerged that sexual dysfunction may need to be counted among the potential negative consequences of the caregiving experience (Litz, Zeiss, & Davies, 1990). Given the risks associated with caregiving, and especially the challenges inherent in the experience for men (who may be more likely to be caring for cognitively impaired spouses), it seems we should be rightfully concerned for the well-being of male caregivers like those addressed in our research. Such individuals are frequently caring for Alzheimer's patients and at the same time may attempt to mask the stress and strain that they experience as caregivers.

Stress, Burden, and Personal Well-Being of Male Carers

Men's subjective experience of burden as family carers (i.e., their appraisal of the cognitive and emotional changes accompanying stress and strain) appears to be a good indicator of compromised well-being. Asked to rate the degree of burden associated with various caregiving tasks, the men in our sample maintained that hands-on, personal care (e.g., bathing, toileting, dressing, and grooming the frail elder) was most stressful. This was the very same category of tasks that they found to be least satisfying to perform. They also felt least competent performing these functions. On the other hand, a mixture of affective and instrumental forms of assistance including the provision of emotional support and companionship, shopping, providing transportation, and dealing with behavioral problems were rarely mentioned as stressful caring activities. These men were discovered to perform frequently an exceedingly wide range of tasks associated with elder caregiving, from hand-holding to home repair. In contrast to the stereotype that male caring is primarily instrumental in nature, these men reported performing tasks associated with the provision of social and emotional support most frequently, most competently, and with the greatest degree of satisfaction. Such activities as listening to the problems of the care recipient, engaging in interpersonal problem solving, and dealing with the intimate and often emotional issues associated with financial planning were performed more often than a variety of concrete home maintenance, case management, and personal care tasks.

Contrary to conventional wisdom, the men in our research apparently derived considerable satisfaction from the experience of caring at an emotional level for another individual. These men appeared to be motivated as much or more by an "ethic of caring" as they did by an "ethic of justice and obligation" or simply "doing the right thing" (Gilligan, 1982). Indeed, we surmise that these men realized considerable emotional benefit from caregiving, which, in turn, could serve to offset, at least in part, the distressing and burdensome aspects of caring for an infirm individual. On the other hand, as documented in previous research, they exhibited a strong tendency to avoid engagement in the performance of those tasks requiring close physical contact.

Regression analysis examined those factors that would best explain differences in the burden felt by the men in our research. Burden was measured by a shortened version of Zarit, Reever, and Bach-Peterson's (1980) Burden Scale, which assesses the extent to which caregivers experience personal stress and strain during the course of caring for another person. The perceived quality of these men's relationships with other members of their families as well as with the recipients of their care proved to have the strongest influence on caregiver burden explaining 14% and 11% of the variance in burden scores respectively. Put differently, a positive and close relationship with other family members served best to reduce significantly the distress that these men associated with family caring. It is noteworthy that six additional variables also proved to influence these men's stress levels to a significant, though lesser, degree. They were (in the order of their importance): the intensity of perceived psychological and social barriers to caregiving (10% of variance explained); their receipt of community services (8% of variance explained); their financial status (6% of variance explained); whether they lived with their care recipient (5% of variance explained); the frequency of task performance (5% of variance explained); and the mental health (i.e., behavioral orientation) of their care recipients (4% of variance explained). Put differently, those men who felt more substantial role conflict did not receive outside community agency assistance, were less financially secure, lived with their care recipient, were more heavily engaged in caring activities, and cared for more disoriented persons experienced greater levels of distress.

Although men and women may experience comparable levels of strain during the course of caregiving, some researchers maintain that women are actually more likely to report signs of emotional distress and related negative outcomes during the course of family caring (Barusch & Spaid, 1989; Bordon & Berlin, 1990; Young & Kahana, 1989). However, this may not always be the case. Grove (1988), Jutras and Veilleux (1991), and Miller (1991) did not find significant sex differences in caregiver distress and burden levels. Zarit, Todd, and Zarit (1986) found female caregiver stress levels initially higher but not significantly different at the end of a 2-year follow-up. Jutras and Veilleux (1991) found that although burden levels were equivalent for men and women, men had more difficulty assuming responsibilities associated with multiple roles and women have adopted new roles in addition to the traditionally ascribed caregiving role. Hinrichsen (1991) argues that the coping patterns between the two sexes appear different when it comes to caregiving. Men (and husbands in particular) may make the best adaptation to caregiving stress and demands. Our data, which serve to document moderate levels of expressed burden by male carers, suggest that men do indeed cope with the stress and strain of caregiving relatively well. However, they may at the same time, in accord with the findings of Barusch and Spaid (1989) and others noted above, be quite adroit at masking the difficulties they are experiencing by presenting a stoic, stiff upper lip to those who are observing or assessing their efforts as carers. As one male caregiver in our research noted, "Having to go through it all; having to take the responsibility. It's something that had to be done and it isn't enjoyable, but I can tolerate it."

Our data and that of other caregiving researchers also document that caregiving is in large part a spousal experience, especially for men (Stoller, 1990). Furthermore, husbands are more likely to be identified as the primary or major carers as compared to other men (Stone, Cafferata, & Sangl, 1987). Husbands who assume the role of carer are also usually older than their female counterparts, tend to have more health problems of their own, perform more caregiving tasks, and care for more disabled persons (Barusch & Spaid, 1989). Indeed, spousal caregivers appear to be more adversely affected by providing care than nonspousal caregivers (George & Gwyther, 1986).

Spousal caregivers may well be vulnerable in particular to mental health stress. Across all indicators of mental health, spousal caregivers have been found to be more depressed, express higher levels of negative affect, are more likely to use psychotropic drugs, have more symptoms of psychological distress than the general population, and suffer from more physical health problems (particularly diabetes, arthritis, ulcers, and anemia) (Pruchno & Potashnik, 1989).

Caring for a spouse also appears to be more demanding in many respects than the act of caring for other relatives. And, as our data confirmed, the caring experience for husbands tends to be long-term with limited help offered by other members of the family. We found that respondents in our research had been performing family caregiving functions for considerable periods of time. More than 95% of our sample had been carers for more than 1 year. Almost two thirds had been family carers for 3 years or longer and one third had been performing in this capacity for more than 5 years. The vast majority (almost 90%) had served as the primary or major carer throughout their tenures as carers. For these men, caring also consumed substantial amounts of time in their lives. More than half of these men were providing in excess of 60 hours of caring during the course of the average week. An additional 24% reported caregiving involvement levels between 21 and 60 hours a week.

These extended hours of caring were required due to the substantial functional incapacity of those being cared for. The most difficult activities for these impaired elders to perform included handling money, shopping for groceries, getting to places beyond walking distance, and preparing meals. In particular, the mental and emotional health status of care recipients was judged to be poor. Assessments of their behavioral orientation by their male carers confirmed that among the most common behaviorally inappropriate actions by care recipients were instances of mental confusion, disoriented behavior, and expressions of inappropriate fear and anxiety. Given that 81% of the men in this research believed they were caring for Alzheimer's disease victims, such behavior is to be expected. It should be clear that these persons were severely mentally incapacitated. A notable positive association was found between the frail elders' functional capacity level and the mental health status of the men who cared for them. The relationship between these two variables is considered worrisome as it suggests that these men may be increasingly vulnerable to the strain of caring at the very time when their services are needed most. These men's capacity to tolerate greater levels of disability even in the face of increased responsibility for caregiving becomes a testimonial to their commitment to the caring function.

Discussion

It was stated earlier that the subjects in our research had been or were currently involved as caregiver support group participants. There is the possibility that their experiences differ from male caregivers who have not been associated with support groups (whose experiences, for example, may be less stressful, making it unnecessary for them to seek out support). Because we did not employ a control group of male caregivers who were never associated with support group programming, it is impossible to speak with full confidence of the widespread generalizability of our findings to all caregiving men. Caution in the interpretation of our data is therefore warranted. Even so, given the traditional attitudes regarding the types of domestic labor that might be expected of older men, the range and intensity of expressive tasks performed by the men in our research is notable. Indeed, the earliest research in the field of informal care emphasized the predominant role played by women in caring for both children and incapacitated adults. More recently, however, research appears to be documenting a greater role played by men in the caring process at both ends of the life cycle. Our data underscore men's capacity to assume and maintain the caring role even in the face of exceedingly demanding physical and emotional conditions.

More generally, the amount of time that fathers spend with and care for their children appears to be increasing (Leslie, Anderson, & Branson, 1991; Yogev & Brett, 1985), and the difference between the time that husbands and wives spend in child care has been found to lessen as women assume more hours of employment (Darling-Fisher & Tiedje, 1990; Leslie, Branson, & Anderson, 1989; Pleck, 1985). Furthermore, husbands appear to believe that their level of responsibility for child care is greater than that which is attributed to them by their spouses (Berk & Shih, 1980; Leslie et al., 1991).

Investigators have also discovered that men may tend to increase their involvement in expressive types of work at home when they retire (Coverman & Shelby, 1986; Rexcoat & Shehan, 1987; Stoller & Cutler, 1992). Some of the most intensive types of care are actually provided by spouses, with husbands as likely to be involved as wives (Parker, 1989). Arber and Gilbert's (1989) analysis of the British experience showed that over 90% of married persons helped with both domestic and personal care tasks needed by their spouses. Husbands were almost equally likely to assist their severely disabled wives as compared to their female spousal counterparts.

Our research suggests that once men have assumed the role of primary caregiver, especially in a spousal caring situation, the differences between their experience and that of female carers lessens considerably. Enright's research (1991) appears to support this observation. He, too, found that spousal caregivers devoted large amounts of their time to caregiving and that husbands spent no less time at it than did wives. The men in his research, as ours, engaged in rather intimate, long-term caregiving efforts. During the course of this commitment, they performed a broad spectrum of caring functions with only limited help from family, friends, and community service organizations.

Male caregiving spouses may even be emerging as that cohort of men who perform the most intensive and demanding range of caring functions in the family unit. Dwyer and Seccombe (1991), applying a family labor framework, found that husbands (when compared to wives) report spending more time with and performing a greater range of caregiving tasks. On the other hand, daughters as compared to sons reported their caregiving responsibilities were greater. The authors suggest that family position may confound interpretations regarding the association between gender and family caregiving. Other research has found that men are equally or more likely than women to experience four types of potentially conflicting roles during the course of caregiving. These were spouse, paid worker, adult child of aging parent, and parent (Spitze & Logan, 1990). The ability to document this evolution in men's involvement in caring tasks, and especially the experience of male spouses, opens important areas for further research and thinking on gender and caregiving.

Of particular concern for analysts of men's experience as carers should be the risk that spouses, in particular, expose themselves to when assuming caregiving responsibilities. Spousal caregivers, who are aging themselves, are a vulnerable cohort. They are at considerable risk for a host of mental and physical health problems. In fact, this category of caregivers may be in no better health than their care recipients. For men who tend to downplay their incapacities and the burden associated with caregiving, this experience may eventually be a particularly disabling one, subjecting the care provider to a variety of potentially negative consequences (Pruchno & Potashnik, 1989). Indeed, the marital caregiving system can be simultaneously intense and fragile. Alzheimer's caregivers, more likely to be men than women, appear to be at particular risk of illness that in turn undermines their ability to continue in the caregiving role (Alzheimer's Association, 1991).

The movement of men into primary caregiving roles has been explained by Grbich (1990) as the consequence of inadequate socialization or resistance to societal norms, a response to a crisis situation that threatens family survival, and required maximization of the division of labor of the family unit. Under these circumstances, rapid social change in individual behavior can be expected. Grbich creates this context to explain the movement of men in intact nuclear families into primary caregiver roles for their preschool aged children. Grbich discovered that early male socialization with its emphasis on the performance of instrumental tasks did not restrict the males in her study in making the role choice they made. In similar fashion, the men in our research appear to have become firmly embedded in the family caring function with older adults.

The men studied in our sample saw no apparent boundary between "caring for" and "caring about" another person. Dalley (1988), in mounting a theoretical analysis of the ideologies that underlie care provision, has argued that the separation of these two processes—caring for and caring about someone—has traditionally been far more common for men than women. Public perceptions have reinforced women's obligatory performance of tasks for those they care about. This integration of caring for and about someone by women has not, according to Dalley, been assumed to be a natural state of affairs for men who are able more easily to disentangle one process from the other. Are the men in our research therefore atypical in this respect or simply reflecting the feelings and experiences of individuals, regardless of gender, who come to assume primary caregiving responsibilities for another individual? Further investigation is warranted in this area.

There are several major trends that may ultimately impact on the availability and willingness of men to perform family caring functions in greater numbers in the future. First, the momentum building toward what has been conceived as the new familism, which is likely, in turn, to encourage men's continuing assumption of what were formally rather stigmatizing and even taboo feminine functions in the home. As the barriers serving to thwart men's inclinations to care for others continue to weaken, we anticipate that the assumption of the familial helping function by men will be accomplished with lesser degrees of role incongruence and conflict. We believe that the role transforming child care activities engaged in by younger fathers in increasing numbers can also be expected to serve a preparatory function for those men who will eventually be pressed to assume elder carer responsibilities later in life. We anticipate as well that the male carers in our research, and others like them, will represent influential role models for succeeding generations of males in their own family lines.

A second trend is reflected in a series of demographic thrusts that appear, at first glance, to serve as countervailing forces that challenge the premise of the new familism. Referred to here is a series of long-term shifts toward smaller families, delayed childrearing, more women in the workforce, more chronically impaired elderly, higher divorce rates, the growth of single-headed households, and increased family mobility, all of which may suggest that fewer primary family caregivers will be available in the future and that they will have to provide this care with less informal support (Alzheimer's Association, 1991; Brubaker & Brubaker, 1992; Cicirelli, 1990; Worobey & Angel, 1990). Brody (1990) points out that one of the consequences of these demographic shifts is that adult children are providing more care to more and increasingly frail and vulnerable individuals for longer periods of time than ever before. Stone (1987) maintains that this set of sociodemographic transformations will, by necessity, demand that more adult sons, in particular, take responsibility for various aspects of family care.

A third noticeable trend supportive of men's entry into the world of caregiving is the gradual emergence of increasing numbers of "family friendly" companies with personnel policies that reflect greater sensitivity to the needs of employees with children and elderly relatives. Such dependent care policies and programs as information and referral programs in child and elder care, educational seminars, part-time work, flextime and meal breaks, job sharing, family care and illness leaves for mothers and fathers, and employer-supported child and adult day care centers should serve to reinforce employed men's (and women's) inclinations to fulfill a familial caring function at the same time that workplace obligations continue to be satisfied. Reflective of this trend is the recent announcement by 137 national companies and organizations of the formation of the American Business Collaboration for Quality Dependent Care. This group will be spending $25.4 million in the next 2 years to fund child care and elder care programs in 25 states and the District of Columbia (Levin-Epstein, 1992). Unfortunately, there is evidence to suggest that female employees are more likely than male employees to be provided with family care benefits by their employers. That is, men may be discouraged from engaging in family care activities, including both child care and elder care, because of gender-biased dependent care workplace policies (Society for Human Resource Management, 1992). Even so, we know that large proportions of both male and female employees have elder care responsibilities. One in four employees have some elder care responsibility according to a survey by Neal, Chapman, and Ingersoll-Dayton (1988). Furthermore, their number and needs as both salaried workers and unpaid family helpers are expected to grow in the future (Anastas, Gibeau, & Larson, 1990).

In the final analysis, elder caregiving may be seen as providing men with an opportunity to reconceptualize the meaning of gender. It may, in fact, provide the same opportunity as household labor does for the expression, confirmation, and even transformation of the meaning of gender (Coltrane, 1989). In Coltrane's research, married men who practiced child care were perceived to be significantly transformed by the experience. By "doing gender" in the context of the family unit, parents were found to gradually construct images of fathers as sensitive and nurturing caregivers. When household functions were equally shared among mother and father, so-called maternal thinking was found to develop in fathers too. Thus, the social meaning of gender began to change.

Just as the meaning of gender may be undergoing a transformation based on men's experience caring for children, so too may our rethinking of gender be influenced as a consequence of men engaged in greater numbers as nurturing carers of frail older adults. That experience may also serve to redefine the boundaries of socially acceptable behavior for men who may subsequently model nurturant behavior for the next generation of men who can be expected to be called on to assume increasing family care responsibilities.

References

Alzheimer's Association. (1991, April). *Time out! The case for a national family caregiver support policy.* Washington, DC: Author.

Anastas, J. W., Gibeau, J. L., & Larson, P. J. (1990). Working families and eldercare: A national perspective in an aging America. *Social Work, 35,* 405-411.

Arber, S., & Gilbert, N. (1989). Men: The forgotten carers. *Sociology, 23,* 111-118.

Aronson, J. (1985). Family care of the elderly: Underlying assumptions and their consequences. *Canadian Journal on Aging, 4,* 115-125.

Barusch, A. S., & Spaid, W. M. (1989). Gender differences in caregiving: Why do wives report greater burden? *The Gerontologist, 29,* 667-676.

Berk, S. F., & Shih, A. (1980). Contributions to household labor: Comparing wives' and husbands' reports. In S. F. Berk (Ed.), *Women and household labor* (pp. 191-228). Beverly Hills, CA: Sage.

Blankenhorn, D. (1991). *The good family man: Fatherhood and the pursuit of happiness in America* (Working paper). New York: Institute for American Values.

Borden, W., & Berlin, S. (1990). Gender, coping, and psychological well-being in spouses of older adults with chronic dementia. *American Journal of Orthopsychiatry, 60,* 603-610.

Brody, E. M. (1990). *Women in the middle: Their parent-care years.* New York: Springer.

Brubaker, T. H., & Brubaker, E. (1992). Family care of the elderly in the United States: An issue of gender differences? In J. I. Kosberg (Ed.), *Family care of the elderly: Social and cultural changes* (pp. 210-231). Newbury Park, CA: Sage.

Carlson, K. W., & Robertson, S. E. (1990). The influence of impairment on the burden experienced by spouses of partners with dementia. *Canadian Journal of Rehabilitation, 3,* 213-222.

Cath, S. H., Gurwitt, A., & Gunsberg, L. (1989). Introduction. In S. H. Cath, A. Gurwitt, & L. Gunsberg (Eds.), *Fathers and their families* (pp. xv-xxiii). Hillsdale, NJ: Analytic Press.

Cicirelli, V. G. (1990). Family support in relation to health problems of the elderly. In. T. H. Brubaker (Ed.), *Family relationships in later life* (2nd ed., pp. 212-228). Newbury Park, CA: Sage.

Coltrane, S. (1989). Household labor and the routine production of gender. *Social Problems, 36,* 473-490.

Commonwealth Fund, Americans Over 55 at Work Program. (1992, June 25). *The nation's great overlooked resource: The contributions of Americans 55+.* New York: Commonwealth Fund.

Coverman, B., & Shelby, J. F. (1986). Change in men's housework and child-care time, 1965-75. *Journal of Marriage and the Family, 48,* 413-422.

Dalley, G. (1988). *Ideologies of caring: Rethinking community and collectivism.* London: Macmillan.

Darling-Fisher, C. S., & Tiedje, L. B. (1990). The impact of maternal employment characteristics on fathers' participation in child care. *Family Relations, 39,* 20-26.

Dwyer, J. W., & Seccombe, K. (1991). Elder care as family labor: The influence of gender and family position. *Journal of Family Issues, 12,* 229-247.

Enright, R. B., Jr. (1991). Time spent caregiving and help received by spouses and adult children of brain-impaired adults. *The Gerontologist, 31,* 375-382.

George, L. K., & Gwyther, L. P. (1986). Caregiver well-being: A multidimensional examination of family caregivers of demented adults. *The Gerontologist, 26,* 253-259.

Gilligan, C. (1982). *In a different voice.* Cambridge, MA: Harvard University Press.

Grbich, C. (1990). Socialisation and social change: A critique of three positions. *British Journal of Sociology, 41,* 517-530.

Grove, L. (1988). *Psychological distress of caregivers to spouses with Alzheimer's disease.* Unpublished doctoral dissertation, Northwestern University, Evanston, IL.

Harper, S., & Lund, D. A. (1990). Wives, husbands, and daughters, caring for institutionalized and noninstitutionalized dementia patients: Toward a model of caregiver burden. *International Journal of Aging and Human Development, 30,* 241-262.

Hinrichsen, G. A. (1991). Adjustment of caregivers to depressed older adults. *Psychology and Aging, 6,* 631-639.

Jutras, S., & Veilleux, F. (1991). Gender roles and care giving to the elderly: An empirical study. *Sex Roles, 25*(1/2), 1-18.

Kaye, L. W., & Applegate, J. S. (1989). *Unsung heroes? A national analysis and intensive local study of males and the elderly caregiving experience* (Final report to the AARP Andrus Foundation). Bryn Mawr, PA: Bryn Mawr Graduate School of Social Work & Social Research.

Kaye, L. W., & Applegate, J. S. (1990a). *Men as caregivers to the elderly: Understanding and aiding unrecognized family support.* Lexington, MA: Lexington Books.

Kaye, L. W., & Applegate, J. S. (1990b). Men as elder caregivers: Building a research agenda for the 1990s. *Journal of Aging Studies, 4,* 289-298.

Kaye, L. W., & Applegate, J. S. (1990c). Men as elder caregivers: A response to changing families. *American Journal of Orthopsychiatry, 60*(1), 86-95.

Leslie, L. A., Anderson, E. A., & Branson, M. P. (1991). Responsibility for children: The role of gender and employment. *Journal of Family Issues, 12,* 197-210.

Leslie, L. A., Branson, M. P., & Anderson, E. A. (1989). The impact of couples' work profile on husbands' and wives' performance of child care tasks. *Family Perspective, 22,* 327-344.

Levin-Epstein, M. (Ed.). (1992, September 15). *The National Report on Work & Family.* [Available from Business Publishers, Silver Spring, MD.]

Litz, B. T., Zeiss, A. M., & Davies, H. D. (1990). Sexual concerns of male spouses of female Alzheimer's disease patients. *The Gerontologist, 30,* 113-116.

Miller, B. (1991). Elderly married couples, gender, and caregiver strain. *Advances in Medical Sociology, 2,* 245-266.

Montgomery, R. J. V., & Datwyler, M. M. (1990, Summer). Women & men in the caregiving role. *Generations,* pp. 34-38.

Neal. M. B., Chapman, N. J., & Ingersoll-Dayton, B. (1988, October). Elder care, employees, and the workplace: Findings from a survey of employees. Report at the forum *Stepping up to elder care: A major corporate challenge for the 1990s,* Portland, OR.

Olesen, V. L. (1989, March). Caregiving, ethical and informal: Emerging challenges in the sociology of health and illness. *Journal of Health and Social Behavior, 30,* 1-10.

Parker, G. (1989). Unending work and care. *Work, Employment & Society, 3,* 541-553.

Pett, M. A., Caserta, M. S., Hutton, A. P., & Lund, D. A. (1988). Intergenerational conflict: Middle aged women caring for demented older relatives. *American Journal of Orthopsychiatry, 58,* 405-417.

Pleck, J. H. (1985). *Working wives/working husbands.* Beverly Hills, CA: Sage.

Pruchno, R. A., & Potashnik, S. L. (1989). Caregiving spouses: Physical and mental health in perspective. *Journal of the American Geriatrics Society, 37,* 697-705.

Rexcoat, C., & Shehan, C. (1987). The family life cycle and spouses time in housework. *Journal of Marriage and the Family, 49,* 735-750.

Society for Human Resource Management. (1992). *SHRM work & family survey report.* Alexandria, VA: Society for Human Resource Management.

Spitze, G., & Logan, J. (1990). More evidence on women (and men) in the middle. *Research on Aging, 12,* 182-198.

Stoller, E. P. (1990). Males as helpers: The role of sons, relatives, and friends. *The Gerontologist, 30,* 228-235.

Stoller, E. P., & Cutler, S. J. (1992). The impact of gender on configurations of care among married elderly couples. *Research on Aging, 14,* 313-330.

Stone, R. I. (1987). *Exploding the myths: Caregiving in America.* A Study by the Subcommittee on Human Services of the Select Committee on Aging (HR Comm. Pub. 99-611). Washington, DC: Government Printing Office.

Stone, R. I. (1991). Defining family caregivers of the elderly: Implications for research and public policy. *The Gerontologist, 31,* 724-725.

Stone, R., Cafferata, G. L., & Sangl, J. (1987). Caregivers of the frail elderly: A national profile. *The Gerontologist, 27,* 616-626.

Stone, R. I., & Kemper, P. (1989). Spouses and children of disabled elders: How large a constituency for long-term care reform? *The Milbank Quarterly, 67,* 485-504.

Tennstedt, S., Cafferata, G. L., & Sullivan, L. (1992). Depression among caregivers of impaired elders. *Journal of Aging and Health, 4,* 58-76.

Whitehead, B. D. (1992, Summer). A new familism? *Family Affairs,* 1-5.

Worobey, J. L., & Angel, R. J. (1990). Functional capacity and living arrangements of unmarried elderly persons. *Journal of Gerontology: Social Sciences, 45,* S95-S101.

Yogev, S., & Brett, J. (1985). Patterns of work and family involvement among single- and dual-earner couples. *Journal of Applied Psychology, 70,* 754-768.

Young, R. F., & Kahana, E. (1989). Specifying caregiver outcomes: Gender and relationship aspects of caregiver strain. *The Gerontologist, 29,* 660-666.

Zarit, S., Reever, K., & Bach-Peterson, J. (1980). Relatives of the impaired elderly: Correlates of feelings of burden. *The Gerontologist, 20,* 649-655.

Zarit, S. H., Todd, P., & Zarit, J. (1986). Subjective burden of husbands and wives as caregivers: A longitudinal study. *The Gerontologist, 26,* 260-266.

11

Sexual Adaptations
Among Gay Men With HIV

RICHARD TEWKSBURY

The spread of HIV and AIDS has brought numerous cultural, political, and social changes. Although many of these changes have created modifications in the structure and institutions (i.e., medicine, education, religion, the family, the workplace) of our culture, there are perhaps no more serious consequences of this disease than those experienced by the individuals who live with HIV disease. However, present knowledge of the lives of these persons is incomplete and selective. For reasons of practicality and convenience, a majority of the social science research regarding HIV and its effects on gay men has been conducted in or near the major urban centers where the disease has taken its greatest numerical toll—New York, San Francisco, Los Angeles. There is, however, an emerging body of literature addressing the impacts of the epidemic in smaller cities (see Bell, 1991; Kelly et al., 1990; Ruefli, Yu, & Barton, 1992; Silvestre, 1992). This chapter adds to this broadening focus by addressing the experiences of HIV+ gay men in the Midwest.

Researchers have generated an ever-increasing amount of data about rates of HIV infection, diagnosed cases of AIDS, and the sexual behaviors of high-risk groups (especially men who have sex with men). Qualitative research on homosexual and bisexual sexual behaviors in relation to HIV has been slower to emerge. Qualitative understandings—in-depth analyses of the experiential components of behavior, attitudes, and societal responses—are critical for transforming quantitative data and research findings into applied and meaningful conclusions (see Carey & Smith, 1992). Such an approach is referred to as a contextual understanding.

AUTHOR'S NOTE: This research was supported in part by a grant-in-aid from the Society for the Psychological Study of Social Issues.

Such understandings of the impacts of illness on afflicted men's lives has been one of the areas receiving the least attention from researchers. Researchers have established that other medical conditions such as cancer (Auchincloss, 1991; Beutel, 1988; Jenkins, 1988; Smith & Babaian, 1992) and heart disease (Gendel & Bonner, 1986) are known to introduce disruptions to sexual desire, functioning, and satisfaction. However, the ways these disruptions are experienced have largely remained a matter for rehabilitative therapists and those intimately involved with the terminally ill or seriously injured. Perhaps most importantly, Gendel and Bonner argue that attention to sexual concerns may significantly assist patients in their overall recovery process.

Related to HIV disease, Parker and Carballo (1990) have called for increased contextual understandings to be generated by qualitative social science research related to (a) the social context of sexual conduct, (b) the documentation of sexual practices, and (c) the interpretation of behavioral changes. This chapter addresses all three of these needs. The emphasis in this work is not on identifying the specifics of the sex lives of HIV+ gay men. Instead, this chapter first explores the processes by which they retain, modify, or abandon their sexual lives (including sexual activity). Secondarily, this work explores the way these men experience sex and sexuality, and looks at how those who have experienced changes in their sexual lives incorporate these changes into their lives.

Based on the results of in-depth interviews with 45 HIV+ gay men, this chapter will discuss the adaptational processes these men experience in adjusting to life with HIV disease. First, the relevant literature on the impact of HIV and other illnesses on men's sexuality is reviewed. This is followed by a brief description of the methods by which this research was carried out. After this the study's major findings are presented and interpreted, the processes of adaptation and experiential components of these adaptations are highlighted. Finally, some conclusions are drawn regarding the role of illness in the sexual lives of HIV+ gay men.

Review of the Literature

It is well-known that a key impact of HIV on sexual behavior is that gay and bisexual men are engaging in sex with somewhat fewer partners (Martin, 1987; Ruefli et al., 1992; Siegel & Raveis, 1993; Silvestre, 1992; Stall, Coates, & Hoff, 1988). However, the rates of unsafe sexual behaviors remain high, especially among young gay men (Gold, Skinner, &

Ross, 1994; Hays, Kegeles, & Coates, 1990; Stall et al., 1992). Recent concern, however, has focused on preventing relapses into high-risk sexual behavior (Adib, Joseph, Ostrow, Tal, & Schwartz, 1991; Ekstrand & Coates, 1990; Godfried et al., 1988; Kelly et al., 1991). Additionally, concerns about targeting prevention messages for specific categories of men, such as African American men (Peterson et al., 1992; Stevenson & Davis, 1994), incarcerated men (Baxter, 1991; Marcus, Amen, & Bibace, 1992), and men in substance abuse treatment (Paul, Stall, & Davis, 1993) have become increasingly prevalent. More specifically Gochros (1992), relying on 4 years of experience as a support group facilitator for HIV+ gay men, concludes that although HIV often interrupts gay men's sexual lives, sexual desires and activities are often revived following periods of abstinence (see also Gold, Skinner, & Ross, 1994; Meyer-Bahlburg et al., 1991). However, Gochros emphasizes that interruptions occur for numerous reasons. Identified as reasons why HIV+ gay men may cease sexual activities are physical factors, an absence of a willing sex partner, a lack of privacy in housing, perceived or actual loss of attractiveness, guilt regarding sexual orientation, depression, a lack of community support for continuing sexual activities, and the fear of infecting sexual partners (Gochros, 1992). Consequently, these factors, combined with the belief that the complex emotional and social dynamics can only be fully appreciated by someone who also has HIV disease, lead many HIV+ gay men to a preference for romantic relationships with other HIV+ men (Hoff, McKusick, Hilliard, & Coates, 1992).

The social science literature has largely (and implicitly) accepted that physical factors have been the primary reasons for HIV+ gay men (or all HIV+ persons) to terminate sexual activities (Weitz, 1991). However, some researchers have suggested that declining sexual functioning may be either a direct consequence of HIV or "mediated by the men's affective response to the AIDS epidemic and the preventive measures taken" (Meyer-Bahlburg et al., 1991, p. 23). Although physical problems may indeed be a reason for curtailing one's sexual activities, it is also necessary to consider issues of sexual interest and pleasure when examining HIV+ gay men's sexual activities (Meyer-Bahlburg et al., 1991) as well as interruptions that HIV and HIV status disclosure may have upon an individual's relationships. Early research regarding HIV's impact on sexual desire and functioning focused on case studies (Lippert, 1986; Nurnberg, Prudic, Fiori, & Freedman, 1984), with few recent investigations focusing on samples of HIV+ men (Hoff et al., 1992; Meyer-Bahlburg et al., 1991). Regardless of why some HIV+ men may reduce or abandon sexual activities, it is important to recognize that some researchers have found HIV+ men to have rates of sexual activities essentially similar to those of HIV- men (Gold et al., 1994; Meyer-Bahlburg et al., 1991).

Although some HIV+ gay men do maintain sexual interests and desires, many have concluded that it is easier and safer to discontinue sexual activities rather than significantly modify such behaviors (Weitz, 1991). As a consequence, many gay men actively, but unenthusiastically, choose to remain abstinent. For other gay men, it is not abstinence that is chosen, but instead curtailment of selected activities (Connell & Kippax, 1990). Not all persons informed of their HIV+ status alter their high-risk behaviors, however (Landis, Earp, & Koch, 1992; Osmond et al., 1988). Godfried et al. (1988) report that gay men are most likely to terminate participation in oral sex, not anal sex. Cleary, Devanter, Rogers, and Singer (1991) report that 2 weeks after being informed of their HIV+ status, nearly two thirds of a diverse sample had suspended unsafe sexual behaviors. However, Meyer-Bahlburg et al. (1991) and Gold et al. (1994) report HIV+ and HIV- gay men do not necessarily have significantly different rates of anal, oral, or other forms of sexual behaviors. Furthermore, even for those who desire to bring their sexual activities into line with safer sex guidelines, many persons (including gay men) do not possess sufficient knowledge to practice safer sex properly (Martin, 1990; Tewksbury & Whittier, 1992) or have significant difficulties controlling their sexual behaviors (Exner, Meyer-Bahlburg, & Ehrhardt, 1992; Pincu, 1989; Quadland & Shattls, 1987).

When sexual behavior is controlled, the losses of physical and emotional intimacy may lead to significant emotional distress. Therefore, the impact on HIV+ individuals can be seriously debilitating. Folkman, Chesney, Pollack, and Phillips (1992) suggest that those most likely to engage in unsafe sex are those for whom sex provides an important mechanism for coping with stress. Or, as Gold et al. (1994) found, HIV+ gay men's most common justification for engaging in unprotected anal intercourse is a perception of "having nothing to lose." Somewhat similarly, uninfected gay men may consciously elect to have unprotected intercourse based on perceptions of limits of risk of a partners' likelihood of infection, to show love (Levine & Siegel, 1992), or because they redefine their sexual acts' degree of risk (Offir, Fisher, Williams, & Fisher, 1993).

Sex, although often a central component to the lives of gay men, must be reviewed and reevaluated when one learns of his HIV infection. For some gay men, sex has traditionally been an important, self-affirming life component. This may mean that it is necessary to discover new ways for establishing self-esteem, whereas for others it may mean finding new ways of establishing friendships and intimate relationships. For other gay men, sex may stand as a primary mode of recreation; this may carry over to HIV+ gay men seeing unprotected sex as a form of "adventure and excitement" (Gold et al., 1994, p. 72). Men involved in relationships, both gay and straight, may encounter additional stresses of informing partners of their HIV status (Mays et al., 1993). Despite some men's temptation to withhold such information, the vast majority of HIV+ gay men do inform their primary sex partners of their status (Schnell et al., 1992). For those men who succumb to the temptation not to tell their partners, most such relationships terminate in short order (Coates, Morin, & McKusick, 1987; Schnell et al., 1992).

However, these research findings and conclusions still do not inform us of the way such events are experienced. What do gay men feel about curtailing their sexual activities? Is it possible to remain sexually active and not think about one's HIV status? These are the types of questions that remain to be answered. This study examines the way these issues impact the context of HIV+ gay men's lives.

Methods

The data in this analysis are drawn from a series of in-depth, semi-structured interviews with 45 HIV+ gay men[1] conducted between 1991 and 1993. Interviewees are all volunteers who learned of the project through one of two methods.[2] Community organizations in Ohio and Kentucky, devoted either to providing services to HIV+ persons or to public education, assisted with recruitment. Organizations published announcements of the research project in newsletters, made announcements at meetings, and most important, personally referred clients and contacts. Also, some interviewees were obtained through a snowball technique. At the conclusion of each interview a request was made to refer others to the researcher; several networks of acquaintances were accessed in this manner.

The data in the present analysis are drawn from a larger project of interviews with all varieties of HIV+ persons. All interviews lasted between 1.5 and 4 hours and focused on interviewees'(a) medical conditions, (b) social networks, (c) experiences with family, friends, workplace, medical providers, and significant others, and (d) personal social and psychological experiences with their disease.

All interviews were transcribed in full and conceptually coded using a multiple reading technique. Analysis follows the procedures of grounded theory development (Glaser & Strauss, 1967).

The Sexual Adaptations of HIV+ Gay Men

The discussion that follows focuses on identified patterns and commonalities of experiences across gay-identified, HIV+ men ($N = 45$).[3] The sample includes both men with asymptomatic HIV infection and those diagnosed with AIDS. The analysis focuses on the experiences of individuals rather than on an aggregated interpretation of data; a full understanding of changes in men's perceived experiences necessitates a look at individuals and how they have or have not altered their behavior over time (Joseph, Adib, Koopman, & Ostrow, 1990). Where different patterns of experiences have been identified between men diagnosed with AIDS and those who remain asymptomatic, these are noted.

The most striking finding to arise from this examination of HIV+ gay men was the frequent abandonment of sexual activities. One third (31.1%) of respondents reported that they no longer engaged in sex. This was more common among gay men diagnosed with AIDS (45%) than among asymptomatic HIV+ gay men (20%). For some men the loss of sexual relations represented a major loss in life satisfaction, although for some this loss was seen as little more than an expected consequence of disease or advancing age. The important conclusion, though, is that sexual behaviors and perspectives have changed. Generally, changes in perceptions and values were perceived as distressing and stress inducing. This is well illustrated in the comments of Victor, a 40-year-old HIV+ man who said,

> So much of it is funny how much you take for granted in life, even the sexuality part. How much I've taken for granted! It's changed though. I can no longer take it for granted. If I'm going to be with somebody it's not going to be like before, because it's simply not like before.

The majority (68.9%) of HIV+ gay men continued to be sexually active; this was especially true (80%) for men who are seropositive, but otherwise healthy. These men, though, have modified their behaviors leading them to perceive sexual interactions as less fulfilling than previously. Only 15% of the men diagnosed with AIDS reported not having significantly altered their sexual lives. Among the HIV+ asymptomatic gay men, only 20% reported no significant negative impacts to their sexual lives.

It is important here to recognize that these reports pertained specifically to these men's perceptions of their sexuality and sexual activities. This says nothing of how these men perceived impacts to their status as men (i.e., their masculinity). However, although data directly assessing gender identity impacts was not gathered, it is possible to interpret such impacts from the perspectives these men have offered. Throughout the discussion that follows, the impact of their illnesses on conceptions and constructions of masculinity (as mediated by direct impacts on sexuality) will be highlighted. Generally speaking, when illness affects an HIV+ gay man's gender identity it is in a manner that leads him to question his masculinity and often to modify or reconstruct core elements of that identity.

Losing or Abandoning
One's Sexual Life

In the eyes of HIV+ gay men who have experienced changes in their sexual lives, such changes were "inevitable." HIV disease, as well as many of the social consequences of the disease, could not have been averted, even though nearly all of these men yearned for some degree of control over their disease. The losses mounted in these men's lives, and the loss of sexual opportunities and activities only added to the distress of living with HIV disease. This was typically added to the stresses of watching friends, family, lovers, and others become ill and lose their abilities, appearances, work, friends, and eventually their lives. Sexual losses, then, came in addition to numerous other inevitable psychological stresses.

Sex, often a central component to a man's self-esteem and definition of self, was likely to be forfeited or severely restricted for the good of both oneself and others. This, however, was almost never an easily made forfeiture. With few avenues available for establishing self-esteem—due to societal homophobia—oftentimes gay men sought their pathways to success within their own communities. One of the most easily accessed, and for some most desirable, ways to pursue success had been to pursue an elusive goal of physical attractiveness and accumulated sexual conquests. However, HIV infection quickly made both of these goals more difficult, if not impossible, to achieve.

As an impact on the individual's masculinity, a loss of control can be highly significant. Traditional constructions of masculinity have included an ability to control one's self and surroundings and demonstrable achievements of success. HIV+ gay men have lost significant measures of control. Success in physical attractiveness and sexual conquests have been forfeited or significantly reduced. Hence, two central measures of masculinity slipped out of HIV+ gay men's reach. Maintaining a strong sense of masculinity, then, became increasingly difficult. At the very least, alternate avenues had to be found for maintaining displays and self-affirmations of masculinity.

Sometimes sexual opportunities and activities were abandoned by choice and other times this was something foisted upon the individual, despite objections. Forced celibacy most frequently was initiated during a time period when health concerns and daily living matters demanded so much energy and attention that the absence of sexual activity went essentially unnoticed. It was typically only after recovering from a serious opportunistic infection or adjusting to a physical disability that a man realized his sexual opportunities had been sacrificed. Sex tended to be forfeited during a time of crisis, and often the consequences of the physical crisis left the individual physically debilitated or psychologically unwilling to risk either transmitting the virus or suffering personal rejection.

For those men who voluntarily and consciously chose to abandon their sexual lives, this choice came as a result of careful deliberations and concerns regarding the welfare of others. The decision to move beyond sexual acts (and presumably to a focus on intimacy rather than behavior) often developed only after attempts to manage a safer sex life. Oftentimes, however, such efforts proved frustrating and disappointing, therefore leading the man to opt for the truly safe route of no sex rather than the probably safe route of carefully restricted sex. This process was clear in the experiences of Charlie, a 44-year-old man who battled numerous opportunistic infections for nearly 3 years. In Charlie's eyes, the worst thing about having AIDS was "not having sex." As he explained, though,

> My choice at this point . . . is not to have sex. . . . Initially, in the very early stages, I certainly took the precautions that were appropriate and it ultimately just became a burden and I just decided that I didn't want to live that way. It was easier to do without and I continue that today. And I'm okay with that. . . . It's my choice, I understand that, but I'm a very sexual person.

Somewhat similar, yet different because he had not (yet) completely abandoned sexual activities, were the recounted experiences of self-described punk artist and AIDS activist, Jarvis. Rather than suggesting that his lack of sexual encounters was a conscious choice, Jarvis explained that his inability to find other, similarly situated (socially and healthwise) sex partners led to the cessation of his sex life.

> It really hasn't affected my libido, you know, I masturbate all the time. But yeah, it's a huge effect. I mean, occasionally I will have encounters with people that vaguely resemble sex without telling them of my health status. Usually like S & M scenes. . . . Casual sex, that's a big loss. . . . I do have encounters that somewhat resemble sex. It's very antiseptic encounters. But hopefully I'll be able to meet other people in my same boat, you know, someone else who's horny as hell! Then I can go back to having sex, I really miss it.

For Jarvis, Charlie, and other HIV+ gay men who once had active, satisfying sex lives, the loss of such outlets only added to the distress of their disease. Both of these men are examples of how HIV+ gay men had forgone a major element of self-constructed masculinity, the central element of sexuality. Their sense of masculinity had to be refocused; sexuality no longer provided a foundation on which to build a gender identity. However, sexuality remained a part of these men's lives, only in a different form than they previously knew. The sexual lives of HIV+ gay men may continue, only without the participation in sex acts. HIV impacted not only physical health but also social interactions, psychological functioning, and gender constructions.

Factors Associated With Sexual Losses

The loss or declining frequency of sexual activities for HIV+ gay men could be attributed to several factors. First, some men, such as Charlie, have consciously chosen to discontinue sexual activities. Other men have found the complications of their disease directly contributed to their sexual losses (20%). For some HIV+ gay men, losses were a result of losing a significant other to HIV disease (11%) and remaining celibate following his death. Although these men were not forced into celibacy by their *own* disease, their celibacy stood as a consequence of HIV. Additionally, some HIV+ gay men's sexual losses were a result of psychological changes brought about by their disease or their fears of transmitting HIV to others.

Physical Factors

The physical factors that contributed to a termination of sexual activities ranged from paralysis and major physical impairment to the simply bothersome side-effects of medications. A common report was that sex drives greatly decreased following the onset of their disease. It was the belief of most men with decreased sexual drive that this came about due to one of two factors. First, decreased sexual drive may have been the result of the changes that HIV brings to bear on the physical body. Second, and more commonly proposed by HIV+ gay men, physiological changes imposed by their numerous medications were believed to have reduced their sex drive. Xing, a 45-year-old, first-generation Chinese American who had recurring bouts with serious opportunistic infections for more than 3 years, believed his sexual drive has been decreased by the new medicines: "I'm taking five antibiotics all at the same time. I think it pretty much kills the sexual desire. . . . Very, very once in a while I feel aroused, but not like before."

Again, sexual activities and physical abilities were restricted or removed, thereby restricting resources available for constructing and maintaining avenues to achievement (as a means of validating one's masculinity).

For some men, though, decreased sexual activities and desires appeared to be directly related to HIV itself. Various opportunistic infections and changes to the body made sex seem less desirable than previously. Men diagnosed with AIDS were most likely to report decreased desire. This is logical, because they have experienced more numerous and significant physiological changes. Timothy, a 40-year-old retired public relations executive who lost a lover to AIDS 1 year earlier, responded to questions about his present sex life saying,

> The sexual part of it? By gosh, I guess this is the time to be totally honest. I mean, I have numbness in my arms and in particular I can feel that same numbness in my penis. I'll be perfectly honest. So, when I masturbate it feels very different than it used to and it's not quite as enjoyable as it used to be.

Although many HIV+ gay men acknowledged a loss of sexual drive, diminished enjoyment, and less frequent sexual activities, those men not in a relationship did not usually report this as a major disruption to their lives. Correspondingly, these physical factors may have been somewhat less significant to these men's masculine identity constructions. Sex was less a matter of achievement or conquest and more emotionally based. Self-esteem and perceptions of external value and validation were accessible from a relationship partner. This may have offset some of the erosion nonpartnered men experienced in the foundation on which they build a gendered identity. However, for men in a relationship with a highly sexual, HIV- significant other, a contrasting consequence occasionally resulted.

Illustrative of this experience was Frank, a 46-year-old retired social worker who reported losing interest in sex since becoming HIV infected. Frank recommended to his partner, a 27-year-old HIV- man, "taking a lover on the side." The contrasting values they attributed to sex—as intimacy versus activity-achievement—introduced problems to their relationship. Of course, such a difference in perspective can arise for many reasons. The following account from Frank highlighted his frustrations in this regard.

> We just had this glorious sex [and] afterwards, of course we had to strip the bed and wash the sheets and he had to take a shower. He wasn't interested at first in hearing that I didn't want to pursue it because I didn't feel good. He had to show me, just like a little kid. He said, "Well, let's just fool around." I said I didn't want to. But he said, "Oh, c'mon, what the hell?" I didn't feel like arguing, so I said, fine, I'll show ya. You know, I have diarrhea really bad, so I didn't feel like having sex. But, he learned.

For those men who did remain sexually active, physical factors seriously detracted from their experiences. For some HIV+ gay men there have been physical changes in their bodies that have caused them to lose much of the sensation in various parts of their bodies. When physical pleasures have been forfeited, sexual activity, for many, became very unappealing. Additionally, sexual losses due to HIV brought special challenges to some men's sense of masculinity. Attempts to overcome emerging physical obstacles led to disappointment and consequently motivated an eventual abandonment of sexual activities. This, in turn, may well have led to a need to reestablish a base on which to construct masculinity.

Loss of Self-Esteem

For some HIV+ gay men, decreases in sexual desire followed as a consequence of decreasing self-esteem. Oftentimes men who abandoned sex due to declining self-esteem pointed to their anguish over the changing outward appearances of their bodies. Men with Kaposi's sarcoma (KS) typically did not believe they were sexually attractive, either to themselves or others. Martin said that despite having a partner for the last 14 years, KS triggered the death of his sex life. Specifically Martin explained that

> my sex life pretty well died in '90 when I got my first lesion and had to deal with the self-esteem and the fact that it wasn't just a concept anymore of being HIV-infected. There was physical proof, something very tangible that people

could see. . . . I had so many lesions that it was not something you could just kind of hide or say "oh, that's just a bruise."

More simply, Timothy, who above explained how numbness in his penis decreased his sexual desire, also reported losing over 40 pounds through the course of his disease. As a consequence Timothy said, "I look in the mirror and I used to have a butt, now I have three wrinkles of skin where my butt used to be." This, in Timothy's experience, meant that "I have pretty low self-esteem in terms of how I think I look with my clothes off, so that bothers me and reduces the drive somewhat."

Appearance is among the most highly valued components of sexual attractiveness in our culture, especially among gay men. When one's physical appearance is radically, and negatively, altered, it is not surprising that a gay man's self-esteem, and, consequently, his sexual drives, are lowered. The attack such a change brought to some HIV+ gay men's masculinity was clear: When they lost self-esteem they believed they had lost status. When they lost status, how could they remain "a man"? Physical attractiveness, long associated with women's constructions of femininity, influences men's constructions of self as a gendered being as well. This may be especially true for gay men, who have long lived in communities where youthfulness and attractiveness have been highly valued. The HIV+ gay man, however, has lost his attractiveness and his status as terminally ill has redefined him as old (nearing the end of life). Therefore, HIV+ gay men lose the social status their body provided them, as well as slowly losing their bodies.

Fears of Transmitting HIV

Although the impacts of the physical disease on both one's body and mind were important factors that led many HIV+ gay men to abandon or significantly curtail their sexual activities, these were not the most common reasons for such actions. Rather, fear of transmitting HIV to others was the factor that most frequently induced HIV+ gay men to self-impose sexual restrictions. For some, the fear of transmitting HIV was overwhelming, whereas for others it was merely a recurring but manageable distraction. As one might expect, all HIV+ gay men reported that they wished they had not become infected. Not only did they see themselves with an incurable, stigmatizing, fatal disease but they also have experienced or anticipated experiencing a significant loss in social status. HIV+

gay men faced questions regarding their masculinity because of their sexual orientation (as a result of homophobia). With the addition of HIV to their lives they also encountered losses of activity, ability, and attractiveness. These losses, in turn, may have called their masculinity into question even more.

Because they have experienced the multitude of losses that accompany HIV disease, HIV+ gay men unanimously reported that they would never want to think they were responsible for infecting someone else. Consequently, behaviors known to transmit HIV, such as sex, were reportedly approached only with great trepidation.

Fears about infecting others were clearly expressed by a majority of HIV+ gay men. First, Don, a 38-year-old African American man whose disease has forced him to move back into the home of his parents, stated that, "I wouldn't mind having a real companion. . . . But as far as sex, I'm way beyond that. . . . I would not ever do that to anyone. I simply would not. I couldn't be that cruel."

Or, even more direct were the comments of Charlie, who battled several opportunistic infections before being forced to retire. He declared, "I don't want to live with the burden that I might, even innocently, pass this on." Yet more specifically, Lon, a 45-year-old man who migrated to the city from his rural home to escape homophobic prejudice and discrimination, and who was diagnosed 5 years earlier, related the following story:

At first I was even afraid to have, well if I met someone and then we would have mutual masturbation, I thought, "My god, I can't do that either because what happens if he has a cut on his body and this cum gets into that cut and it gives him this disease?" So I wiped that out. Then I thought, well, there's condoms. Then I thought, what happens if we're having sex and it breaks and I give this guy a disease? Naw, just forget it. Just live in your fantasy world, which I did.

Some HIV+ gay men, however, have succeeded at managing their fears and remained (relatively happily) sexually active. It was, however, only a minority of men that claimed they could continue sexual activities. These were the men for whom sex and sexuality appeared the most central in self-constructions of masculinity. When sex was sustained, the overall level of sexual satisfaction was typically decreased. In the words of many HIV+ gay men, sex and HIV came to be so intertwined that they were unable to engage in sex without thinking about their HIV. Jeremy, whose partner was also HIV+, affirmed this experience:

> No, I can't forget about it. I wish that could happen, but you know, you're being intimate with someone and the whole time, you're concerned about infecting the partner and you know, I guess that takes precedence over bringing pleasure to your partner.

Similarly, Gaston, whose partner was HIV-, maintained that

> It makes it much more difficult since he is negative. . . . I mean it's there in the back of your mind. But I can relax more if I know that I'm doing something that isn't putting him at risk. Then I can enjoy it and not let it affect my performance or whatever. But at first it was on my mind all the time. . . . It's still there, don't get me wrong. I've just kind of learned to deal with it.

Realizations that one's sexual acts can have fatal consequences for others had a significant, sobering psychological impact on most HIV+ gay men. Because of their fears regarding the consequences of sex, most HIV+ gay men terminated sexual activities, but often only after attempts to actively manage their fears and risks to others.

Experiencing the Loss of Sex

The behavioral changes involved for men who have stopped engaging in sex with others did not always represent significant changes for those men's lives. When changes were perceived as significant, this introduced important sources of stress, dissatisfaction, and, sometimes, identity questions to their lives. The small minority (7%) of men who reported not altering their sexual behaviors as a consequence of their HIV status were all men who were involved in relationships, usually with other HIV+ gay men. Mike, a 37-year-old former realtor who lost his eyesight to herpes shingles, and who was involved in a 4-year relationship with another HIV+ gay man, said that, "as far as Tom and I go as a couple, we still have sex, because where's it going to go?" Although not a medically advisable position due to the likelihood of continuing reinfection, this is nonetheless an example of the types of choices HIV+ gay men have had to make. Mike and his partner have elected to pursue psychological well-being and a sense of normalcy in their lives, perhaps at the expense of their physical health. Views such as Mike's were definitely in the minority; most HIV+ couples chose to eliminate, reconstruct, or make safer their sexual encounters in attempts to protect their health. In these instances, normalcy has had to be redefined, as has masculinity.

For most men who have found it necessary to limit their sexual activities, these changes were viewed as one of the many hard-hitting losses imposed by their disease. Sex is central to many men's self-concept, self-esteem, and gender identity. When one's sense of identity is challenged, all elements of social life may be questioned or reconfigured. Because self-esteem and sex are intimately intertwined for some gay men, the loss or heavy restrictions on sex has meant that one has had to forfeit a central aspect of one's identity. This perspective was seen again in Jarvis's words:

> Sex was the best thing in my life. It's the purest form of communication between two people for me, and I really didn't get a lot of love as a kid or affection, but a lot of abuse. So I was really, you know, sex was really good for me. It really did a lot for me psychologically and emotionally. So, it makes it a lot harder to cope. You don't have that out, that stress reduction, that beautiful thing. Or, if you do, it's fraught with worry.

However, other men who have made the conscious choice to limit their sexual activities in light of their HIV infection have found it possible to adopt a more optimistic approach to such changes. For some of these men the necessity of changing one's specific sexual activities and number of sex partners offered opportunities to explore new areas of sexuality and personal growth. This meant that these men were able to view such changes as, at least partially, positive in nature. These were men who adapted their constructions of masculinity, not those whose definitions were static and rigid. If an HIV+ gay man could locate new methods of fulfilling masculine criteria, he may have avoided identity dissonance. As an example, some HIV+ gay men, especially those in long-term relationships, have replaced sex acts with heightened levels of emotional intimacy, achieved in nonsexual interactions. Frank, who both knew of his HIV status and had been in a relationship with the same man for over 8 years, reported that

> we haven't had sex in over 4 years. . . . Okay? We haven't had sex. There's no reason for it. Why do you have to have sex in a relationship? That's an added, extra bonus. If you've got love, honesty, and trust, you don't need anything else. Snuggling at night, being close, you don't have to have sex just to have a relationship. No one does. That's the problem with most gay relationships, as

well as straight relationships. . . . You have to set your priorities, and sex is way down on the bottom.

Although many may have expected that those who chose, or were forced, to abandon sex perceived such changes in a negative light, these men's experiences actually revealed a contrasting result. It appeared that those who have given up sex were, on the whole, more positive about such changes than those who merely reduced their range of sexual activities and partners. As discussed previously, those who abandoned sexual activities were most commonly in more advanced stages of disease, while asymptomatic men were more likely to have adopted the less extreme management attempt of limiting their sexual activities. This may suggest, then, that progression of disease is accompanied by acceptance of disease (and its inevitable consequences). This may be most obvious for men whose disease had brought them more serious physical and social implications. Those men who were still relatively healthy live lives that were, in many ways, no different than those they knew prior to learning of their HIV+ status. This also meant healthier HIV+ gay men could be expected to hold more traditional (or, less modified) perceptions of masculinity. The imposition (often self-imposed) of changes to central life elements could, therefore, be more difficult to accept for HIV+, but healthy, gay men. However, as time passed and the individual incorporated his new (HIV+) status to his identity complex, his sexual behavior most likely became modified. Sex tended to lose some of its meaning as these men developed new identities. Additionally, sex also came to be viewed as cumbersome and less than fulfilling. Aaron, a 28-year-old man who knew of his HIV+ status for over 3 years, discussed his sex life, saying,

> I'm more cautious I guess. Not being able to just kind of dive right into, you know, the whole sex act and just get carried away with it and enjoy yourself. It's like, it's so technical sometimes. It's like, okay, well we gotta stop here because we gotta do this now. . . . Now there's rules and regulations, or now it's so technical to have sex and it should be something that you should be able to do any way you want, anywhere you want, you know, and not have to worry about anything. . . . You could be totally enjoying what's going on and then all of a sudden, it's like, okay, before we do that everybody's got to get ready now. And the moment's gone, so to speak.

Aaron recognized the importance and necessity for practicing safer sex, but obviously did not have a positive attitude regarding such. Instead, as was common among HIV+ gay men, sex came to be viewed as unnatural. Sex took on "rules and regulations"; therefore, spontaneity was restricted. Sexual freedom, enjoyment, and the accompanying impact on these men's definitions of self, and masculinity were modified in light of their perceptions of self and potential transmission of HIV to others. Therefore, new avenues of recreation, interactions, and methods for building self-esteem and maintaining a sense of masculinity have had to be discovered. Those men who adopted celibacy showed greater success in these paths; those who worked to maintain and manage their sexual activity repertoires did not.

Not all HIV+ gay men, as evidenced by numerous sensationalized media stories, have been concerned about the welfare of their sexual partners. One somewhat surprising finding of the present research was that only a small minority of HIV+ gay men (9%) were willing to report a sexual encounter in which he did not inform his partner of this HIV status.[4] One man, a self-reported prostitute, although advocating safer sex, reported that if he told clients of his HIV status, they would not patronize him. He reportedly urged clients to use condoms, but a majority refused. Several other men did, however, report having friends or acquaintances (whom they named) who continued sexual activities while not informing their partners of their HIV status. Usually, such other men were viewed very negatively, and often friendships with such men were strained or eventually terminated. As Reginald, whose face and body are covered with KS lesions, reported,

> I had a friend that had a lot of problems with that. He found out he had AIDS, and he was pretty sickly. He still went out to the baths and was still going out and picking up boys . . . and not using condoms. I really had a problem with that. He said, "Well, you know, I've got it and I'm going to die and I don't care." That really bothered me. I talked with him about it and said, "It's not fair. What if you got it that way?"

A few HIV+ gay men (7%) reported that whereas they actively took steps to make sexual activities safer, they did not believe it was their responsibility to tell their sexual partners about their HIV status. Rather, because of widespread education regarding HIV's modes of transmission and safer sex, some men believed their sex partners were responsible for their own health. In these instances, rather obviously, sex was an encounter with an objectified other, not an intimate experience. Rodney, whose lover died with AIDS, recounted having had men literally get up out of bed when he told them of his infection. Rodney's partners, it would appear, perceived him in an objectified manner; when learning of his infection, Rodney became damaged goods (in his partners' eyes). When the object is damaged, just as when buying goods, the value is decreased. Consequently, Rodney believed that if he limited himself to safer sex he need not disclose his status. In this way, even though he may be objectified by his partners, he retained his value (as an object). As he explained his perspective,

> I don't think I should have to tell anybody. . . . Is that really fair though? I keep coming back with, "Yes, damn it, it is fair." . . . I mean, that's really something personal and of course, here goes some ethics, but I might only be with you for a few hours, so why should I share something so personal?

The attitudes expressed by Reginald and Rodney, however, did not represent the full range of HIV+ gay men's attitudes. Rather, what these men's stories made clear was that not all HIV+ gay men necessarily believed they had a responsibility to be concerned about informing their sex partners about their HIV status. Although these men may have felt a personal responsibility to protect others, they did not equate this with a perceived need to publicly announce their health status. When objectified, or when objectifying others, responsibilities were minimized.

Most notably, several of the men interviewed (13%) knew (or believed they knew) that they were originally, knowingly infected by men with whom they shared a relationship. Men infected via this route, somewhat surprisingly, very rarely expressed negative feelings for their partners. Jeremy, while sitting in the same room as his lover, calmly reported how he was knowingly infected. Claiming to accept his infection as a "risk of being gay," Jeremy related the following story:

> When we first met we talked about it and I asked him if he'd ever been tested. He said, "No." . . . But once we were together and we talked more about it, he knew how important it was to me. When we finally had the discussion he came to me and said, "Jeremy, I did something today." I said, "Okay, what did you do?" And he said, "I went to the doctor and I got my results. I had a test done. . . . I'm positive." And the only thing that I could think of was the suffering he was gonna have to go through. You know, it didn't matter to me at that point that he'd lied to me in the beginning and that we weren't being safe. Because at that same point he told, he goes, "I don't know if I'd told you this or not, but I had been tested before, three and a half years before." . . . I've loved him from the beginning and I forgave him for what happened. I've also realized that it just wasn't his responsibility, it was mine too.

What Jeremy's story exemplified is that many HIV+ gay men are faced with serious and difficult decisions about not only their health but also their social lives. It appears that there are two primary, healthy adaptations that are available to HIV+ gay men. First, they could incorporate their status as an HIV+ gay man (and look forward, not to the past and how their lives *might* have been different), or they could alter (sometimes radically) or avoid what some believe to be normative gay (sexual) lifestyles found in many urban gay communities. For some HIV+ gay men, this may lead to a role as an activist, focusing on gay rights, AIDS, or a combination of issues. For many men, such as Jeremy, the decision of how to react to one's newfound status was mainly an intellectual exercise. Once he was infected, it could not be changed; therefore, he looked at his current life situation and decided how to manage his life, both sexually and otherwise.

Conclusion

The sexual lives of HIV+ gay men studied in this research were almost always significantly altered as a result of HIV disease. In contrast to the impacts on sexuality of other terminal or debilitating diseases, it is not simply the disease itself that has brought on changes. Instead, these alterations and losses have been the result of conscious choices to protect oneself and others from infection or psychological changes within the individual. Although the impact of HIV (and opportunistic infections) on the physical body certainly brings about modifications or a cessation of sexual drives and activities for HIV+ gay men, this may have been the least common impetus for change in these men's sexual lives. Of more importance, at least in the eyes of these men, have been the effects of medications for combating HIV and other infections. However, even these physical changes are not at the heart of the impact of HIV disease on sexual lives of HIV+ gay men.

In addition to changes in sexual activities and sexuality, these men also experienced changes in their experiences of masculinity. HIV compelled these men to reexamine and redefine masculinity. Because some of the changes brought by HIV center on areas in which masculinity had traditionally been established (sex, achievement, self-control, environmental control, and physical attractiveness), these HIV+ gay men have had to identify new ways to define masculinity, or risk losing their masculine self-identities. When sex is forgone, many gay men lose a critical means of achieving success and personal-environmental control. Sex contributes to the definition of masculinity; therefore, when sex is abandoned, both sexuality and masculinity need to be reconfigured.

What have easily and obviously been the most common reasons for HIV+ gay men to abandon or restrict sexual activities have been the cares and concerns these men have felt regarding their roles as potential trans-mitters of HIV. The stigma of HIV disease and the universal concern about transferring the stigma (along with the virus) to others led them to rethink and, most often, restructure their sexual lives. Consequently, choices were made to impose hardships on themselves to avoid both drawing others into the grip of HIV and feeling responsible for their disease. Identification of these concerns and motivations for sexual behavior change has not been surprising. Instead, this stood as confirmation that the experience of HIV disease can be seen as an extension of a more general experience of sexuality and gay political identity. This is supported by the similarity between the findings in the present study and Siegel and Raveis's (1993) analysis of gay men's adoption of celibacy as a preventive measure. In their work, Siegel and Raveis found that five themes explained celibacy in gay men: (a) a desire for truly safe sex, (b) emotional distress concern-ing possible transmission, (c) a desire for more than sex from a relation-ship, (d) a dislike of safer sex, and (e) a fear of being unable to limit one's sexual outlets.

These changes have seemed, on the one hand, only appropriate and proper. After all, without at least modifying their sexual behaviors, HIV+ gay men are highly likely to infect others. However, on the other hand, there is an ironic twist here. Whereas this chapter has discussed a category of persons most commonly defined not by their personal or social char-acteristics but instead by their presumed sexual activities and frequencies, it has now become clear that such conceptions are clearly off target. HIV+ gay men can no longer be accurately defined by their sex lives: Sex as they knew it has been either abandoned or restructured. HIV+ gay men generally do not have sex lives similar to gay men without HIV disease. These differences have not necessarily been welcomed, as Martin, a self-described celibate AIDS activist, succinctly said,

Sex . . . continues to be a great frustration for me, and I think for most people with AIDS. It seems kind of a cruel irony that most of us were infected through sex and now we don't get any or very little sex at all.

HIV+ gay men were found to be fundamentally different than their noninfected counterparts physically, socially, and often psychologically. The roles sex played both prior to and after knowledge of infection are different. Sexual lives are just one of the many elements of life impacted by HIV. Life changed for these gay men when HIV entered the picture. Adaptations, including sexual adaptations, were common and significant experiences. This is the context of living with HIV. Changes occurred but were not always experienced the same by those who were changed.

Notes

1. The total sample of 45 HIV+ gay men includes 20 men diagnosed with AIDS and 25 HIV+, asymptomatic men.

2. Difficulties in accessing persons living with HIV disease are numerous and often impose methodological difficulties and implementation restraints on researchers. Perhaps the most difficult barrier to overcome is not convincing persons with HIV to be interviewed, but working through the structural and personal difficulties social service providers face in assisting researchers (Fleishman, Mor, Cwi, & Piette, 1992).

3. All identifications of interviewees are pseudonyms. Unless noted otherwise, all references in this work to "men with HIV" or "HIV positive men" refer to gay men.

4. However, see Meyer-Bahlburg et al. (1991), Martin (1987), Exner et al. (1992) and Gold et al. (1994) for discussions of HIV+ gay men who do continue to practice unsafe sex.

References

Adib, M., Joseph, J. G., Ostrow, D. G., Tal, M., & Schwartz, S. A. (1991). Relapse in sexual behavior among homosexual men: A 2-year follow-up from the Chicago MACS/CCS. *AIDS, 5,* 757-760.

Auchincloss, S. (1991). Sexual dysfunction after cancer treatment. *Journal of Psychosocial Oncology, 9*(1), 23-42.

Baxter, S. (1991). AIDS education in the jail setting. *Crime & Delinquency, 37*(1), 48-63.

Bell, N. K. (1991). Social/sexual norms and AIDS in the South: Ethics and the politics of AIDS: Lessons for small cities and rural areas throughout the U.S. *AIDS Education and Prevention, 3*(2), 164-180.

Beutel, M. (1988). Male sexuality and cancer. In W. Eicher & G. Kockott (Eds.), *Sexology* (pp. 283-289). Berlin: Spring-Verlag.

Carey, M. A., & Smith, M. W. (1992). Enhancement of validity through qualitative approaches. *Evaluation and the Health Professions, 15*(4), 107-114.

Cleary, P. D., Van Devanter, N., Rogers, T. F., & Singer, E. (1991). Behavior changes after notification of HIV infection. *American Journal of Public Health, 81*(12), 1586-1590.

Coates, T. J., Morin, S. F., & McKusick, L. (1987). Behavioral consequences of AIDS antibody testing among gay men. *Journal of the American Medical Association, 258,* 1889.

Connell, R. W., & Kippax, S. (1990). Sexuality in the AIDS crisis: Patterns of sexual practice and pleasure in a sample of Australian gay and bisexual men. *Journal of Sex Research, 27*(2), 167-198.

Ekstrand, M. L., & Coates, T. J. (1990). Maintenance of safer sexual behaviors and predictors of risky sex: The San Francisco Men's Health Study. *American Journal of Public Health, 80,* 973-977.

Exner, T. M., Meyer-Bahlburg, H. F., & Ehrhardt, A. A. (1992). Sexual self control as a mediator of high risk sexual behavior in a New York City cohort of HIV+ and HIV- gay men. *Journal of Sex Research, 29*(3), 389-406.

Fleishman, J. A., Mor, V., Cwi, J. S., & Piette, J. D. (1992). Sampling and accessing people with AIDS. *Evaluation and the Health Professions, 15*(4), 385-404.

Folkman, S., Chesney, M. A., Pollack, L., & Phillips, C. (1992). Stress, coping, and high-risk sexual behavior. *Health Psychology, 11*(4), 218-222.

Gendel, E. S., & Bonner, E. J. (1986). Sex, angina, and heart disease. *Medical Aspects of Human Sexuality, 20,* 18-36.

Glaser, B. G., & Strauss, A. L. (1967). *The discovery of grounded theory.* Chicago: Aldine.

Gochros, H. (1992). The sexuality of gay men with HIV infection. *Social Work, 37*(2), 105-109.

Godfried, J. P., van Griensven, E., DeVroome, M. M., Tielman, R. A. P., Goudsmit, J., van der Noordaa, J., de Wolf, F., & Coutinho, R. A. (1988). Impact of HIV antibody testing on changes in sexual behavior among homosexual men in the Netherlands. *American Journal of Public Health, 78*(12), 1757-1577.

Gold, R. S., Skinner, M. J., & Ross, M. W. (1994). Unprotected anal intercourse in HIV-infected and non-HIV-infected gay men. *Journal of Sex Research, 31*(1), 59-77.

Hays, R. B., Kegeles, S. M., & Coates, T. J. (1990). High HIV risk-taking among young gay men. *AIDS, 4,* 901-907.

Hoff, C. C., McKusick, L., Hilliard, B., & Coates, T. J. (1992). The impact of HIV anti-body status on gay men's partner preferences: A community perspective. *AIDS Education and Prevention, 4*(3), 197-204.

Jenkins, B. (1988). Patients' reports of sexual changes after treatment for gynecological cancer. *Oncology Nursing Forum, 15*(3), 349-354.

Joseph, J. G., Adib, M., Koopman, J. S., & Ostrow, D. G. (1990). Behavioral change in longitudinal studies: Adoption of condom use by homosexual/bisexual men. *American Journal of Public Health, 80*(12), 1513-1514.

Kelly, J. A., Kalichman, S. C., Kauth, M. R., Kilgore, H. G., Hood, H. V., Campos, P. E., Rao, S. M., Brasfield, T. L., & St. Lawrence, J. S. (1991). Situational factors associated with AIDS risk behavior lapses and coping strategies used by gay men who successfully avoid lapses. *American Journal of Public Health, 81*(10), 1335-1338.

Kelly, J. A., St. Lawrence, J. S., Brasfield, T. L., Stevenson, L. Y., Diaz, Y. E., & Hauth, A. C. (1990). AIDS risk behavior patterns among gay men in small Southern cities. *American Journal of Public Health, 80*(4), 416-418.

Landis, S. E., Earp, J. L., & Koch, C. G. (1992). Impact of HIV testing and counseling on subsequent sexual behavior. *AIDS Education and Prevention, 4*(1), 61-70.

Levine, M. P., & Siegel, K. (1992). Unprotected sex: Understanding gay men's participation. In J. Huber & B. E. Schnieder (Eds.), *The social context of AIDS* (pp. 47-71). Newbury Park, CA: Sage.

Lippert, G. P. (1986). Excessive concern about AIDS in two bisexual men. *Canadian Journal of Psychiatry, 31,* 63-65.

Marcus, D. K., Amen, T. M., & Bibace, R. (1992). A developmental analysis of prisoners' conceptions of AIDS. *Criminal Justice and Behavior, 19*(2), 174-188.

Martin, D. J. (1990). A study of the deficiencies in the condom-use skills of gay men. *Public Health Reports, 105*(6), 638-640.

Martin, J. L. (1987). The impact of AIDS on gay male sexual behavior patterns in New York City. *American Journal of Public Health, 77*(5), 578-581.

Mays, V. M., Cochran, S. D., Hamilton, E., Miller, N., Leung, L., Rothspan, S., Kolson, J., Webb, F., & Torres, M. (1993). Just cover up: Barriers to heterosexual and gay young adults' use of condoms. *Health Values: Achieving High Level Wellness, 17*(4), 41-47.

Meyer-Bahlburg, H. F., Exner, T. M., Lorenz, G., Gruen, R. S., Gorman, J. M., & Ehrhardt, A. A. (1991). Sexual risk behavior, sexual functioning, and HIV-disease progression in gay men. *Journal of Sex Research, 28*(1), 3-27.

Nurnberg, H. G., Prudic, J., Fiori, M., & Freedman, E. P. (1984). Psychopathology complicating acquired immune deficiency syndrome. *American Journal of Psychiatry, 141,* 95-96.

Offir, J. T., Fisher, J. D., Williams, S. S., & Fisher, W. A. (1993). Reasons for inconsistent AIDS-preventive behaviors among gay men. *Journal of Sex Research, 30,* 62-69.

Osmond, D., Bacchetti, P., Chaisson, R. E., Kelly, T., Stempel, R., Carlson, J., & Moss, A. R. (1988). Time of exposure and HIV infection in homosexual partners of men with AIDS. *American Journal of Public Health, 78*(8), 944-947.

Parker, R. G., & Carballo, M. (1990). Qualitative research on homosexual and bisexual behavior relevant to HIV/AIDS. *Journal of Sex Research, 27*(4), 497-525.

Paul, J. P., Stall, R., & Davis, F. (1993). Sexual risk for HIV transmission among gay/bisexual men in substance-abuse treatment. *AIDS Education and Prevention, 5*(1), 11-24.

Peterson, J. L., Coates, T. J., Catania, J. A., Middleton, L., Hilliard, B., & Hearst, N. (1992). High risk sexual behavior and condom use among gay and bisexual African-American men. *American Journal of Public Health, 82*(11), 1490-1494.

Pincu, L. (1989). Sexual compulsivity in gay men: Controversy and treatment. *Journal of Counseling and Development, 68*(10), 63-66.

Quadland, M. C., & Shattls, W. D. (1987). AIDS, sexuality and sexual control. *Journal of Homosexuality, 14*(1/2), 277-298.

Ruefli, T., Yu, O., & Barton, J. (1992). Sexual risk taking in smaller cities: The case of Buffalo, New York. *Journal of Sex Research, 29*(1), 95-108.

Schnell, D. J., Higgins, D. L., Wilson, R. M., Goldbaum, G., Cohn, D. L., & Wolitski, R. J. (1992). Men's disclosure of HIV test results to male primary sex partners. *American Journal of Public Health, 82*(12), 1675-1676.

Siegel, K., & Raveis, V. H. (1993). AIDS-related reasons for gay men's adoption of celibacy. *AIDS Education and Prevention, 5*(4), 302-310.

Silvestre, A. (1992). *HIV rates and differences in behavior over time among men entering an HIV disease cohort study.* Unpublished doctoral dissertation, University of Pittsburgh.

Smith, D. B., & Babaian, R. J. (1992). The effects of treatment for cancer on male fertility and sexuality. *Cancer Nursing, 15*(4), 271-275.

Stall, R., Barrett, D., Bye, L., Catania, J., Frutchey, C., Henne, J., Lemp, G., & Paul, J. (1992). A comparison of younger and older gay men's HIV risk-taking behaviors: The communication technologies 1989 cross-sectional survey. *Journal of Acquired Immune Deficiency Syndromes, 5,* 682-687.

Stall, R., Coates, T. J., & Hoff, C. (1988). Behavioral risk reduction for HIV infection among gay and bisexual men. *American Psychologist, 43,* 878-885.

Stevenson, H. C., & Davis, G. (1994). Impact of culturally sensitive AIDS video education on the AIDS risk knowledge of African-American adolescents. *AIDS Education and Prevention, 6*(1), 40-52.

Tewksbury, R., & Whittier, N. (1992). Safer sex practices in samples drawn from nightclub, campus and gay bars. *Sociology and Social Research, 76*(4), 10-15.

Weitz, R. (1991). *Life with AIDS.* New Brunswick, NJ: Rutgers University Press.

12

Testicular Cancer and Masculinity

DAVID FREDERICK GORDON

How do men cope with illness that threatens their reproductive organs or their sexual functioning? How does such an experience affect their thoughts about themselves as men? Testicular cancer is a disease that enables us to investigate both questions. Its physical consequences include the loss of a testicle and, in many cases, subsequent changes in sexual functioning. Because men who have testicular cancer are likely to survive the disease, they must integrate these changes into their lives and into their self-concepts.

In this chapter I will argue that cancer of the testes usually does not alter men's sense of masculinity. Part of the masculine coping process involves defining the cancer experience in a way that reaffirms masculine identity. Although this process can have benefits, for some men it has serious drawbacks as well.

Testicular Cancer

When a testicular tumor is discovered, the affected testicle is removed in what is called an *orchiectomy*. If there is suspicion that the tumor has metastasized to the abdominal lymph nodes, an additional operation, called a *lymph node dissection,* is performed to remove these lymph nodes. This is a lengthy operation that leaves a large abdominal scar. It is also common for the nerves that control ejaculation to be damaged during this operation.

AUTHOR'S NOTE: My thanks to Don Sabo for his helpful comments on an earlier draft of this chapter. This research has been supported by the Geneseo Foundation.

If this occurs, the patient is left with a dry ejaculation. Ejaculation is normal except that no semen or fluid is ejaculated. This condition can reverse itself after several years if the nerves are able to regenerate. In many cases, though, the loss of an ejaculate is permanent. Depending on the type of cancer cell that was found in the testicular tumor, surgery can be followed by either radiation or chemotherapy to kill any stray cancer cells left in the body. A newer approach, used in some cases in which the tumor is in an early stage, is to forgo therapy following surgery. Instead, the patient is monitored closely to watch for any further evidence of cancer (Pizzocaro et al., 1986; Sogani et al., 1984).

Testicular cancer is relatively rare in the general population, with approximately 6,800 new cases per year (American Cancer Society, 1994, p. 6). It is, however, the most common cancer in white men between the ages of 20 and 34 and the second most common between the ages of 35 and 39 (National Cancer Institute, 1987). This is a period when men typically are making commitments to careers, spouses, and families, and a life-threatening disease at this stage could have serious effects on these commitments. Testicular cancer is highly curable,[1] but surgery, chemotherapy, or radiation therapy can physically limit sexual functioning and fertility,[2] and the cultural meanings associated with sexual function, testicles, and potency, especially for young men, make this a potentially serious issue for masculine identity.

Studies of the psychosocial consequences of testicular cancer have found that most men who have had testicular cancer make positive long-term adjustments (Gorzynski & Holland, 1979; Rieker, Edbril, & Garnick, 1985; Tross, Holland, Bosl, & Geller, 1984). In her review of studies of psychological adjustment to testicular cancer, Tross (1989) states,

> There is general agreement that the cancer experience does not impair the major areas of function of the survivor's life, such as employment, marriage, or economic status. When explicit questions are asked about mood, especially depressed and anxious states, increased subjective distress is observed among these survivors, but it is subtle and nonimpairing. (p. 242)

There is evidence that some men's outlook on life in general was improved by having experienced testicular cancer (Rieker et al., 1989). These findings are generally consistent with studies of the long-term quality of life of other cancer survivors (de Haes & Van Knippenberg, 1987).

The evidence related to sexuality and masculinity is mixed. Although some studies have found that testicular cancer threatens sexual potency and masculinity (Gorzynski & Holland, 1979), others have found no significant differences in sexuality between men who have received an orchiectomy and those who have not (Blakemore, 1988). There is evidence, however, that up to 30% of testicular cancer survivors experience problems with sexual functioning, body image, or infertility as a result of the treatments for testicular cancer (Gritz et al., 1989; Moynihan, 1991; Rieker et al. 1989; Schover, 1987; Schover, Gonzales, & Eschenbach, 1986). Those who experience ejaculatory impairment are also at greater risk for concern about sexual functioning, especially as the years since the treatment increase (Rieker et al., 1985).

Although these studies have produced important findings, they leave some important questions unanswered. First, they do not reveal *how* most men arrive at positive long-term adjustments to these physical changes in their bodies. Second, they do not reveal how men who experience physical problems deal with these problems. Third, even though some of the existing studies gathered responses from both survivors and their wives (Gritz et al., 1989), they did not investigate the gender-related processes by which men and their partners attempted to cope with the experience of cancer and its aftermath. As Fife, Kennedy, and Robinson (1994) point out, in studies of cancer,

> little research pertaining to the variable of gender has been done with respect to either the stress of the illness or an individual's adjustment to the crisis. Although many studies concerning the impact of cancer on individuals' psychosocial well-being have focused on women, few have focused predominantly or exclusively on men or on a comparison by gender. (p. 2)

The present study was undertaken to investigate the ways in which men and those close to them attempt to adjust to and make sense of the experience of having testicular cancer, especially as it influences their thoughts about themselves as men. The study's most general finding is that testicular cancer created a transitional phase that encouraged men to reassess their priorities (Gordon, 1990). In the course of this reassessment, they drew on cultural meanings and engaged in social practices that in one way or another reaffirmed their masculine identities. The paradox is that although losing a testicle, and in some cases the ability to conceive children, they maintained or strengthened their sense of being men.

The Male Sex Role

One way in which to conceptualize masculinity is through sex roles. According to Pleck (1981), the sex role paradigm claims that

> the individual is preprogrammed to learn a traditional sex role as part of normal psychological development; thus culturally defined sex roles do not arbitrarily restrict individuals' potential—on the contrary, they are necessary external structures without which individuals could not develop normally. (p. 4)

The central characteristics of the male sex role in American society were summarized by Brannon (1976) as follows:

1. No Sissy Stuff: the need to be different from women
2. The Big Wheel: the need to be superior to others
3. The Sturdy Oak: the need to be independent and self-reliant
4. Give 'Em Hell: the need to be more powerful than others, through violence if necessary

Earlier, Parsons and Bales (1953) formulated the distinction between male instrumental, technical roles and female expressive, supportive roles. Harrison, Chin, and Ficarrotto (1992) summarize the resulting socially prescribed male role as one that "requires men to be noncommunicative, competitive and nongiving, and inexpressive, and to evaluate life success in terms of external achievements rather than personal and interpersonal fulfillment" (p. 272). Although there is some debate over specific elements of this role, I will use the previous characteristics as an approximate description of what I will refer to as the traditional male sex role.

The concepts of sex roles in general and the male sex role in particular have been heavily criticized by men's studies. First, the use of the sex role paradigm in social science is seen as conceptually imprecise, too static, politically conservative, overly simplistic, and inconsistent with social reality (Carrigan, Connell, & Lee, 1987; Kimmel, 1987; Pleck, 1981). The second type of objection to this approach is that there are psychological and behavioral problems created when men use the idea of a masculine sex role to form their own identities or to evaluate themselves as men. This becomes a particularly serious problem when one set of masculine characteristics becomes dominant in the culture. On the one hand, this "hegemonic masculinity" is used by men to their advantage to legitimate their power in relation to women (Carrigan et al., 1987). On the other hand, because the hegemonic male sex role is based on stereotyping and an unrealistic conception of masculinity, few men are able to live up to its standards. This leads to feelings of inadequacy, attributions of deviance, and hypermasculine compensations such as rape and other forms of violence and aggression (Pleck, 1981). In addition, hegemonic masculinity fosters behaviors such as risk taking that are harmful to men's health (Harrison et al., 1992; Waldron, 1976). In sum, the men's studies critique of the male sex role argues that rather than furthering normal male development, using the standards of hegemonic masculinity as norms to guide ones behavior and to judge ones adequacy as a man leads to both psychological and physical problems for men.

The question in relation to testicular cancer is, to what extent and with what results do men who contract this disease employ the norms of hegemonic masculinity? Before addressing this question, I will describe the methods used to perform this study.

Methods

Twenty face-to-face intensive interviews were conducted with men who have had testicular cancer at some point in their lives.[3] This method was selected as a means of investigating the question of *how* men had adjusted to testicular cancer. The men were selected by several methods. Some were identified through a tumor registry at a cancer center. These men contacted me in response to a letter sent to them by the cancer center. Other men had participated in a support group for testicular cancer and were identified by the group's organizer. These men were contacted by phone, and all of them readily agreed to be interviewed. Others were found by word of mouth and referrals by acquaintances. These men also initially were contacted by phone. All but one of the interviews were conducted in the homes of the men. Five of the interviews were joint interviews, including both husband and wife together.[4] The interviews lasted approximately 1.5 hours each. In all except two cases, the interviews were tape-recorded and later were transcribed verbatim. Two of the interviews were reconstructed from jotted notes immediately after they were completed.

A semistructured, open-ended interview guide was used, and the men were encouraged to talk about what they considered important. Questions in the interview guide were organized into four general categories: (a) medical aspects, (b) social relationships, (c) self-concept, and (d) a general overview of the experience. The early interviews began with the general question, Has testicular cancer changed your life in any way? Later interviews began with the question, What was it like to have testicular cancer? The goal of the interviewing was to discover how testicular cancer patients interpreted various aspects of this experience rather than to discover how widely these interpretations were distributed among such patients (McCracken, 1988).

The research methods used in this study have particular strengths and weaknesses. I am a testicular cancer survivor myself, and in every case but one, the men I contacted were enthusiastic about discussing their experiences with me. In many cases, I was the *first* person with whom they had discussed their experiences with testicular cancer. My first-hand familiarity with the disease and its treatment combined with my ability to relate some of my own experiences to the men resulted in interviews that were very personal and candid. On the other hand, if there are psychological processes at work such as denial of fears and anxieties, my own personal involvement could have made it more difficult for me to recognize these or to probe effectively into some areas of the experience. In the final analysis, this study is based on what men were willing or able to tell me about their experiences and how they defined them.

Another crucial aspect of the methods resulted from the relative rarity of this disease in the population. This required the use of a convenience sample that was largely self-selected, thus making any generalizations extremely tentative. What I have attempted to do, instead, is to examine the processes by which these men successfully (as defined by them) coped with the disease and its various effects on their lives. Although these processes may not exhaust all of the possible ways in which this can be accomplished, they do provide insights into several types of strategies that are related to gender. I describe these strategies in the remainder of the chapter.

Focusing on Performance

Following their diagnosis for testicular cancer, the men went through three major stages of adjustment. The first, and usually the shortest stage, was intense fear. This included fear of death, fear of disfigurement, and fear of suffering. The second stage was the process of working through what this experience meant to them and to their lives. This stage generally began once they knew that their chances of survival were very high. The third stage was an (at least tentative) arrival at a set of meanings that allowed them to make sense of the experience. This stage was usually arrived at some time after treatment was completed. Although there was considerable overlap among these stages, they can be distinguished on the basis of the concern that was most prominent at a particular time.

One of the questions in the interview guide asked, Has this experience had any effect on the way you think about yourself? This was followed with probes asking, as a person, as a man, as a husband/lover/father? If the man did not specifically discuss masculinity in his response, I also asked, Do you feel any less masculine in any way?

None of the men who were interviewed for this study reported feeling uncertain or concerned about their masculinity by the time they reached stage three. One important reason for this is that once men have completed treatment for testicular cancer, they are almost always able to return to whatever activities they were involved in prior to the cancer. This enables them to leave the dependency of the sick role, and it enables them to construct a presentation of self that they and others typically use to impute masculinity. For example, none of the men lost their jobs or suffered from lost occupational status, all those who were married remained married, and most reported returning to what they considered a normal sex life. Furthermore, the physical traces of treatment, such as the loss of a testicle and surgical scars, are not visible when the men are dressed.

On the other hand, these traces *are* visible when men are undressed. In addition, treatment frequently leaves men with dry ejaculations, infertility, and feelings of decreased attractiveness (Gritz et al., 1989). If there is an effect of testicular cancer on masculinity, then one would expect it to arise from feelings related to sexual performance, fertility, and physical attractiveness.

It was not uncommon for men to report that they had felt less masculine immediately following surgery or chemotherapy, because at this point they were unable to function normally sexually. Once normal functioning was restored, however, these feelings disappeared. Often, the wife's supportive attitude helped men through this period, but even in cases of unmarried men, the return of sexual functioning was usually enough to allow them to feel "back to normal" and to overcome any doubts about their masculinity.

For some men, the second stage was more difficult than for others. A college administrator in his 40s described his struggle:

> The ejaculation is not there. That by itself bothered me initially, the sensation, the sexual side of it. I got some counseling on that because I didn't know how to handle it. Pretty dramatic, phew!

Even he reached what he considered a satisfactory adjustment eventually. A more typical response came from a 34-year-old computer programmer. He said,

> At the beginning, when I first lost my testicle, I thought, Oh my God, I'm only half a man now. But that really went away quickly. Once I had been through my surgery and stuff like that, and after I was feeling better, we went back to, you know, making love. It was easy. I didn't feel stifled. I was having a normal ejaculate, which I think made a difference.

Although the loss of a testicle was itself distressing to some men, in many cases it led them to a reassessment of their ideas about masculinity. The computer programmer continued,

> As a matter of fact, I think if I lost my other testicle and was not able to ejaculate or even have an erection, I don't even feel at this point that I would feel it was a threat to my masculinity because I realize there's so much more involved now than just the sexual.

One of the men had lost both testicles as the result of two unrelated testicular tumors. He reported feeling no less masculine than before he had cancer, and his wife commented that the hormone injections he was taking actually made him even "friskier" than he had been before. A 34-year-old electrician pointed out that because you do not really need two testicles, he did not lose something all that important. He went on, "The thing is, I had cancer. That's what bothered me, not the testicular part. Who cares?" Only one man I interviewed bothered to get a prosthesis to replace the lost testicle. He was a single man in his 20s, and he said that he did it to look normal so that he could tell women about the cancer when he wanted to rather than when he was having sex. He did not, however, feel any less masculine as a result of the experience.

Men who were married prior to their diagnosis commonly reported that their wives' continued support and sexual interest in them made it easier for them to adjust to the physical changes in their bodies. A 41-year-old technician described his appearance while he was undergoing chemotherapy. In describing his wife's reaction, he said,

> And seeing that she could look at me when I could look in the mirror and I couldn't stand what I was seeing, and she could still hug me and make love to

me. The whole ability to get through it, I think, was because of her support and that feeling of that nonchanging love regardless of physical condition.

Although focusing on performance worked as a strategy for maintaining masculinity, there were also expressions of ambivalence toward this approach. A high school teacher who had been divorced just prior to discovering the cancer said,

I think what it's done is make me focus on what it means to be a man, and one of the men in the support group said it's who you are on the inside that makes you a man. That's true, but at the same time sometimes you think, well, that's a lot of bullshit. I'd like another testicle, you know. But at the same time you recognize that, hey, sexually I'm able to function as well as I could before.

The ability of the men to return to their precancer activities, including sexual activities, as well as the support of their wives, made it possible for them to minimize the effects of the disease on their definitions of themselves as men. Beyond this general experience, men employed two different strategies in thinking about their masculinity. The first strategy was to define the experience as reaffirming a traditional version of masculinity. The second strategy was to adopt a less traditional view of masculinity.

The Traditional Strategy

One criticism of the sex role paradigm is that it presents an image of normal masculinity that is unattainable by most men. In addition, if one does accept the traditional definition of masculinity, it is difficult to know when and if one has attained it. As Orrin Klapp (1969) points out,

Of course, modern man does not hanker for primitive initiation rites; but what many people seem to be striving for in strenuous and dangerous play—not to say sex and other things not usually thought of as sports—is some kind of ritual by which to prove themselves, some test which requires a person to extend his whole self, not merely play a role. . . . The majority of roles a man takes are "grown into" or contracted without his ever having a clear impression of himself as having "made it," or having been created, remade, reborn—without, in other words, a distinct experience: "I am a new man." (p. 34)

The experience of surviving testicular cancer provided just such an opportunity for men to test themselves and to feel reborn.

The Good Fight

Arthur Frank (1991), a sociologist who has written about his own experience with testicular cancer, points out that people with other diseases are sick, but people with cancer "fight" it. This idea was prominent in the accounts given by the men I interviewed. Many of them defined the experience as a serious fight in which they displayed courage in the face of fear. When asked to characterize his experience with testicular cancer, a 39-year-old high school teacher said,

> Yeah, I mean scary. Just this frightening experience. . . . Yeah, being forced to stay in there, being forced into a situation where you had to assert yourself against it . . . basically that sense of being frightened and not running from the fear.

This feeling emerged even in men who had not feared for their lives. A 42-year-old man who owned his own store described how the experience had increased his confidence level even though

> I didn't feel my life was threatened in any way, so I didn't think that. I didn't really believe that I was going to die any younger than the average person. I just knew I wasn't guaranteed anything. Also, my confidence level went up. No question about it. [Just because you had gotten through the experience?] Yeah. Some of the John Wayne attitude, you know. Tough it out and prove that you can do it.

Several of the men spoke of facing and conquering the fear of castration. A 32-year-old college professor said,

> It's a kind of defiance. I mean it is very much Oedipal. It is very much that kind of defiance of castration. And I like that . . . I like being able to say to myself, You know, you've had cancer and you beat the son of a bitch. . . . So it was in a way a kind of test of courage and hanging together, and that I didn't just go all scrambled with it in one form or another.

This feeling of having been tested in a dangerous contest outweighed any challenges to masculinity that may have been created by the actual loss of a testicle or the loss of fertility. It is important to note that not only did these men feel victorious and self-confident but that they also felt they succeeded by "toughing it out" and not going "all scrambled." In every case, the men I interviewed regarded keeping their emotions under control as very important.

The nature of the turning point that this experience created in men's lives was summarized by the high school teacher quoted above. He said,

> But there's that sense, clearly it's a rite of passage. There are other rites of passage, but somehow this one seems to be a rite of passage which almost reveals itself as such, both because it involves one's masculinity, one's sense of masculine self-image, and because of the mortality and because it happens to younger men, primarily.

Body Image

Although the physical losses experienced by these men did not result in them feeling less masculine, the surgeries and treatments did have negative effects on their thoughts about their bodies. The aftereffects of treatment that were troubling to men included the loss of an ejaculate, the inability to father children, scars from surgery, the general loss of physical capacity, and the loss of a testicle. Survey studies of testicular cancer survivors have found that these effects are associated with elevated levels of psychological distress (Gritz et al., 1989; Rieker et al., 1989; Schover, 1987; Schover et al., 1986). A 33-year-old machinist who had several serious complications from surgery said,

> I feel almost like an old man sometimes with my legs being the way they are. And that really bugs me the most because I was always an athletic person. I like playing sports. I like being competitive. And that was all taken away from me.

The electrician quoted above, who said that losing a testicle did not particularly bother him, gave up his weight lifting because any ache or pain that he developed frightened him that cancer was returning. Several of the men felt a shame for having had cancer. A salesman in his 20s said,

> I didn't want anybody to know that I had testicular cancer because a lot of people, my friends, guys and girls, they really don't know. When they hear testicular cancer they think maybe you had everything chopped off.

When the wife of a 27-year-old manager said that her husband was self-conscious about his abdominal scar, he replied,

> I don't know if it's as much the scar or that someone's going to ask you what's the scar from. And then you have to go and explain it to them and you talk to

strangers or something like that. It's not something you just feel comfortable talking about.

Even though most of the men did not feel that their sense of masculinity was diminished because of the cancer, there were these lingering feelings of a less positive body image and some feelings of shame and stigma associated with the cancer.

Emotional Work and Gender

How did the men handle these and other negative feelings associated with having testicular cancer? The blunt answer is that in most cases they handled it like men. That is to say, they attempted to deny or hide their feelings. When I asked the machinist when he started feeling better mentally, he responded, "I haven't. I haven't yet. I mean I make the best out of situations, but I try to block out a lot of this." A 39-year-old college professor, who clearly was bothered by the loss of a testicle, said, "And you think about that. I don't let it bother me now as much, because you can't let it bother you. You can't, you know, you move on to other things."

A 30-year-old manager, who was married with one child, wanted additional children. He and his wife both attempted to downplay his infertility. He said,

> Occasionally you just start thinking about it, that you can't father children, and I just play some games with that. Other than that, I really don't think about it [the testicular cancer] that much any more. It's been six years and I've pretty much adjusted to it. It was hard for a little while but now it doesn't bother me.

His wife added, "Yeah, it's something that happened and it's over with. It could have been worse. That's our standard thing we say."

Joking was a common way for the men to cope with the loss of a testicle. A 42-year-old man said,

> I feel that it's probably helpful living here in New York, so if you get kicked in the nuts you probably won't miss half . . . you have a 50% chance of escaping [laughs].

Other men denied the seriousness of the event by returning to activities such as sports and work as soon as possible. According to a college administrator in his 40s,

I remember I wanted to do every sport that I did before cancer. And I said I want to do it within 1 year. Not 2 years or 3 years or 4 years. One year! And that summer I did everything.

A 27-year-old father of three said, "Within a week I got out, did some snowmobiling and sledding . . . I went right back to work. I was back to work, in one week." His wife added, "Yeah, but he would go and do something and then end up in bed for 4 hours." Later in the interview he discussed how he felt about losing the testicle. He said,

I joked about it for a while. I pretended I was lefty for a while. You pretend things don't bother you but losing a testicle is part of one's, to me, a male, I don't want to say ego, but, yeah in a sense, it's part of your manliness and so it's a big thing. But I usually get over it, getting out and snowmobiling the first week after surgery. I try to get things behind me very quickly. I'm not one to put a lot of thought into things.

As this statement suggests, the men may have been feeling more of a threat to their masculinity than they were willing to admit. This man's hesitations in these comments suggest that he was having difficulty making this admission. This was, however, the only such statement in the interviews.

Men avoided confronting their feelings by trying not to think about them, by joking, and by returning to previous activities as soon as possible. What happened to the feelings that many of these men were attempting to keep hidden? In many cases, the men's wives were left to do the emotional work for them. A common theme in the wives' comments was that they did not really know what their husbands were thinking or feeling as they went through the experience. The wife of the man who went snowmobiling said,

I guess the hardest part was not knowing what I can do to make him feel better, to help him get through this. He's not a very open person with people around him because he's not very open with himself a lot of times. I think he could be the most open with me as he could with anybody else, but I don't think he would tell me his fears because he wouldn't want me to worry.

This man was maintaining the strong, silent approach for himself as well as for his wife. This leaves his wife, who is attempting to be supportive of him, to do whatever emotional work needs to be done. This aspect of the experience is evident in the comments of the wife of a 35-year-old plumber. She said,

> I can tell you I'm a worry wart, but I think of it all the time. Jim's much more casual than I am. I think he went through the whole thing, even though it was his body, much more easily than I did.

The men themselves were aware of this pattern and talked about it freely. When I asked the store owner, who referred to his "John Wayne" attitude, if he talked with his wife about the surgery and treatments as he was going through them, he said,

> Oh yeah. I'm sure we did. I'm more the quiet type. Betty is the questioning type, and she wants to know what's going on and how you feel. So I was used to that. So yeah, we did talk about it and her concerns.

Even when they did discuss the experience, then, it was at his wife's urging and over *her* concerns. Some of the men justified this pattern by saying that they were attempting to protect their wife's feelings. One of the single men attempted to protect his mother's feelings by not revealing the facts about his illness to her. He said,

> I didn't want to give her any more troubles, so I kind of kept things in. Just right in the hospital and stuff I only let her know certain things so that it wouldn't bother her so much.

In summary, the men who used this approach to make sense of their testicular cancer experiences interpreted their survival as a fight they had won by displaying courage and toughness. This John Wayne approach was often accompanied by displays of physical strength (returning to sports, snowmobiling) and inexpressiveness. In effect, they arrived at a secure sense of their masculinity by defining themselves through several of the key characteristics of the traditional male sex role. Their inexpressiveness also forced their wives, who were already trying to be supportive, to become more emotional, further polarizing their relationships with women into male instrumental behavior and female expressive behavior. This strategy enabled them to avoid feeling less masculine, but it also prevented them from working through the negative emotions that were created by the changes in their bodies. Fife, Kennedy, and Robinson (1994) found a very similar pattern in their study of over 300 cancer patients. Based on responses to a self-report questionnaire, they compared men's and women's coping strategies at various points following a cancer diagnosis. They found that the men used a more task-oriented approach and the women focused on altering their emotions and mobilizing family support. The authors argue that the outcome of this difference was that the men made a less positive psychosocial adjustment than did the women.

The Nontraditional Strategy

The existence of the traditional strategy does not mean, however, that men cannot cope in other ways. As we have seen, during the second stage of their adjustment to testicular cancer, men wrestled with the question of what it is that makes them masculine. Although one strategy was to draw upon elements of the traditional male sex role in answering this question, another strategy was to define masculinity in nontraditional terms. These two strategies do not necessarily correspond to different individuals, because in some cases individual men used elements of both strategies simultaneously.

Using the nontraditional strategy, men defined themselves as more emotionally expressive, more concerned about personal relationships, and more empathetic to others. A 35-year-old man, who works in research and development for a large corporation, talked about how he had always coped with problems by not talking about them. He said,

> And my wife has tried over the years to get me out of that, and up until the cancer I would still be that way with my own family. Whereas it's easier for me not to be that way with my own family since the cancer.

The most commonly expressed change in the men was the feeling that since the cancer experience, personal relationships had become more important to them. For example, the college administrator said,

> I think you start thinking more about yourself as to how you are as a person in your relationships to other people. It's not so much of a me attitude. It's us. And you know we all count in this world. I remember, I don't think I ever hugged anybody all that much. My father was never a hugger. But I'll tell you, since I've been through this, I've hugged more people in the past six years than I had in my entire life.

The man who worked in research and development pointed out that he now put his family first and his job second:

> Before the cancer I probably didn't have as much of an appreciation for my own family and for my own well-being, and I probably put my job up there at a little higher point. It [the cancer] certainly put that in perspective, and now myself and my family come first, and my job is second or third on the list.

Others limited this greater concern for others to those with cancer. Many of them became active in volunteer programs that involve talking with current cancer patients to help answer their questions and to offer support. A PhD recipient with two children took a job with a human service organization. Referring to his experience with testicular cancer, he said,

> It makes you appreciate other people's suffering more. I think in that sense it makes you feel like you can relate to others better, so you can relate to your children better.

Men who employed elements of this strategy reported feeling better about themselves and better about life in general. As the college administrator said, "Certainly as a result of all this I feel that I'm a better person than I was. I certainly have a much more sensitive feeling for people." The young salesman said, "I appreciate my health and just being alive and everything I do. That's the major thing, just being a better person toward other people."

Even though this second strategy moved away from traditional masculinity to some extent, for most of the men it was somewhat limited. First, men often used elements of both traditional and nontraditional masculinity simultaneously. Second, when these men's statements of greater sensitivity are examined closely, they reveal very few expressions of emotion, and only one of the men actually cried while being interviewed for this study. Many of the statements express a desire to offer practical (instrumental) help to others, such as the volunteer and service programs mentioned above. Frequently, this desire to help was seen as a form of repayment for having survived. A final indication of the limited nature of this movement away from traditional masculinity is that none of the men questioned the idea of gender identity or masculinity.

Conclusion

Testicular cancer is a disease that results in the loss of a testicle. In addition, it can lead to the loss of an ejaculate, sterility, and large abdominal scars. Despite the cultural association between testicles, fertility, and masculinity, none of the men who were interviewed in this study reported feeling less masculine by the time their physical recovery had been completed. These results can be understood by examining the meanings that the men used to interpret their cancer experiences and the resulting changes in their bodies.

One approach employed by almost all the men who were interviewed was for them to focus on their ability to perform their major roles following physical recovery from the cancer. This allowed them to interpret the cancer as an interruption to their lives (Charmaz, 1991). Beyond this approach, there were two different strategies that the men used.

The first strategy of interpretation was to draw upon elements of the traditional male sex role. One traditional element involved defining the testicular cancer as a fight in which the men had been required to exert themselves against a potentially deadly foe ("Give 'Em Hell"). This approach to dealing with cancer is reinforced by the cultural assumption that cancer is something that one fights against in a win or lose contest (competitiveness). Some men also used rapid returns to physical activities and to work as ways of proving their toughness.

Another element of the traditional approach was for the men to define themselves as stoical, unemotional, and protective toward their women ("The Sturdy Oak"). This casts the women in the expressive role of providing emotional support for their men as well as becoming emotionally agitated themselves.

A third element of the traditional strategy was for the men to focus on their sexual performance and to rely on their wives or lovers to treat them as still desirable sexual beings. Pleck (1981) refers to these latter two elements as powers that men have granted to women and that men have come to depend on: the power to express emotions and the power to validate masculinity.

Constructing a traditional masculine identity had both positive and negative effects for the men. Using the traditional model to interpret their cancer as a struggle that proved their courage and toughness enabled them to feel more self-confident and more masculine. Traditional masculinity can also help maintain advantaged positions within marriages (Sabo,

1990; Sattel, 1992). The most important negative effect evident in these interviews was difficulty in coping with a less desirable body image.

The second strategy the men used was to employ nontraditional masculine characteristics in defining themselves. The men who employed this strategy interpreted the testicular cancer experience as having changed them in one or more of three ways: becoming more emotionally expressive, becoming more relationship oriented, and becoming more concerned about the well-being of others. Men who employed elements of this strategy did not report feeling less masculine, but rather redefined masculinity to include these characteristics. They also reported feeling better about themselves, and there were no apparent negative effects from this strategy.

The findings of this study have several theoretical implications for the study of gender and men's health. First, when faced with a serious health crisis, creating a satisfactory self-definition became crucially important for these men. The potential threat to masculinity posed by testicular cancer led to attempts to define themselves as men, and having a clear-cut masculine identity of some kind became very important. Although most of the men were influenced by the traditional model of masculinity and focused on some of its features, this was not their only alternative.

The presence of the nontraditional strategy indicates that it is possible for men to choose to follow a different model. Not only was the nontraditional strategy effective in satisfying men's desire for a gender identity but it also enabled them to cope more effectively with the experience of testicular cancer.

Finally, men were able to exercise some individual control over the process of self-definition. Whether they used traditional, nontraditional, or a combination of both types of masculine characteristics, the men seemed to be attempting to create the most advantageous set of interpretations for themselves personally. This suggests that masculinity is not conferred by nature or biology and that it is not fixed. Rather, it is constructed by actors within a meaningful social context and in response to life experiences.

Notes

1. The present rate of cure is approximately 93% (American Cancer Society, 1994, p. 17).

2. See Tross (1989) for a review of studies on the frequency of various types of sexual dysfunction among testicular cancer survivors.

3. The ages of the men at the time of interview ranged from 26 to 58 years (average = 38). The ages at the time of diagnosis ranged from 24 to 40 years (average = 32). The time since treatment at the time of interview ranged from 1 to 24 years (average = 6.4). At the

time of the interview 18 of the men were married and 14 of them had one or more children. All had received orchiectomies, 15 had received lymph node dissections, 9 had received chemotherapy, 2 had received radiation therapy, 3 had received both chemotherapy and radiation therapy, and 6 had received neither chemotherapy nor radiation therapy.

Testicular cancer is rare in men of African descent. Increased risk for testicular cancer also is associated with higher occupational status (Haughey et al., 1989; Murphy, 1983). The men interviewed for this study all were white, and all but three were employed in white-collar and professional occupations. The three exceptions were skilled laborers.

4. The presence of the wives in these five interviews could have biased the men's descriptions. I had set up these joint interviews as an experiment to test whether the type or amount of information would, in fact, be different than that obtained from individual interviews. As far as I can tell, there was little difference except that the joint interviews tended to yield more detail concerning specific events. I am currently reinterviewing the men and their wives separately.

References

American Cancer Society. (1994). *Cancer facts and figures—1994.* (Available from the American Cancer Society, 1599 Clifton Rd., NE, Atlanta, GA 30329-4251)

Blakemore, C. (1988). The impact of orchidectomy upon the sexuality of the man with testicular cancer. *Cancer Nursing, 11*(1), 33-40.

Brannon, R. (1976). The male sex role: Our culture's blueprint of manhood, and what it's done for us lately. In D. David & R. Brannon (Eds.), *The forty-nine percent majority* (pp. 1-45). Reading, MA: Addison-Wesley.

Carrigan, T., Connell, B., & Lee, J. (1987). Toward a new sociology of masculinity. In H. Brod (Ed.), *The making of masculinities—The new men's studies* (pp. 63-100). Boston: Allen and Unwin.

Charmaz, K. (1991). *Good days, bad days: The self in chronic illness and time.* New Brunswick, NJ: Rutgers University Press.

de Haes, J., & Van Knippenberg, F. (1987). Quality of life of cancer patients: Review of the literature. In N. Aaronson & J. Beckmann (Eds.), *The quality of life of cancer patients* (pp. 167-182). New York: Raven.

Fife, B. L., Kennedy, V. N., & Robinson, L. (1994). Gender and adjustment to cancer: Clinical implications. *Journal of Psychosocial Oncology, 12*(1), 1-21.

Frank, A. (1991). *At the will of the body.* Boston: Houghton Mifflin.

Gordon, D. F. (1990). Testicular cancer: Passage to new priorities. In E. Clark, J. Fritz, & P. Rieker (Eds.), *Clinical sociological perspectives on illness & loss* (pp. 234-247). Philadelphia: Charles Press.

Gorzynski, J., & Holland, J. (1979). Psychological aspects of testicular cancer. *Seminars in Oncology, 6*(1), 125-129.

Gritz, E. R., Wellisch, D. K., Wang, H., Siau, J., Landsverk, J. A., & Cosgrove, M. D. (1989). Long-term effects of testicular cancer on sexual functioning in married couples. *Cancer, 64,* 1560-1567.

Harrison, J., Chin, J., & Ficarrotto, T. (1992). Warning: Masculinity may be dangerous to your health. In M. Kimmel & M. Messner (Eds.), *Men's lives* (2nd ed., pp. 271-285). New York: Macmillan.

Haughey, B. P., Graham, S., Brasure, J., Zielenzny, M., Sufrin, G., & Burnett, W. S. (1989). The epidemiology of testicular cancer in upstate New York. *American Journal of Epidemiology, 130*(1), 25-36.

Kimmel, M. (1987). The contemporary "crisis" of masculinity in historical perspective. In H. Brod (Ed.), *The making of masculinities—The new men's studies* (pp. 121-153). Boston: Allen and Unwin.

Klapp, O. (1969). *Collective search for identity.* New York: Holt, Rinehart & Winston.

McCracken, G. (1988). *The long interview.* Newbury Park, CA: Sage.

Moynihan, C. (1991). Testicular cancer. In M. Watson (Ed.), *Cancer patient care: Psychosocial treatment methods* (pp. 238-259). Cambridge, UK: British Psychological Society.

Murphy, G. P. (1983). Testicular cancer. *CA-A Cancer Journal for Clinicians, 33,* 100-104.

National Cancer Institute. (1987). *Testicular cancer-research report* (NIH Pub. No. 87-654). Washington, DC: Public Health Service.

Parsons, T., & Bales, R. F. (1953). *Family, socialization and interaction process.* London: Routledge & Kegan Paul.

Pizzocaro, G., Zanoni, F., Milani, A., Salvioni, R., Piva, L., Pilotti, S., Bombardieri, E., Tesoro-Tess, J., & Musumeci, R. (1986). Orchiectomy alone in clinical stage I nonseminomatous testis cancer: A critical appraisal. *Journal of Clinical Oncology, 4,* 35-40.

Pleck, J. (1981). *The myth of masculinity.* Cambridge: MIT Press.

Rieker, P., Edbril, S., & Garnick, M. (1985). Curative testis cancer therapy: Psychosocial sequelae. *Journal of Clinical Oncology, 3,* 1117-1126.

Rieker, P., Fitzgerald, E. M., Kalish, L. A., Richie, J. P., Lederman, G. S., Edbril, S. D., & Garnick, M. B. (1989). Psychosocial factors, curative therapies, and behavioral outcomes: A comparison of testis cancer survivors and a control group of healthy men. *Cancer, 64,* 2399-2407.

Sabo, D. (1990). Men, death anxiety, and denial: A radical feminist interpretation. In E. Clark, J. Fritz, & P. Rieker (Eds.), *Clinical sociological perspectives on illness & loss* (pp. 71-84). Philadelphia: Charles Press.

Sattel, J. (1992). The inexpressive male: Tragedy or sexual politics? In M. Kimmel & M. Messner (Eds.), *Men's lives* (2nd ed., pp. 350-358). New York: Macmillan.

Schover, L. (1987). Sexuality and fertility in urologic cancer patients. *Cancer, 60,* 553-558.

Schover, L., Gonzales, M., & Eschenbach, A. C. (1986). Sexual and marital relationships after radiotherapy for seminoma. *Urology, 27,* 117-123.

Sogani, P., Whitmore Jr., W., Herr, H., Bosl, G., Golbey, R., Watson, R., & DeCosse, J. (1984). Orchiectomy alone in the treatment of clinical stage I nonseminomatous germ cell tumor of the testis. *Journal of Clinical Oncology, 2,* 267-270.

Tross, S. (1989). Psychological adjustment in testicular cancer. In J. C. Holland & J. H. Rowland (Eds.), *Handbook of psychooncology* (pp. 240-245). New York: Oxford University Press.

Tross, S., Holland, J., Bosl, G., & Geller, N. (1984, March). A controlled study of psychosocial sequelae in cured survivors of testicular neoplasms. *Proceedings of the American Society of Clinical Oncology, 3*(74), Abstract C-287.

Waldron, I. (1976). Why do women live longer than men? *Social Science and Medicine, 10,* 349-362.

13

Identity Dilemmas
of Chronically Ill Men

KATHY CHARMAZ

Consider this story. A 45-year-old man had had a serious heart attack 3
years before while cycling. Being a competitive cyclist had complemented
and extended his identities as a hard-driving, no-nonsense businessman,
a former military man, and the traditional breadwinner and head of his
household. These masculine identities—male athlete, competitive businessman, Vietnam veteran, and breadwinner—formed the boundaries and
content of his self-concept. A business failure just before his heart attack
forced his wife to go to work. After his heart attack, his doctor prescribed
a strenuous cardiac rehabilitation program. Without my asking, he stated,
"I didn't know who I was for a while. I'd kind of [think], 'God, if I can
do this exercise, I'll die again . . . [doing the exercise frightened him
because having a heart attack while cycling vigorously almost killed him].
How to identify?' " I then asked, "How did you come to identify yourself?" He replied with the following:

AUTHOR'S NOTE: Portions of this article appeared in a different form in *The Sociological
Quarterly, 35*(2), 269-288. © 1994 by the Midwest Sociological Society; permission granted.
The paper was also presented at the annual meeting of the Society for the Study of Social
Problems in Pittsburgh, August 18-20, 1992. I am indebted to Candee Nagle, Norman K.
Denzin, David F. Gordon, Mark Mikkelson, Don Sabo, and three anonymous reviewers for
their comments on an earlier draft. I thank David F. Gordon and Don Sabo for encouraging
me to work in this area.

Well, what's the alternative? If death is on the one end, or do you want repeated heart attacks? We had one of our friends in the group [cardiac rehabilitation] who was in there for the second heart attack and he lasted 2½ years and he's my age but he let himself go—back to smoking and drinking and bad eating habits. So there is—I've heard this before—you get this invulnerable feeling—this invincible feeling and all of a sudden the hardest thing to accept is, "Hey, you are vulnerable. You can be hurt. You can die," you know, which you never thought of that before, or I never did. So that's still in the back of your mind.

Caught within the identity dilemma of forecasting himself as a potential dead man who had exercised hard or as a cardiac invalid who had not, this man had felt trapped in a web of uncertainty for months. However, like other men who participated in cardiac rehabilitation programs, this man eventually gained a sense of leaving death behind and regained a feeling of moving on with his life. But reminders of the fragility of life come more frequently and forcefully, as occurred with the sudden death of his friend. The earlier victory over death fades, the regained sense of invincibility crumbles, and the consciousness of uncertainty again heightens.

This story illustrates two essential properties of men's experience of chronic illness: (a) Illness can threaten masculine identities and lead to identity dilemmas, and (b) these dilemmas, like the illnesses themselves, can be recurrent and chronic.[1] Identity dilemmas for men revolve around the following oppositions: active versus passive, independent versus dependent, autonomy versus loss of control, public persona versus private self, and domination versus subordination.

Identity dilemmas ripple upon each other. Should the man above give up his exercise program, he would also relinquish his masculine identity as an athlete. He would face the identity dilemma of active athlete versus passive patient. Subsequently, if he adopted the identity of passive patient, he would also face identity dilemmas between having been the traditional breadwinner and decision maker and becoming the dependent partner in his marriage.

Chronic illness frequently comes to men suddenly with immediate intensity, severity, and uncertainty. Typically, men contract more serious and life-threatening chronic illnesses than women, who experience a higher incidence of degenerative diseases such as arthritis and multiple sclerosis (Conrad, 1987; Verbrugge, 1989; Verbrugge & Wingard, 1987). Therefore, men have more heart attacks and strokes earlier in life and die significantly more frequently and quickly than women (Verbrugge, 1985). Thus, the suddenness of illness, its intensity, and timing in the life course (usually middle age and older) pose special identity dilemmas for men.

Identities define, locate, characterize, categorize, and differentiate self from others. Identities develop both in stable roles and in emergent situations (Goffman, 1963; Weigert, 1986). Following Hewitt (1989), social identities derive from cultural meanings and community memberships that others confer upon the person. Personal identities define a sense of location, differentiation, continuity, and direction by and in relation to self. When identities of either type are internalized, they become part of the self-concept, what Turner (1976) defines as the relatively stable, coherent organization of characteristics, evaluations, and sentiments that a person holds about self (cf. Charmaz, 1991; Gecas, 1982). Identity dilemmas result from losing valued attributes, physical functions, social roles, and personal pursuits and their corresponding valued identities, that is, positive definitions of self, including socially conferred and personally defined positive identities. These dilemmas arise as people experience complicated problems, defined incapacities, and hard decisions that result from such identity losses.

Masculine identities reflect lifelong participation in the gender order (Connell, 1987) and are taken for granted by men when these identities remain stable. Chronic illness can undermine all the taken-for-granted identities that support and sustain a man's place in the gender order, including his place in the male dominance hierarchy among men (cf. Messner & Sabo, 1990; Sabo & Panepinto, 1990). To wit, chronic illness can alter or end men's participation in work, sports, leisure, and sexual activities. Hence, illness can reduce a man's status in masculine hierarchies, shift his power relations with women, and raise his self-doubts about masculinity. Consequently, chronic illness can relegate a man to a position of "marginalized" masculinity in the gender order (Connell, 1987; Messner & Sabo, 1990; Sabo & Gordon, 1992).

To date, the sociological literature has not addressed the circumstances that chronically ill men face. Nor have earlier researchers looked at these men's experience from the standpoint of gender-based conceptions of masculinity. Instead, the literature has largely remained gender-neutral and thus not only missed seeing the particular emergent structure of men's experience of chronic illness but also the identity dilemmas that they confront (see, e.g., Charmaz, 1987, 1991; Corbin & Strauss, 1988; Johnson, 1991; Kelleher, 1988; Kleinman, 1988; Strauss et al., 1984).

What is it like to be an active, productive man one moment and a patient who faces death the next? What is it like to change one's view of oneself accordingly? What identity dilemmas does living with continued uncertainty pose for men? How do they handle them? When do they make identity changes? When do they try to preserve a former self?

This chapter explores these questions by initiating the discussion of gender and male identity in chronic illness and by looking at four major processes that men with chronic illnesses experience: (a) awakening to death after a life-threatening crisis, (b) accommodating to uncertainty as men realize that the crisis has lasting consequences, (c) defining illness and disability, and (d) preserving self to maintain a sense of coherence while experiencing loss and change.[2] These categories build on each other, although accommodating to uncertainty, modes of defining illness, and ways of preserving self often reflect implicit meanings rather than explicit strategies. Here, uncertainty means awareness of imminent or eventual recurrence, degeneration, or death. Although uncertainty has long been a key theme in the chronic illness literature, the focus has been on uncontrollable embarrassing, incapacitating, or painful symptoms and further episodes (cf. Reif, 1975; Schneider & Conrad, 1983; Wiener, 1975). By also studying men who suffer potentially life-threatening conditions, uncertainty in relation to death in chronic illness becomes explicit.

Awakening to Death

Death. The first identity dilemma comes when men realize that death could occur—now. Clinging to former identities in hope of minimizing the symbolic threat of death by defining illness as minor could risk their lives. Acknowledging the threat of death could cost them their most valued identities. When wholly unanticipated, the threat of death shakes men to their very core. Within moments or brief hours, the disruptive crisis removes them from familiar former identities to that of patient, possibly of dying patient. Crisis can overtake them without earlier warnings. Even illnesses such as diabetes or cancer may not become manifest until a crisis.[3] Occasionally, as the athlete above, another man's crisis awakens or re-awakens a man to his own vulnerability, aging, and death (cf. Karp, 1988).

Some men invoke gender-based reasoning such as the male midlife crisis (Jaques, 1965; Levinson, Darrow, Klein, Levinson, & McKee, 1978; Sabo, 1990) to account for what happens to them even as illness develops. One man believed he was having a midlife crisis—that his life was falling apart, "There's a point I was thinking, 'This is a midlife crisis; this is just a state, or this is a stage you're going through.' " Later, his doctor told him that his aorta was literally ripping apart.

Awakening to death comes as an unbelievable shock when a man (a) sees himself as too young to die, (b) defines himself as exceptionally healthy, or (c) has had no earlier episodes or heralding symptoms. Young clinical psychologist Neil A. Fiore (1984) sought help for what he believed was an infection on his testicle only to find the physician talking "calcification," "surgery," "cancer," "death." When younger men have heart attacks, particularly the first one, they often do not know what is happening to them (cf. Cowie, 1976; Frank, 1991; Johnson, 1991). The athlete above recounted his heart attack at age 42:

> I was on my bicycle going on just a routine ride for me and . . . I just went down. I didn't know what happened. . . . So I had no indication that I [was having a heart attack]—no chest pains, no shortness of breath, no the typical [symptoms of] how you feel. I couldn't even tell you what it feels like.

He awoke in the hospital to find himself partly paralyzed, which did not faze him, but the news that he had had a heart attack infuriated him. When I asked him what raised his fury, he juxtaposed the finality of heart disease with the injustice of having paid his dues already by stopping smoking, limiting drinking, getting in shape, and losing weight. All this work and then, the biggest injustice, "It's just I'm too young. . . . Why me?"

Once men realize or are told what has happened, identity dilemmas emerge. When men believe that they have narrowly survived their crisis, at least at first they assume it means vulnerability, a greatly increased risk of dying, a radically altered life. A substantially foreshortened future? Death? Now real and perhaps soon. They now connect death with personal identity. Several men made statements such as the following: "I know that I am mortal." "We all 'know' that we are going to die, but when you come close to death, you see it is true." "I am not immune to death."

The prospect of immediate death darkens the present and shades the future. While in crisis, men see living and dying as discrete categories. Their sense of betrayal by their bodies evokes anger, self-pity, and envy of the healthy. Once certain futures now look uncertain, even ended. Though premature death now seems possible, these men remain unaware of lasting illness and disability if they are unfamiliar with their diagnoses, their disease process, and other men who have the same condition (cf. Charmaz, 1991).

When men define awakening to death as only a discrete, immediate event, they limit the critical period to the initial crisis. As Speedling's (1982) men who had heart attacks, such men initially view getting through this crisis as the passage to an unchanged future. Several men who had had bypass surgery or other circulatory procedures questioned whether they were suitable subjects for a study of experiencing chronic illness. They believed their surgery had effected the necessary repairs. For them, not only the threat of death was over, but also the illness. A referral to my study, especially if by their nurse, undermined their construction of illness as an acute episode.

Eventually, men's routine interactions and unforeseen daily obstacles turn early glimmers of awareness into growing cognizance that illness remains. They learn lessons in chronicity during everyday routines that have become much more arduous and time-consuming than before. For example, buttoning a shirt or tying a shoe becomes a formidable task to a man whose stroke has affected his dominant side. Playing his usual round of golf becomes impossible for a man who had a recent serious heart attack. Lessons in chronicity can challenge men's assumptions about male mastery and competence, thereby leading them into depression (cf. Dahlberg & Jaffe, 1977; Hodgins, 1964). Treating illness and its consequences as problems to solve is consistent with men's gender-related behavior (Tannen, 1990). Inability to solve these problems erodes their personal identity. A 45-year-old man with heart disease disclosed that for 6 months, "I thought my life was over. Cardiac Cripple."

The identity issues emerging in awakening to death are not limited to men, but they are embedded in the medical diagnoses these men received and the social conditions they experienced. Women responded similarly when they found themselves facing unanticipated life-threatening crises. However, women, even heart patients, reported much more difficulty in getting physicians to view their symptoms as real. Subsequently, practitioners, relatives, and the women themselves wondered if they fabricated their symptoms. Hence, these women met serious diagnoses with relief (cf. Charmaz, 1991). In contrast, men who had crises acknowledged their symptoms but initially glossed over their present or potential seriousness. Further, they seldom had trouble in getting practitioners to attend to their developing symptoms.[4]

What mitigates the overwhelming implications of awakening to death for identity? When might a man gain through having a crisis?

Awakening to death can result in direct, positive consequences for identity. Not only do moments of crisis crystallize when defined and met with a spouse or partner, so also do identities. During crisis and its immediate aftermath, most married men felt tremendous affirmation of their valued identities in the family as they awakened to death (cf. Johnson, 1991;

Speedling, 1982). They received an outpouring of care, comfort, and love from their wives and families. These men often bragged about how supportive and helpful their wives had been. Even men who had had troubled marriages felt that their wives affirmed, valued, and supported them. Statements such as, "Marge was right there every minute; she even stayed at the hospital those first few nights" were common ones. To these men, their wives had provided the essence of "being there" for them. They were vigilantly attentive, helpful advocates, and loving companions throughout the crisis. These women provided their husbands with a continuing link to both past and future identity through the intensity of their involvement in the present.

Thus, these men received identity validation that not only confirmed positive social identifications and private self-definitions but also implicitly affirmed their gender identities as men in the household. Paradoxically, that validation came when they were most physically dependent but derived from their central positions as husbands (which also validates the wife or partner's identity and role as helpmate and caregiver).

Identity supports to provide validation for unattached single men, however, usually were much less available. They weathered crises largely on their own. Here, their situations resembled those of single women who often had to fend for themselves during crises and within the health care system. Older widowed and divorced women, however, typically received more caring and comfort from adult children than their male counterparts. The occasional exception occurred when divorced men's first wives, or gay men's friends gave them care and support through their crises.[5] Generally, if single men had no caring children or close friends, they were particularly bereft. Thus, constructing a personally valued and socially validated identity became more problematic for them than for those who had ready access to families.

Accommodating to Uncertainty

In which ways do men define and handle uncertainty? A casual observer might find that men often accommodate to uncertainty by ignoring, minimizing, or glossing over it. But what do such actions mean to men who do so? Their way of accommodating to uncertainty assumes "bracketing" (Husserl, 1970) the event that elicited it. Bracketing means setting this event apart by putting a frame around it and treating it as something separate and removed from the flow of life. The impact of the event upon identity lessens when this event is separated from social and personal identity. Through bracketing, men define uncertainty as having boundaries —those limited to flareups and crises.[6] To the extent that men bracket uncertainty, they avoid letting it permeate their thoughts and alter their identities. Thus, bracketing raises identity dilemmas because it poses maintaining past identity at cost to health against taking illness into account at risk to social and personal identity.

Bracketing reduces awareness of uncertainty. But why might men who remain at least partly aware of continued uncertainty not make prescribed lifestyle changes because of it? First, these men cannot envision themselves as dead and may see themselves as risk takers and winners. Second, their earlier habits merge with their conception of masculine identity. Third, they have lost hope of genuinely effecting change and decide to live on their own terms for whatever time they have left. In each case, they usually do not foresee the possible kind or degree of disability and debility. Rather, they see themselves as remaining the same or as dead. Yet men can use uncertainty to retain power and privilege in their homes. Then, wives who cajole and try to control them get responses such as, "Why should I care what I eat? I'm going to die anyway." Fertile grounds for marital strife develop in each case (cf. Peyrot, McMurray, & Hedges, 1988). Subsequently, identity dilemmas arise when spouses disagree on bracketing or acknowledging uncertainty.

Eventually most men realize that their bodies have changed. Subsequently, they become aware of uncertainty—uncertain episodes, uncertain treatment effects, uncertain complications—an uncertain life. Awakening to death and acknowledging continued uncertainty is sobering. Reappraisals follow. These reappraisals can lead to epiphanies marking major turning points for men and their families (cf. Charmaz, 1991; Denzin, 1989; Gordon, 1990). When men acknowledge continued uncertainty, their reappraisals bring reflection and self-appraisal. Men who had attended much more to their work than to their families decide to devote more time to the latter. Men who describe themselves as driven by their Type A behavior believe that they have to relinquish it before it kills them. The man above who had viewed himself as a cardiac cripple for 6 months saw his heart attack quite differently 2 years later:

I would say, "Thank you, thank you," type of thing. But you know, had it not been for my heart attack—I'm grateful it happened now, 'cause it changed my life considerably and so [I] have a lack of words [to describe it]. Yeah, I thank my heart attack for that. In one way I'm grateful.

Reappraisals of productivity, achievement, relationships all alter what these men defined as valuable. Their forced reappraisals led to setting priorities, making decisions, and also, coming to terms with their pasts and presents. A middle-aged executive regretted his behavior in his first two marriages and resolved to maintain his third. These appraisals lead to assessments of self and identity. The middle-aged attorney reflected:

> When you are on the brink, so to speak, you begin to look at what things in your life are valuable and which aren't. And you begin to—and one of the things is real clear was I was glad that I did work where I tried to help other people rather than having a garage full of Mercedes. And it made me feel not like a saint, or anything, but it made me feel like not a bad person, not even like I was a good person. But I was all right; I was all right.

A resolve to live in the present frequently follows these initial reappraisals. The man above said, "I reflect on the past, leave the sadness and parts of myself that I don't consider functional anymore and try to live in the present." A young man believed that his earlier struggles to sift through and to sort out the past had kept him from attending to the immediate present and from knowing himself within it.

For young men, reappraisal can open paths to self-discovery. Getting a kidney transplant and being released from triweekly dialysis treatments resulted in reappraisal by the young man above. At that point, he suddenly had much more unstructured time. He reflected:

> And part of it is getting used to myself. . . . Getting used to my self, yeah, two words, because I didn't really have that much time to find out who I was before. I'd get glimpses now and again, and I'd go, "Oh, yuck," or "yeah, far out," you know, or "Maybe," you know. [I] caught a lot of those [glimpses].

Not uncommonly, men will be shaken by the initial crisis then gradually resume normal lives. Concurrently, they normalize their symptoms and regimens if they follow one. But before they resettle into a normal routine, they reappraise their lives and their actions.

After awakening to death and defining uncertainty, lifestyles, and also habits, rapidly change—at least for a while. Men quit working, change jobs, renegotiate their work assignments, or retire early. They follow a regimen, lose weight, stop smoking, and reduce drinking. Making permanent changes, however, means acknowledging uncertainty and treating its consequences as lasting. Several men with diabetes disclosed that they had not attended to their conditions until shocked by a diabetic crisis. One middle-aged manager previously had ignored his diet, his doctor's warnings, and his wife's nagging. After a harrowing struggle against death followed by loss of his foot, he not only acknowledged his own uncertain future but also tried to instruct unaware relatives and friends about the negative consequences of their lifestyles, "because, look what happened to me."

As young men grow older, their accommodations to uncertainty can form the foundation of their identities. As he looked back on having been a diabetic for more than two decades, a professor viewed his regimen as not only the means of reducing uncertainty by staving off further complications but also as the way he identified himself:

> I would not want to have to be preoccupied with it the way I was the first year or so. Ah, but at the same time, it is the ground of my life. *I have no idea who I would be, in a way, if I hadn't become diabetic.* . . . Just to have to internalize this regime must have made a great difference to my personality, I think . . . I was a person who didn't eat unless someone sort of sat him down. And, I like to drink and drink and sometimes got quite intoxicated. Stay up all night, and not sleep, go days without sleeping. And I've now become the opposite of all that, like a field and ground thing [emphasis mine].

Defining Illness and Disability

As they accommodate to uncertainty, how do men define their conditions? How do these definitions affect their personal identity? These men viewed their conditions in four major ways: (a) an enemy, (b) an ally, (c) an intrusive presence, and (d) an opportunity. Definitions of illness as an enemy or an ally personify and make illness tangible. Definitions of it as an intrusive presence or an opportunity reveal the connectedness between body and self. At different points in time, a man may hold each definition. Similarly, different contexts that call forth different identities can elicit disparate, even paradoxical views of illness. Thus, a man can curse his illness as the enemy that ruined his life, but treat it as an ally deserving of respect when he attempts to obtain a disability benefit. Such seeming inconsistencies can reveal the extent to which illness has permeated a man's self-definition and self-concept. In any case, these definitions reflect and simultaneously shape narratives of knowing self through illness (Frank, 1993; Herzlich & Pierret, 1987) and, therefore, can result in raising or resolving identity dilemmas.

Definitions of enemies and allies both explicitly create personifications. However, viewing one's illness as an enemy objectifies and externalizes it and thus distances and separates it from at least personal, if not also, social identity (cf. Goffman 1961, 1963). Viewing illness as an ally emphasizes subjectivity and identification with it and thus integrates it with personal and, if disclosed, social identity. Illness as an intrusive presence brings it into the body as an unwelcome occupant that insidiously has become part of self rather than remaining external to it. Illness as an opportunity allows for reevaluation, redirection, and reconstruction of self.

Changing definitions and revising the stories that frame them reveal new identifications. Yet these definitions are not always stories of self-change as Frank (1993) describes. Rather, definitions of illness as an enemy typically testify to a man's continuity of self. Here, the narrative framing of the man's definition proclaims that he remains the same though his body and situation may have changed.

Definitions of the illness spread to specific symptoms, treatments, and even to the body itself. A young man who had defined the dialysis machine as an enemy tried to make an ally of his new kidney transplant, which his body began to reject. To him, the transplant meant a direct route to his preferred identity as an involved graduate student. He said:

> Rejection is a very scary time . . . a very scary time because you have all these hopes and then the kidney—your body is saying, "Well, I don't agree with you, you don't need—this isn't your kidney." And you're saying, "Well, agree with me, this is . . ." and you get into conversations, I got into conversations with my kidney and my body.

Images of enemies and allies are present, although sometimes implicit, in the competitive discourse of victories and losses that middle-aged and younger men frequently invoke when talking about their illnesses. Norman Cousins (1983) titles his chapter on dealing with his heart attack, "Counterattack." Lee Foster (1986) states, "The record for longevity on a kidney machine, the last time I checked, was fourteen years, and if I stay on dialysis I aim to break the record" (p. 526). Arnold R. Beisser (1989), a psychiatrist who became quadriplegic due to poliomyelitis, took a similar stance toward his disability:

> When I became disabled, I even tried to turn my disability into a competitive sport. I did everything possible to deny the cripple in me. I had no use for him, and no place in my concept of myself for disability. Much of what I have written

here has been about my search to find something of worth in that image of the cripple, something with which I could identify without regret. (p. 80)

Beisser wrote his book at age 62; he became ill at 27. Visible disabilities, such as Beisser's wheelchair use, result in social identifications that cause or complicate problems in self-definition. If so, definitions of illness and disability as an intrusive presence are likely to follow. Anthropologist Robert F. Murphy had had a productive career before a benign tumor left him progressively paralyzed. He (1987) comments:

> [F]rom the time I first took to the wheelchair up to the present, the fact that I am physically disabled has been in the background of my conscious thoughts. Busy though I might be with other matters and problems, it lingers as a shadow in the corner of my mind, waiting, ready to come out at any moment to fill my meditations. It is a Presence. I, too, had acquired an embattled identity, a sense of who and what I was that was no longer dominated by my past attributes, but rather by my physical defects. (p. 104)

Murphy's wheelchair use permeated his consciousness of self, as well as others' consciousness of him, and symbolized his loss of power. Other meanings and symbols emerge when the context and situation are different. When first ill, Beisser (1989) laid flat on his back for a year. He recalled when he first sat in a wheelchair, "I felt as though my power had been restored. I had far greater difficulty in breathing, and it lasted only three or four minutes. But who cared! It was position that counted, and I associated this one with being able to take care of myself " (p. 24).

Later, Beisser's disability elicited rudeness, stigma, invaded space, and loss of privacy, which raised and reinforced identity dilemmas. Like Beisser, several of my middle-aged and younger interviewees took years to reconcile the identity dilemmas that illness thrust upon them. Older working-class men were resigned to their situations and built lives around illness. Middle-class men sought to make illness and disability meaningful, to recast them into something through which positive identification could be made. Their quest resembled that of the younger and middle-aged women respondents (both middle and working class), but these women ordinarily articulated their concerns more directly and arrived at positive conclusions more readily. Nonetheless, by seeking to make illness meaningful, these men changed their definition from illness as an enemy or an intrusive presence to an experience with positive consequences. The professor above first received his diagnosis while he had a diabetic crisis and nearly died. Afterward, he viewed both his body and his illness as enemies who were trying to kill him. But over the years, his definition changed:

> It's [his illness] an enemy that I've made an ally of. Really, I don't think I'd still be here, if I hadn't been diabetic. It's like the paradox of the return of the prodigal son. It kicked me out of Eden alright, having to, you know, be on my best behavior so much and think about when to shoot up and all that. But it was what I needed.

From this vantage point, this man learned how central being diabetic was to his sense of identity. He remarked, "Probably if I were less narcissistic and obsessive, I would be a poorer diabetic. It's sort of like diabetes and me, we were made for each other."

By making illness an ally, men can use it as an opportunity for reflection and change. Arthur Frank (1990) refers to illness explicitly as "an opportunity, though a dangerous one" (p. 1). He writes, "Illness takes away parts of your life, but in doing so it gives you the opportunity to choose the life you will lead, as opposed to living out the one you have simply accumulated over the years" (p. 1).

Whether men treat their conditions as enemies, allies, intrusions, or opportunities, their definitions are seldom mutually exclusive or static. That is, a man who sees illness as an ally because it led him to set priorities can still see it as an intrusive, even ominous presence in his life. Similarly, a man can treat his illness as an ally for a number of years only to redefine it as an increasingly intrusive presence if it steadily limits his activities. Which definition holds sway depends on the context and situation, the man's self-definition, and his responsibilities, actions, values, goals, and plans. As a result, many men appreciate what they learn while ill, but still struggle with preserving defining aspects of self from the past before illness.

Preserving Self

Although certain major identities change, such as that of worker to part-time retiree, men with chronic illnesses try to lead normal lives. In doing so, they implicitly, and often explicitly, devote much effort to preserving self—aspects of a self known and valued in the past (see also, Charmaz, 1991; Johnson, 1991). Preserving self means maintaining essential qualities, attributes, and identities of this past self that fundamentally shape the self-concept. Thus, ill people relinquish some identities but retain others. By preserving self, men reconcile the identity dilemmas that chronic illness thrusts upon them. Johnson (1991) stresses roles and lifestyles in preserving self, but it means more than that. Rather, preserving self means maintaining a way of being in the world and a way of relating to and knowing self, others, and social worlds. Doing so reduces the marginalizing effects of illness. Through preserving self, men maintain continuity throughout the past, present, and future. Although he had to take a disability benefit, Ernest Hirsch (1977), a clinical psychologist with multiple sclerosis, still maintained identity continuity through remaining in the same organization, community, and close friendships. His former employer provided him with free office space and clerical help to enable him to do research and writing. Despite earlier worries about losing his masculinity and independence, he managed to preserve essential qualities of self although he endured profound physical and social losses. He writes:

> Whatever changes have occurred in me do not touch the core of my "self," which has remained pretty much the same. As far as other people are concerned, I think I've remained much as always. Although I realize some changes have occurred, I feel a continuity with the past and have no difficulty recognizing myself as myself, and neither does anyone else. (pp. 169-170)

As men come to terms with illness and disability, they preserve self by limiting encroachments from illness in their lives and controlling definitions of their illness and any disability, as suggested above. They also intensify control over their lives when they can and develop strategies that minimize the visibility and intrusiveness of illness, which I discuss briefly below. This reconciling of identity dilemmas takes illness into account, whether others believe that these men do it in a healthy way.

Recapturing the Past Self

Before men learn these new ways of preserving self, many of them assume that they will recapture the past self, or explicitly aim to do so. Here, they aim to reclaim the same identities, the same lives that they had before illness. Nothing less will do. For these men, their "real" selves are and must be only the past self (Charmaz, 1991; Turner, 1976). They lapse into invalidism and despondency if they cannot recapture their past selves.

Jean B. Zink (1992), who has long been disabled and now suffers from postpoliomyelitis syndrome, compares herself with a male friend:

> Disability came to Bill in his mature life, which was full of fun and freedom, and he feels he was robbed of it. Bill's future is now in the past. Disability robbed me of a carefree youth but not of youth itself, which was full of innocence and idealism. My future was before me. Bill yearns for the past. I prayed for a future. . . . Bill lost the life that was precious to him, and now he ages with regret. I age with gratitude, regardless of the struggle, not because I am better than Bill but because my experience as I perceive it has demanded this of me. Bill seems to believe that the way things *were* should be pursued relentlessly. Bill uses his psychic energy to recapture the past. I use my psychic energy to maintain the present. (p. 60)

Except for women whose diseases caused severe mental impairment, women showed more resiliency and resourcefulness than men in preserving aspects of self, even though women were less likely to have spouses to bolster their efforts (see also, LeMaistre, 1985; Lewis, 1985; Pitzele, 1985; Register, 1987; Wulf, 1979). Women rarely persisted in tying their futures to recapturing their past selves when they defined physical changes as permanent. Quite possibly, women's earlier roles and identities fostered greater adaptability to illness.

Trying to recapture the past self does provide strong incentives to fight illness and to stave off death. When men believe in their doctors and in their treatment, their resolve to struggle maintains their hope. If so, then a man assumes that his past self will be preserved when his physician promises marked improvement. A middle-aged father of young sons commented about having cardiac bypass surgery:

> I felt—I was going to do everything I did before; otherwise, it wasn't worth having the surgery. . . . I wanted to be just the same as before. And, like for these children, it would be really devastating to them if I were to go ahead and say, "Well, I can't do this because of my heart; I can't do that," you know. You don't want to teach young children to be like that.

Attempting to recapture the past self has its pitfalls when all valued social and personal identities remain in an irretrievable past. Being unable to measure up to the past self results in further preoccupation with it, and heightens identity dilemmas. Arnold Beisser (1989) recalls how his desire to recapture his past self affected his courtship:

[O]ne big thing separated us. I was in love with someone else. That someone else was me, or rather my image of what I used to be. My past was my standard and I carried it with me like a Pepsi generation commercial. And, of course, I assumed that everyone else, including Rita, was attracted to that same image. (p. 56)

Drastic lifestyle changes following illness such as reduced employment, forced retirement, rigid regimens, and broken marriages erode or collapse former identities entirely, one after another, like dominoes. Simultaneously, despondency about not recapturing the past self increases and renders preserving valued aspects of self more arduous. A middle-aged man with heart disease felt overwhelmed, immobile, and depressed when he compared his present precarious physical, financial, and marital statuses with his past fitness, financial security, and stable marriage. His fear of another heart attack combined with his lassitude led him to withdraw from everyone. He said, "I'd say I hit rock bottom about October, November last year. I got to where I don't care what happens to me, you know; I don't care what happens to anybody."

The distance increases between a man's past self, by now reconstructed in memory in idealized form, and present identities, as valued former identities collapse and new ones are viewed as negative. With each identity loss from chronic illness, preserving valued past "masculine" identities becomes more difficult. Not surprisingly then, Brooks and Matson (1982) found that the self-concepts of men with multiple sclerosis changed more negatively over time than those of women. Men draw upon the existing cultural logic that currently defines masculinity as they try to make sense of their altered selves and situations (cf. Denzin, 1991). When sexual performance forms the foundation of their conception of masculinity, impotency undermines their identities as men.

Preserving a past identity becomes particularly problematic when the basis for that identity is lost. After his heart attack, the man above was financially devastated. Both he and his wife valued traditional roles but he could no longer work full-time. Subsequent crises put more responsibility on his wife to get a full-time job, as his identity as the wage earner rapidly eroded. He said:

She was fine throughout that [the financial crisis]—she didn't work [before then]; she worked part-time; now she's working full-time. So yeah, she blamed me for that, me being the provider and that type of thing. That hurts me too, you know.

Under these conditions, illness becomes the symbol of identities lost and the reason why attempts to preserve self flounder. This man explained, "This is the worst year of my life. In one month I lost health, a career. In a year I lost my capital; I almost lost my marriage—you could almost say that year I lost my marriage. My oldest daughter moved."

Problematic health strains an already strained marriage. It also strains a stable marriage when erosion of valued identities continues. As with retirement, chronic illness allows men who cut back or leave work to become new critics of their wives' and children's activities. Loss of control outside of the home leads to efforts to preserve self by exerting more control within it. To the extent that a man takes for granted that masculinity is embedded in power, the more likely he will tighten his control within the household as access to other arenas decreases. For example, as a retired bartender became housebound, his scrutiny of his wife's day increased and he became more critical and controlling. She could incur his wrath by failing to anticipate or to satisfy his dictates about the smallest household or personal care task.

Such men want to be in control. At this point, they implicitly realize that illness has marginalized their sense of masculinity (cf. Connell, 1987; Messner & Sabo, 1990). They cannot accept physical dependence, except, perhaps, upon wives. The demeaning nature of seeking help, being evaluated ("his doctor found out he was smoking again and read him the riot act"), of living on new, much less on someone else's, terms does not come easily. Rather than give up old habits, these men may flaunt them. If they cannot control their health, they may try to control someone else's response. To do this, they take risks—often many of them—and likely cast their wives and physicians as adversaries to outwit. In this way, they maintain their assumed status in the hierarchy of men and simultaneously exert dominance over women (cf. Sabo, 1990). At such a point, they also risk being identified as obstreperous, unmotivated, and mentally unstable by their practitioners (cf. Albrecht, 1992; Plough, 1986).

Dependency strains relationships and plays havoc with identity. But identity develops and is maintained through interaction. Partners often find themselves in an elaborate dance around dependency. Wives and partners may find themselves anxiously trying to protect shreds of their husbands' former identities while feeling overwhelmed by the escalating demands placed upon them (see, e.g., Lear, 1980; Strong, 1988).

These women provide pivotal identity supports for their partners that mute the identifying effects of dependency and loss. In contrast, dwindling identity supports accelerate dependency and loss in single men. Death, divorce, and distance left a 38-year-old man with advanced multiple sclerosis institutionalized and without family contact. After years of life-threatening crises, he felt disconnected from the world and from almost everyone. He said, "I don't think of death as gloomy; I see it as a release."

This man disdained the self he witnessed in illness. To him, it was not worth preserving. When talking about his teenaged years, his present immobility contrasted strikingly with his past activity. He said in wonder, "You know, I could do anything I needed to do. Like baseball, or football, or basketball. You know I did all those things—swimming. Now it's no more."

For him, the halcyon days of healthy youth remained in a faded past. But for others, the disparity between past and present identity enfolded the immediate present and foretold the future. A young man whose kidney transplant was failing questioned the value of living on the dialysis machine. The middle-aged attorney alluded to previously discovered that his condition was far more serious and complicated than he had initially thought and probably had resulted in minimal brain damage. Another surgery became necessary, but his health had deteriorated too much to risk doing it. Losses accrued. No stamina for backpacking. Memory losses canceled work. Social Security denied his disability claim. A legal victory against Social Security still did not force processing his claim. Pleas for more painkillers were refused. Increased blood pressure medications sapped his energy and drained his spirit. Despondent and unable to function as in the past, he said, "I don't do anything but sleep now." Six months later, he hanged himself in the room that had come to be his bedroom, office, and sanctuary.

These three men saw their lives shrinking and their chances for creating valued identities diminishing. Under these conditions, they each saw suicide as a reasonable way of resolving the identity dilemmas in which they found themselves.[7] In contrast, possibilities of expanding identities foster hope and desire to stave off disability and death. The self to be preserved is a developing self, ripe with potential for new, positive identities. For example, one man had recently won an award that brought him substantial recognition and travel, in addition to renewed friendships. The world was opening up to him, not closing down upon him. Quite spontaneously, he disclosed, "I don't want to die, I'm just a baby, a 52-year-old baby boy. I'm just starting; I don't want to die."

Preserving a Public Identity, Changing a Private Identity

Some men claim public identities that reaffirm their pasts and demonstrate continuity with that past. They offer a public narrative of their lives in which chronic illness plays a minor or past role. In that way, they attempt to maintain their earlier position in the gender order. But to keep their public narrative creditable, they may have to devote vast amounts of energy to keeping illness contained and disability hidden or cloaked (cf. Charmaz, 1991). Their efforts are founded on assumptions of preserving masculinity. A man with diabetes could not manage both his wheelchair and a tray in the cafeteria. Because he could not bring himself to ask his coworkers for help, he skipped lunch and risked a coma rather than request help.

Simultaneously, men may maximize the significance of illness and disability in their private lives. At home, illness and disability engulf them and may engulf the entire household. Roger Ressmeyer (1983) found that he involved himself in unwise relationships because he needed a partner's support and backup work. Ironically, the independent public man can transform himself into a dependent patient at home. This stance allows the tyranny of the sickroom, promotes self-pity, and encourages physical dependence. Even when men do not become overly dependent, wives add hours to their day as they prepare special diets, assist in bathing, dressing, grooming, completing the daily medical regimen, and provide rides (cf. Corbin & Strauss, 1984; Gerhardt & Brieskorn-Zink, 1986).

Strategies for Preserving Self

Whether a complete disjuncture exists between the public and private identities, most men try to mute the effects of illness on socializing or working. They draw upon both taken-for-granted actions and explicit strategies to preserve their earlier selves and thus, maintain or re-create public and private identities. Their strategies involve careful timing, pacing, and staging to maintain appearances to others, and often, to self.

When they needed to keep working, men attended closely to ways they could quite literally preserve themselves to do so. These men planned and managed their appearance because looking sick could cost them their bosses' confidence, coworkers' support, or even their jobs. When they felt that they would be disadvantaged in their hierarchy of men, they told no one that they had a serious illness (see also Ressmeyer, 1983), avoided disclosing further episodes, or minimized their significance. One middle-aged man with renal failure discovered that his cronies of 30 years turned against him for receiving less strenuous tasks for a few months after he had a heart attack. This man decided not to be beaten by his coworkers' attitudes and kept his job. But he refused his supervisor's offers to reassign him to easier jobs to prove that he could still do the strenuous work.[8]

Being able to control the logistics for doing work, as well as the amount and type of work itself, allows men to preserve their work and themselves, including their assumptions about masculinity. Part of that control rests on also being able to control other people and the definition of the situation. An executive masked leaving the office early for his dialysis treatments by "attending meetings out of the office." Not even his secretary knew he was a dialysis patient. He believed that knowledge of his illness in the business community would reduce his stature as an aggressive competitor in the hierarchy of businessmen (cf. Sabo & Gordon, 1992). A salesman completed his sales calls in the morning when he felt and looked fresher, and did paperwork at home in the afternoons when he could take rest breaks. A professor referred questions to several bright students when he felt short of breath. An administrator moved his office to a wing closer to the parking lot. In all these cases, controlling time, pace, space, information, and people gave these men more control over ensuing interaction, impression-management, and identity.

How do men preserve self when they cannot exert this type of control? Their embarrassment about visible markers of illness resulted in avoiding encounters beyond their inner circles. The executive above maintained a policy of not socializing with business associates. By not attending cocktail or swim parties, he hid his restricted diet and his dialysis shunt. A craftsman with emphysema hid how hard walking had become. He lagged behind anyone who might observe him struggling to climb a few stairs. Later, as his coughing and spitting fractured ordinary conversation, he refused social invitations and reduced his work to a few projects that he could complete alone at home.

Not everyone assumes that illness and disability will become melded with identity. Some men remain strikingly resourceful in finding ways to remain vitally involved and simultaneously, to avoid having a stigmatized identity. Wheelchair use, for example, can give rise to developing a host of clever strategies for preserving self. One man arrived at social events early to position himself in an opportune location to see and greet friends. He found that people treated him as a commanding male when seated across from him but did not when they towered over him. When others were seated, he could position his body more forcefully in ways associated with manliness (Connell, 1983; Whitson, 1990). Such strategies preserve self as known in the past and, moreover, preserve assumptions about masculinity.

Discussion

Traditional assumptions of male identity, including an active, problem-solving stance, emphasis on personal power and autonomy, and bravery in the face of danger create a two-edged sword for men in chronic illness. On the one hand, these assumptions encourage men to take risks, to be active, and to try to recover, which certainly can prompt re-creating a valued life after serious episodes of illness and therefore bolster self-esteem. On the other hand, these assumptions narrow the range of credible male behaviors for those who subscribe to them. Hence, they foster rigidity in stance and set the conditions for slipping into depression. Men's assumed difference between masculine identity and the "lesser" identities of women and children shrink as they lose ordinary masculinizing practices (Connell, Ashenden, Kessler, & Dowsett, 1982; Whitson, 1990).

Thus, an uneasy tension exists between valued identities and disparaged, that is, denigrated or shameful, ones. A man can gain a strengthened or a diminished identity through experiencing illness. These are not mutually exclusive categories. Men often move back and forth depending on their situations and their perceptions of them. The grieving process in men may be negated or cause those who witness it such discomfort that they cannot give comfort. Men express their grieving in fear and rage as well as in tears and sorrow. But for many men who experience progressive illness and disability, grieving, instead of being a process, sinks into becoming a permanent depression. If so, they will likely abandon constraining medical regimens that erode their sense of mastery. Life becomes struggling to live on their own terms while waiting to die.

What are the conditions that shape whether a man will reconstruct a positive identity or sink into depression? Certainly, whether a man defines having future possibilities makes an enormous difference. The men in my study primarily founded their preferred identities in action. Subsequently, if they saw no valued realm of action available to them and no way to preserve a valued self, the likelihood increased that they would become despondent.

In summary, awakening to death causes men to face their mortality. Whether they view their illness as a discrete event or as causing continued uncertainty depends in part on whether their concepts of masculinity allow them to construct flexible roles and valued identities as men who have chronic illnesses. Otherwise, they accommodate to uncertainty by bracketing illness to acute episodes and crises, or they refuse to accommodate to it. In this sense, men take more individualistic stances toward their illnesses than do women, who are tied to a network of relationships that shape how they manage their illnesses. Acknowledging uncertainty as lasting, however, does prompt reappraisals and redirection for both men and women and shapes how they define illness and disability. Men more often view illness as an enemy to overcome or as an intrusive presence to control than do women. Visible disability may reduce men's stature in the hierarchy of men more than its analogous consequences for women. If so, then men have greater incentives than women to try to recapture the past and their respective masculine identities in the past. Similarly, then, men have perhaps a greater stake in preserving self than women and the public identities that support this self.

A final point: A more exacting look at the differential experience of men and women who suffer from serious chronic illnesses will deepen sociological and professional understandings of how they make sense of their lives. As the research in chronic illness grows, studying men and women comparatively in conjunction with marital, age, and social class statuses, in addition to the type of illness, can substantially refine sociological interpretations of the narratives of chronically ill people.

Notes

1. Chronic illness means experiencing ongoing or intermittent, recurrent, irreversible, and often, degenerative, symptoms of a disease process (cf. Freund & McGuire, 1991). I focus on what it means to have a disease, not on objectivist medical definitions, and address two of Conrad's (1987) subtypes of chronic illness: "lived-with-illnesses" (e.g., multiple sclerosis, chronic fatigue syndrome, renal failure, diabetes, postpoliomyelitis syndrome), which force adapting without immediate life threat, and those "mortal illnesses" (e.g., heart attack, stroke, cancer) that sufferers view as life-threatening and have lasting consequences whether or not they (a) know about these consequences and (b) experience immediate symptoms.

2. The data for this study are derived from 40 in-depth formal interviews of 20 men, 7 of whom were interviewed more than once, informal interviews, and a collection of personal accounts. Comparisons were made with 80 interviews with chronically ill women. The criteria for being interviewed included (a) adult status (over 21 years of age), (b) a diagnosis

of a serious but not terminal chronic illness, (c) a disease with an uncertain course, and (d) effects of illness on daily life. When I first met the men, their ages ranged as follows: three under 40; six between 40 and 50; four between 50 and 60; five between 60 and 70, and the remaining two men were 73 and 85. Ten men worked at least part-time; others had retired or were too ill to work. In social class, they ranged as follows: eight men were working class or poor; six were middle class, and four were upper-middle class. Ten men were married. Status attributes of the one half of the sample with whom I kept in touch (5 to 8 years) changed slightly over time (e.g., financial and marital). All of the men were white.

Grounded theory methods were used to analyze the data (Charmaz, 1983, 1990; Corbin & Strauss, 1990; Glaser, 1978; Glaser & Strauss, 1967; Strauss, 1987). The steps included (a) examining the interviews for gender differences, (b) studying men's interviews and written accounts for themes, (c) building analytic categories from men's definitions of and taken-for-granted assumptions about their situations, (d) conducting further interviews to refine these categories, (e) rereading personal accounts from the vantage point of gender issues (e.g., Fiore, 1984; Hirsch, 1977; Hodgins, 1964; Kelly, 1977; Murphy, 1987; Zola, 1982), (f) studying a new set of personal accounts (e.g., Beisser, 1989; Frank, 1990; Zink, 1992), and (g) making comparisons with women on selected key points. The processes in the major themes served to integrate the analysis.

3. Also, men report fewer illnesses and doctors' visits than women; men may not seek early care or routine checks that might result in averting crises (Freund & McGuire, 1991; Nathanson, 1989; Verbrugge, 1989; Verbrugge & Wingard, 1987; Waldron, 1976). Some men disattend to conditions such as diabetes or high blood pressure until they become crises.

4. Note that I refer to *initial* crises here. A man who becomes identified as a troublemaker, crock, mental case, mental incompetent, or an alcoholic will be hard-pressed to have his symptoms and views of treatment taken seriously (cf. Albrecht, 1992; Leiderman & Grisso, 1985; Millman, 1976; Plough, 1986).

5. The few gay men with whom I talked did not currently have love relationships.

6. The disease process affects the kind of the uncertainty that people experience. Laura Nathan (1990) points out that initially cancer patients and their families focus on recovery, but they cannot be sure when and if that recovery has occurred; they face continued uncertainty.

7. Kotarba (1983) details the story of a man in chronic pain who suffers one loss after another and commits suicide. His story reveals parallel conditions to those these men faced.

8. Most working-class jobs permit little flexibility. Middle-class jobs, in contrast, allow men more control over timing, scheduling, pacing, and using space during work. Kotarba (1983) suggests that working-class laborers may be relatively unconcerned about staying on the job because they can net 80% of their pay if they can claim a job-related disability. Ten years later, many working-class jobs are without access to benefits and even if they are available, workers are hard-pressed to prove that their illnesses or disabilities are job related. Thus, workers try to remain in their jobs.

References

Albrecht, G. L. (1992). The social experience of disability. In C. Calhoun & G. Ritzer (Eds.), *Social problems* (pp. 1-18). New York: McGraw-Hill.

Beisser, A. R. (1989). *Flying without wings: Personal reflections on being disabled.* New York: Doubleday.

Brooks, N. A., & Matson, R. R. (1982). Social psychological adjustment to multiple sclerosis. *Social Science and Medicine, 16,* 2129-2135.

Charmaz, K. (1983). The grounded theory method: An explication and interpretation. In R. M. Emerson (Ed.), *Contemporary field research* (pp. 109-126). Boston: Little, Brown.

Charmaz, K. (1987). Struggling for a self: Identity levels of the chronically ill. In J. A. Roth & P. C. Conrad (Eds.), *Research in the sociology of health care: The experience and management of chronic illness* (pp. 283-321). Greenwich, CT: JAI.

Charmaz, K. (1990). Discovering chronic illness: Using grounded theory. *Social Science & Medicine, 30,* 1161-1172.

Charmaz, K. (1991). *Good days, bad days: The self in chronic illness and time.* New Brunswick, NJ: Rutgers University Press.

Connell, R. W. (1983). *Which way is up?: Essays on class, sex and culture.* Sydney, Australia: Allen and Unwin.

Connell, R. W. (1987). *Gender & power: Society, the person and sexual politics.* Stanford, CA: Stanford University Press.

Connell, R. W., Ashenden, D. J., Kessler, S., & Dowsett, G. W. (1982). *Making the difference: Schools, families and social division.* Sydney, Australia: Allen and Unwin.

Conrad, P. (1987). The experience of illness: Recent and new directions. In J. A. Roth & P. C. Conrad (Eds.), *Research in the sociology of health care: The experience and management of chronic illness* (Vol. 6, pp. 1-31). Greenwich, CT: JAI.

Corbin, J. M., & Strauss, A. L. (1984). Collaboration: Couples working together to manage chronic illness. *Image, 4,* 109-115.

Corbin, J. M., & Strauss, A. L. (1988). Unending work and care: Managing chronic illness at home. San Francisco: Jossey-Bass.

Corbin, J. M., & Strauss, A. L. (1990). *Basics of qualitative research.* Newbury Park, CA: Sage.

Cousins, N. (1983). *The healing heart: Antidotes to panic and helplessness.* New York: Avon.

Cowie, B. (1976). The patient's perception of his heart attack. *Social Science & Medicine, 10,* 87-96.

Dahlberg, C. C., & Jaffe, J. (1977). *Stroke: A doctor's personal story of his recovery.* New York: Norton.

Denzin, N. K. (1989). *Interpretive biography.* Newbury Park, CA: Sage.

Denzin, N. K. (1991). *Images of postmodern society.* Newbury Park, CA: Sage.

Fiore, N. A. (1984). *The road back to health.* New York: Bantam.

Foster, L. (1978). Man and machine: Life without kidneys. In H. D. Schwartz & C. F. Kart (Eds.), *Dominant issues in medical sociology* (pp. 522-526). Redding, MA: Addison-Wesley.

Frank, A. (1991). *At the will of the body.* New York: Houghlin Mifflin.

Frank, A. (1993). The rhetoric of self-change: Illness experience as narrative. *Sociological Quarterly, 34,* 39-52.

Freund, P. E. S., & McGuire, M. B. (1991). *Health, illness, and the social body.* Englewood Cliffs, NJ: Prentice Hall.

Gecas, V. (1982). The self-concept. *Annual Review of Sociology, 8,* 1-33.

Gerhardt, U., & Brieskorn-Zink, M. (1986). The normalization of hemodialysis at home. In J. A. Roth & S. B. Ruzek (Eds.), *Research in the sociology of health care: The adoption and social consequences of medical technologies* (Vol. 5, pp. 271-317). Greenwich, CT: JAI.

Glaser, B. G. (1978). *Theoretical sensitivity.* Mill Valley, CA: Sociology Press.

Glaser, B. G., & Strauss, A. L. (1967). *The discovery of grounded theory.* Chicago: Aldine.

Goffman, E. (1961). *Encounters.* New York: Bobbs-Merrill.

Goffman, E. (1963). *Stigma.* Englewood Cliffs, NJ: Prentice Hall.

Gordon, D. (1990). Testicular cancer: Passage to new priorities. In E. J. Clark, J. M. Fritz, & P. P. Rieker (Eds.), *Clinical sociological perspectives on illness & loss* (pp. 234-247). Philadelphia: Charles Press.

Herzlich, C., & Pierret, J. (1987). Illness and self in society. Baltimore: Johns Hopkins University Press.

Hewitt, J. (1989). *Dilemmas of the American self.* Philadelphia: Temple University Press.

Hirsch, E. (1977). *Starting over.* Hanover, MA: Christopher.

Hodgins, E. (1964). *Episode: Report on the accident inside my skull.* New York: Athaneum.

Husserl, E. (1970). *The crisis of the European sciences and transcendental phenomenology.* Evanston, IL: Northwestern University Press.

Jaques, E. (1965). Death and the midlife crisis. *International Journal of Psychoanalysis, 46,* 502-514.

Johnson, J. L. (1991). Learning to live again: The process of adjustment following a heart attack. In J. M. Morse & J. L. Johnson (Eds.), *The illness experience* (pp. 13-88). Newbury Park, CA: Sage.

Karp, D. (1988). A decade of reminders: Changing age consciousness between fifty and sixty years old. *The Gerontologist, 28,* 727-738.

Kelleher, D. (1988). Coming to terms with diabetes: Coping strategies and non-compliance. In R. A. Anderson & M. Bury (Eds.), *Living with chronic illness* (pp. 155-187). London: Unwin Hyman.

Kelly, O. E. (1977). Make today count. In H. Fiefel (Ed.), *New meanings of death* (pp. 181-194). New York: McGraw-Hill.

Kleinman, A. (1988). *The illness narratives: Suffering, healing, & the human condition.* New York: Basic Books.

Kotarba, J. A. (1983). *Chronic pain: Its social dimensions.* Beverly Hills, CA: Sage.

Lear, M. (1980). *Heartsounds.* New York: Simon & Schuster.

Leiderman, D. B., & Grisso, J-A. (1985). The Gomer phenomenon. *Journal of Health and Social Behavior, 26,* 222-231.

LeMaistre, J. (1985). *Beyond rage: The emotional impact of chronic illness.* Oak Park, IL: Alpine Guild.

Levinson, D., Darrow, J. C., Klein, E., Levinson, M., & McKee, B. (1978). *The seasons of a man's life.* New York: Knopf.

Lewis, K. (1985). *Successful living with chronic illness.* Wayne, NJ: Avery.

Messner, M. A., & Sabo, D. F. (1990). Toward a critical feminist reappraisal of sport, men and the gender order. In M. A. Messner & D. F. Sabo (Eds.), *Sport, men, and the gender order: Critical feminist perspective* (pp. 1-15). Champaign, IL: Human Kinetics.

Millman, M. (1976). *The unkindest cut.* New York: William Morrow.

Murphy, R. F. (1987). *The body silent.* New York: Henry Holt.

Nathan, L. E. (1990). Coping with uncertainty: Family members' adaptations during cancer remission. In E. J. Clark, J. M. Fritz, & P. P. Rieker (Eds.), *Clinical sociological perspectives on illness & loss* (pp. 219-233). Philadephia: Charles Press.

Nathanson, C. (1989). Sex, illness, and medical care: A review of data, theory, and methods. In P. Brown (Ed.), *Perspectives in medical sociology* (pp. 46-70). Belmont, CA: Wadsworth.

Peyrot, M., McMurry, J. F., Jr., & Hedges, R. (1988). Marital adjustment to adult diabetes: Interpersonal congruence and spouse satisfaction. *Journal of Marriage and the Family, 50,* 363-376.

Pitzele, S. K. (1985). *We are not alone: Learning to live with chronic illness.* New York: Workman.

Plough, A. (1986). *Borrowed time: Artificial organs and the politics of extending lives.* Philadelphia: Temple University Press.

Register, C. (1987). *Living with chronic illness.* New York: Free Press.

Reif, L. (1975). Ulcerative colitis: Strategies for managing life. In A. L. Strauss (Ed.), *Chronic illness and the quality of life.* St. Louis, MO: C. V. Mosby.

Ressmeyer, R. (1983, July 10). A day to day struggle. *San Francisco Examiner and Chronicle,* pp. 1-5 [California Living Sec.].

Sabo, D. F. (1990). Men, death anxiety, and denial: Critical feminist interpretations of adjustment to mastectomy. In E. J. Clark, J. M. Fritz, & P. P. Rieker (Eds.), *Clinical sociological perspectives on illness & loss* (pp. 71-84). Philadelphia: Charles Press.

Sabo, D. F., & Gordon, D. (1992, August). *Rethinking men's health and illness: The relevance of gender studies.* Paper presented at the Society for the Study of Social Problems, Pittsburgh, PA.

Sabo, D. F., & Panepinto, J. (1990). Football ritual and the social reproduction of masculinity. In M. A. Messner & D. F. Sabo (Eds.), *Sport, men, and the gender order: Critical feminist perspectives* (pp. 115-126). Champaign, IL: Human Kinetics.

Schneider, J. W., & Conrad, P. (1983). *Having epilepsy.* Philadelphia: Temple University Press.

Speedling, E. J. (1982). *Heart attack: The family response at home and in the hospital.* New York: Tavistock.

Strauss, A. (1987). *Qualitative analysis for social scientists.* New York: Cambridge University Press.

Strauss, A., Corbin, J., Fagerhaugh, S., Glaser, B. G., Maines, D., Suczek, B., & Wiener, C. (1984). *Chronic illness and the quality of life* (2nd ed.). St. Louis, MO: C. V. Mosby.

Strong, M. (1988). *Mainstay.* Boston: Little, Brown.

Tannen, D. (1990). *You just don't understand: Women and men in conversation.* New York: Ballantine.

Turner, R. (1976). The real self: From institution to impulse. *American Journal of Sociology, 81,* 989-1016.

Verbrugge, L. M. (1985). Gender and health: An update on hypotheses and evidence. *Journal of Health and Social Behavior, 26,* 156-182.

Verbrugge, L. M. (1989). The twain meet: Empirical explanations of sex differences in health and mortality. *Journal of Health and Social Behavior, 30,* 282-304.

Verbrugge, L. M., & Wingard, D. L. (1987). Sex differentials in health and mortality. *Women and Health, 12,* 103-145.

Waldron, I. (1976). Why do women live longer than men? *Social Science and Medicine, 10,* 349-362.

Weigert, A. J. (1986). The social production of identity: Metatheoretical foundations. *Sociological Quarterly, 27,* 165-183.

Whitson, D. (1990). Sport in the social construction of masculinity. In M. A. Messner & D. F. Sabo (Eds.), *Sport, men, and the gender order: Critical feminist perspectives* (pp. 19-30). Champaign, IL: Human Kinetics.

Wiener, C. J. (1975). The burden of arthritis. In A. L. Strauss (Ed.), *Chronic illness and the quality of life* (pp. 71-80). St. Louis, MO: C. V. Mosby.

Wulf, H. H. (1979). *Aphasia, my world alone.* Detroit, MI: Wayne State University Press.

Zink, J. B. (1992). Adjusting to early and late-onset disability. *Generations, 16,* 59-60.

Zola, I. K. (1982). *Missing pieces: A chronicle of living with a disability.* Philadelphia: Temple University Press.

14

Men Who Survive a Suicidal Act

Successful Coping or Failed Masculinity?

SILVIA SARA CANETTO

In the United States men engage in fewer acts of suicidal behavior than women. It has been estimated that there are 240,000 to 600,000 acts of nonfatal suicidal behavior per year, and that the male to female ratio is one to three. Men are, however, more likely to die as a result of a suicidal act than women by a ratio of four to one (McIntosh, 1993).

Evidence suggests that culture and gender socialization contribute to the low rates of nonfatal suicidal behavior and the high rates of suicide mortality of U.S. men. First of all, this pattern is not universal. According to a review of the international literature by Canetto and Lester (1995b), men's rates of nonfatal suicidal behavior outnumber women's rates in India, Poland, and Helsinki, Finland; furthermore, men's rates are similar to women's in Sri Lanka.

Second, there is evidence that in the United States, surviving a suicidal act is viewed as "unmasculine." Additionally, men who survive a suicidal act are considered less deserving of sympathy than women (Canetto, 1992-1993, 1995). Interestingly, it is men who are most critical of other men who survive a suicidal act (White & Stillion, 1988). According to White and

AUTHOR'S NOTE: The author is grateful to Eric R. Dahlen, Jeremy Gersovitz, and David B. Wohl for their editorial assistance. I also thank Michael Kimmel and the editors, Don Sabo and David Gordon, for inviting me to contribute to this important volume. Correspondence should be addressed to Silvia Sara Canetto, Department of Psychology, Colorado State University, Fort Collins, CO 80523.

Stillion, "attempted suicide by troubled males may be viewed by other males as violations of the sex-role messages of strength, decisiveness, success, and inexpressiveness" (p. 365).

Finally, identification with, or adoption of, behaviors considered feminine in the United States is associated with high risk for nonfatal suicidal behavior. This means that nonconformity to conventional gender expectations is associated with risk for nonfatal suicidal behavior in males but not in females (Harris, 1983). In other words, "feminine" males are more likely to be suicidal than "masculine" females.

A prevalent theory in the U.S. professional literature is that men become suicidal due to impersonal reasons, such as health and work problems (see Canetto, 1992-1993; Kushner, 1993, 1995, for reviews). There is evidence, however, that this theory is based on culture-specific beliefs about men and suicide. The assumption is that men do not become suicidal because of relationship losses. For example, a study exploring the role of gender and context (athletic versus relationship failure) in the perceived acceptability of suicidal death found that males who killed themselves because of an achievement failure were rated as more well-adjusted than males who killed themselves because of a failed relationship (Lewis & Shepeard, 1992).

One consequence of these cultural beliefs about men and suicide is that very little research has been conducted on men who survived their suicidal acts. Furthermore, available research on men's suicidal behavior has tended to focus on impersonal factors, to the neglect of interpersonal factors. Insufficient information is then mistaken for confirmation of traditional assumptions about men and suicidal behavior.

In this chapter, I critically examine the literature on males who survive a suicidal act. A brief discussion of the nomenclature of suicidal behavior precedes the review of studies. Finally, case studies of suicidal men are presented and discussed in light of theory and available evidence.

Nomenclature of Suicidal Behaviors

In this chapter, suicidal behaviors are classified in terms of outcome rather than intent. The expression *nonfatal suicidal behavior* is used to refer to suicidal acts with a nonfatal outcome, in lieu of terms such as *suicide attempt* and *parasuicide*. *Fatal suicidal behavior* and *suicide mortality* are reserved for those suicidal acts that result in death, instead of the terms *completed* or *successful suicide*. The expression *suicidal behavior,* not otherwise specified, is used whenever information about outcome is not available or relevant. An advantage of this nomenclature is that it makes no assumptions about the suicidal person's intent. Not all persons who survive a suicidal act expected to live; conversely, not all suicidal deaths are intended. My nomenclature also avoids the implication that killing oneself means being successful, whereas surviving a suicidal act means failing (see Canetto, 1992; Diekstra, 1990; Lester, 1989, for a discussion of suicidal behavior terminology).

Studies of Men and Nonfatal Suicidal Behavior

The Nature and Limitations of the Data

Information on nonfatal suicidal behavior is usually available through local epidemiological surveys. No country maintains an ongoing, nationally comprehensive record of nonfatal suicidal behaviors. Thus, information on nonfatal suicidal behavior is neither historically nor geographically comprehensive. A large proportion of nonfatal suicidal acts never reaches the attention of the medical and psychological community. Of those that do, some may never go beyond the individual private clinician. According to studies reviewed by Jack (1992), as much as one third of all suicidal persons do not visit a hospital for treatment, and at least 10% of those who do are discharged from the emergency room without an inpatient admission. Studies of nonfatal suicidal behaviors do not usually cross-classify information about gender, age, and ethnicity. Therefore, important comparisons across specific gender-age-ethnic groups are impossible.

The main limitation on available data results from variations in definitions of nonfatal suicidal behaviors. There are no standardized definitions of nonfatal suicidal behaviors. De Leo and Diekstra (1990) note that "suicidal acts with a non fatal outcome are labeled either suicide attempts, attempted suicides, parasuicides or acts of deliberate self-harm, depending upon the country of origin of the author(s) or the 'school' he or she adheres to" (pp. 178-179). Although some authors consider these terms synonyms, other authors distinguish between attempted suicide and parasuicide, the former implying intent to kill oneself and the latter encompassing acts in which there is no conscious lethal intention. This lack of agreed upon terminology makes it difficult to draw comparisons across studies.

Furthermore, reporting practices and criteria used for the determination of suicidal behaviors also vary. Recording a self-destructive act as suicidal is likely to be influenced by the clinician's training and beliefs, the social consequences of suicidal behavior, the characteristics of the suicidal person (e.g., gender, age, ethnicity), and the circumstances of the suicidal action (e.g., method used, antecedents).

There is evidence suggesting that men's nonfatal suicidal acts are particularly susceptible to underreporting and misclassification. For example, according to Whitehead, Johnson, and Ferrence (1973), the lower rates for males, as compared with females, may be an artifact of biased data collection. Their Canadian study shows that men's and women's rates of nonfatal suicidal behavior are similar if one includes the data from jails. Because it is assumed that surviving a suicidal act is feminine (Canetto, 1992-1993), and because nonfatal suicidal behavior in males is often associated with alcohol and illegal substance abuse (Beck, Lester, & Kovacs, 1973; Fernandez-Pol, 1986), clinicians may be reluctant to recognize suicidal clues in a man's nonfatal overdose. Finally, because it is generally believed that relationship problems are not a masculine reason for suicidal behavior (Canetto, 1992-1993), men who become suicidal over relationship problems may be motivated to hide their suicidal actions or to report impersonal precipitants.

Given the variations in the comprehensiveness, criteria, and methods of data recording, one ought to view the available data on nonfatal suicidal behavior as providing conservative and possibly biased estimates. With these caveats, I move to an analysis of studies of men's nonfatal suicidal behavior. From now on, my review uses only data from the United States, in recognition of the cultural specificity of the meaning of suicidal behaviors and masculinity.

Ethnicity and Culture

Rates of nonfatal suicidal behaviors vary depending on ethnicity and culture. Data from a five-site U.S. study (Moscicki et al., 1988) indicate that whites are more likely to engage in nonfatal suicidal behavior than nonwhites. However, Puerto Ricans in East Harlem were found to have rates of nonfatal suicidal behavior two to three times higher than either blacks or whites (Monk & Warshauer, 1974).

The relationship of gender and ethnicity is variable. According to a study of the lifetime prevalence of suicidal ideation and attempts in a community sample of Spanish-speaking (Hispanic) individuals and non-Spanish-speaking (non-Hispanic) whites, fewer men of both ethnic groups reported suicide attempts than women of either ethnic group (Sorenson &

Golding, 1988). However, among Puerto Ricans, men were found to have similar (Fernandez-Pol, 1986) or higher (Monk & Warshauer, 1974) rates of nonfatal suicidal behavior than women.

Finally, studies of ethnicity and suicidal ideation and behavior with male adolescent samples found that racial-ethnic minorities tended to be overrepresented in the suicidal group. Specific patterns of suicide risk and ethnicity vary by region of the country. One study of adolescents conducted in the greater Miami, Florida, area (Vega, Gil, Warheit, Apospori, & Zimmerman, 1993) found that African Americans had the highest prevalence of 6-month ideation, whereas Haitians had the highest nonfatal suicidal behavior. Non-Hispanic whites reported the highest ideation and the lowest nonfatal suicidal behavior frequencies, a pattern that is congruent with conventional expectations about men and suicide in the United States. Interestingly, foreign-born adolescents had higher frequencies of nonfatal suicidal behavior than natives. Another study of adolescent and young adult gay males conducted in the Los Angeles area noted that a history of suicidal ideation or behavior was most common among Latinos (Schneider, Farberow, & Kruks, 1989). However, among people over age 60, nonfatal suicidal behavior seems to be more common among whites (Frierson, 1991).

Age

According to a recent review of the literature by Canetto and Lester (1995b), suicidal persons tend to be under 30 years of age. The 1987 National Adolescent Student Health Survey found a history of nonfatal suicidal behavior in 11.1% of males and 17.5% of females from a national random sample of eighth and tenth grade students (American School Health Association, 1989). Studies of age, gender, and nonfatal suicidal behavior suggest that male rates of nonfatal suicidal behavior decline after age 44 (e.g., Frierson, 1991; Pederson, Awad, & Kindler, 1973; Sorenson & Golding, 1988).

Education, Employment, Social Class, and Economic Resources

Nonfatal suicidal behavior appears to be most prevalent among unemployed (Moscicki et al., 1988), uneducated (Petronis, Samuels, Moscicki, & Anthony, 1990), poor (Guyer, Lescohier, Gallagher, Hausman, & Azzara, 1989), and lower socioeconomic status individuals (Lyons, 1985; Moscicki et al., 1988; Pederson et al., 1973). The association between unemployment, low social class, and nonfatal suicidal behavior has been confirmed for males. In a study of Puerto Rican suicide attempters (51% males), 98% reported being unemployed (Fernandez-Pol, 1986). Black suicidal males aged 20 to 35 treated at an emergency medical service in Detroit were more likely to come from a disadvantaged socioeconomic background than a nonsuicidal control group (Kirk & Zucker, 1979).

Personal Relationships

The evidence regarding the relationship status of suicidal men is equivocal because studies have typically not looked at the evidence for women and men separately. A recent epidemiological study of five U.S. communities by Petronis et al. (1990) found that being separated or divorced was associated with an increased risk of nonfatal suicidal behavior. Similarly, a study of ethnicity and nonfatal suicidal behavior found that individuals who were divorced, separated, or married with an absent spouse reported the highest rates of ideation and attempts (Sorenson & Golding, 1988). An earlier study of gender and nonfatal suicidal behavior noted that suicidal men were as likely as suicidal women to have experienced a marriage breakup (Beck et al., 1973).

Similarly, there is very little information about the personal background of suicidal men, as distinguished from suicidal women. One study of self-reported suicidal behavior among Navajo adolescents found that suicidal males tended to have a history of sexual abuse, whereas suicidal females had a history of physical abuse (Grossman, Milligan, & Deyo, 1991). On the other hand, suicidal ideation among gay adolescent and young adult males was associated with a history of physical abuse, paternal alcoholism, and family rejection of homosexuality (Schneider et al., 1989).

Method

The choice of suicidal method is influenced by familiarity, accessibility, and perceived cultural acceptability (Marks & Abernathy, 1974). In the United States, the majority of nonfatal suicidal acts involves medically prescribed psychotropic drugs (Canetto & Lester, 1995b). Such choice of suicidal method is not surprising given that women, who are more likely than men to engage in nonfatal acts of suicidal behavior, are also more likely to be prescribed psychotropic drugs by physicians (Cooperstock, 1982; Fidell, 1982). One early study of method by gender (Beck et al., 1973) found that men were more likely than women to use self-laceration and to engage in nonfatal suicidal behavior outdoors. Furthermore, a recent hospital-based study of nonfatal suicidal behavior among the elderly found that men were more likely than women to have used a gun as a suicide method (Frierson, 1991). It has sometimes been argued that for each method, men injure themselves more than women. However, Lester (1990) did not find any gender differences in the severity of injury of suicidal persons who jumped.

Mental Disorders

Several studies have confirmed an association between suicidal behavior and the diagnosis of mental disorder (Frierson, 1991; Grossman et al., 1991; Moscicki et al., 1988; Sorenson & Golding, 1988). For example, Moscicki et al. (1988) found that persons who had a lifetime diagnosis of mental disorder had the highest risk for nonfatal suicidal behavior. Similarly, Sorenson and Golding (1988) reported that individuals with a mental disorder diagnosis were more likely to think about killing themselves and to engage in nonfatal suicidal behavior than those without such a diagnosis. One potential confound, however, is that the diagnosis of mental disorder is often given because of the suicidal ideation or behavior, rather than independently. The most common major clinical diagnosis assigned to suicidal persons is depression (Frierson, 1991; Sorenson & Golding, 1988; Weissman, 1974; Wolff, 1969), accounting for 35% to 79% of all cases (Weissman, 1974). An early study (Wolff, 1969) found that among older male inpatients, suicidal ideation was associated with psychotic depression.

Another clinical condition frequently found in suicidal persons is alcohol or substance abuse (Canetto, 1991). A recent study of five United States communities (Petronis et al., 1990) found that the risk for suicidal behavior was associated with being a cocaine user but not with the illicit use of marijuana, sedative-hypnotics, or sympathomimetic stimulants. One study (Beck et al., 1973) reported that suicidal males are more likely to be diagnosed as alcoholics or as having a history of alcohol abuse than suicidal females. Furthermore, a recent study of a multiethnic sample of seventh and eight grade males found an association between nonfatal suicidal behavior and psychoactive drug use among Hispanics, non-Hispanic whites and African Americans. However, substance abuse did not seem to play a role in nonfatal suicidal behavior among elderly psychiatric inpatients (Lyness, Conwell, & Nelson, 1992).

Personality

Suicidal persons have been described as anxious, mistrusting, self-critical, impulsive, dependent, and unable to tolerate frustration (see Canetto, 1991, for a review). It has been suggested that suicidal persons have difficulties in expressing and regulating aggression. The diagnoses of borderline and antisocial personalities are often associated with nonfatal suicidal behavior. One limitation of available studies is that they did not look at the data on men and women separately, making it impossible to examine the unique personality characteristics of suicidal men.

Summary

Information about rates and patterns of nonfatal suicidal behavior in men is very limited because studies do not usually break down the data by gender, nor do they use all-male samples. A majority of national studies find that men have lower rates of nonfatal suicidal behavior than women. Rates of men's nonfatal suicidal behavior vary, however, according to age and ethnicity. Ethnic minority (especially Haitians, Puerto Ricans, Cubans, and other Latinos) and foreign born males are overrepresented among suicidal adolescents, whereas white males are predominant among the suicidal elderly. Men who engage in nonfatal suicidal behavior typically come from lower socioeconomic backgrounds. An association between unemployment and nonfatal suicidal behavior has also been confirmed for men. Information about the personal and family relationships of suicidal men is scarce. An early study showed that suicidal men were as likely as women to have experienced a marriage breakup. Recent evidence suggests an association between male suicidal behavior and a history of sexual abuse, physical abuse, and paternal alcoholism.

Case Studies

Two case studies of suicidal males from two age groups are presented following. These cases were selected from a sample of hospitalized suicidal persons recruited for a study of suicide and couple interaction. The data were obtained from interviews with the suicidal males and their female partners (see Canetto & Feldman, 1993; Canetto, Feldman, & Lupei, 1989, for details on the study's sample and interview methodology).

Case 1. John, a 34-year-old white, separated male, was hospitalized in the inpatient unit of a psychiatric hospital following an overdose of Valium and Ritalin. John had a history of depression, drug abuse, and psychiatric treatment. He had recently quit his job as a high school teacher because, according to his wife, "the principal did not like him." Two months before his suicidal act, John had completed a substance abuse program, but had quickly relapsed. When his wife realized he was back on drugs, she talked to him about divorce and moved with their young son to her parents' house. In his interview, John explicitly stated he overdosed to avoid feeling "the pain of her leaving." He admitted he did not really want to die, he just wanted "to get back together" with his wife. After taking the drugs, John called his psychiatrist, who arranged for him to be admitted to the hospital; John then called his wife, who took him to the hospital.

This case is representative of some of the trends noted in studies of male nonfatal suicidal behavior. Consistent with epidemiological trends, John was separated and had a history a drug abuse. He also had recently become unemployed. However, an archival study of John's case could have missed an important interpersonal dynamic. By the patient's own admission, the most important precipitant of his suicidal behavior was not his drug problem nor his unemployment, but his wife's leaving him.

Does John's behavior represent a failed suicide attempt? If it is true, as has been speculated (see Canetto & Lester, 1995a, for a review), that a majority of suicidal acts aim at improving one's life circumstances, not at dying, then it is dying that should be viewed as "failing" at suicide. Therefore, John's surviving his own suicidal behavior could be viewed as a sign of successful coping.

Case 2. In some ways, Richard's suicidal behavior followed the conventional patterns predicted for a man his age. It occurred late in life, at age 70, within a year of his experiencing retirement and a deterioration in physical health (he had a stroke and hip replacement surgery, which left him with limited mobility). Other aspects of his situation, however, did not quite fit textbook patterns. For one, he did not kill himself, as is typical of older white males who engage in a suicidal act. In fact, he attempted to jump out of a window while his wife was at home and within view of the suicide note he had left on the table. Second, he was neither isolated nor living alone, having married for the third time 2 years earlier.

Durkheim (1987/1951) has argued that women do not kill themselves as often as men because they are not imaginative and intellectually complex enough, and because they passively accept the blows of life more readily than men. Is Richard's behavior an indication of dullness, passivity, and lack of courage? Can it be a sign of *failed masculinity*? Or does his behavior represent true imagination, action, and courage? If it is true, as suggested by psychological autopsy studies, that older men who kill themselves are unusually emotionally and cognitively rigid (Clark, 1993), being willing to survive a suicidal action may be an indication of psychological flexibility. This is not to argue that engaging in a nonfatal suicidal act is a marker of psychological health. Nonetheless, being willing to survive a suicidal act may be an indication of psychological resilience, especially in men, in that male survival from suicide is so negatively viewed.

Conclusions

Most literature on suicidal behaviors defines death by suicide, a typically male outcome, as a "completed" or "successful" suicide. By contrast, surviving a suicidal act is defined as a "failed" suicide attempt. As discussed previously, in the United States, surviving a suicidal act is considered unmasculine; males are most critical of other males who express suicidal feelings. The assumption implicit in this terminology and these theories is that men who survive a suicidal act not only fail at suicide but also at masculinity. Thus, by defining nonfatal suicidal behavior as a female activity, experts also assume that men who survive a suicidal act are entering the female sphere.

It may be because of the association of nonfatal suicidal behavior with femininity that very little research has been conducted on males who survive a suicidal act. As in the case of depression (Nolen-Hoeksema, 1987), the parameters of typical nonfatal suicidal behavior have been based on conventional interpretations of the phenomenology and dynamics of female suicidal behavior. Male nonfatal suicidal behavior has come to be viewed as atypical and infrequent, and therefore unworthy of study.

This review of the literature shows that little is known about male nonfatal suicidal behavior. It also demonstrates that theory and research on male suicidal behavior need to go beyond the traditional attention to external, impersonal events, such as losses in income, employment, and health, and include a serious analysis of these men's interpersonal histories and needs (Canetto, 1994). For some suicidal men (as in the case of John described above), as for some women, external losses may be secondary to interpersonal losses.

Finally, this literature review shows that an analysis of the gendered priorities and identities of suicidal males in different cultures may be important to understanding male suicidal behavior. For some men (as in the case of Richard, possibly), an external loss, such as retirement or a minor physical disability, however normative, may be uniquely stressful because it threatens their sense of masculinity. Furthermore, adapting to such a loss may be viewed as unmasculine. For example, a recent study found that older men who killed themselves were so "fiercely proud and independent" that they appeared unable to "bend in the way of most older adults when life confront[ed] them with the ordinary stressors of aging, . . . [such as] increasing limitations on physical and mental functioning or [the] increasing need to rely on others for help with activities of daily living" (Clark, 1993, p. 24). For these suicidal men, external changes, such as returning to perfect health, even if desirable, are simply unfeasible. A shift in their gender identity and assumptions could be a key to their survival. A focus on gender can thus broaden possibilities for the prevention of male suicidal behavior.

References

American School Health Association. (1989). *The National Adolescent Student Health Survey: A report on the health of America's youth.* Oakland, CA: Third Party Publishing.

Beck, A. T., Lester, D., & Kovacs, M. (1973). Attempted suicides by males and females. *Psychological Reports, 33,* 865-866.

Canetto, S. S. (1991). Gender roles, suicide attempts, and substance abuse. *Journal of Psychology, 125,* 605-620.

Canetto, S. S. (1992). Gender and suicide in the elderly. *Suicide and Life-Threatening Behavior, 22,* 80-97.

Canetto, S. S. (1992-1993). She died for love and he for glory: Gender myths of suicidal behavior. *Omega, 26,* 1-17.

Canetto, S. S. (1994). Gender issues in the treatment of suicidal individuals. *Death Studies, 18,* 513-527.

Canetto, S. S. (1995). Elderly women and suicidal behavior. In S. S. Canetto & D. Lester (Eds.), *Women and suicidal behavior* (pp. 215-234). New York: Springer.

Canetto, S. S., & Feldman, L. B. (1993). Overt and covert dependence in suicidal women and their male partners. *Omega, 27,* 177-194.

Canetto, S. S., Feldman, L. B., & Lupei, R. A. (1989). Suicidal persons and their partners: Individual and interpersonal dynamics. *Suicide and Life-Threatening Behavior, 19,* 237-248.

Canetto, S. S., & Lester, D. (1995a). Women and suicidal behavior: Issues and dilemmas. In S. S. Canetto & D. Lester (Eds.), *Women and suicidal behavior* (pp. 3-10). New York: Springer.

Canetto, S. S., & Lester, D. (1995b). The epidemiology of women's suicidal behavior. In S. S. Canetto & D. Lester (Eds.), *Women and suicidal behavior* (pp. 35-60). New York: Springer.

Clark, D. C. (1993). Narcissistic crises of aging and suicidal despair. *Suicide and Life-Threatening Behavior, 23,* 21-26.

Cooperstock, R. (1982). Research on psychotropic drug use: A review of findings and methods. *Social Science and Medicine, 16,* 1179-1196.

De Leo, D., & Diekstra, R. F. W. (1990). *Depression and suicide in late life.* Toronto, Ontario: Hogrefe & Huber.

Diekstra, R. F. W. (1990). An international perspective on the epidemiology and prevention of suicide. In S. J. Blumenthal & D. J. Kupfer (Eds.), *Suicide over the life cycle: Risk factors, assessment, and treatment of suicidal patients* (pp. 533-569). Washington, DC: American Psychiatric Press.

Durkheim, E. (1951). *Suicide* (J. A. Spaulding & G. Simpson, Trans.). Glencoe, IL: Free Press. (Original work published 1897)

Fernandez-Pol, B. (1986). Characteristics of 77 Puerto Ricans who attempted suicide. *American Journal of Psychiatry, 143,* 1460-1463.

Fidell, L. S. (1982). Gender and drug use and abuse. In I. Al-Issa (Ed.), *Gender and psychopathology* (pp. 221-236). New York: Academic Press.

Frierson, R. L. (1991). Suicide attempts by the old and very old. *Archives of Internal Medicine, 151,* 141-144.

Grossman, D. C., Milligan, C., & Deyo, R. A. (1991). Risk factors for suicide attempts among Navajo adolescents. *American Journal of Public Health, 81,* 870-874.

Guyer, B., Lescohier, I., Gallagher, S. S., Hausman, A., & Azzara, C. V. (1989). Intentional injuries among children and adolescents in Massachusetts. *The New England Journal of Medicine, 321,* 1584-1589.

Harris, J. (1983). Parasuicide, gender, and gender deviance. *Journal of Health and Social Behavior, 24,* 350-361.

Jack, R. (1992). *Women and attempted suicide.* Hillsdale, NJ: Lawrence Erlbaum.

Kirk, A., & Zucker, R. (1979). Some sociopsychological factors in attempted suicide among urban black males. *Suicide and Life-Threatening Behavior, 9,* 76-86.

Kushner, H. I. (1993). Suicide, gender, and the fear of modernity in nineteenth-century medical and social thought. *Journal of Social History, 26,* 461-490.

Kushner, H. I. (1995). Women and suicidal behavior: Epidemiology, gender and lethality in historical perspective. In S. S. Canetto & D. Lester (Eds.), *Women and suicidal behavior* (pp. 11-34). New York: Springer.

Lester, D. (1989). The study of suicide from a feminist perspective. *Crisis, 11,* 38-43.

Lester, D. (1990). Sex difference in severity of injury in attempted suicides who jump. *Perceptual and Motor Skills, 71,* 176.

Lewis, R. J., & Shepeard, G. (1992). Inferred characteristics of successful suicides as function of gender and context. *Suicide and Life-Threatening Behavior, 22,* 187-198.

Lyness, J. M., Conwell, Y., & Nelson, J. C. (1992). Suicide attempts in elderly psychiatric inpatients. *Journal of the American Geriatrics Society, 40,* 320-324.

Lyons, M. J. (1985). Observable and subjective factors associated with attempted suicide in later life. *Suicide and Life-Threatening Behavior, 15,* 168-183.

Marks, A., & Abernathy, T. (1974). Toward a sociocultural perspective on means of self-destruction. *Suicide and Life-Threatening Behavior, 4,* 3-17.

McIntosh, J. L. (1993). *U.S.A. suicide: 1990 official final data.* Denver, CO: American Association of Suicidology.

Monk, M., & Warshauer, M. E. (1974). Completed and attempted suicide in three ethnic groups. *American Journal of Epidemiology, 100,* 333-345.

Moscicki, E. K., O'Carroll, P., Rae, D. S., Locke, B. Z., Roy, A., & Regier, D. S. (1988). Suicide attempts in the epidemiologic catchment area study. *Yale Journal of Biology and Medicine, 61,* 259-268.

Nolen-Hoeksema, S. (1987). Sex differences in unipolar depression: Evidence and theory. *Psychological Bulletin, 101,* 259-282.

Pederson, A. M., Awad, G. A., & Kindler, A. R. (1973). Epidemiological differences between white and nonwhite suicide attempters. *American Journal of Psychiatry, 130,* 1071-1076.

Petronis, K. R., Samuels, J. F., Moscicki, E. K., & Anthony, J. C. (1990). An epidemiological investigation of potential risk factors for suicide attempts. *Social Psychiatry and Psychiatric Epidemiology, 25,* 193-199.

Schneider, S. G., Farberow, N. L., & Kruks, G. N. (1989). Suicidal behavior in adolescent and young adult gay men. *Suicide and Life-Threatening Behavior, 19,* 381-394.

Sorenson, S. B., & Golding, J. M. (1988). Suicide ideation and attempts in Hispanics and non-Hispanic whites: Demographic and psychiatric disorder issues. *Suicide and Life-Threatening Behavior, 18,* 205-218.

Vega, W. A., Gil, A., Warheit, G., Apospori, E., & Zimmerman, R. (1993). The relationship of drug use to suicide ideation and attempts among African American, Hispanic, and white non-Hispanic male adolescents. *Suicide and Life-Threatening Behavior, 23,* 110-119.

Weissman, M. M. (1974). The epidemiology of suicide attempts, 1960 to 1971. *Archives of General Psychiatry, 30,* 737-746.

White, H., & Stillion, J. M. (1988). Sex differences in attitudes toward suicide: Do males stigmatize males? *Psychology of Women Quarterly, 12,* 357-372.

Whitehead, P. C., Johnson, F. G., & Ferrence, R. (1973). Measuring the incidence of self-injury: Some methodological and design considerations. *American Journal of Orthopsychiatry, 43,* 142-148.

Wolff, K. (1969). Depression and suicide in the geriatric patient. *Journal of the American Geriatric Society, 17,* 668-672.

Author Index

305

Subject Index

Accidental death, 34
    among males, 23, 24, 27
    as leading cause of death, 51, 52, 68
    decrease in, 27
    male behavior and increased risk of, 6, 8
    male employment and, 25, 34, 35
    See also Accidents *and* Motor vehicle
      fatalities
Accidents:
    among African American males, 123
    gender differences in, 24, 27, 34, 35,
      37, 38, 39
    See also Accidental death
African American communities:
    alcohol advertising in, 136
    church's role in, 127-128
    hazardous waste sites in, 123
    male shortage in, 122-123
    tobacco advertising in, 136
    See also African American males
African American males:
    accidents among, 123
    AIDS/HIV among, 122, 130-132, 133,
      135, 136, 141, 149
    alcoholism among, 13, 122, 132-133,
      134, 135, 136

    as homicide victims, 11, 54, 121, 122,
      123, 124-125, 127, 133, 136
    biogenic factors in health of, 122
    cancer among, 123, 124
    cirrhosis among, 134
    coping mechanisms of, 132-133
    crack cocaine use by, 127
    diabetes among, 123
    drug abuse by, 123, 132-136, 149
    drug-related homicides among, 127
    gangs and, 127
    high mortality rate of, 122, 123
    inadequate hospital treatment of, 123
    incarceration of, 136
    life expectancy among, 122, 123, 135
    major causes of death among, 122, 123,
      125, 128
    "masculine mystique" among, 123
    occupationally related diseases among,
      123
    polydrug use by, 136
    poor health status of, 11
    poverty-level incomes among, 136
    school dropouts among, 136
    strokes among, 123
    suicides among, 52, 53, 127-130

About the Contributors

Jeffrey S. Applegate is Associate Professor in the Graduate School of Social Work and Social Research at Bryn Mawr College. He has published numerous journal articles on men's roles as caregivers across the life cycle and is a coauthor of the book *Men as Caregivers to the Elderly: Understanding and Aiding Unrecognized Family Supports*. He is also a consulting editor for the *Clinical Social Work Journal* and the *Child and Adolescent Social Work Journal*.

Silvia Sara Canetto is an Assistant Professor in the Department of Psychology, Colorado State University, Fort Collins, Colorado. Dr. Canetto is the author of numerous articles on gender, life-threatening behaviors, family, aging, and the editor of a book (with David Lester) on *Women and Suicidal Behavior*.

Kathy Charmaz is Professor and Chair of the Sociology Department at Sonoma State University. Her research interests include the experience of chronic illness, the development and change of self, and the sociology of time. These interests are reflected in her book, *Good Days, Bad Days: The Self in Chronic Illness and Time*, which won the 1992 Charles Horton Cooley Award for the Society for the Study of Symbolic Interaction and the 1992 Distinguished Scholarship Award from the Pacific Sociological Association. Currently, she has several projects, including an empirical study of bodily experience in health and illness, didactic works on qualitative research, and epistemological critiques of postmodernism.

Thomas J. Gerschick is an Assistant Professor of Sociology at Illinois State University. His research focuses on identity and marginalized and alternative masculinities.

David Frederick Gordon is Associate Professor in the Department of Sociology at the State University of New York at Geneseo. His research focuses on the self and its relationship to major transitions in life such as joining new religious groups and surviving cancer. He is a survivor of testicular cancer himself, and he is continuing to interview other survivors of this disease. He has published articles in *Urban Life and Culture, Qualitative Sociology, Sociological Analysis, Journal of Community Health,* and *Journal for the Scientific Study of Religion.*

Vicki S. Helgeson is Associate Professor in the Department of Psychology at Carnegie Mellon University. Her research interests include how the socialization of men and women contributes to their psychological and physical health and how cognitions (perceived control, optimism, deriving meaning from the experience) enhance adjustment to chronic illness such as heart disease, cancer, and diabetes. She has published articles in *Journal of Personality and Social Psychology, Journal of Applied Social Psychology, Journal of Social and Clinical Psychology, Personality and Social Psychology Bulletin, Personal Relationships, Psychological Bulletin,* and *Sex Roles.* She is also a member of the editorial board of *Health Psychology* and is a consulting editor for the *Journal of Men's Studies.*

Alan M. Klein is Professor of Sociology-Anthropology at Northeastern University. His areas of research include sport ethnography, Latin American sport, masculinity, and political economy. His recent publications include *The Owls of the Two Laredos: Baseball and Nationalism on the Texas-Mexican Border, Little Big Men: Bodybuilding Subculture and Gender Construction,* and *Sugarball: The American Game, the Dominican Dream.*

Lenard W. Kaye is Professor at Bryn Mawr College Graduate School of Social Work and Social Research. He received his bachelor's degree from the State University of New York at Binghamton, his master's degree from New York University School of Social Work, and his doctorate from the Columbia University School of Social Work. He is the author of *Home*

Health Care, the coauthor of *Resolving Grievances in the Nursing Home* and *Men as Caregivers to the Elderly,* and the coeditor of *Congregate Housing for the Elderly* and *Part-Time Employment for the Lower Income Elderly: A Promising or Problematic Trend?* He has published more than 70 journal articles and book chapters on issues in elder caregiving, long-term care advocacy, home health and adult day care, marketing techniques in the human services, retirement lifestyles, and social work curriculum development. Dr. Kaye sits on the board of the *Journal of Gerontological Social Work.* He is a board member of numerous community organizations, the Past President of the New York State Society on Aging and of Understanding Aging, Inc., and a Fellow of the Gerontological Society of America. He has recently conducted research on self-help support groups for older women and on the delivery of high technology home health care services to older adults.

William G. McTeer is Associate Professor in the Physical Education Department at Wilfred Laurier University in Waterloo, Ontario, Canada. His research focuses on sport and physical activity from a sociological perspective. He has published articles recently in the *International Review for the Sociology of Sport* and the *Journal of Sport Behavior.*

Adam S. Miller is a graduate student in journalism at the University of Michigan. His research focuses on issues of masculinity for men with physical disabilities.

Carol Polych, MScN, is currently working as a Nurse Practitioner at Anishnawbe Health Toronto, an Aboriginal Community Health Center. She teaches in the Nursing and Midwifery programs at Ryerson Polytechnic University in Toronto. She also facilitates a weekly support group for injection drug users at Parkdale Community Health Center. She is working toward her doctorate in Nursing from Wayne State University with minors in Health Policy and Anthropology. Her research has centered on the areas of abuse of health care workers, heroin injection, and the end-of-life issues. She serves as a Board Member of the Prisoners with HIV/AIDS Support and Action Network (PASAN), which provides advocacy and support to prisoners across Canada in relation to HIV issues.

Donald Sabo is a Professor of Sociology at D'Youville College in Buffalo, New York. He has coauthored *Humanism in Sociology, Jock: Sports and Male Identity,* and *Sport, Men, and the Gender Order: Critical*

Feminist Perspectives. His most recent book, with Mike Messner, is titled *Sex, Violence, & Power in Sports: Rethinking Masculinity.* He writes regularly for *Changing Men Magazine,* edited a special issue of *Men's Studies Review* on men in prison, and studies psychosocial aspects of health and illness. He has conducted an array of national surveys on women's sports and fitness and is a trustee of the Women's Sports Foundation. He has appeared on the "Today Show" and is frequently quoted by national media (e.g., *USA Today, Los Angeles Times, Sports Illustrated, The Washington Post, Glamour* magazine, and *Self* magazine). He is a parent and fitness enthusiast.

Robert Staples is Professor in the Graduate Program in Sociology, University of California, San Francisco. His current research is a comparative analysis of indigenous groups in Australia and New Zealand with African Americans and Native Americans in the United States. His latest publication is *Black Families at the Crossroads* (with Leanor Johnson), and he is working on a book on masculinity and racial identity.

Judith M. Stillion is Professor of Psychology and is currently serving as Vice-Chancellor for Academic Affairs at Western Carolina University in Cullowhee, North Carolina. She is past President of the Association for Death Education (ADEC) and still serves that organization as strategic planner. In 1992, she was awarded ADEC's Outstanding Death Educator award. Dr. Stillion is also a member of the International Work Group on Death, Dying, and Bereavement, the American Association of Suicidology, the American Psychological Association, and several other national organizations. She has conducted an ongoing series of studies on attitudes toward suicide, which received national attention when presented at the American Psychological Association national conference. Her first book, *Death and the Sexes: An Examination of Differential Longevity, Attitudes, Behaviors, and Coping Skills* brought together her expertise in the psychology of sex differences and her work in death and dying. Her second book, *Suicide Across the Life Span: Premature Exits* (with Eugene McDowell and Jacque May) was the first to bring a developmental perspective to the study of suicide. In addition to presenting more than 100 keynote addresses, workshops, and presentations, Dr. Stillion has published over 50 articles and chapters in death and dying over the past 20 years.

Richard Tewksbury is Assistant Professor in the School of Justice Administration at the University of Louisville. His research interests center on issues of men's sexuality, psychosocial experiences of HIV disease, gender constructions, and institutional corrections. Dr. Tewksbury is active in HIV prevention programming, correctional education proramming, and child sexual abuse advocacy. His recent publications include "Speaking of Someone with AIDS: Identity Constructions of Persons with HIV Disease," "A Dramaturgical Analysis of Male Strippers," and the forthcoming text, *Introduction to Corrections*.

Ingrid Waldron is a Professor of Biology at the University of Pennsylvania. Her primary research interests are the causes of gender differences in mortality, effects of employment on women's health, and psychosocial influences on smoking.

Philip G. White is Associate Professor in the Department of Kinesiology at McMaster University, Hamilton, Ontario, Canada. His research interests include sport and the gender order, critical issues around the fitness-health movement, and sport and social stratification.

Kevin Young is Associate Professor of Sociology at the University of Calgary, Alberta, Canada, where he teaches and researches in areas such as sport, deviance, social control, and mass media. His published work has probed the roles law, culture, gender, and media play in sports violence. He is currently researching experiences of pain and injury for both male and female athletes, and contradictions in the contemporary health movement. He has recently completed a 5-year term on the editorial board of the *Sociology of Sport Journal*.